SOCIOLOGICAL REVIEW MONOGRAPH 26

The Sociology of Literature: Applied Studies

Issue Editor: Diana Laurenson

Managing Editors: W. M. Williams and Ronald Frankenberg
University of Keele
April 1978

The Sociology of Literature: Applied Studies
Monograph 26
Editor Diana Laurenson

Contents

University of Keele, Keele, Staffordshire

Michele Barrett BA, MA, DPhil
Lecturer, Department of Social Science and Humanities, City
University

Ian Birchall MA, BLitt
Senior Lecturer, Faculty of Humanities, Middlesex Polytechnic

Mike Brake BA, MSc (Econ), PhD
Lecturer, Department of Social Policy, Social Administration and
Social Work, University of Kent at Canterbury

Terry Eagleton MA, PhD
Fellow, Wadham College, Oxford

Paul Filmer BA
Principal Lecturer, Department of Sociology, Goldsmiths' College,
University of London

Ronald Frankenberg BA, MA (Econ), PhD
Professor, Department of Sociology, University of Keele

Mary Horton BA
Senior Lecturer, Department of Psychology, Hatfield Polytechnic

Diana Laurenson BA, PhD
Late Lecturer, Department of Sociology, North East London
Polytechnic

Terry Lovell BA
Lecturer, Department of Sociology, University of Warwick

John Orr BSocSc, PhD
Lecturer, Department of Sociology, University of Edinburgh

Frank Pearce BA, MPhil
Lecturer, Department of Sociology, University of Essex

Helen Roberts BA, DPhil
Lecturer, School of Social Analysis, University of Bradford

Mike Rustin BA
Head of Department, Department of Sociology, North East London
Polytechnic

Alan Swingewood BSc, PhD
Lecturer, Department of Sociology, London School of Economics
and Political Science

Cover Design by Cal Swann FSIAD

Note

All the material in this Monograph is copyright under the terms of the Brussels Convention and the Copyright Act 1956.

Manuscripts to be considered for publication in the form of *Monographs of the Sociological Review* and contributions to be considered for inclusion in *The Sociological Review* should be sent to Professor Ronald Frankenberg, Managing Editor, University of Keele.

Acknowledgments

The article by John Orr is reprinted by kind permission of Macmillan Publishers Ltd., London and Basingstoke, from his book *Tragic Realism and Modern Society*, 1978.

Copyright 1978
ISBN 0 904425 05 3

Printed and bound in Great Britain
by Wood Mitchell & Co. Limited, Hanley, Stoke-on-Trent, Staffs.

Memorial to Diana Laurenson

Many memories and incidents come crowding into my mind whilst writing this brief memorial to Diana Laurenson, who edited this monograph shortly before her tragic accidental death last June. How to possibly convey to the readers the range of her scholastic commitments which cannot be disassociated from her personal qualities. It is these that often take precedence when evaluating a close friend and colleague.

Long before she became a 'vocational' sociologist she had acquired a deep understanding of literature from her father, an examiner in Greats at Oxford. Her wide reading, coupled with her enthusiasm, gave her the ability to communicate this excitement to her friends and students alike. She brought to her academic knowledge of the sociology of literature an involvement in a wide range of interests and her personal experience. More recently she was developing a wide interest in the literature emanating from the Third World. She was able to draw upon the experience of her secondment of a year in Jamaica which enabled her to make a deeper analysis of the political and economic problems faced by Third World writers.

Her scholarship, however, was not of the 'ivory tower' kind – no student felt inhibited or unable to contact Diana, at any time and for whatever reason, personal or private. Her role in North East London Polytechnic was the organization of the Social Psychological teaching and running the Sociology of Literature course in our department. The other interests she brought to the Department were psycho-analysis and group dynamics, which she developed through her involvement in Tavistock (Institute) conferences and study groups and in other ways. Diana enabled many students to explore these areas, and helped some to a lasting professional interest in this field.

However, her interests ranged much wider to the cause of women's rights, and in this field she was closely associated with the work being done by the committee set up by the British Sociological Association. She took an active interest in her trade union – NAFTHE – and she always showed a willingness to be involved in a whole range of issues.

Diana reminds one of those intrepid women travellers of the nineteenth century – no unchartered regions would have daunted her. She came into 'academia' as a mature student, sailed through her first degree with an upper second class honours (at the then Regent Street Polytechnic) and then went on to do her PhD at the London School of Economics under Professor MacRae. An endearing incident from our undergraduate days comes to mind, the time when she almost got locked into the library because of being completely engrossed in Plato's

'Republic'. Probably, the only under-graduate to have become that absorbed in this work. During the war she was an ambulance driver in the East End and many a male colleague quaked at the idea of a lift from her. But we 'braver' mortals miss these flirtations with danger.

In our Department at NELP we truly feel our loss. Diana was a scholar, in the old-fashioned sense of finding knowledge stimulating and making this quest her life's inspiration. We miss the exciting exchanges of ideas, the care she bestowed on her students, her individuality and idiosyncracies. Hers was, indeed, a life cut down in its prime.

Claire Bland
North East London Polytechnic

Current Research in the Sociology of Literature: Introduction

Diana Laurenson

I *Uneven Developments in the History of Method*
The recent upsurge of interest in the sociology of literature is itself of interest to sociologists. Long established in Europe, it has been treated here with neglect and suspicion. Not only did the link with Marxist analysis and the grudging acceptance accorded to sociology itself nurture this taboo; it was also cold-shouldered by sociologists themselves who were busy with empirical activity, preferring data more amenable to statistical analysis and more measurably relevant to popular social problems. It received opprobrium from literary specialists who feared encroachment if not occupation, scenting crude reductionism and over-determined casual 'explanation', not without reason. Amongst general readers it faced a spectrum of views ranging from indifference to protective possessiveness based on an image of art and literature as the sacred preserve of an initiated élite.[1] Assumptions that 'great' literature should be saved from iconoclastic denigration by irreverent and irrelevent meddlers, while 'popular' reading provides escapist entertainment unsuitable for serious analysis, die hard and are still with us. Those exploratory studies of art and society appearing in England during the 1930s did little to shift this entrenched view,[2] although the work of F. L. Leavis and his school, itself avowedly anti-Marxist and lacking academic recognition, was responsible for some informed studies of literature in a social context.[3]

After the explosive expansion of sociology during the 1950s, students wishing to research into the sociology of art and literature were often deflected; at most allowed to undertake occupational studies of professional groups, or commercial activities such as publishing, and gently manœuvered away from what was considered a soft option for an innumerate (if not idiotic) fringe. Significantly, the work of Raymond Williams developed in the ambience of an English department (extra-mural).

Why, then, this spectacular shift? The sociology of literature is now ensconced in many academic departments and attracts large numbers of students and general readers. The growing critique of positivism, the proliferation of empirical studies, ambiguities of grappling with the complexities of protest and crises both in sociology and daily life, and an awareness of the relevance of literature and art to the understanding of social reality are some of the more obvious factors. Frederick Jameson points to the demise of profoundly anti-social modernism in the arts and an emergent 'new modernism', quoting 'John Cage's music, Andy Warhol's films, novels by Burroughs, plays by Becket, Godard, Camp, Norman O. Brown, psychedelic experiences.' To this North American list we can add at random the Beatles, Joan Littlewood, the film 'Blow Up', the plays of Tom Stoppard, the novels of Doris Lessing, happenings at the Roundhouse and Middle Earth. All of these are relatively 'social', far removed from the agonised isolation of the works of Kafka or late abstract art as condemned by Lukács, and cannot conveniently be ignored by sociologists.

At a deeper level we can look to the alienating boom conditions of the fifties, the fetishistic consumer society which intensified a need for both escape and support. For many, art is an opportunity temporarily and relatively to transcend alienation: 'the works of culture come to us as signs in an all-but-forgotten code, as symptoms of diseases no longer recognised as such, as fragments of a totality we have long since lost the organs to see.'[4] The erosion of other escape routes (such as religious participation or large family life) accentuates this turn to literature and art for the provision of self enhancement and revitalisation: a role as potent in economic boom as in the inflationary crises of the 1970s.

Political movements and events have likewise challenged the model of a consensus society. Many of these have generated their own literature and culture which cannot be neglected. The civil rights struggles of blacks, women, homosexuals, mental patients, prisoners and other groups, the Vietnam War, blatant evidence of corruption amongst the powerful, culminating in Watergate and the CIA exposures, reverberate in literature and art throughout the world, demanding an exploration of values on the same scale as those undertaken by Goethe, Tolstoy, Balzac and George Eliot. There has been a welcome two-way expansion in areas of access for sociologists: not only is there now encouragement to explore 'contemporary culture'[5] but also, as this monograph bears witness, there is licence to reassess 'classical' authors. Articles here presented are not only on styles of recent criticism, Doris Lessing's novels, Godard's *La Chinoise*, gangster films, Gay literature and women's popular fiction, but also on Conrad, Emily Brontë, Jane Austen, Dickens, Dostoevsky and Emile Zola. Interestingly this allocation between the contemporary and the historical was fortuitous rather than planned.

Academic shifts and developments have also been conducive to the recognition of the subject as fit for serious study. The spread of linguistics and semiology,[6] the application of structural analysis to myth and folklore[7] and new approaches in deviancy studies[8] are examples.

The first two areas have depended much on translations from abroad which are now accelerating (accompanied by greatly needed texts in the sociology of literature itself); they overlap both with each other and with sociology, drawing on disciplines as diverse and similar as Marxism and psychoanalysis, especially in France and Germany where demarcation is less parochial. The 'New Deviancy' studies are prominent in this country and the United States: a reliance on subjective accounts being the initial link with literature.

So a new generation of students is now encouraged to turn to literature and art of all kinds to clothe the dry bones of the social survey and to fill the contours of conceptual models. In addition literature departments are now more open to the added dimensions of considering works sociologically. In *Contemporary Approaches to English Studies*, 1977, Raymond Williams stresses that writers work *within* society: 'society is not something fixed beyond them but their activity is an activity *within* it.'[9] Hitherto this has not been invariably a commonplace on 'Eng. Lit.' courses. Academic bias has been softened by a growing sophistication in the research into the relationship between infrastructure and superstructure in adjacent fields,[10] while continental theorists have provided evidence that vulgar and mechanical reductionism is not the inevitable correlate of such studies. Williams writes of the radical change in his attitude to Marxist analysis:

> 'I have always opposed the formula of base and superstructure . . .
> because of its rigid, abstract and static character . . . I came to
> believe that I had to give up, or at least leave aside, what I knew as
> the Marxist tradition: to attempt to develop a theory of social totality
> . . . This being so, it is easy to imagine my feelings when I discovered
> an active and developed Marxist theory, in the work of Lukács and
> Goldmann, which was exploring many of the same areas with many of
> the same concepts, but also with others in a quite different range . . .
> advances have been made, and I want to acknowledge them.'[11]

Some of the authors of this monograph seek to clarify issues not satisfactorily resolved by either Lukács or Goldmann, but most would concur with this somewhat magisterial acknowledgement of contributions to methodology.

Hence, work is now proceeding, albeit of a somewhat fragmented kind. Williams laments the crucial lack of collaborators 'especially of people who did not say or have to say, as we approached the most difficult central problems, that there, unfortunately was the limit of their field.' Few of us can devote more than part-time work to the subject. An article on the sociology of literature in a journal is still a rarity; it does not usually represent a corpus of sustained focus. The area is now perhaps 'safe', where biting rigour of criticism is muted or can be sloughed off with no damage to real reputation which rests on hard sociological publications. Nonetheless a thrust has occurred and prevails.

The phenomenological orientation underlies a number of variants some of which have been labelled 'new deviancy theories', symbolic interactionsm, ethnomethodology or labelling theories. These have in common a stress on subjectivity, an awareness of alternative forms of reality, constructions of other worlds with other normative orders and a desire to obtain vicarious experience in diverse social groupings. Movements of protest from minorities have provided opportunities for such experience. The realisation that a plethora of alternative worlds exists ready to hand in literature has led subscribers to this approach to look there, not only for a source of subjective accounts sufficiently vivid to offer participant experience, but also to feel the contradictions inherent in the habitation of two or more worlds simultaneously. These contradictions are spelled out by Castaneda[12] and in such novelistic documentaries as Oscar Lewis's *Children of Sanchez* but are as present in *Heart of Darkness, Wuthering Heights* or *Pickwick Papers* – films add visual impact and heard dialogue to written script and intensify the embrace.[13] Novels and films provide a universe of meanings and possibilities both removed from and tangential to the 'real', commonsense world.[14] Those of this persuasion have been criticised for failing to develop a theory of total society; the critique has led to a radical re-evaluation, stimulated by recent political events.[15]

It is possible to trace another critique and progression in the sociology of literature relevant to the development of a methodology appropriate to applied studies. Eagleton has accused the early explorers of the 1930s of often 'falling into the Vulgar Marxist mistake of raiding literary works for their ideological content and relating this directly to the class struggle or the economy.' Williams writes: 'it is now widely conceded that what was known, at the beginning of this period, as Marxist cultural theory (which incidentally, for those of us working on it, came through not only as Engels and Plekhanov, or Fox and Caudwell and West, but as Zhdanov) needed radical revision.'[16] It was not until the late 1950s that works of Lukács and Goldmann, together with new translations of Marxist texts began to circulate; students began to grasp a more sophisticated Marxist literary theory. Yet many contributions by the Frankfurt school are still unobtainable; Goldmann's *Towards a Sociology of the Novel*[17] was not published in English until 1975 and much work by Lukács and Sartre is still unavailable. Of course, works of criticism appearing between these two periods increasingly referred to the social dimension of art,[18] research was undertaken into the bases of authorship, book production and readership,[19] and some sociologists looked on literature as a quarry from which insights might be hewn to illustrate their teaching.[20] But the partial nature of many of these contributions (albeit useful and necessary) accentuated the need for what Jameson calls a synchronic theoretical formulation: a total approach which could provide a working methodology for research.

The contributions of Lukács and Goldmann cannot be overlooked: the stress on totality of the one informed the attempt at methodology of the other. 'Genetic Structuralism' claimed to provide a comprehensive and dialectical method avoiding both social reductionism and psychologism. In brief, Goldmann looked first to the text for structures and micro-structures which could subsequently be related to the social class or group to which the author belonged (with its 'world view') and to historical moment and wider sociological context. A working model could then be set up capable of explaining the main structures of the text, refined by continuous oscillating reference to text, changing social structure and the model itself. This method was evolved during Goldmann's study of some works of Racine and Pascal as situated in a complex class situation;[21] it was applied to smaller-scale research on Genet, Malraux and the novels of Robbe-Grillet. The large-scale team research he advocated was realised in the project on Flaubert, interrupted by his death in 1970.

Goldmann provided us with the most comprehensive methodology to date, moreover he applied it consistently to specific works. Yet it cannot be denied that he failed ultimately to avoid the very reductionism he abhorred. In his model the author as conscious creator is submerged; while the view of social class is passive, muting the essentially conflictual and strategic roles of each. Moreover the distinction between World View *(Vision du Monde)* and ideology (expression of the interests of a class) is unclear; while the claim that only 'great' works are suitable for the grist of his model poses a highly problematic task of preliminary categorisation. Nonetheless his influence is evident in this monograph.

A comparison has been made of such so-called 'pure' sociological methodology and a comprehensive Marxist criticism.[22] Although the history of the methodology in the sociology of literature often seems to consist of one position castigating another for Marxist inadequacy or over-emphasis, the progress has not been circular; the signs are that a model will be forthcoming. The necessity of avoiding a diachronic and static economic schema with spurious 'homologies' between various levels of reality is emphasised, together with the need to recognise the *conflictual* characteristics of class-ideologies and author.[22] From another quarter comes a call to relate literature to struggle in order to read texts fully, understand our present and further the production of art forms of value.[23] The whole focus of Williams's work is towards the forging of the intellectual pre-conditions of a socialist culture.[24] It is in the interest of this task that many of the articles in this monograph were written.

II *Ideology in Applied Studies*

At this point some definitions may be helpful. *The sociology of literature* is the study of literature *in* society (or of society *in* literature). It is based on the assumption that literary works: novels, biographies, plays, poetry, film-scripts, documentaries, short stories, etc., do not drop 'like meteorites from heaven' (Taine) or emerge solely from the lower depths of individual creativity. They are created by authors who have a history of socialisation in a particular class, gender and place and who are subject to a range of changing social pulls and pressures. They are created at a particular historical stage of society, which is never static, they are affected by a number of variants such as market situation and readership. *Applied studies* in the sociology of literature discuss individual works or bodies of works in their social context, or study conditions of production and distribution or take literary themes to illuminate sociological concepts (or vice versa). Sociological study implies the avoidance of monocausal 'explanation' or reductionism; modern Marxist methodology claims to incorporate the ever-changing and conflictual nature of economic and social phenomena, thereby avoiding fragmentation and partial study. *Theoretical studies* in the sociology of literature (discussed fully in volume I of this series) research the formulations underlying both Marxist and non-Marxist approaches to the subject. *Methodology* is intricately bound up with both theory and application. Empirical methodology is based on recognised scientific procedures, does not necessarily stress interaction, and often aims at one particular dimension. A Marxist methodology should be dialectical, dynamic and forward looking, different in kind from more static analysis, informed by a total theory of social change. A fully satisfactory programmatic methodology has not yet been formulated.

Ideology can be used in at least two senses: a neutral and a pejorative sense. It can stand for ideas arising from a given set of material interests held in common by a group or social class. Or, if it is held that individuals do not hold a realistic view of their class, that they are victims of false consciousness, then ideology is defined as false thought

(Marx and Engels) or, as Goldmann put it, as a partial perspective in contradistinction to a comprehensive World View. In popular talk, ideology is often identified with misleading polemics. Of course the ideology of one class is ultimately antagonistic and opposed to that of another; although if the ideology of a ruling class is accepted as 'normal reality' or 'commonsense' by subordinates a situation of *hegemony* exists. A work of art is often imbued with ideology or ideologies; indeed sociologists would stress the importance of understanding both manifest and latent elements. A recent work helpful to this task is John Berger's *Ways of Seeing.* [25]

One view of 'great' realist art is that it alone can grasp fully the total structure of society, can present an organic picture of the ideological clash and struggle of different classes of divergent economic and social interests. Since writers have been usually members of the bourgeoisie (or petty bourgeoisie), the majority sons of professionals,[26] this view holds that it was easier for them to achieve this when their class was ascending and successful than when it was threatened politically and economically.[27] The conscious ideology of a writer is not crucial: Balzac (favoured by Marx) was royalist and conservative yet his structural grip was such that he could present the real dynamics of his society, the corrupt bourgeoisie and the sufferings of the deprived. Indeed he unconsciously condemned the ideology of the former and sympathised with that of the latter. A 'great' artist, can give premonitions of social and ideological changes to come (Shakespeare and Dante) or recapture the unity and harmony of a former age (as in the case of Greek art according to Marx). The 'tragic vision' (world view) underlying some of the works of Pascal and Racine stemmed from the attempt to resolve the ideological conflicts of a marginal social group at a particular historical moment (Goldmann).

The Marxist view of ideology in literature has been problematic. The assumption is that false consciousness would be minimal in a socialist society, therefore true socialist art would not be ideological. Marx and Engels were steeped in literature to an astonishing degree[28] and valued the works of the great bourgeois writers. The picture of Marx with his daughters and friends making the three hour walk to and from Dean Street and Hampstead Heath reciting Dante and Shakespeare is founded on fact.[29] In no way did they encourage the view that art must be overtly polemical or narrowly representative of the working class; although Marx argued for the unity of form (languages and devices) and content, disliking both those Romantic works whose sensational content overwhelms form (to the extent of burning some of his own unrestrained poems) and formalistic literature which over emphasises style and technique at the expense of content. He held that changes in literary form occur with developments in ideology: the novel form parallels changes in the interests of the rising bourgeoisie (he cites *Robinson Crusoe* as an apt example).[30] Eagleton, however, stresses that there is no simple, symmetrical relationship between changes in form and ideology, a view emphasised by Trotsky.[31] Literature, he argues, has a high degree of independence. It is affected, not only by dominent ideological structures but by 'relatively autonomous' traditional forms as well as by relations between author and readers. 'It is the dialectical unity between these elements that Marxist criticism is concerned to analyse.' The extent to which the literary forms change at any particular time depends on 'whether at that point in history "ideology" is such that they must and can be changed.'[32]

With the rise of Stalin, the views of Marx, Engels, Lenin and Trotsky concerning literature were superseded by a severe censorship which insisted that literature should be simplistic and polemical: 'tendentious, party-minded, optimistic and heroic.' An ideological content was enforced by Zdhanov, who justified his actions by misinterpreting Lenin's call for *party* literature to become 'a cog and a screw of one single, great, democratic machine.' The fact that Lenin did not intend this remark to apply to imaginative literature was (and is) conveniently ignored. This has driven much Russian literature underground, reverting to a pre-revolutionary situation where writers were forced to use codes and allegories to avoid censorship.[33] In Britain this extreme situation existed during the eighteenth and nineteenth centuries: those works of Blake and Shelley which attacked the dominant ideology of the ruling class often contained allegories and obscurities to hide their republican and socialist ideas;[34] while later the lending libraries enforced a stultifying political and moral code on authors. Sociologists need to decode the language of ideological disguise in order to discern the interplay of contending dominant and revolutionary ideologies and to know the classes and groups whose interests are expressed ideologically.

Ideology is, therefore, a crucial concept for the understanding of both form and content in art and literature of all periods. It is an indispensable tool for applied study in the sociology of literature, particularly for understanding the novel which is a crucible of ideological interplay, a kind of ideological laboratory. Jameson goes further:

'The stress Marx laid on individual works of art and the value they had for him (as for Hegel before him and Lenin after) were very far from being a matter of personality: in some way, which it is the task of Marxist theory to determine more precisely, literature plays a central role in the dialectical process. I might also add that the realm of literature, the experimental or laboratory situation which it constitutes with its characteristic problems of form and content and of the relationship of superstructure to infrastructure, offers a privileged microcosm in which to observe dialectical thinking at work.'[35]

If (following Roland Barthes) we as readers create our own texts, by observing total ideological interplay we can experience the dialectic at work also within ourselves.

III

The articles in this monograph represent a variety of theoretical perspectives: the thread which links them is the use of ideology as a tool of analysis. There are some obvious gaps: we were particularly sorry not to include work on the new African and Caribbean literature for example. The authors are to be congratulated for conveying their analytic intensity and excitement in a manner likely to spur students to explore further for themselves.

Ideology is the clue which enables Terry Lovell to resolve a contradiction which has baffled those critics who read their own values into Jane Austen's novels. A careful examination of the 'bourgeois class' (blanket term) of her day reveals Austen's position: a woman member of the threatened lesser gentry, concerned with the moral regeneration and economic retrenchment of that class, intimately interested in the maintenance of landed estates. Hence both her asperity towards 'trade' and instrumentality, and her confirmation of orthodox and conformist values; the latter only appearing excessive and anomalous in *Mansfield Park*, an estate threatened by the consequences of moral laxity. Lovell unravels Jane Austen's ideology of reformist conservatism, thus confuting her reputation of being 'a Marxist before Marx', exposing the economic basis of behaviour with an ironic smile (Daiches).

Alan Swingewood, with Goldmann and Walter Benjamin 'in mind', distinguishes three phases of development in the work of Doris Lessing and distinct sets of basic structures in the texts of each. Swingewood links the transitions with the groups to which Lessing belonged (the Communist Party, dissident communists grouped around *The New Reasoner*. Laingian psychoanalysis, Eastern mysticism – Sufiism – and the 'Counter-culture') but he departs from Goldmann by not attempting to establish homologies with wider economic changes. He does not view the novel as a direct expression of bourgeois class interests, but as a form shaped by bourgeois class hegemony in a complex balance of forces within a still strong civil society.

Terry Eagleton bids us beware of the ease with which an 'ideological' text yields insights for a materialist criticism, but his intrinsic and closely argued treatment of the interplay between components of the text and components of ideology in Conrad's *The Secret Agent* is far from simplistic. He details the process of displacement and re-casting, of contradictions mutually engendering conflict and change, the complex relations between forms and ideologies, formal elements and ideological sub-ensembles, aesthetic devices and codified perceptions within the text. He presents the game quality of this continuous movement which ends in a statement which on one level is a resolution (and vice versa), yet avoids the 'methodological circularity' and 'mirrorlike-image reciprocity' between 'approach' and 'object' against which he warns. His piece is a useful corrective to those of us who under-rate the relative autonomy of the text or the intricacies of such an analysis.

Paul Filmer starts from the concept of 'social world', stressing the centrality of language, both under-emphasised by Realism which assumes only referent reality. In the world of *Pickwick Papers* an alternative reality develops and holds sway: that of Pickwickian knowledge and sense, created by Dickens through the device of a surreal language. This game, shared by his readers, takes on its own life and has to be defused at the end. Filmer argues that until language becomes central, sociology can have little of human relevance to say to us about art.

Nineteenth century France was noted for the controversy around 'Naturalism' in literature, to the extent of protagonists wearing badges for or against Zola, the prominent representative of this school. Ian Birchall champions Zola's novels, in particular *Germinal*, against the verdict of Lukács, which, together with the condemnation of modernism, he sees as a blind spot in an otherwise significant achievement. He argues that Lukács's accusations of biological mysticism, over-detailed reportage, aloofness and trend to dehumanisation are misplaced. Lukács had not read much Zola, he was following Lafargue, Engels, and increasingly the Stalinist line; in fact the novels do not contravene the Lukácsian canons: their continued popularity bears witness to their value.

John Orr also dissents from the verdict of Lukács, who ignored the later work of Dostoevsky. *The Devils* ostensibly attacks both liberal and revolutionary ideologies in the Russia of the 1860s, but a dialectical tension emergies between 'tendenz' and actuality, resulting in the emergence of a'demonic tendenz'. This subverts the polemics, and the novel springs into life. The result is prophetic, demonstrating the potentiality for evil in Russian society; Dostoevsky is clearly situated in the category of 'great' critical realists according to Lukács's own criteria.

There are two articles on criticsm in this monograph. Ronald Frankenberg takes us on a comparative tour of analysis of *Wuthering Heights* from Caudwell through Wilson, Kettle, and Q. D. Leavis to Raymond Williams ('the agonised left outsider of the '50s'), Eagleton, Musselwhite and finally Kermode. In his own view, Heathcliffe symbolises woman's demand to be a person, a demand threatening both to the Heights and to Victorian capitalist society. Frankenberg stresses the continual re-reading and re-writing of the text by critics; the process of production continuing each time the text is read (following Barthes). Only theoretical clarity combined with practice can break this persistent generative chain of structures in which we are all embedded.

Extremes of adulation and denigration are represented in Virginia Woolf criticsm. Michèle Barrett exposes the superficiality of the latter in critics from Edel, E. Hardwick, W. Allen and Q. D. Leavis through Daiches, A. J. P. Taylor and Bradbury to Marder and Bazin. The fact that Virginia Woolf opposed patriarchial institutions such as war, religion, royalty, marriage, the family and middle-class psychiatry in both novels and prose is conveniently ignored by those, both right and left wing, who label her as aloof from the material world, constrained by class and gender and even unoriginal.

Although Drabble and Weldon challenge the traditional romanticised stereotype of women, Helen Roberts shows how the old image is still perpetuated in women's magazines and popular fiction. Examining the three themes of romantic love, role conflict and role distance, and fate and chance, from the beginning of the century – in the work of Mrs. Humphrey Ward, Marie Corelli, E. M. Delafield, Winifred Holtby, Dorothy Sayers, Edna O'Brien and in the magazine *Woman* she finds little evidence of progressive change. Those later examples which express ambiguity implicitly endorse the old view and no alternative model is provided.

Mike Brake traces the image of the homosexual from the Aesthetic Movement to its eclipse after the Wilde trial, through its resuscitation with Bloomsbury and Ronald Firbank (disguised or underground, E. M. Forster's *Maurice* was not published until 1971) and on to Isherwood and the overt challenge to heterosexual hegemony. He points to the quality of new lesbian novels which avoid Gay sexism; this he links with differential organisation of consciousness.

The 'Literature of Alienation' is a successful example of the 'quarry' approach in which literary examples are chosen to illustrate a theme or concept. Mary Horton distinguishes six themes of psychological alienation in literature, the Insider, the Outsider, the Detached Man, the Hollow Man, the Wasteland and the Possessed; the latter is divided into Escape, Embrace and Metamorphosis. The cumulative effect is powerful.

Godard's *La Chinoise* was an attempt to work out an aesthetic which could provide a form for revolutionary work, prescient of events to come. Michael Rustin discusses the role of semiology: in this film colour (particularly red), lighting and stationary camera. The iconographic consistency of metaphors, mixed with documentary shots, provides the setting for five students in a Paris flat learning to be revolutionaries. Violence builds up to assassination; the art of this film is one of contradictions and fragments which match the complicated and self-contradictory problem of revolution at that time.

Finally Frank Pearce presents a comprehensive survey of Gangster films whose iconography portrays a world of violence, where 'nature has been transformed, not to aid man's development, but to produce an oppressive cage which dwarfs and intimidates him.' In this man-made city of ruthless competition, only the tough can survive: the gangster emerges as 'what we want to be and what we are afraid we may become.' Pearce links this world with the politics and corruption of American society at large.

These papers stand for themselves; together they indicate some of the areas in which applied work is now proceeding. They discuss social context, interplay of ideology, class structures and hegemony, language and other worlds, textual analysis, semiology and iconography. Our present task, building on the work of such theorists as Lukács, Goldmann, Benjamin, Brecht, Machery and others, is to refine a satisfactory methodology for a dynamic sociology of literature. In this work, applied studies have a crucial place.

Current Research in the Sociology of Literature: Introduction

1. See Matthew Arnold: *Culture and Anarchy*, Cambridge University Press, London, 1960, for the Nineteenth Century view; and T. S. Eliot: *Notes towards the Definition of Culture*, Faber, London, 1948.

2. See the work of Ralph Fox, Arnold Kettle, Christopher Caudwell and others. Ronald Frankenberg discusses their criticisms of *Wuthering Heights* on pp. 112-20.

3. In particular Q. D. Leavis: *Fiction and the Reading Public*, Chatto and Windus, London, 1932.

4. Frederic Jameson: *Marxism and Form*, Princeton University Press, New Jersey, 1971, p. 416.

5. As, for example, the Birmingham Centre for Cultural Studies which publishes *Cultural Studies*.

6. See the work of Roland Barthes, published in English by Jonathan Cape.

7. See the work of Claude Lévi-Strauss, published in English by Jonathan Cape, and note the structural analysis of *Wuthering Heights* by Frank Kermode discussed on pp. 135-7.

8. In particular those by Stanley Cohen, Laurie Taylor and Jock Young.

9. Raymond Williams: *Contemporary Approaches to English Studies*, ed. Hilda Schiff, Heinemann Educational Books, London, 1977.

10. Such as social history and politics. See for example E. P. Thompson: *The Making of the English Working Class*, Pelican, Harmondsworth, 1968, and the work of Christopher Hill.

11. Raymond Williams: 'Introduction' to Lucien Goldmann's *Racine*, Rivers Press, London, 1972.

12. Carlos Castaneda: *Tales of Power*, Penguin, Harmondsworth, 1974. See also the three earlier accounts – *The Teachings of Don Juan*, *A Separate Reality* and *Journey to Ixtlan*, Penguin, Harmondsworth.

13. Compare for example *Quai des Brümes*, *The Seven Samurai*, *One Flew Over the Cuckoo's Nest* and Lina Wertmüller's *Seven Beauties*.

14. Both the hermeneutic and icongraphic approaches to art are here relevant. See Janet Wolff: *Hermeneutic Philosophy and the Sociology of Art*, Routledge and Kegan Paul, London, 1975.

15. A summary of this process is given by Peter Archard: 'Critical Criminology: a Velvet Glove without an Iron Fist', (unpublished paper, read before S.I.P. conference) 1977.

16. Raymond Williams: 'Notes on Marxism in Britain since 1945' *New Left Review*, No. 100, 1977, p. 88.

17. Lucien Goldmann: *Towards a Sociology of the Novel*, Tavistock, London, 1975.

18. Such as R. Wellek and A. Warren: *Theory of Literature*, Peregrine Books, Stevenage, 1963; E. Auerbach, *Mimesis*, Princeton, New Jersey, 1963; H. Levin: *The Gates of Horn*, Oxford University Press, London, 1963.

19. See for instance D. F. Laurenson: 'A Sociological Study of Authorship', *British Journal of Sociology*, Volume XX, No. 3, 1969; R. D. Altick: 'The Sociology of Authorship, *New York Public Library Bulletin*, 1962 and *The English Common Reader*, Chicago Press, Illinois, 1957; R. K. Webb: *The British Working Class Reader*, Allen and Unwin, London, 1955.

20. As in Lewis Coser's *Sociology Through Literature*, Prentice-Hall, Hemel Hempstead, 1963.

21. Lucien Goldmann: *The Hidden God*, Routledge & Kegan Paul, London, 1964.

22. Jameson: op. cit., Chapter 5.

23. Terry Eagleton: *Marxism and Literary Criticism*, p. 70. He stresses 'Marxist criticism is not just an alternative technique for interpreting *Paradise Lost* and *Middlemarch*. It is part of our liberation from oppression, and that is why it is worth discussing at book length.'

24. *New Left Review*, Editorial, No. 100, 1977, p. 4.

25. John Berger: *Ways of Seeing*, BBC and Penguin, Harmondsworth, 1972.

26. Laurenson: op.cit.

27. Georg Lukács: *Realism in Our Time*, Torchbook Paperbacks, 1964 (preface by George Steiner); and Roland Barthes: *Writing Degree Zero*, Cape Edition, London, 1967, p. 66.

28. S. S. Prawer: *Karl Marx and World Literature*, Clarendon Press, Oxford, 1977.

29. David McLellan: *Karl Marx, his Life and Thought*, Paladin, London, 1976, p. 267.

30. This process is spelled out by Ian Watt: *The Rise of the Novel*, Penguin, Harmondsworth, 1957.

31. Leon Trotsky: *Literature and Revolution*, Ann Arbor Paperbacks, 1971.

32. Eagleton: op.cit., pp. 24-27.

33. D. F. Laurenson and A. Swingewood: *The Sociology of Literature*, MacGibbon and Kee, St. Albans, 1971, pp. 98-100.

34. David Erdman: *Blake, Prophet against Empire*, Princeton University Press, New Jersey, 1969; and Richard Holmes: *Shelley, the Pursuit*, Penguin, Harmondsworth, 1976. This situation resulted in a totally false popular image of these poets: Shelley the lyrical poet of *To a Skylark* and Blake of *Songs of Innocence* submerged Blake and Shelley the revolutionaries.

35. Jameson: op.cit.

Jane Austen and the Gentry: A study in Literature and Ideology

Terry Lovell

I

> 'Her comedy is a little sly, a little prim,
> more often than not, a little sharp, and
> entrancing in its felicity of expression.
> To me it is the dash of lemon juice which
> makes the sauce supreme.'[1]

D. W. Harding's justifiable famous essay[2] on Jane Austen was an attempt to rescue her from the 'Janeites'; those who saw her satire as amiable laughter directed at people whom she liked, despite, even because of, their comic foibles. He drew attention to the 'unexpected astringencies' contained in the novels, which are lost in complacent Janeite readings. For Harding, the novels express 'regulated hatred' of her narrow class society and its values – regulated because Jane Austen was emotionally and economically dependent on that society, and could not afford to express her antagonism more openly. Harding exaggerated his case in an attempt to provoke readers into a recognition of these jarring elements in the novels. But his thesis has been echoed, modified, and added to by other critics whose more extreme interpretations are offered as accurate renderings of the themes of the novels. Marvin Mudrick finds Jane Austen's characteristic detached irony exactly suited to expose 'the polished surface of the bourgeois world to its unyielding material base.'[3] David Daiches, in exploring the economic values of the novels, discovers in them 'a Marxist before Marx', who 'exposes the economic basis of social behaviour with an ironic smile.'[4] All variants of this approach share the belief that Jane Austen was subversive of the accepted values of her class and society. They have performed a valuable task in directing attention to aspects of her novels which any critical interpretation must acknowledge. She makes acid comment on the gallery of minor characters who people her fictional world, and if that world is representative, she is not flattering to its human product.

The novel which creates most difficulty for what has been called the 'subversive school' of Jane Austen criticism is *Mansfield Park*. Criticism of it from this quarter too frequently amounts to little more than a display of spleen. Its heroine, the timid, moralising Fanny, is taken to be her author's spokeswoman, in the absence of any obvious distancing devices; and Fanny is anything but subversive. Totally conformist, she struggles to defend the moral order established at Mansfield. This is exposed as fragile in Sir Thomas's absence, undermined by the defective moral character of most of its natural custodians, the Bertram children. Q. D. Leavis, more sympathetic to this novel than critics of the subversive school, nevertheless agrees with them in discerning in this novel alone an unnatural censure of Jane Austen's own standards of judgement, of her instinctive values, 'a determination to sponsor the conventional moral outlook . . . to persuade herself that she feels as she believes she ought to feel.'[5] Mudrick resorts to biographical inference (although he does not give any direct supportive evidence) to explain the difference between Jane Austen's 'characteristic' self, and that displayed in *Mansfield Park.* The anomalies of the novel are put down to (hypothetical) social and moral pressures which Jane Austen may have been under at the time, 'to produce a work of uncompromising moral purpose, whatever the bent of her taste and imagination.' To this end, she betrayed her characteristic self, as well as her art.[6] It is left to Kingsley Amis to express this view most forcefully and crudely: 'Her judgement and her moral sense were corrupted. *Mansfield Park* is the witness of that corruption.'[7]

'Uncharacteristic'; a craven submission to social convention; a betrayal of art and self; corrupt. Any general account of the novels of Jane Austen which is forced into such exceptionalism in relation to this one novel is hardly a serious contender for a critical theory of her work. Yet if *Mansfield Park* is *not* exceptional, then the subversive thesis cannot be retained, since that novel supports and affirms the most orthodox values of gentry society. This paper is an attempt to assess the sociological significance of Jane Austen's writings, by placing them within their contemporary ideological context. An interpretation is needed which gives due recognition to the sharply critical nature of much of her comment, but which locates that criticism more convincingly as part of a wider world-view.

II

'The large Austen household, well-born but not well-off, well-educated, singularly united, with tentacles of kinsfolk reaching out into great houses, parsonages, rich and poor, Bath and London, the navy and the militia . . .'[8]

Since Ian Watt's pioneer work[9] it is a commonplace to link the rise of the novel with the rise of the bourgeoisie, among sociologists and Marxist critics alike. When all its various sections have been identified and distinguished, 'the rise of the bourgeoisie' becomes less seductive as an explanation, for it was not one, but a series of events which began as early as the sixteenth century, and was not completed until the early nineteenth century. This lack of historical specificity is compounded by the sociologist's array of dichotomous types used to characterise the state of society before and after some historically vague, but epochal social change: a kind of moveable historical feast, invoked to explain an ever increasing variety of social and cultural changes, shifting in time according to need, over some three hundred years. It is a pseudo-event, generated by juxtapositioning the terms of a typology. For our purposes, the changes to which the novels are to be related must be more narrowly translatable into real historical events. If we turn to the Marxist tradition we find, at worst, a similar propensity to blur distinctions. The blanket label of 'bourgeois ideology', applied indiscriminately to any and every cultural manifestation, is at the present time a common substitute for analysis. We need to differentiate clearly the various, and often sharply opposed, forces within the bourgeoisie itself and the even greater variety of expression within its ideological product. Further, the analysis of the social reality from which the novels emerged must be extended beyond a description of class structure and relations, in recognition that society is differentiated along equally salient lines of sex.

Jane Austen was born in 1775. Her father was a country clergyman, and on his death, his widow was left with an income of only £210, raised to £450 per annum by contributions from her sons, to support herself and her unmarried daughters. Jane Austen's perception of the social meaning of this income may be gleaned from her description of the Dashwood family in *Sense and Sensibility*. Mrs. Dashwood, with three daughters, was left with £500. The dependent and unfavourable position in which this left them, both with respect to the maintenance of gentry life-styles, and to the paramount duty of a mother to arrange suitable marriages for her daughters, is very clear in the novel. The Austen family, before and after the death of its head, depended on the patronage of wealthier kin and connections to make good its status claims, and to place its sons and daughters in the world. Such patronage was used to good effect, at least as far as the sons were concerned. Two of Jane Austen's brothers became admirals, two more followed their father into the church and another was adopted by a distant cousin, and became heir to a valuable estate in Kent. The girls were less fortunate than their fictional counterparts, given that a 'good' marriage was the only realistic aspiration for women in gentry society. In fiction, good sense, wit, lively intelligence and beauty could be more readily be made to compensate for a small portion than in reality. The Austens had innumerable family connections with wealthier gentry, and as such they were typical of those who followed professions in the church, law, or the armed services.[10] They should properly be seen as a subaltern section of the dominant gentry class, rather than as an independent social stratum. We shall next consider what kind of class the eighteenth century gentry were.

It is generally recognised that a capitalistic development of society must be looked for not only in the transformation of the relations of production of industry but also those of agriculture, and that from the sixteenth to eighteenth centuries in Britain agrarian capitalism was in the process of formation. For our present purposes we are concerned with the status and behaviour of only *one* of the classes engaged in this process, the rural gentry. E. P. Thompson has remarked the difficulty experienced in conceiving a rural landed class as a capitalist class, but argues forcefully that this indeed was the nature of the eighteenth century gentry, which he describes as 'a superbly successful and self-confident ruling class.'[11] In this he agrees with Anderson, who wrote that the landed aristocracy had in the seventeenth and eighteenth centuries, 'become its own capitalist class.'[12] To what extent is it accurate or useful to speak of the gentry as a capitalist class? Farming in the eighteenth century and beyond was based on the tripartite division between gentry landowner, tenant farmer and landless labourer. The landlord provided the land and the fixed capital – buildings, etc. The 'improving' landlord additionally encouraged better practices and methods on the part of his tenant and supervised the accounts of the estate personally. The landlord's role in the 'agricultural revolution' was in organisation and management of the estate. He was also responsible for important long-term large-scale investments, such as enclosures, marling, drainage, land reclamation, etc. Working capital was provided exclusively by the tenant, and conservative and radical commentators alike are agreed that the spearhead of the 'agricultural revolution' was the wealthier tenant farmer, who pioneered most of the important innovations of the period. As employers of wage-labour, producing commodities for a growing market, the wealthy tenant farmer was the capitalist of the countryside *par excellence*. Notwithstanding the arguments of Mingay, Chambers and others as to the persistence of the smallholder in agricultural production,[13] it seems clear that the *dominant* sector of agriculture, determined not by numbers but by productivity and output, was increasingly the capitalised sector.[14]

The contribution of the gentry class to this process was mixed. Land, whose ownership they almost monopolised, had become a commodity which could be bought and sold on the market more freely, in the wake of the Reformation, and of the changes introduced after the revolution of 1640. But in the succeeding decades the gentry class instituted legal devices (entail, the strict settlement) which severely restricted the market in land. In theory the gentry class was open to anyone who had the purchase price of an estate, but in practice estates came fairly rarely on to the market[15] and land could not easily be alienated. Yet a free market in land, the transformation of land, like labour, into a commodity, is one of the hallmarks of the full institutionalisation of the capitalist mode of production in agriculture. And while the rent roll of the landlord represented in part a share in capitalist profits, it is misleading to suppose that the social characteristics of the gentry owed much to its role in agrarian capitalism. The large estate, with its small 'home farm', and its compact units for rent, was the transformed eighteenth century version of the old feudal manor. It provided an essential basis for the revolution effected by the capitalist entrepreneur, the wealthy tenant, which could not have been provided by a property structure of small peasant holdings. But while the great estates lent themselves to capitalist exploitation in this manner, the contribution of their owners to this process was masked by the passive nature of that role. Just as the physical organisation of the estate owed a great deal to the feudal inheritance, so did the social and cultural characteristics of the gentry, in their life-styles, patterns of interaction, and paternalistic values. The gentry remained a class of consumers, rather than of capitalist investors, thoroughly atypical as a capitalist class. Its members had a powerful incentive to make capitalist investment in 'improvements' in the enhanced level of rents which were the result. But farm rents rose generally in the last part of the century, on the estates of improvers and traditionalists alike. The landlord class was never in the position of the pioneers of capitalist commodity production, of dependence on continued investment and re-investment of profits in production. Its members were never constrained to behave like the classical Weberian entrepreneur, the early capitalist whose slogan was, and had to be: 'Accumulate, accumulate. This is Moses and the prophets.'[16] As befitted a class of gentlemen, they were dilettante in this their most professional concern. Some were enthusiastic innovators; all were improvers or not at will. Their income might diminish over generations if they neglected their estates, but many survived, often turning to capitalist rationalisation only when the encumbrances on the estate made this an essential expedient. Typically, trustees would then be appointed, who would overhaul the affairs of the estate while its owner absented himself on a continental tour. It is not surprising that the gentry were little marked by the puritanism which Max Weber and others associated with the rise of capitalism. Such attitudes are characteristic of those who find themselves entering the ranks of capitalist producers in a modest way; chronically short of capital, with no alternative source of investment open to them, and forced therefore to accumulate out of the profits of the enterprise. The gentry had far more attractive investments open to them, in overseas trade, the money market, and in wealthy city heiresses.

The controversy in the 1960s between Anderson and Thompson concerned the nativity of the gentry class. Thompson argued that Anderson failed to take seriously his own contention that the gentry was a capitalist class. If it was, then the struggles of the early nineteenth century, culminating in political reform, cannot be seen as an inter-class struggle at all. For Thompson, it was an internecine struggle against a 'secondary complex of predatory interests – Old Corruption';[17] a contest in which the older agrarian capitalists adjusted to the claims of the newer industrial sections. Capitalism became more plural, with land 'becoming only one interest beside cotton, railways, iron and steel, coal, shipping, and finance.' The early nineteenth century struggle was a jockeying for position *within* the capitalist class and a growing class struggle *between* capitalists and the rising proletariat. Thompson's argument depends on the assertion that the gentry was a capitalist class like any other, but we have seen that this was not the case. Moreover, it dominated political power and social influence throughout the eighteenth century. Gentry hegemony was unquestioned and unshared. The change occasioned by the rise of industrial capitalism was therefore far more traumatic than Thompson's account allows: the gentry had been, at best, capitalist by whim or expedient. A fully developed capitalist society had to wait the advent of the industrial revolution. After this there was no place for dilettantism; the gentry found itself in the nineteenth century a junior partner in a dominant class, in which they had formerly held exclusive primacy, and committed willy nilly to a capitalist ethos which they had never fully understood nor endorsed. A new group of industrialists and merchants appeared who remained true to the source of their wealth and who could compete in material terms with the great landlords. Not unnaturally, they sought a different kind of legitimating ideology to that of the period of gentry dominance. Paternalism and *noblesse oblige* was challenged by an ideology of utility.

The gentry class thus played a crucial, if largely passive, role in the development of agrarian capitalism and this transformation of agriculture was one of the principal conditions for the subsequent and more spectacular transformation which took place with the industrial revolution. The rise of capitalism in the countryside took place, so to speak, behind the backs of the gentry class, whose dominance on the land and ability to borrow large capital sums against their estates, nevertheless facilitated that development. Agrarian capitalism affected genty life-styles and values but little. Socially and culturally, the English gentry had more in common with their unreformed Irish cousins, who estates were anything but capitalistic, than they had with the class of industrial capitalists who were beginning to appear on the historical stage. With the rise of *industrial capitalism* the new order could no longer be ignored, and there was a rude awakening for the gentry to the nature of the new society which they had helped to forge and in which their traditional life-styles and values were increasingly anachronistic. Different sections of the gentry class were able to adapt to their new social role with varying degrees of ease or hardship. Squeezed between the rising capitalist tenant-farmer and the upper gentry, whose estates had been consolidated and increased in size at their expense, the lesser gentry, to which Jane Austen's family belonged, was in a more exposed position. A position from which the perception of a general threat to their class might be perceived, from which the social and ideological *differences* between traditional rural society and the new urban capitalist order would appear very great. A woman in this section of the gentry class might be especially sensitive to the dangers in this period. The perception that her class was threatened from within was a displacement on to the moral plane of the changes within and between rural and urban economies, which had transformed the nature and role of the gentry class.

The late eighteenth and early nineteenth century was a critical time both for the continued development of capitalism and for the development of more sharply defined consciousness of class on the part of actors in this historical process. Harold Perkin points out the vertical links of kinship and patronage which had hitherto cut across class boundaries. The transformation of this 'old society' into a 'viable class society' in the nineteenth century, by the way of the industrial revolution, was preceded by a period of intense ideological and political strife. It is the ideological aspect of this struggle which provides the context in which we shall look at Jane Austen's novels.

III

The moral concerns of a class whose position and privileges are largely unquestioned are different from those of the same class when its hegemony is under challenge. MacIntyre sees periods of social stability as marked by a moral discourse, concerned with 'my station and its duties.'[19] In periods of social upheaval, this gives way to a discourse in which moral concepts are dissociated from those social roles which initially defined them, and more abstract questions as to the nature of 'right', 'duty', 'good' etc., are raised. What was novel in the moral discourse of the eighteenth century was the development of journals such as the *Spectator*, *Rambler*, *Tatler*, whose self-imposed task was to mould the sensibility, taste and moral judgement of the cultivated gentleman. John Locke's political and moral philosophy had laid the foundations for legitimation of gentry dominance. It was left to more popular writers such as Johnson and the third Earl of Shaftsbury to teach the gentry its morals and manners.

Jane Austen was born towards the close of a century of gentry hegemony and began to write when the French Revolution and the industrial revolution signalled its end. A direct defensive outcome of that situation was the birth of modern conservatism, to which Jane Austen was an early contributor. Her urgent imperative is for the moral self-regeneration of her class to legitimate its ascendancy. This concern shows her to have been a creature of her time as clearly as any more overt references in the novels to contemporary history would have done.[20]

Two recent contributions to Jane Austen scholarship have explored the novels from the perspective of their conservative ideology. Alistair Duckworth takes up a little noted theme, that of estate improvement, and interprets it as the major vehicle of that ideology in the novels.[21] The eighteenth century was the century of estate improvement, both in the management and organisation of estates and in house-building and alteration and the landscaping of parks and gardens. The 'improvement' theme in the novels centres on these latter, peripheral forms of improvement. Jane Austen is silent about the more technical business of running the estate where the capitalist underpinning of the rural economy might be revealed. Her male heroes, Knightley and Darcy, properly devote their time to business, but offstage. Estates and their owners feature at the centre of each of the novels and their moral and social worth is indicated by the physical and financial state of their inheritance. *Mansfield Park*, from this point of view, is less of a problem novel and Duckworth makes it central to his interpretation. The estate in eighteenth century England was the pivot of gentry society, which Habakkuk refers to as 'a federation of country houses . . .'. What more appropriate symbol for conservative defenders of that order? Attitudes towards estate improvement by various characters are used as signs of moral and personal worth. Henry Crawford, the 'villain', favours drastic remedies for the neglected Sotherton, which horrify Fanny and Edmund. The estate, with all its faults, represents a fundamentally sound traditional order and had better not be tampered with by rationalistic improvers. Like the avenue of trees which are to be sacrificed by Crawford and Rushworth, the estate, and the traditional order it stands for, is an 'organic' growth, which may be destroyed but not replaced at will. Duckworth links the theatricals episode to this theme, noting how the play acting progressively invades the space of Mansfield. The physical disruption which it brings symbolises the moral disruption which threatens to undermine the order of Mansfield. The danger arises from Sir Thomas Bertram's failure to educate his children in sound moral principles. At the beginning of the novel, this failure is pointed up by the parlous finances of the estate, which are caused by the extravagance and dissipation of the elder son and heir. The difficulties are compounded by losses on Sir Thomas's West Indian estates, which occasion his absence in Antigua during the first part of the novel. The weakness of the moral order which he has established at Mansfield is revealed in his absence. To be maintained it needed his own stern presence. The agents of the threat, the Crawfords, have come to Mansfield as a result of Tom's extravagance, since the parsonage at Mansfield had been intended to provide a living for Edmund but is disposed of to Dr. Grant instead to help pay for Tom's pleasures. Sir Thomas finally recognises his own failures and the moral order is re-established at the close of the novel. Tom is reformed in the course of a serious illness, Maria is banished, the repentant Julia rescued for respectability and Fanny has become a favoured surrogate daughter. This moral regeneration is accompanied by the restoration of the estate's finances to a sound basis. The threat has been contained.

Jane Austen is politically less perceptive than Burke, who saw that the threat to the gentry and the traditional values it upheld was chiefly an external one. For Jane Austen it was *internal* decay which undermined the traditional order: the bad trustees, inadequate stewards of the traditional order, who insisted upon the privileges but avoided the responsibilities of their inheritances; Sir Walter Elliot, Henry Crawford, the Rushworths, etc. Darcy and Knightley are exemplary in the conduct of their estates, a necessary quality in an

Austenian hero. Elizabeth Bennett has her first intimation that she has misjudged Darcy when she is conducted over his estate at Pemberley. Significantly, both the fine timbers and the absence of any merely fashionable improvements are remarked upon. The analysis of social ills in terms of the moral failings of individuals is a time-honoured one for conservatism. If the structure of society is fundamentally sound, then manifest social disturbances may only be attributed to one of two sources: external forces, or internal debasement. This formula was invoked time and again in Confucian China, that other bastion of traditionalism. Reform was never envisaged as requiring any far-reaching structural change, merely the removal of corrupt officials, and a renewal and re-affirmation of the old values and practices.[22]

Jane Austen's remedy for the threat is, according to Duckworth, the injection of a properly socialised moral individualism into traditional society, usually in the form of a heroine, who has to undergo a series of moral trials before she may marry the hero and assume her roles as mistress of an estate or parsonage and moral leader of her society. It is here that Marilyn Butler who also sees the novels as vehicles of conservative ideology, differs from Duckworth. She sees the context of Jane Austen's novels as the 'war of ideas' of the late eighteenth century between Jacobin and anti-Jacobin writers.[23] Jane Austen is placed firmly in the second camp, despite the protests of many critics that Jane Austen is no mere creature of party. The distinguishing feature of the anti-Jacobin vision, for Butler, is its pessimistic view of human nature and its deep suspicion of, and hostility to, all forms of individualism. The lesson of the anti-Jacobin is the necessity of submission of the self to the social, to a moral order which stands outside of and above the individual, to objective moral and religious values which must be learnt in a sound moral education and which are not revealed to individual intuition. The individual cannot rely on his own judgement and emotions in such matters but must submit to the inherited and superior wisdom of traditional society. The remedy of the novels is not the revitalisation of traditionalism with moral individualism but, on the contrary, the conquest of dangerous assertions of self. The moral education of the protagonists leads to the submission of self to social guidance.

Butler's perspective leads to interpretations of the novels which differ considerably from the received accounts. It is *Pride and Prejudice* which succeeds *Mansfield Park* as problematic, while the latter fits her interpretation relatively easily. Duckworth's approach to *Pride and Prejudice* can be readily accommodated to the usual view of that novel, which sees it as a contrapuntal in structure. Darcy (traditionalism) and Elizabeth (individualism, vitality) learn to recognise their respective errors of pride and prejudice and, suitably chastened, to appreciate their opposed virtues: it is a union of opposites. Their virtues, like their vices, complement each other. Butler sees this as a common *mis*reading of the novel. Darcy and Elizabeth are alike both in their virtues and their vices. 'Pride' and 'Prejudice' are vices which go hand in hand and which each character displays. Both learn the same moral lesson in the course of the novel. But Darcy's sins are more venial than Elizabeth's and it is *her* moral education that we witness, not his. In Butler's opinion, the mistaken interpretation arises because *emotions* which the protagonists arouse in the reader escape the control of the author and work against the *judgements* which she is asking one to make. The modern reader frequently fails to perceive the extent to which Jane Austen was critical of Elizabeth Bennet's rebelliousness and iconoclasm, because he/she identifies with Elizabeth and assumes that the author does so too. Conversely, modern readers find it difficult to identify with the colourless Fanny in *Mansfield Park*, and the misinterpretation of *Pride and Prejudice* adds to this difficulty. The two heroines are so very different that they cannot both be taken as authorial figures: Elizabeth is iconoclastic, vigorous, self-reliant; Fanny is timid, conformist and moralistic. Either Jane Austen was inconsistent (Mudrick argues that she oscillated between social criticism and craven conformism), or we are mistaken in taking one or other heroine as authorial. Fleischmann resolves the problem by inserting a considerable distance between *Fanny* and her author;[24] Butler, while not wanting to say that Jane Austen intends us to approve everything Fanny says and does, insist that it is *Elizabeth* who is at the greater distance from her author and whose actions and speech in the early part of the novel are meant to be judged critically, despite the reader's and the author's affection for her. This interpretation certainly reduces the apparent inconsistencies which have troubled many commentators. Unfortunately, it is achieved at the expense of a certain one-sidedness. It is not only Elizabeth who mocks the inhabitants of her social world but also her author. Some of the most cutting remarks come not from the lips of Elizabeth but in direct authorial comment, including the celebrated judgement of Mrs. Bennet: 'She was a woman of mean understanding, little information and uncertain temper.'[25] Butler cites Jane Austen's prayer of Christian humility, which recommends self-examination and control combined with tolerance towards the faults of others, but fails to cite equally telling evidence that Jane Austen often honoured the second half of this injunction more in the breach than in the observance. Those who have seen a likeness between Jane Austen and Elizabeth Bennet surely are not wrong – the letters are pure and unreformed Elizabeth Bennet. Similarly, many of the virtues which we are asked to admire in Fanny are emphatically not those of her author – her timid romanticism for instance, as well as her moralism. The kernel of truth in Mudrick's interpretation must not be lost. Austen *is* critical of the people in the novels who ought to be bearers of traditional values, but they provoke her to laughter rather than moral outrage. She is not, of course, subversive of the values themselves and to suggest that she is, is a major misinterpretation.

Duckworth and Butler are correct in identifying Jane Austen's world-view with modern conservatism. But they mark off the boundaries, between that conservatism and co-existing ideologies, too sharply. There is a danger in doing this of forcing the novels into too narrow a mould. In England, the class that was the bearer of conservative ideology, the gentry, occupied a fundamentally ambivalent position in the capitalist society which it had helped to forge, so it is not surprising if its ideology is likewise full of contradictions. We may expect to find evidence at this level of interconnections which match the more celebrated interpenetration of the gentry with industrial and commercial capitalism. Butler speaks of 'progressive' and 'reactionary' ideologies, but they were so within the general context of a society which had experienced a bourgeois revolution 150 years previously and whose subsequent capitalist development was one in which 'progressive' industrialists and 'reactionary' gentry alike were deeply implicated. Nevertheless, the ideological differences were recognisable well enough and, at this juncture in the relationship between industrial and agrarian capitalism, the tendency was towards emphasis on their differences rather than as later in the nineteenth century novel, on their complementarity.

In labelling Jane Austen anti-Jacobin, Butler is opposing the common interpretation that she trod a middle road. She is particularly opposed to the view of Jane Austen as mediator between the Jacobin and anti-Jacobin views of human nature and sees the novels as a clear expression of orthodox Christian pessimism. In my view, Jane Austen presents a more complex, structured view of her characters, in which human nature as such plays a subordinate but important part, as shown in Figure I.

Figure I

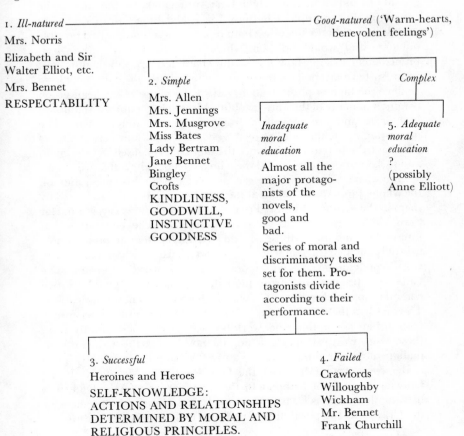

1. *Ill-natured* ———————————————————— *Good-natured* ('Warm-hearts, benevolent feelings')

Mrs. Norris

Elizabeth and Sir
Walter Elliot, etc.

Mrs. Bennet

RESPECTABILITY

2. *Simple*

Mrs. Allen
Mrs. Jennings
Mrs. Musgrove
Miss Bates
Lady Bertram
Jane Bennet
Bingley
Crofts
KINDLINESS,
GOODWILL,
INSTINCTIVE
GOODNESS

*Inadequate
moral
education*

Almost all the
major protago-
nists of the
novels,
good and
bad.

Series of moral and
discriminatory tasks
set for them. Pro-
tagonists divide
according to their
performance.

Complex

5. *Adequate
moral
education*
?
(possibly
Anne Elliott)

3. *Successful*

Heroines and Heroes

SELF-KNOWLEDGE:
ACTIONS AND RELATIONSHIPS
DETERMINED BY MORAL AND
RELIGIOUS PRINCIPLES.
Social and Moral leadership at
apex of local society.

4. *Failed*

Crawfords
Willoughby
Wickham
Mr. Bennet
Frank Churchill

RESPECTABILITY

Maximum possible good which may be achieved within each category is
indicated in capitals.

This is a schematic presentation, which does not include all the subtle gradations and distinctions which Jane Austen makes within most of the categories. For example, Charlotte Lucas and Jane Fairfax do not fit exactly any of these categories; both represent less than the best possible outcome and would fall somewhere between 3 and 4. But it is immediately striking how few of the characters are thoroughly bad; Jane Austen may be pessimistic about the ability of many people to achieve the highest possible good, but she lacks the Manichean vision common to many of the anti-Jacobins. Most of her 'failures' amount to very little and are prevented from doing very much harm. The interesting division is not between 'good' and 'bad' but between those who have the potential to achieve the highest level of self-development and social responsibility and those who have not. The latter are almost all minor characters (with the exception of Jane and Bingley) and, on the whole, Jane Austen laughs at them rather than being scandalised by them in the manner of Fanny Price. The laughter, however, is often far from kindly, as Harding correctly perceived. The characters that interest her, and us, are those who do have high potential; on the whole it is only such characters who are taken seriously – whose failures are worth condemning or whose moral struggle is worth recording. The Crawfords present one of the most interesting cases. There are two common approaches to the Crawfords, both of which are misleading. The first sees them as essentially evil, a threat to Mansfield because of their urban corruption and worldliness.[26] The second, mostly from those who are unsympathetic to the novel, sees the Crawfords as maligned by their author and/or Fanny.[27] What is less frequently noted is the counterpoint between the Crawfords and Mansfield. If the Crawfords represent a threat to the moral order at Mansfield, it is because that order is weak and exposed; and Mansfield represents for the Crawfords the possibility of realising their own better natures:

> Mrs. Grant: 'You are as bad as your brother, Mary; but we will cure you both. Mansfield shall cure you both – and without any taking in. Stay with us and we will cure you.'[28]

The Crawfords are more sharply perceptive about the inhabitant of Mansfield than either Fanny or Edmund, which enables them to exploit the weaknesses they detect in Maria, Julia and others. Their judgement is sound. Both are sensible of the indignities suffered by Fanny and, during the theatrical episode, Mary Crawford is warm and kind in defence or Fanny against Mrs. Norris.[29] They are, at first, detached observers bent only on enjoyment and mischief. A mark of the

Crawfords' high potential is their recognition of the superior worth of Edmund and Fanny, to whose influence they submit, in Mary's case unwillingly, in Henry's with a facility which cannot be maintained when he is away from Fanny. Both emotional attachment and sound judgement pull them towards Fanny and Edmund but these are not strong enough to overcome the corrupting effects of their education and upbringing when the Crawfords move out of the orbit of Mansfield and back to London. Perhaps Jane Austen drew back from the slow process of re-generation which the Crawfords had begun under the guidance of Fanny and Edmund because of the imbalance between the two pairs. Fanny and Edmund are so lacking in forcefulness that it is impossible to imagine them gaining any lasting ascendancy and leadership in their relationships with people so energetic and vital as the Crawfords. The moral threat which they represent for Mansfield is in the end greater than the normal power of Mansfield over the Crawfords. Jane Austen is wise to dimiss them rather than to try to reform them.

IV

Jane Austen's world is depicted from the point of view of her heroines. The women in her fictional world can only hope to play the role of moral and social leadership if they are both fortunate and discriminating in the crucial choice of a marriage partner. If they choose unwisely, then however exemplary they may be, their role can only be a modest one, as the case of Anne Elliot's mother illustrates. They can temper the faults of their husbands, and help to ensure their respectability.

> 'In the eighteenth century society, daughters came to be of more consequence to a father than his younger sons. Daughters were the key to family connexion and influence.'[30]

The business of negotiating a marriage alliance and agreeing a settlement was often difficult and protracted, and many a proposed union came to nothing because the terms could not be agreed. Entail and the strict settlement were devices by which the gentry protected their interests as a rentier class against the encroachments of commodity capitalism on the land. The marriage settlement provided a jointure for the woman, should she outlive her husband, and marriage portions for any daughters, plus provision for younger sons. The terms, often the subject of delicate negotiations by family lawyers, would normally depend on the fortune which the wife herself brought to the union, an important source of liquid funds for the estate, and the income of the husband. The norm was of 'equal alliance' and that the calculation was exact may be inferred from the opening lines of *Mansfield Park*:

> ' . . . Miss Maria Ward of Huntingdon with only seven thousand pounds, had the good luck to captivate Sir Thomas Bertram of Mansfield Park . . . All Huntingdon exclaimed on the greatness of the match, and her uncle, the lawyer, himself allowed her to be at least three thousand pounds short of any equitable claim to it.'[31]

J. F. G. Gornall has explored the novels for what they reveal of eighteenth century attitudes to marriage and finds that they recommend both equal alliance and mutual affection; a reading gained by the expedient of giving all utterances of all characters, plus authorial comment, equal weight as 'evidence'.[32] When Jane Austen's fictional alliances are examined with due weight to her use of irony and comment, a different picture emerges. All her heroines, with the exception of Emma, have relatively small portions – relative that is to the hope of marriages which would yield incomes sufficient to maintain gentry life styles: a minimum of £500 per annum; £1,000 for comfort; and £2,000 for style. The only heroine whose fortune is not disclosed is Anne Elliot, but we may assume that it is small, given the extravagance of her father and sister and the fact that their heir to the Kellynch estate (entailed away from them in the absence of a son) scorns Elizabeth in favour of a lady with more cash. Jane Austen puts the term 'equal alliance' into the mouth of Sir Walter but the context makes it clear that the equality in question is not of material wealth but of birth. Sir Walter has such a high opinion of his baronetcy that he believes honour to be all on one side in marrying his penniless daughters to men of wealth but (slightly) inferior birth. Jane Austen does seek 'equal alliance' in her marriages but not *materially* equal alliances. The equality sought and valued is first of all of affection, intelligence, taste and moral principle. Secondly, she recognises the claims of birth, as the following discussion between Anne Elliot and Mrs. Smith about the first marriage of Mr. Elliot, the heir, indicates:

Anne:	'But was she not a very low woman?'
Mrs. Smith:	'Yes: which I objected to, but he would not regard. Money, money was all that he wanted. Her father was a grazier, her grandfather had been a butcher . . . not a difficulty or a scruple was there on his side, with respect to her birth.'[33]

And thirdly, Jane Austen is hard-headed about the need for material prosperity. In *Mansfield Park* she makes it almost a condition of the development of moral and intellectual worth in the contrast drawn between Mansfield and Portsmouth. The moral order of Mansfield may be precarious, but it is the only viable locus of such order. In *Sense and Sensibility*, the sensible Elinor and the romantic Marianne differ only in the size of income thought necessary; for Marianne 'a mere competence' of £1,800-£2,000, for Elinor 'wealth' of £1,000. *Persuasion* is equivocal on the need for material security where affection is strong. Anne Elliot, persuaded at nineteen against her engagement to Captain Wentworth because his only hope of a fortune lay in his naval career, is at twenty- seven;

> '. . . eloquent . . . on the side of early warm attachment, and a cheerful confidence in futurity, against the over-anxious caution which seems to insult exertion and distrust Providence! – She had been forced into prudence in her youth, she learned romance as she grew older – the natural sequel of an unnatural beginning.'[34]

But although Jane Austen generally recognises the need for material prosperity, she is altogether indifferent to the question of material *equality* between the two partners. If Gornall's norm of equal alliance were upheld, then Catherine Morland had no business to fall in love with Henry Tileny and his father, the general, was after all correct, if a little brutal, to turn her out of doors when he discovered the size of her fortune. Elinor and Marianne, with £1,000 apiece, could not have aspired to Willougby, who expected if he toed the line to inherit a valuable estate from his aunt, or Edward Ferrars, an elder son, destined by his family for an heiress worth no less than £30,000. The Bennet daughters were similarly placed; yet Elizabeth married Darcy, worth £10,000 per annum, and Jane married Bingley, with an inherited fortune of £100,000. Interestingly, Darcy's objection to the Bennet girls as marriage partners was not directed against their low fortunes, but their 'undesirable' connections – an uncle in trade, and the singularly vulgar mother and sisters. The portionless Fanny in *Mansfield Park* is courted by, but rejects, the wealthy Henry Crawford. Superiority of wealth is clearly held to be no compensation for inferiority of moral principle.

Jane Austin is merciless at the expense of those who make material considerations the *sole* determinant of marriage choice. Edward Ferrars is disinherited by his mother in favour of his younger brother, and the family ambition to annex the fortune of Miss Morton shifts accordingly:

> '"We think now" – said Mr. Dashwood, after a short pause, " of *Robert's* marrying Miss Morton!" Elinor, smiling at the grave and

decisive importance of her brother's tone, calmly replied,
"The lady, I suppose, has no choice in the affair."
"Choice! – how do you mean?"
"I only mean, that I suppose from your manner of speaking, it must
be the same to Miss Morton whether she marry Edward or Robert."
"Certainly, there can be no difference; for Robert will now to all
intents and purposes be considered the eldest son: and as to anything
else, they are both very agreeable young men, I do not know that one
is superior to the other.'"[35]

The values which Jane Austen celebrates in her fictional marriages
are fully commensurate with her conservative ideology. Due
recognition of its material basis makes her not 'progressive' or
'subversive' but a realist in terms of the class and individual interest of
her protagonists. However, what her heroines bring to these alliances is
the moral and intellectual strengths to the lack of which she had
attributed the main threat to gentry society. The heroines guarantee the
renewal of gentry society by marriages into it.

V

It is not easy to determine how much the novels of Jane Austen owe to
any specifically female consciousness. They are strictly limited to that
section of her class and its activities which she knew from her own
experience, and this accounts for the fact that the relationships of
production are not depicted. She does not stray from her own class and
its internal relations even to portray such inter-class relations as might
be compatible with conservative paternalism. Peasants, impoverished
villages, servants, are notable for their absence, except where they
(anonymously) help the plot along (Emma's sick cottagers). It is true
that her male heroes suffer by comparison with the heroines; they tend
to be flat, fictional stereotypes. We have to take on trust Darcy's
reformation in the course of the novel, but we are party to Elizabeth's
painful re-education. Courtship and marriage are the subject of these
novels; but one which was shared by the novel in general at that time
and was not exclusive to women writers. Jane Austen portrays her
women sympathetically, and from within, but her attitude to them does
not differ from that of her class. Marriage to the right man – that is, one
who is affectionate, principled, intelligent, well-born and in good
circumstances – is the only worthwhile project for a woman; although
family relations, especially between siblings, are also highly prized. If
this idea fails – and the almost uniformly laughable *established* marriages
with which the novels are littered suggests that it must fail frequently –
then a stoical acceptance is prescribed – to make the best of poor

circumstances and to be of use to others by mitigating their folly. Anne Elliot embodies this stoicism among the heroines but it is all present in other women who have made less than ideal alliance – Anne's mother, Charlotte Lucas, etc. As Hazel Mews put it: 'A sensible woman', in such circumstances, 'can still make something of her own life, and her duty is to help her husband make the best of his by her quiet and intelligent influence.'[36] However, the suggestion of possible tragic outcomes for women in their narrowly circumscribed lives, their lack of education and means of independent livelihood, is muted. The heroines uniformily achieve the ideal marriage and presumably live happily ever after. The fate of her less fortunate sisters, within her class, is not dwelt upon. Jane Austen has been criticised for her failure to write a novel in which characters in the situation of Miss Bates or Jane Fairfax were brought more to the fore. Such portraits must have been well within her scope, such lives only too depressingly familar to her. The only work with a heroine in such a position is the fragment *The Watsons* and all the signs are that Emma Watson, like Jane Fairfax, was destined to be rescued by marriage. The reason for Austen's failure to explore the situation of such women in depth may lie in her ideological limitations. She had chosen to understand the crises of her class as a *moral* crises and could therefore only attribute deep-seated and manifest evils to moral and human failings, not to structural causes. Emma's rudeness to Miss Bates is the turning point of *Emma*. She is roundly criticised for it by Knightley, who is persistently kind to Miss Bates. But the rudeness of Emma and others is not the cause of Miss Bates's plight, and while 'kindness' may mitigate that plight, it is rooted in the structure of gentry society itself which offers such women no independent role. Any serious examination of it must necessarily lead to a different analysis of that society than Jane Austen's. She instinctively avoids such dangerous territory, aware perhaps that the injunction to be kind to the Miss Bateses of her world hardly measured up to their need and the ingenuity of their situation. The materials of the novels are carefully selected and arranged in such a way that the weaknesses and contradictions of their vision will not be exposed. Perhaps this is why objects of charity do not feature, as they do in the novels of eighteenth century writers who influenced Jane Austen, such as Fanny Burney. The strength of Jane Austen's fiction lies in the portrayal of the nuances of social relationships. In the case of such inter-class relations, either the ideology or fictional veracity would have had to be abandoned. Only in intra-class relations could the two be kept in harmony, and a focus on internal relations was consistent with her sense that her class was threatened with corrosion from within.

Against this record of feminine conservatism must be set the fact that in her own life Jane Austen transcended the narrow role allotted to women of her class, against all the odds. The education of women was cursory in the eighteenth century, limited to the superficial acquisition of drawing room accomplishments; it was an education in manners. Jane Austen's formal schooling ended when she was nine, the remainder of her education was in the hands of parents and older brothers. Novel writing was perhaps the only literary activity for which such an education was not too great a handicap, for it gave her leisure to pursue the best possible apprenticeship, that of wide reading of contemporary literature: family readings, in which new works were subjected to collective scrutiny and criticism. Q. D. Leavis has shown the extent to which this apprenticeship in reading and criticism informed her work: also the sheer intellectual labour behind the polished surface of her novels.[37]

If inadequacies in the education which women of her class received was turned to account by Jane Austen, so too was the second restriction under which she suffered, the narrowness of the milieu in which she passed her life. The lack of reference to contemporary history has often been noticed, but this was a deliberate choice. She limited herself to the world which she knew at first hand. In a letter to a niece making her first attempt at authorship she wrote: '. . . we think you had better not leave England. Let the Portmans go to Ireland: but as you know nothing of the manners there you had better not go with them. You will be in danger of giving false representations. Stick to Bath and the Foresters. There you will be quite at home.'[38] The ability to create a fictional world from such limited materials, without similarly restricting the breadth and depth of the world-vision it carried, is a measure of her creative genius.

A third and equally serious impediment to literary achievement was the nature of the day-to-day life of her class and sex. She was of course 'a woman of leisure' – paid employment was barred. But it does not follow that her time was her own. The social round of visiting and entertaining could not be avoided. Sick relatives had to be attended (her mother suffered from ill-health), charities dispensed, the poor visited, etc. Her own conservatism dictated submission to these demands on her time. The house was small and she wrote in a sitting-room, not in a private study, constantly at the mercy of chance interruptions. This problem was exacerbated by her desire to keep her authorship secret. The novel was the form most open to intervention by women at that time, and women made a contribution unprecedented in any other art before or since. Poetry demanded a less informal education, while drama was less socially acceptable. An essayist required greater breadth of experience and knowledge of public affairs. The rise of the novel marked a shift from patronage to a market nexus. This did not happen overnight, and the dedication of *Emma* to the Prince Regent is an indication of residual forms of patronage. But women of Jane Austen's class, constrained to lead sheltered lives in which any public notice would be unacceptable, could survive more readily in a market system in which their anonymity could be preserved. Needless to say, Jane Austen's relationship to the literary market was very different from that of many of her male contemporaries, who turned to it as a means of livelihood. Scott in Britain and Balzac in France were both prolific because they were trying to write their way out of indebtedness. Jane Austen's talent was not of a kind to survive total dependence on the market. In all, she made only about £700-£1,000 from her work. She depended, like all women of her class, on the support of family and kin. Her submission to the conditions under which she produced was then doubly determined – by ideological acceptance and economic dependence.

The falling away of major contributions to fiction by women in the late nineteenth century probably had more than one cause. The field of occupations open to women become more diverse, so that creative energies which in the earlier period could have found almost no other outlet, may have been diverted into other pursuits. Moreover, as novel-writing became more fully professionalised, women must have competed for such a career on the same unequal terms which account to this day for their underrepresentation in *all* the professions.

Charlotte Brontë wrote in *Jane Eyre* that,

> 'Women are supposed to be very calm generally: but women feel just as men feel: they need exercise for their faculties and a field for their efforts as much as their brothers do: they suffer from too rigid a restraint, too absolute a stagnation, precisely as men would suffer; and it is narrow-minded in their more privileged fellow-creatures to say that they ought to confine themselves to making puddings and knitting stockings, to playing on piano and embroidering bags.'

Paradoxically, Jane Austen endorsed the narrow view of women in the conservative ideology of her novels while simultaneously denying it by the act of writing them.

University of Warwick.

REFERENCES

1. W. K. Rugg: 'Of Jane's Good Company', *Christian Science Monitor*, 1952.

2. D. W. Harding: 'Regulated Hatred: An Aspect of the Work of Jane Austen', *Scrutiny*, VIII, 1940; reprinted in I. Watt (ed.): *Jane Austen: a Collection of Critical Essays*, 1963, and elsewhere.

3. Marvin Mudrick: *Jane Austen: Irony as Defence and Discovery*, Princeton, London, 1952, p. 36.

4. David Daiches: 'Jane Austen, Karl Marx, and the Aristocratic Dance', *American Scholar*, 17, 1948.

5. Q. D. Leavis: 'A Critical Theory of Jane Austen's Writings', *Scrutiny*, 1941-1942.

6. Mudrick: op.cit., p. 171.

7. Kingsley Amis: 'Whatever Became of Jane Austen?', *Spectator*, October, 1957; reprinted in Watt: op.cit.

8. Leavis: op.cit.

9. Watt: op.cit.

10. cf. William and Richard A. Austen-Leigh: *Jane Austen: her Life and Letters*, New York, 1965.

11. E. P. Thompson: 'Peculiarities of the English', *Socialist Register*, 1965.

12. Perry Anderson: 'The Origins of the Present Crisis', *New Left Review*, 23, 1964.

13. G. E. Mingay: *English Landed Society in the Eighteenth Century*, London, 1963; J. D. Chambers: *The Agricultural Revolution 1750-1880*, Batsford, London, 1966.

14. cf. J. Saville: 'Primitive Accummulation . . .', *Socialist Register*, 1969.

15. cf. Mingay: op.cit.

16. K. Marx.

17. Thompson: op.cit.

18. Harold Perkin: *The Origins of Modern English Society, 1780-1880*.

19. Alasdair MacIntyre: *A Short History of Ethics*, London, 1966.

20. The silliest of all criticisms of Jane Austen is the one which blames her for not writing about the battle of Waterloo and the French Revolution'. Arnold Kettle.

21. Alistair Duckworth: *The Improvement of the Estate*, Baltimore, 1971.

22. J. Levenson: *Confucian China and its Modern Fate*, three volumes, London, 1958-65.

23. Marilyn Butler: *Jane Austen and the War of Ideas*, Oxford University Press, London, 1975.

24. Fleischman: op.cit.

25. *Pride and Prejudice*, R. W. Chapman (ed.), Oxford University Press, London, 1923. All references to the novels are to the Chapman edition.

26. e.g. Duckworth: op.cit.; Butler: op.cit.; A. Walton Litz: *Jane Austen: a Study of her Artistic Development*, Chatts, 1965.

27. e.g. Mudrick: op.cit.; Fleischman: op.cit.

28. *Mansfield Park*, Chapman edition, Vol. III, p. 47.

29. ibid., p. 147.

30. Mingay, op.cit., p. 29.

31. *Mansfield Park*, p. 3.

32. J. F. G. Gornall: 'Marriage, Property and Romance in Jane Austen's Novels', *History Today*, 17, 1967.

33. *Persuasion*, Chapman edition, Vol. V, p. 202.

34. ibid., p. 30.

35. *Sense and Sensibility*, Chapman edition, Vol. V, p. 296.

36. Hazel Mews: *Frail Vessels*, 1969.

37. Leavis: op.cit.

38. Austen-Leigh: op.cit., p. 356.

Structure and Ideology in the Novels of Doris Lessing

Alan Swingewood

This paper is a preliminary exploration of the relation of form and content with the specific socio-historical context in the imaginative fiction of one writer. The analysis is not comprehensive; it is intended only as a first step towards a Marxist theory of the modern novel.

The starting point is Lucien Goldmann's much criticised sociology of the novel. Goldmann's position in this programmatic text is similar to other twentieth century critics who identify the 'decline' or 'death' of the novel form with trends towards a collectivist society and the necessary elimination of liberal individualism.[1] However, Goldmann's main point was not the dissolution of liberal ideology as the basic element for maintaining the novel form but the steady decline within contemporary capitalism of these independent social *groups* which alone constitute the real creators of literature. For Goldmann the modern writer becomes isolated and alienated, a problematic individual existing on the fringes of society, his artistic vision deterministically related to the *total* structure of society. Now there is here an important parallel between Goldmann's thesis of 'organised capitalism' and the pessimistic social theory of the Frankfurt school (Adorno, Horkheimer, Marcuse), especially Horkheimer's description of modern capitalism as 'rationalised, automated, totally managed' in which all significant *mediating* social institutions (the family, political parties, trade unions) no longer exercise any independent role in the cultural and political socialisation of the individual. In the face of modern technology and mass communications the potentially revolutionary proletariat of Marx's theory are integrated into the alienated world and reified consciousness of capitalist mass culture. The result is the virtual elimination of 'every vestige of even a relative autonomy for the individual.'[2]

The whole thrust of these arguments is to show that as 'civil society' grows progressively weaker the state (or 'political society' in Gramsci's terms) develops into a totalitarian structure dominating every sphere of human activity. Yet the actual sociological evidence for such negative conclusions remains thin in the work of Goldmann, Adorno and Marcuse: institutions such as trade unions, political parties and education have played an increasingly independent role in capitalism; class conflict and struggle, far from disappearing, have taken new forms and the experience of inflation during the past few years has clearly shown as vacuous the sociological concept of 'organised', 'totalitarian' capitalism. The class structure of contemporary capitalism is not atomised but constitutes a complex and dense structure of mediating institutions and it is precisely within this *hegemony* that the separate fractions of social classes, professional and occupational associations, literary and political groups retain their resilience and independence. These institutions and the groups which constitute them thus act as the crucial mediation between individual and society as a whole.[3]

Goldmann's sociology of the novel, then, is rooted in a model of society profoundly historicist: historical economic laws and trends work irresistibly towards definite social, cultural and political ends and they do so independently of the specific 'moments' and conjunctions of class struggle and opposition. The origin of these ideas can be traced to Lukács's *History and Class Consciousness* (1923) with its depiction of capitalist economy and culture as a dehumanised, reified and *total* system which dominates the individual to the exclusion of those institutions of 'civil society' such as trade unions in which the working class did struggle against capitalist domination. The result is a social and cultural theory lacking any genuine grasp of hegemony; by definition 'mass society' and 'organised capitalism' are societies ruled by 'direct domination' through a powerful state and state apparatus. Goldmann's sociology of the novel is therefore no sociology at all since it has no theory or even concept of social structure. Goldmann has thus removed any consideration of the complex, dialectical relation of literary texts to *specific* social structure in favour of broad homologies between text and society as a whole, thus reducing literary content and form to mere mimetic reflection of inevitable economic trends; the unity and coherence of a text therefore hinges on the *accurate* representation of such trends. The problematic hero disappears and is replaced by collective heroes; the novel form more and more approximates to a factual and conceptual rather than fictional structure. It is in this way, of course, that Goldmann, like Adorno and Benjamin, locates modernism (Kafka, Joyce, Robbe-Grillet), not as an irrational response to capitalism and pessimism (as in Lukács's theory of realism), but as a necessary artistic mode of representing capitalist alienation and therefore to be praised. There is, too, a striking similarity between Goldmann's *theory* of the novel form (based on Lukács's idealist *Theory of the Novel*), as distinct from his sociology of the novel, and Walter Benjamin's argument that the novel, as a form of cultural communication historically linked with bourgeois social organisation (the isolated, privatised, individualistic middle-class reader, capitalist printing, mass communications and technology), is gradually

transformed into a new mode of communication which replaces
narrative and the story element in fiction:

> It took the novel, whose beginnings go back to antiquity, hundreds of
> years before it encountered in the evolving middle class those elements
> which were favourable to its flowering. With the appearance of these
> elements storytelling began quite slowly to recede into the archaic; in
> many ways, it is true, it took hold of the new material, but it was not
> really determined by it. On the other hand, we recognise that with the
> full control of the middle class, which has the press as one of its most
> important instruments in fully developed capitalism, there emerges a
> new form of communication which, no matter how far back its origins
> may lie, never before influenced the epic form in a decisive way . . . it
> . . . brings about a crisis in the novel. This new form of
> communication is information.[4]

Benjamin's is therefore an argument about modernism, that the
traditional novel form contains within it elements which, over the
course of capitalist economic and technical development, transforms
the novel into non-art, into reportage.[5]

Thus unlike the formal arguments of literary development which
rigidly demarcate 'critical realism' from 'uncritical' and decadent
modernism (Lukács, Caudwell, Fischer) Benjamin's theory of the novel
allows for the contradictory, immanent structure of the form itself.
More precisely it retains the dialectical element in fictional structure by
linking *form* with specific socio-economic processes. With this, and
Goldmann's *theory* of the novel form in mind I will explore the fiction of
Doris Lessing.

First, however, I wish to suggest the following hypotheses:

1.   The novel form is closely related to large scale economic and social
changes but its specific content and character cannot be explained
adequately unless it is analysed in terms of social groups with whom the
writer is associated. The specific location of such groups within the class
structure and the ways in which they mediate the hegemonic structure
of contemporary capitalism will constitute one of the most important
structures in sociological-literary analysis.

2.   English cultural history is characterised by traditional forms and
structures; a profound hegemony has resulted in the persistence of the
realist novel form over modernist and experimental fiction. The tension
between the novel as story, and the novel as information, although both
are implicit within the form itself, emerges only at moments of acute
crisis. And this crisis is ultimately one of values and practice closely
bound up with the social position of the writer's group or groups.

3.   Fiction which emerges from such crisis will approximate to the *open*

rather than the *closed* form which is so characteristic of nineteenth century realism and English fiction in general. In the open form the novel remains ambiguous in its inner structure, values and ending. The closed form is challenged both by the immanent tendency within fictional form itself towards information rather than story and the increasingly problematic nature of bourgeois hegemony.

4. The *problematic hero* will tend to disappear from modern fiction; a collective hero and conceptual structure become important structural elements in the novel form.

Doris Lessing's novels fall into three distinct phases of development.

1. *The Grass is Singing* (1950), the first three volumes of the *Children of Violence* sequence *(Martha Quest*, 1952, *A Proper Marriage*, 1954, *A Ripple from a Storm*, 1958) and *Retreat to Innocence* (1956). These fictions are typical realist novels built around a knowable community and biographical structure. The form is non-problematic.

2. A transitional phase which is characterised by a problematic, self-questioning of the novel form itself with consequent shifts in focus and time; individual heroine and straightforward narrative structure is replaced by a collective hero, conceptual structure and a trend to information: the central text in this transition is *The Golden Notebook* (1962).

3. And finally a return to realist narrative form but with a rejection of community and individual biography as basic constituent elements in favour of isolated and fragmented individuals and an experience which is no longer essentially social and concretely historical but mystical and apocalyptic. The beginnings of this development are located in the last two volumes of the *Children of Violence* sequence (*Landlocked*, 1965, and *The Four Gated City*, 1969) and in Doris Lessing's more recent writings (*Briefing for a Descent into Hell*, 1971, *Memoirs of a Survivor*, 1974).

The question of schematisation is extremely important for while it is true that like other writers Doris Lessing's novels are characterised by certain recurring themes and preoccupations (madness in *The Grass is Singing*, *The Golden Notebook*, and *Briefing for a Descent into Hell;* political commitment in the *Martha Quest* novels and *The Golden Notebook;* sexual emancipation and the struggle for an autonomous self) the treatment of these themes varies significantly from one group of novels to another. And it is precisely this specific element which any sociological method should seek to preserve in its analysis. To synthesise the apparently similar thematic material from a number of novels into 'a style of thought' or 'structure of feeling' is to reduce the (often) complex and contradictory unity of a text to a straightforward reflection or emanation of an ahistorical abstraction. To grasp the structure and meaning of a literary text it is essential that its historical specificity and complex determinations (social and literary) are placed at the heart of sociological methodology.

Doris Lessing's first published novel, *The Grass is Singing*, [6] explores with great subtlty and insight the relationship of white settler ideology to the realities of African life. The basic structure of the novel is one which will dominate her later work, that of the clash of ideals between the individual and the collectivity and the impossibility for the individual to realise his ideals. In *The Grass is Singing* genuine selfhood and individual autonomy are impossible in a society which demands total adherence to its ideology. The individual is integrated into the white community and self is defined by *its* ideology (social, political and sexual norms are simply accepted) and is never allowed to develop any inner autonomy. The novel describes the empty, sterile and futile lives of two people brought by circumstances into a hopeless marriage, and whose values are unrealisable, their ambitions too large for their small world, living in a hostile environment which destroys them both. Caught in the trap of white settler poverty, with all hope for the future gone, the wife becomes a vegetable totally dependent on the African servant, incapable of any independent course of action. She retreats to madness as the only 'refuge' against the destruction of her life and self and in the end it is the African who emerges as the dominant force, 'powerful and sure of himself.' (p. 177). In a society in which the vast majority are excluded as subhuman ('munts'), where there is no contact except that of master and servant, this total ideology must destroy those who necessarily practice it although themselves living in poverty and spiritual degradation. The twelve year marriage ends in murder and madness.

The narrow, although concentrated focus of *The Grass is Singing* with its total pessimism and depiction of the individual as the sum of total social pressures exemplifies the realist, closed fictional form. The first three volumes of the *Children of Violence* sequence are equally realist and closed in form but go beyond the first novel by attempting a more ambitious rendering of the whole society both in terms of its class structure and ideology and the possibility of a radical alternative. *Martha Quest* is symbolic both of a heroine who, at the outset inexperienced and relatively 'innocent,' is seeking her selfhood and 'authentic' values in the 'degraded' world of white colonial Africa, and the wider question of the individual's relation with society as a whole.

The fictional universe of the first three volumes is characterised by a largely uncritical acceptance of the Communist Party and Martha's search for authenticity and meaning in life is ultimately bound up with the political community of socialist intellectuals and workers she identifies with in the second and third volumes. Central to the structure of these novels is the belief that meaningful relationships are possible only through action based on socialist values; the future is thus linked with these values and to affirm selfhood it is essential that the individual lives in the world and struggles to achieve and realise his values.

This is a fairly optimistic vision of the world. *The Golden Notebook* represents a transition to almost total pessimism and despair within a more problematic fictional form. In this novel experience is no longer evolving progressively, no longer expanding in rhythmn with Martha Quest's optimistic search for 'authentic' values but is deeply problematical because the values which invest experience with meaning are now seriously questioned. *The Golden Notebook* is a transitional work for its structure is bound up with Doris Lessing's abandonment of the Communist Party (which she left in 1957) and Marxism; but unlike other 'dissident' or disenchanted Communists (such as Koestler, Silone) she does not embrace anti-Communism so that her ideological standpoint remains fluid. In this connection it might be argued that the function of mental illness in the novel (in the life of Anna Wulf) is to prevent a coherent alternative to Communism and Marxism being formed: it is only in the next phase of development that Doris Lessing forges such an alternative. But perhaps more significantly the rejection of Marxism is depicted as a gradual rather than abrupt process and it is this which suggests that neither Martha Quest of the earlier novels nor Anna Wulf really understood or were deeply committed to Marxism as a world view.

Unlike the first three novels of the *Children of Violence* sequence *The Golden Notebook* approaches an open rather than closed form. As the major tradition of the English novel the closed form portrays the self in the process of continual discovery, of affirming itself through new experiences, but these experiences are 'closed off' at the end in such a way as to unify the complex and often contradictory material. In contrast, the open form refuses to contain the experience in a conveniently ideological ending; there is no 'closing off,' the ending and ultimate meaning remain ambiguous and problematic. But the fact that a novel has to end necessitates a choice:

1. All the contradictory or 'disturbing' experiences are ended or closed off in the manner of the nineteenth century realists; this

often means that material which cannot be resolved is resolved ideologically rather than artistically.

2. The experiences remain problematic and although the hero strives to transcend them and assert *his values* he fails to do so.[7]

Now it is the open form of the novel which characterises so much of modern fiction (Gide, Lawrence, Kafka, Conrad, Nabokov, Borges) and the importance of *The Golden Notebook* is that it is both open and closed and approximates to the novel as information. It is both open and closed in that although portraying a problematic world of experience, chaos and fragmentation and the impossibility of reconciling the many conflicts and tensions the novel nonetheless does 'close off' these contradictory elements at the end. Anna Wulf's madness and alienation are rendered non-problematical by the act of joining the Labour Party and taking up social work.

It can be seen from this brief discussion how closely Doris Lessing's novel approaches Goldmann's sociological theory of the novel: in *The Golden Notebook* there is no longer a heroine capable of affirming self and thus values through meaningful action but rather individuals alienated from and dominated by the external social world; it is no longer possible for values to invest life with meaning since the values themselves are deeply problematical and doubtful.

The post-*The Golden Notebook* novels are a return to the completely closed form although with one important difference from the early *Children of Violence* novels. The vision now is one of total despair but without the sense of the self seeking to affirm itself through social forces, striving to transcend fragmentation and chaos. In *The Four-Gated City* there is no longer a belief in a future created through human activity but a fatalistic acceptance of historical inevitability: the characters become mere puppets, enjoying no semblance of autonomy; experience is no longer problematical as in *The Golden Notebook* but contained and 'closed off.'

I shall now attempt a preliminary structural analysis of these novels relating them to the above discussion.

1. *Martha Quest, A Proper Marriage, A Ripple from a Storm*

There are three basic structures informing these three novels:

i. A rejection of bourgeois values and bourgeois community in favour of socialist values and socialist community.

ii. Romantic individualism: Martha Quest is aware of literature, her self partly 'formed by poetic literature,' one 'of that generation who had formed themselves by literature.'[8] The first two volumes are taken up with a contrast between Martha's subjective ideals and mundane reality: for example, sexual love: 'Martha, final heir to the long romantic tradition of love, demanded nothing less than that the quintessence of all experience, all love, all beauty, should explode suddenly in a drenching, saturating moment of illumination.'[9] Instead she marries into the white settler community and a life built around the 'barren' and monotonous activities of the local 'Sports Club' and 'set.' Like the heroine of *The Grass is Singing* Martha enjoys an 'appalling feeling of flatness, staleness and futility.'[10] She is like Emma Bovary whose values by their nature were impossible to realise in the world she inhabited. Thus the first two volumes chronicle Martha's futile attempt to translate values into action through a community which by its nature is hostile to them (the bourgeois community – the Magistrate, civil servants, professional groups). This conflict, which is unresolvable, is linked to the third structure.

iii. Passivity. Martha is not autonomous: at the beginning her job in the city is arranged through the Cohen brothers, she drifts into marriage, and later into socialism. After agreeing to marry Douglas, the following morning Martha decides 'she did not want to marry at all' but she does. Earlier she reflects on the need for Josh to guide her and much later on she thinks that 'what she actually wanted . . . was for some man to arrive in her life, simply take her by the hand, and lead her off into this new world.' (of socialism).[11]

These three structures express themselves in many ways but it should be obvious that there is a contradiction between the first and the other two. This question of unity is best approached through the elements which constitute the third structure:

(a) The individual is expected to conform on all levels: thus Martha conforms to her husband's anti-semitism and anti-communism, to the 'set,' to gossip, the running of the household, to her mother as the person organising her life. In short Martha does what others want her to do.

(b) When she realises that her marriage to Douglas is 'a foolish mistake' she does nothing but accept the sterile relationship; when she has the same experience with Anton Hesse her passivity is still the dominant feature of the relationship.

(c) Martha's attitude to the Communist party and to Marxism is one of uncritical acceptance. The Communist Party is defined in terms of organisation and dogma. There is nothing to suggest a genuine grasp of Marxist thought or socialist history and Martha's commitment takes place in a political and theoretical vacuum.

The basic contradiction, therefore, lies between the awareness of socialist community for political practice and the individualistic ideals of the heroine. Martha's quest for meaning and freedom necessarily flows from her relation with the community; it cannot be an individualistic quest. In *Martha Quest* the idea 'of separate things interacting and finally becoming one, but greater . . .' is perhaps the key to Martha's sense of freedom. It is possible only with and through a group; and yet collectivities absorb the individual, demanding conformism to the norms and thus the elimination of genuine individuality. It is this contradiction which dominates these three novels: within the network of the bourgeois community Martha's 'odd' socialist ideas are tolerated as 'deviant'; within the Communist group she retains and accepts her female role 'dreaming persistently of that man . . . who would allow her to be herself.'[12] The novels develop a strict homology between the structure of the community and sexual relations: when Martha joins the Communist group her sexual and emotional life remain unfulfilled precisely because Anton exemplifies the bureaucratic Stalinist approach to politics which then dominated the international Communist movement. The Party comes first and the personal lives of individual members must fit in with Party work; Anton defines Communism in austere, elitist terms and his attitude to persons is one of contempt.[13] And because there is no real grasp of the historical roots of Stalinism, or of Marxism, Martha must fail to reconcile her individualism with bureaucratic organisation. The overriding impression is that Martha becomes a Communist for personal, emotional reasons and her commitment remains on this plane. The failure to grasp Marxism is expressed by the concept of practice as welfare: there is an enormous gulf between this isolated Communist community and those Communist groups in Europe who, linked to the broad labour movement, were far more deeply involved in serious political activity.

These three novels are minor works of fiction: within them there is no real grasp of serious politics, Marxism, sexuality and mental health. They depict a largely non-problematic social world through the evolving biographical experience of the heroine. All this changes with the sudden qualitative transition to Doris Lessing's most important fiction, *The Golden Notebook*.

2. *The Golden Notebook*

There are four basic structures within this novel:
  i. A rejection of Marxism, revolutionary socialism and community in favour of a positive affirmation of individualistic values. Central to

this structure is the necessity to compromise: the values are therefore realistic and not romantic.

   ii. Social isolation, fragmentation, reification.

  iii. Passivity.

  iv. Information.

The most significant difference between the first three volumes of the *Children of Violence* sequence and *The Golden Notebook* is that it is now no longer possible to believe in a future brought about through collective action and inspired by collective ideals. The pervasive optimism and belief in human potential of the former novels has given way to irrational forces and unrestrained egotism: in *The Golden Notebook* there is an increasing emphasis on violence for its own sake and the hopelessness of human communication. In the earlier novels elements such as violence, egotism, sexuality and illness were integrated as an organic part of an evolving experience, but in *The Golden Notebook* they appear as destructive and irrational forces, no longer mediated by social relations but flowing from man's nature. There is, here, a decisive shift from the social and historical to the innate: violence, egotism, sexuality and illness are forces which, for the Marxist writer, are necessarily integrated and transcended as individualistic phenomena in the socialist community. This is an important point since Doris Lessing has consciously set the novel among Marxists and socialists 'because it has been inside the various chapters of socialism that the great debates of our time have gone on.'[14] Thus the question is one of analysing these various elements as they function within the totality of the novel. I will now illustrate briefly the ways in which the four structures identified above shape and condition three dominant themes: political commitment, sexual emancipation and finally mental breakdown.

(a) Political choice, values and practices are depicted in highly personal individualistic and passive terms. Like Martha Quest, Anna Wulf experiences Communism externally even though a member of the Party: thus although the novel gives an accurate account of the bureaucratic degeneration of the British Communist Party during the 1950s and especially of the isolated and marginal role of the intellectual within it, the whole experience is rendered individualistically. There is never, for example, any deep sense of political commitment or understanding of Marxism and the international Marxist movement. Anna joins the Communist Party 'because they believe in something' yet she soon discovers that the Party consists 'of people who aren't political at all,' but have 'a powerful sense of service.' Her activity is confined to the fringes of the movement, the occasional election campaign and the reading of manuscripts for the Party publishing house: Anna notes that she only meets other Communists and this is one reason why she'll leave. In fact her involvement is entirely passive: she finally leaves the Party not for any specific reason but through gradual disillusionment with the prospects for reforming the bureaucracy.[15]

At the heart of this fictional depiction of Communism is the conflict between the individual and the collectivity: Anna has two personalities, the Communist and the Anna Wulf; she tells her psychiatrist that 'If I could say *we*, really meaning it, I wouldn't be here would I?' She experiences Communism in this way precisely because Stalinism succeeded in imposing a bureaucratic, monolithic apparatus on the movement and an ideology which eliminated the individual except as part of the Party. A monolithic Party must necessarily annihilate every vestige of individuality and impose a stifling conformity. It is this historically specific process of political degeneration, the transformation of the Communist movement into totalitarianism which Anna Wulf cannot grasp and she, and the novel, identifies Stalinism with Marxism and thus with an irreconcilable conflict between the individual and the collectivity. When she leaves the Party, then, she does so on personal not ideological grounds: she writes that a 'stage' of her life was now over and she can turn to other things.[16] And because the commitment was so fragile there is no lurch to the right into anti-Communism as happened with writers such as Koestler and Silone. She comforts herself with a fatalistic interpretation of Communist history as a once in a century 'act of faith' which generates a great leap forward but then 'the well runs dry . . . the cruelty and the ugliness is too strong.'[17] The Communist movement is thus judged almost entirely from a deterministic and ahistorical standpoint. Therefore when Anna Wulf justifies her compilation of newspaper cuttings and her record of the mundane activities of ordinary day to day life as part of her search for truth she identifies *meaning* with information. Her diary, her 'reports' on Communist Party meetings, her notebooks filled with newspaper cuttings are attempts to impose a meaning and pattern on an historical experience which seems beyond the range of the novel form.[18] In an illuminating passage Anna Wulf writes that modern society is far too fragmented to support a novel form given to large philosophical statements (as in nineteenth century realism) and so the novel becomes an art form which 'we read *to find out what is going on.*'[19] Fiction and fact are fused; autobiography and information obliterate the story element.
(b) Anna and Molly are formally 'free women' defining themselves as 'a completely new type of woman.'[20] Yet it soon becomes obvious that

both women, as well as Anna's fictional heroine, Ella, want to get married; more significantly both women accept rather passively the ideological definitions of male/female relationships especially the role of woman. As in the Martha Quest novels the relations of the sexes are homologous with the structure of the community or the lack of community. The bureaucratised nature of the Communist Party which defines relations between people in terms of a fetishised organisation and inevitable historical goal finds its sexual expression in Anna's sterile relationship with the Communist, Willi, in Africa, her passive relationship with Michael for whom she is wholly domesticated ('It is a great pleasure, buying food I will cook for Michael, like the act of cooking itself.') and her highly charged neurotic relationship with the American writer Saul Green. In all three cases Anna is dependent on the man, acquiescing in the ideological notion of an essentialist female self. The fictional Ella, for example, has that 'female intuition' and *knows* by the 'quality' of Paul's voice that he would be her lover; and when he leaves each morning to return to his home and wife, 'to pick up a clean shirt', she passively accepts the situation.[24] The failure to 'connect' pervades all human relations in the novel: at the beginning of 'Free Women' Anna observes what she takes to be a 'perfect understanding' between the milkman and his son', an instinctive form of communication denied to every other character in the fiction. In the absence of any genuine community sexual relations become fraught and unsatisfactory, being reduced to orgasm and egotism. Sexual love is divested of its societal mediations; to love someone is to experience vaginal not clitoral orgasm and neither Anna nor Ella 'connect' in this way. The novel informs its readers thus:

> There can be a thousand thrills, sensations etc., but there is only one real female orgasm and that is when a man, from the whole of his need and desire takes a woman and wants her response. Everything else is a substitute and fake, and the most inexperienced woman knows this instinctively.[22]

The irony of 'Free Women' is especially brought out in Ella's remark that unless they love a man there cannot be orgasm yet men 'get erections when they're with a woman they don't give a damn about.'[23] The idea of innate human characteristics which differentiate men from women and condition their responses to sex, love, self, is clearly ideological and indicates the conservative essence of Doris Lessing's vision. Freedom is defined almost exclusively in terms of the male role and there is never any awareness that the male role itself is *unfree*. The question of freedom should have been linked to socialism and the socialist community but having abandoned that possibility we are left with essentialist notions of human relations.

(c) The problem of mental illness, like that of sexuality, is presented in highly individualistic terms. A fragmented society, the lack of a genuine community, the collapse of values and a belief in the future create a neurotic Anna suffering from anxiety and hysteria, her two distinct selves constituting the crisis of identity which is in effect the illness. In the end the problem of self is resolved partly through a 'Lawrentian' fusion of identities between Saul and Anna as well as in Anna's writing through which she creates other selves.[24] But the crisis of identity is brought about by Doris Lessing's ideological concept of selfhood, her definition of woman as having no separate identity outside the role she plays in relations with men: the passive acceptance of this and the seeking to fuse identities present a highly deterministic, asocial and essentialist notion of human nature. For there is no autonomy, no sense of choice and freedom: women are dominated by a reified notion of role which is cut off from its societal determinations.

There is, then, a complex unity combining in both open and closed forms: at the beginning of the novel Anna observes that 'everything is cracking up,' and as the novel develops a problematic world and self emerges in such a way that no solutions to the problems of politics, sexuality and mental illness seem possible. Yet the novel ends with Molly married and Anna no longer ill but a member of the Labour Party and contemplating social work. The four notebooks had expressed Anna's divided self, the lack of unity in her life and the struggle for truth. In the end truth eludes her and there is compromise. The closed ending clearly relates to the ideological concepts within the novel's various structures and is an attempt to impose a formal unity on the text in the manner of the nineteenth century realists. But no such artistic unity is possible given the nature of the material: the transitional nature of *The Golden Notebook* becomes clearer with Doris Lessing's subsequent fictions.

The experiment with the open form gives way to the closed form in *Landlocked* (1965) where the African Communists are depicted as conforming with white society (Anton Hesse), dying a futile death (Thomas who goes to the people and dies of fever) or rejecting Marxism. All the loose ends are tied together and Martha Quest leaves for England.[25] In the final volume of the *Children of Violence* sequence, *The Four-Gated City* (1969) a new vision emerges: cosmic evolutionism. Of the novel Doris Lessing has said that it is not fantasy but what is likely to happen to a mankind 'corrupted, violent, perverted and cruel.'[26] Marxism and socialism have been finally abandoned in favour of a deterministic philosophy of history and like many other Western intellectuals Doris Lessing has turned from science and rationality, which is identified with industry, urbanism, alienation, mass society and conformism, to Eastern mysticism.[27] The result is a closed fictional form in which the individual characters have no autonomy or freedom, their lives dominated by a pervasive sense of doom. *The Golden Notebook* had eliminated hero/heroine in the traditional sense and this is further developed in *The Four-Gated City*. Martha becomes entirely passive, a cipher and medium for social, historical and psychological movements. She still strives to assert her individuality: 'I want to live in such a way that I don't just – turn into a hypnotized animal,'[28] but the novel shows the complete power of the collectivity over the individual. The collectivity, the Coldridge family, is the 'hero' of the novel, insulating the characters from an alienated society with its mass culture, hedonism and egotism, the mentally ill being the only sane people in an insane society. The paradox is obvious: individualistic values survive only in the collectivity.

The apocalyptic vision expressed in the novel is fundamentally ahistorical and asocial. As in *The Memoirs of a Survivor* (1974) Doris Lessing is rejecting Western society, both capitalism and socialism, and using the novel form as a mode of communicating information about the psychological health of the oversocialised individual in modern mass society, and warning of the possible collapse of 'civilisation.' The result is the subordination of fiction to a conceptual structure of speculative philosophy and information. [29] Character is held in a vice of historical determinism; the imagination is debilitated and the novels are arid and withered in their depiction of human relations. Authenticity comes to mean the inner rather than the outer life which, in *Briefing for a Descent into Hell* (1971) is identified with metaphysical cosmic unity. In this novel Charles Watkins's inner experience (based almost entirely on the theories of R. D. Laing) are the means whereby he transcends his egotistic persona and his divided socialised self; the inner space voyage reunites him with a cosmic whole and a sense of unity which is clearly counterposed to earthy destructive individualism.[30]

These novels are closed forms, claiming an essentialist notion of man, an essence, a truth which lies outside ordinary experience and consciousness. But man's essence is the sum of culture, economy and polity at a given historical moment: in rejecting socialism and the materialist world view which defines the social and historical world as the result of *man's* own actions and accepting a metaphysical, non-historical notion of man Doris Lessing has succeeded in stifling the potentially liberative modernism and autonomy of that part of *The Golden Notebook* which strives to capture the ambiguity, richness and realistic complexity of man's social and historical condition.

Conclusion

I have argued that the three phases of Doris Lessing's career as a novelist can be analysed sociologically in terms of Goldmann's categories and methodology. But whereas Goldman linked the specific fictional structures with large scale economic change I believe it necessary to identify the social and political structures of a group or groups, for modern capitalism is not an atomised mass society but a complex balance of forces within a still strong civil society. The novel, of course, was never a direct expression of bourgeois class interests and although practised by social groups unsympathetic to capitalist political economy its form has been shaped by the fact of bourgeois class hegemony.[31] The resilience of this hegemony is perhaps the most important factor in any sociological study of the English novel and in particular the resistance by writers to artistic modernism. The great tradition of the English novel is realism and its major mode the closed form. Few English novelists have embraced fully the open form of fiction as their European counterparts have done: the significance of *The Golden Notebook* is that it moves towards the open form, towards a conceptual and information dominated structure, but then draws back to the closed form. During the early 1950s Doris Lessing uncritically supported the Communist Party; breaking from it in 1957 she joined the dissident Communists grouped around the magazine *The New Reasoner* but with its transformation into the *New Left Review* at the end of the 1950s she abandoned politics and Marxism; in the 1960s she more and more identified with Laingian psychoanalysis, Eastern mysticism (Sufism) and the 'counter-culture.' In conclusion therefore it might be said that these social groups were neither sociologically nor politically significant enough to provide the social basis of a coherent artistic vision.

London School of Economics & Political Science

1. L. Goldman: *Towards a Sociology of the Novel*, Tavistock Publications, London, 1975.

2. M. Horkheimer; *Critical Theory*, Herder and Herder, New York 1972, p. vii.

3. I have developed these points in greater detail in my *The Myth of Mass Culture*, Macmillan, London, 1977.

4. W. Benjamin: *Illuminations*, Cape, London, 1970, p. 88.

5. ibid, p. 161.

6. D. Lessing: *The Grass is Singing*, Penguin Books, London, 1961.

7. Goldmann, op. cit. p. 50.
On the open and closed forms of fiction see A. Friedman: *The Turn of the Novel*, Oxford University Press, New York, 1966.

8. D. Lessing: *Martha Quest*, Panther Books, London, 1975, p. 61, 184.

9. ibid. p. 202
See also D. Lessing: *A Ripple from a Storm*, Panther Books, London, 1966, p. 247 and 274 for identical feelings on Martha's Part.

10. D. Lessing: *A Proper Marriage*, Panther Books, London, 1966, p. 43. See also p. 78, 227, and *Martha Quest* p. 182.

11. *Martha Quest* p. 246, 222.
See also *A Proper Marriage*, p. 81, 293, 342.

12. *A Ripple from a Storm*, p. 274.

13. ibid, pp. 36-9, 58, 129, 134-6, 192, 204.

14. D. Lessing: 'Preface' to the 1972 edition of *The Golden Notebook*, Panther Books, London, 1973, p. 11.

15. ibid. p. 237, 169-74, 435.

16. ibid. p. 87. Doris Lessing herself left later on after Hungary; she has denied that there was any specific reason for leaving although the discovery of anti-semitism as a tool of policy combined with Khruschev's revelations about Stalin and the labour camps in 1956 must have been significant factors in her decision. See the description of her two CP editors, pp 337-9, an episode which, like many others dealing with the Communist Party is written in terms of information not imagination.

17. ibid, p. 273. A similar explanation is put forward in V. Serge's *The Case of Comrade Tulayev* (1945).

18. ibid, p. 571. Cf. pp 299-301, 466ff.

19. ibid. pp 79-80 (Doris Lessing's emphasis)

20. ibid. p. 26

21. ibid. pp 161-2, 334, 355; and see also pp 199-201, 205-6.

22. ibid. p. 220.
Indicative of Doris Lessing's portrait of 'free women' is the fact that none of them initiates sexual relations except when it doesn't matter.

23. ibid. p. 446.

24. ibid. pp 590-2

25. D. Lessing: *Landlocked*, Panther Books, 1973. All the familiar themes are rehearsed in this novel but the text remains lifeless and predictable.

26. Quoted by P. Schlueter: *The novels of Doris Lessing*, Illinois University Press, Carbondale, 1974. Schlueter and Michael Thorpe (*Doris Lessing:* Longmans for The British Council, London, 1973) argue that similar themes and ideas characterise all the *Children of Violence* novels and they fail to situate Doris Lessing sociologically and historically. Both under-emphasise the political element in her fiction and fail to discuss the question of Marxism and Stalinism.

27. In *The Four-Gated City* Martha rejects Marxism and psychoanalysis as different faiths aiming for the same ends but which have both failed. D. Lessing: *The Four-Gated City*, Panther Books, London, 1973, pp 528-30. And for similar ideas see 'Preface' to *The Golden Notebook.*

28. *The Four-Gated City*, p. 108. The same themes dominate the later, *The Summer Before the Dark*, 1973.

29. For Example, Doris Lessing: *The Memoirs of a Survivor*, The Octagon Press, London, 1974, p. 21.

30. D. Lessing: *Briefing for a Descent into Hell*, Panther Books, London, 1975, Cf. R. D. Laing: *The Divided Self*, Penguin Books, London, 1965, and especially, *The Politics of Experience*, Penguin Books, London, 1967, Chapter Seven, 'A Ten Day Voyage'.

31. For further discussion see my *The Novel and Revolution*, Macmillan, London, 1975 Chapter Two.

Form, Ideology and 'The Secret Agent'

Terry Eagleton

There is a sense in which Conrad's *The Secret Agent* is altogether too convenient a text to select for discussion in this kind of Monograph. For it is, self-evidently, a 'political' novel, and a materialist criticism should not give itself an easy ride by choosing as its object texts which 'spontaneously' conform to its method. Better, surely, to select an 'innocent' work – a Beddoes verse-tragedy or medieval love-lyric – than to risk the perils of methodological circularity, a mirror-image reciprocity between 'approach' and object. *The Secret Agent* may well seem too ideologically 'guilty' a fiction to strain the assumptions of an ideologically-oriented criticism; one may be merely repeating the evasion of the theological critic who works on nothing but Dante and Hopkins, or the semiotician for whom Joyce is the only true literature there is. Yet I am not in fact particularly concerned with the explicitly 'political' dimension of the novel, and certainly not with what might be termed a 'sociological' reading of it. Not that a 'sociology' of the novel can yield us nothing: it is *textually* relevant that a single historical incident is all the evidence there ever was to back up that vision of an anarchist-haunted London which *The Secret Agent* projects. The sociology of anarchism can tell us much about the novel's perceptions – can lead us, for example, to ask why Michaelis should be categorised as an anarchist when he is clearly a Marxist, or how it comes about that the nihilist Professor and time-serving Ossipon can be subsumed under the same political heading. There is nothing in the least empiricist about such questions, but this article will not be concerned with them. For I have chosen *The Secret Agent* because it seems to me a peculiarly paradigmatic example of the complex relations within fiction between forms and ideologies, formal elements and ideological sub-ensembles, aesthetic devices and codified perceptions. That this is so because of the unusual 'foregrounding' of the ideological which the novel effects is doubtless true; but I would claim that what can be observed with peculiar visibility in this self-consciously tendentious text is merely a convenient index of what occurs in the self-structuration of every literary work. We need, then, to beware of the ease with which an 'ideological' text yields us insights for materialist criticism, at the same time as we need to insist that such a text can indeed provide a provisional model for such a materialist method.

The specific form of *The Secret Agent* is composed of a complex amalgam of *genres* – a compound of spy-thriller, Dickensian 'imaginative realism', 'metaphysical' meditation and (in a loose sense of the term) naturalism. Each of these constituent *genres* contributes to an ideological contradiction between the 'exotic' and 'domestic' – a contradiction united in the novel's central character Verloc, the seedy domesticated double-agent. The spy-thriller inserts the fascination of the foreign into the sordidly routine world of *realpolitik;* 'Dickensian' realism involves an imaginative caricaturing of the familiar. The naturalist form produces, and is the product of, the bourgeois illusion of 'normality', of the solid indestructibility of the quotidian world. Yet the laboriously self-parodic quality of that naturalism in *The Secret Agent* intimates its self-contradictory character. For naturalism, in fetishising the material world, dislocates subjectivity from it, banishing it into its own autonomous zone where it inevitably presents itself as mysterious, unmotivated and opaque. The very form selected to produce the 'naturalness' of the world, when pressed to a caricaturing extreme, highlights the 'mystery' of subjectivity and so puts itself into question. This contradiction is vital for the 'ideology of the text' (hence the calculatedly self-parodic nature of its naturalist modes), for while *The Secret Agent* is constrained to defend the 'naturalness' of the quotidian world against the revolutionary dreams of anarchism, it is equally constrained not to do so at the cost of denying the value of subjectivity itself. But here the text encounters further contradiction. The more it confirms the 'naturalness' of the given by raising it to a *metaphysical* level, producing a 'metaphysical materialism' (the 'indestructibility of matter' and so forth), the more it is forced to conspire, as it were, with the 'metaphysical' dreams of the anarchists themselves, inhabiting that world of discourse in its very drive to undermine it. Moreover, the *repellant* vision of the world as a desert of brute matter which such self-parodic naturalism produces is bound to render the views of the anarchists more palatable – to make the grotesque nihilist Professor something more than a madman. The forms of the text, then, produce and are produced by an ideological contradiction embedded within it – a contradiction between its unswerving commitment to bourgeois 'normality' and its dissentient 'metaphysical' impulse to reject such 'false consciousness' for a 'deeper' insight into the 'human condition'.

This contradiction, in fact, arises from the internal conflicts of the Conradian ideology – a form of 'metaphysical' conservatism equally hostile to petty-bourgeois myopia and revolutionary astigmatism. The form of the work is an attempt to 'resolve' this contradiction by operating a naturalist mode which nevertheless, in its self-parodic quality, detaches itself ironically from its own vision. It is, as it were, naturalism to the second power – an Olympian, dispassionate view of reality which then views itself in precisely the same light in order to distance itself sceptically from its own presuppositions. It is for this reason that the familiar Conradian device of 'point of view' cannot be used, since its effect would be both to 'humanise' the action and allow an access to the workings of subjectivity which must be blocked. Yet the Conradian formal device habitually coupled with narrational viewpoint – the dislocation of chronological narrative – *is* used, since the text can preserve its resolute 'objectivity' only by literally *not seeing* events which lie beyond its scope. The killing of Stevie is unpresented – happens, so to speak, in the reader's absence; and the murder of Verloc is presented with extreme obliquity, squinted at sideways rather than frontally encountered. Both events reveal sinister forces capable of destroying the quotidian-forces which must be 'shown' at the same time as the novel proclaims the impossibility of attesting textually to their authentic existence. Yet the device is also calculated to draw our attention to the threatening *reality* of these subterranean forces: the fact that they cannot be shown directly underscores their 'untypicality' at the same time as it shockingly intensifies their effect. The text, indeed, operates here a triple irony on the reader. Its contemptuous caricaturing of the anarchists as conformist parasites or febrile freaks, coupled with its resolute fetishising of social reality, reassures the reader of the anarchists' despicable impotence. But it conspires with that assumption only the more brutally to subvert it: for the anarchists emerge, after all, as repugnant killers, responsible for dismembering a mentally defective child. In a third twist, however, such destructiveness is 'metaphysically' illusory: the dream of negating material reality and re-constructing the world from nothing is itself negated by the stubborn indestructibility of matter, symbolised by the tell-tale surviving pieces of Stevie's flesh.

Yet this 'resolution' of contradiction merely produces another. For that very survival of matter suggests the sickening vision of a universe endlessly, mechanically permutating its various materials – the ideology, in short, of crass bourgeois scientism and positivism which the anarchists set out to explode. The novel's 'metaphysical' symbolism is thus in partial contradiction with its naturalist forms: the former, in raising the ideology of the latter to an unchallengable cosmic vision, at the same time protests in mute horror at its devastating implications. Yet the text confronts a severe problem in selecting the terms in which such a protest is to be couched. For 'humanitarian' protest is ruled out on two opposed grounds: as incompatible with the book's clinical naturalism, and, contradictorily, as a merely feeble reflex of the bourgeois ideology of which that naturalism is the product. On the one hand, the novel exploits naturalist devices to dramatise a bourgeois society from which humane feeling is expelled, and in parodying that society implies a satirical protest against it. But in discerning a 'metaphysical' basis to such behaviour in the neutral, dispassionate cosmos, it enforces its own sense of the pathetic inefficacy of the humane, as part of a 'degenerate' sentimental cult of the human subject. It is, moreover, a cult of which the utopian brotherhood of anarchism is an even more degenerate extension. This contradiction is incarnated in the idiot Stevie, whose human tenderness is at once a function of his muddled, mentally regressive naivety, and a 'mystical' intimation of values critical of bourgeois society – values which are in him, however, literally inarticulable, mere broken murmurs of dissent. The silence of Stevie is ideologically determinate: the text is unable to endorse the callous inhumanity of the social world, but unable to articulate any alternative value because *value itself* is 'metaphysically' trivial, an illusion of false consciousness or (in the case of Winnie's claustral love for Stevie) a mere biological reflex. The text's satire of humanitarianism, then, springs from a 'metaphysical' ideology deeply sceptical of such banal petty-bourgeois pieties – an ideology which, despite its Olympian omniscience, is no more than a 'higher' expression of bourgeois inhumanity itself and a rejection of that utopian humanitarianism which threatens it. The silence of Stevie is the product of the mutual cancellation of the text's ideological contradictions: the text can 'speak' only by *activating* such contradictions, not by surmounting them into a determinate 'solution'. It is for this reason that *irony* is its dominant mode of discourse.

The silence of Stevie, symbolised in his scribbled, spiralling circles of infinity, is 'mystical' because it gestures towards that which can be shown but not stated, a condition of which art itself is for Conrad the prototype. It is in this sense that Stevie, the 'mad artist', defines the status of the text of *The Secret Agent* as a whole. The novel is unable to speak *of* its contradictions; it is, rather, precisely its contradictions which speak. Stevie's silence is 'mystical' in a sense of the term appropriate to Ludwig Wittgenstein's *Tractatus Logico-Philosophicus*. Language, for the *Tractatus*, can do no more than 'show' the structure of the world in the structure of its own world-picturing propositons; it cannot *speak* of reality directly, but can only intimate obliquely, by allowing itself to be cancelled out, the reality which transcends it. There is a figurative analogy here, inexact but instructive, with the relations between text, ideology and history. For it is as though the text, also, cannot speak directly of historical reality, but 'shows' something of its structure in the conflictual ideological structure of its own propositions. Just as for the *Tractatus* language is coterminous with the world, so for the text ideology is coterminous with history, permeating its own sign-systems; and it is for this reason that the text cannot cast a direct glance 'behind' that ideology to the history it signifies. What it can do instead is indicate the presence of that reality by the very sign of contradiction it produces within it. The text, to adapt Marx's comment on Adam Smith, thus does not 'really' resolve problems, but reveals them by contradicting itself – reveals them not merely by failing to resolve them but by its very efforts to do so. *The Secret Agent* may be seen in this sense as a paradigm of a particular case of the text-ideology relationship. As the *Tractatus* must end by lapsing into mystical silence, intimating the real only by inducing its own self-negation, so *The Secret Agent* is constituted by the 'mystical' absence figured above all in Stevie – an absence ideologically defined by the text as metaphysical, but in fact the 'hollow' scooped out by the clash of its contradictions. Constrained at once to consecrate 'normative' reality as a material process on which the subjective is slavishly contingent, and to reject such dreary positivism in the name of those privileged, cataclysmic moments in which the subjective is assertively alive, the novel subsists in a series of 'gaps' – between what can be known and what can be shown, between the discourse of 'experience' and of description, between the styles of metaphysics and social documentation. These gaps, the product of ideological conflict, are then themselves ideologically rendered so as to be accommodated. The text cannot, of course, know them for what they are, for if it did it would cease to exist; it therefore images them as those crevices in ordinary discourse through which the abyss of an infinite silence is to be glimpsed.

It is an abyss on the edge of which the nihilist Professor is continually poised – the Professor who, wired up for instant self-consignment to eternity, is thus a graphic image of the text itself. For the text, too, images itself ideologically as moving at the still point of the turning world, pivoted like Stevie between time and eternity at the prime meridian of Greenwich Observatory, able to reveal the truth of itself only by that ceaseless process of 'self-detonation' which is irony. Only by the 'revolutionary' act of negating its every proposition and reconstructing itself *ex nihilo* could the text articulate reality; yet this, it knows, is impossible, for it is doomed to work with discourses ridden with ideological contradiction, or – as the text itself would say – condemned to the eternal 'inauthenticity' of language itself, which can never crystallise 'pure' truth. Irony is thus both a sign of self-contradiction and a protection against it, a sardonic mode of survival; the final contradiction is that the Professor's nihilism is both metaphysically intelligible and politically impermissable. Whereas the *Tractatus* can ignore the ideological effects of its retreat to the mystical which is the other face of language (for such a retreat leaves everything just as it was), *The Secret Agent* cannot do so – cannot, as a text, allow itself to disappear down the abyss of the unspeakable, permitting its propositions to be retrospectively cancelled, leaving itself with absolutely nothing to say. Its commitment to *discourse* is unavoidably a commitment to the largely 'inauthentic' social practices which such discourse articulates – a commitment, as it were, to the later Wittgenstein world of the *Philosophical Investigations*, with its complacent fetishising of ordinary language-games as the criteria of the real. Such games appear in this text too – indeed 'game' is a central metaphor of *The Secret Agent;* and they appear because language and society must be protected against the minatory invasions of the absolute. More exactly, the arbitrary game of bourgeois legality, in which police and criminals are reversible counters, must itself be absolutised, raised to the status of that greater self-validating game of fixed pieces and endlessly shifting positions which is the universe itself. Since the social game is arbitrary, there is no reason why this, rather than some other piece of gratuitous practice, should not be absolutised; that the rules of any game are both arbitrary and absolute is the novel's metaphorical assurance for this. The novel's own 'game' is then the operation of this ideological effect. In a series of mutually cancelling moves, it satirises Winnie Verloc's blinkered petty-bourgeois viewpoint from the standpoint of the anarchist activity she ignores, while simultaneously satirising the anarchists as petty-bourgeois hypocrites from the standpoint of the 'fanatical' Professor. Conversely, it condemns the Professor's metaphysical 'extremism' by an appeal to the humanity of Winnie and Stevie, while at the same time questioning such sentiments from a 'metaphysical' vantage-point which is at least 'on terms' with that of the Professor himself. This stalemated game is then at once the product, and possible resolution, of the novel's contradictions. For if stalemate suggests non-resolution, it equally suggests a kind of finality which can pass as a solution. Stalemate is both ending and non-ending, completion and unachievement. In one sense, the novel ends on the latter note, bereft of a Victorian 'settlement': the Professor walks away through the London streets, the interdependent forces of legality and criminality continue their reversible cat-and-mouse encounters. But that, precisely, is the point – that the game will *go on*, even though neither side wins. In this sense, incompletion is itself a solution – it is the perpetuity of the social game which matters, to which the only threat is the deathly spectatorial Professor. *His* sense of the game's absurdity must be acknowledged if the text is 'clinically' to transcend its own materials, but it is an insight which can be accommodated within a vision of indestructability which belongs to the same Godlike view. The novel thus 'gets somewhere' even though it appears not to – just as *walking*, one of its dominant images, seems a mere static marching on the spot, but (notably in the case of Verloc's surreal walk to the embassy) *mysteriously* lands you at your destination. Progress, narrative, diachrony are radically questioned by textual forms and images, but not in the end abolished: although they cannot exactly be accounted for within a reified world drained of dynamism, they nonetheless cryptically persist. This internally contradictory image, of motion held within stasis or stasis accommodating motion, is an effect of the formal and ideological contradictions of the text, whereby events are seen at once durationally and *sub specie aeternitatis*. That narrative is possible and chronology viable – in short, that something *happens* – is a mark of the novel's relation to the ideology of bourgeois realism, of its endorsement of the 'normative' assumptions of the bourgeois world. But the naturalist form which puts such narration to work has the effect of 'freezing' and spatialising it, becoming in this sense the reflection, 'on earth' as it were, of that vision of time from eternity which belongs to the novel's 'metaphysical' dimension. That dimension is the ideological product of a radical scepticism about progress, change, causality and temporality which belongs to the 'radical conservative' sub-ensemble which Conrad inhabits, hostile to 'orthodox' bourgeois liberal doctrines yet dependent on the social order they help to sustain. Naturalism manages to 'solve' this contradiction by appearing at once 'temporal' and 'spatial', accommodating 'realist' duration while framing and fashioning it into immobility. In doing so, it fulfills two contradictory functions: it intensifies the stolid 'normality' of the world, but also 'naturalises' the metaphysical viewpoint of it, and so allows that viewpoint to be upheld while rescuing it from the 'unworldly' extremism of the Professor (and to some extent of Stevie). 'Nothing can really be changed' is the message of the book's metaphysical materialism, a message both negative and affirmative in its implications. As against revolutionary metaphysics, it is affirmative; in so far as it necessarily banishes along with such revolutionism any 'spiritual' vision beyond the crassly materialist, it is profoundly pessimistic. This contradiction, and its 'solution', embed

61

themselves in the work in ways we have examined: for violent change (Winnie), motion (Verloc), spiritual vision (Stevie), *do* insist on thrusting themselves into the text, although in ways which can only be enigmatically alluded to. Some ideology of the 'humane' must be obliquely recognised, if a source of value is to be provided from which both the Professor and bourgeois society can be criticised; yet such values are too close to bourgeois sentimentalism and anarchist Romanticism to be countenanced. In other works, Conrad is able to lend such values a concrete location – the 'organic' society of the ship's crew, inimical alike to bourgeois individualism and subversive egalitarianism. But no such court of moral appeal is available in the wholly urbanised society of *The Secret Agent;* and value is thus, as in the *Tractatus*, forced beyond the frontiers of the world, exiled beyond what can be articulated. Yet because it is thus forced beyond the world, everything seems to be left exactly as it was; and this provides the text with a kind of resolution, or, better, with the illusion of one. The world of *The Secret Agent*, as of the *Tractatus*, just is 'everything that is the case'; and in this sense there is no need of a resolution because *there is nothing, it seems, to resolve.* The world goes on: and this is at once the question, and the answer, of the text.

I have tried in this excessively terse and abstract account of Conrad's novel to demonstrate a certain complexity in the text-ideology relation. The Conradian ideology is itself internally complex, compounded of elements of various ideological sub-ensembles (of the 'emigré', Merchant Code, Romantic artist and so on) as well as of major elements of the dominant ideology (imperialism). *The Secret Agent* is also an internally complex formation; but the one formation does not merely 'reflect' the other. The complexity of the text is the product of certain contradictions between its component elements – contradictions which are in turn produced by the mutually conflictual relations of those elements to mutually conflictual aspects of the Conradian ideology *as that ideology is produced by the novel.* If, for example, there are certain contradictions between the aesthetic elements of form and symbolism, this is because the novel so produces ideology as to place them in relation to different ideological 'levels', or indeed to different ideologies. If there are internal contradictions within a single aesthetic element (say, between 'spatial' and 'durational' devices in narrative), this comes about because the text so produces ideology as to place the same aesthetic element in simultaneous relation to different ideologies or ideological 'levels'. If there is contradiction in characterisation, so that, for example, Stevie is a type both of the anarchists themselves and of their innocent victims, this occurs because ideology is so produced as to relate Stevie and the anarchists at once to the same and to different ideologies. And so on: there is no need to list the possible permutations of such a method, or to emphasise how in the textual process any one such permutation overdetermines another, so that the effect of isolating them for purposes of demonstration is inevitably one of a certain crudity. But to give a relatively simple example, with reference to *The Secret Agent:* one aesthetic element (naturalism) may so produce one aspect of ideology (bourgeois 'normality') as to throw it into contradiction with another ideology or level of ideology ('metaphysical nihilism') and thus put itself into contradiction with aspects of another aesthetic element (symbolism). This process, whereby aesthetic elements constantly *displace* and *recast* ideological elements as they are displaced and recast by them, is the very process of the text's 'self-determination', in which each proposition, each 'problem' provisionally 'solved', produces a fresh problem, and that another. It is this *necessity* of the textual process which is the object of scientific literary study.

Wadham College, Oxford.

Dickens, Pickwick and Realism: On the importance of Language to Socio-Literary Relations

Paul Filmer

I

Analysis of works of art involves attempting to grasp a complex of relationships. From a sociological point of view, the complex will be of social relationships and will include those between the artist and his social world, and between the social world(s) of audience(s) and artist. The concept of social world is not a simple one in this context, for the social world of the artist confronts us, as we approach his work, in two ways that need to be distinguished from one another: the first is that of the socio-historical world of the artist – that in which he creates his work, according to the understandings of it that he can negotiate (whether he does so or not[1]) independently of his work with those who share that world with him. This socio-historical world of the artist also has to be negotiated amongst those of us who are his audiences according to our different historical experiences and according to the salient features of the different historical epochs from within which we undertake those negotiations. There will therefore unavoidably be a number of versions of it, though all of them should share some historico-social structural features in common in order to be recognisable as such to one another.

The second way in which the social world of the artist confronts us is in and through the social world of the work itself. This differs from the socio-historical world of the artist in a number of ways, but especially because it is a thoroughly particular understanding of the world, that of the artist. According to the degree that it has, in any judgement we may make of it, the ability to arrest and hold our attention, it works to impose itself upon our existing understandings of our world and, by doing so, it works also to re-direct these understandings in its own terms. A work of art seeks to accomplish this individually by enabling us to realise ourselves in our relations with it, and socially in our relations with others with whom we share its apprehension and the resources from and in which it is created, and with whom, therefore, we relate through it.

Critical analysis of works of art which is primarily aesthetic, and whose orientation is social and/or humanist is grounded upon art's potential ability to accomplish such realisation, whatever the particular mode of inquiry in which the analysis is cast – historical, psychological, political, for example.[2] The work of critical analysis is, first, an exploration of how – and perhaps why, if the two can be separated – works of art are able to achieve amongst us the alterations of our understandings of our world that they do; and secondly, it is a judgement about the value of those alterations of our understandings. It is both an understanding of the way a work of art works with and upon its audience *and* a judgement of the value of the ways in which it does so.

It is possible to offer versions of how and why works of art work in these ways with and upon their audiences without any detailed attention to their content. All that is required is the citation of typical, representative excerpts and features of them which serve to corroborate the fact that the understandings of the world that their contents present to us are understandings which we already share with the artist of the world from within which we receive their presentation and towards which they direct our attention. Such versions provide illustrative examples which are seen as more or less accurately reflecting our existing understandings of what they exemplify. But to accomplish such versions is to deprive art of what is distinctively characteristic about it as a human activity: its active ability to re-direct in its own terms our experiences and understandings of our worlds. And it is to do so by reducing works of art, in whole or in part, to passive illustration of what we know, or ought to know, already. If works of art are rendered into passive illustrations their ways of working are not being attended to as significantly different in kind from the ways of working that enable us, members of their audiences, to understand the worlds of which we are already members. *Ipso facto*, if a work of art is so reduced, it can no longer be critically valued, for it offers us nothing more than its illustrative qualities to be valued about itself. No judgement of critical value is necessary, or even possible, of the ways in which it alters our understandings, for we are relating to it in ways which prevent it from doing that altering work in order that we may preserve it as (merely) illustrative and corroborative of the social world which has produced it, and of which we are already actually or potentially knowing members.

There is a strong temptation, not always resisted, to conduct a sociology of art in this fashion – not least, perhaps, because it would appear to exonerate the sociologist from making judgements of value and thus risking involvement in tiresomely unresolvable debates over ethical neutrality in the systematic study of social relations. I am insisting that to do so, however, is to miss the human and social import of art and, worse, to risk characterisation of one's enterprise by such an excruciating metaphor as that employed, and then disowned, by E. H. Gombrich, who has commented on the relations between the social sciences and art history as follows:

'a social scientist . . . must confine himself to social evidence and this evidence can, in the nature of things, have no bearing on values. To put the matter epigrammatically: the social scientist can always tell us which are the top ten; he cannot commit himself to picking a first eleven. The top ten, as we know, are based on real or pretended statistics of sale; the choice of a first eleven is a matter of past performance – and of faith.'[3]

The inadequacies of such a crude distinction between evidence and evaluation would take more space to refute fully than they deserve here; and a cognate issue will be engaged below on the more salient site provided by realist aesthetics. Suffice it to say at this point that social evidence, before it is that, is social and therefore human experience – and *that* is intrinsically evaluative. To pursue Gombrich's awful metaphor: a sociologist can only select a top ten from a first eleven which have already been selected on grounds and according to criteria that satisfy the practice of sociology as he has negotiated understanding of it with his fellow-members of communities of sociological practice. Statements of social scientific evidence can only be claimed as different from judgements of (sociological) value if the claimant has forgotten, or has never understood, that the latter are the originary grounds of the former, and make possible their formulation as such.[4]

Reduction of works of art to illustrations of the social worlds from which they emanate and to which they refer is accomplished through two linked sets of practices. Firstly, the contents of the work are glossed and summarised as (mere) narrative, rather than treated to detailed analysis under the aegis of the analyst's explicit interpretation of what are their own terms – that is, the claim of the work that it requires our attention in order to attempt a re-direction of our experiences and understandings of our worlds. Secondly, the language of the work – that is, the coherent collection of signs shared between the artist and his audience, from which the artist selects and in whose terms he organises his creative work – is treated as existing in an unproblematically correspondential set of relations with the world to which it refers: indeed, this correspondence version of language is necessary for the work to be glossed and summarised as narrative.

By a correspondence version of language, I mean to write of one which proposes that language and the world to which it refers could be divorced from one another as a matter of practice. This would imply that the world is a world of events and phenomena which are somehow self-evident, and which send out self-identifying signals with which we who observe them need only to align ourselves – and to receive them as our sense-perceptions – in order to produce a correct linguistic description of them. Language is thus seen as a neutral medium which brings our sense-perceptions into correspondence with the self-evident forms of the contents of the world. Such a version of language's relations with its referents is antithetical to art when the latter is considered as an attempt to re-direct the experiences and understandings of their worlds of members of its audiences. Language and the world to which it refers are deeply interrelated in as much as it is only through and in language that we can understand a world of events and phenomena which can take their meaningful places in human experience. To speak or write or in other ways exercise a language is to live in a mode of understanding which itself invests events with their descriptive characteristics. Moreover, languages and their modes of understanding are essentially social phenomena, since to speak or write language is to use words (and to be used by them) in regular and shareable ways. It is, in short, constitutive (and, where it is exercised as art, re-constitutive) of the worlds that are its referents.[5]

II

Somewhere within this complex interpenetration of language, art and the human life of social worlds, of individual biography and social history, the sociology of art and literature must somehow locate itself. The temptation to skirt the mists of interpretive analysis of the contents of particular works, in favour of quasi-determinist explanations of their socio-historical, -economic and -political production is considerable, and has resulted in an emphasis on extrinsic approaches to sociological analysis of literary art in particular.[6]

Apart from the curious practice of some American sociologists[7] of assembling anthologies of literary excerpts, with minimal introductory comments, in the expectation that their use in introductory sociology classes 'should help to teach modern sociology through illustrative material from literature'[8] extrinsic approaches take two predominant forms. One consists in the study of the biography and socio-economic background of literary artists and their works, together, perhaps, with some details of the conditions of the production and publication of their texts and of their critical and public reception. Instances of work of this kind are legion, but their contributions to sociological knowledge are more recognisably in the areas of sociology of occupations, professions and industry and of the history of socio-economic structures than in those of sociology of art and literature, just because the extrinsic character of their approach is such as to avoid any detailed reference of a systematically sociological character to the *contents* of the works themselves.[9] By contrast, the second predominant extrinsic approach to the sociology of literary art, that of realism, is at least literary, for it shares its grounds for making sense of literary works with the literary critical-aesthetic of realism.[10] The trouble with this approach, however, is the correspondential character of the relation which it postulates between the work's contents and the nature of the reality (or realities) from which it emanates, of which it is a part, and to which it refers. This relation is invariably initially proposed – more usually implicitly than explicitly – and thereafter presumed upon throughout analysis of the work. Nor is this a simple matter, since the correspondentiality of the relation between the work's contents and 'reality' is postulated according to certain conventions which also need to be stated. They will operate as a resource for establishing those correspondences on the basis of which the work's interrelations with social reality will be explicated by subsequent analysis. These conventions provide both for ways of seeing the nature of social reality, and for the nature of correspondence between the latter and the contents of works of literary art. A succinct postulation, both of convention and correspondence, in two cases of realism which are difficult to separate, is given thus by Arnold Kettle:

> 'By *Socialist Realism*, in the field of literature, I assume we mean literature written from the point of view of the class-conscious working class, whose socialist consciousness illuminates their whole view of the nature of the world and of the potentialities of mankind. By *Critical Realism* I assume we mean literature written in the era of class society from a point of view which, while not fully socialist, is nevertheless sufficiently critical of class society to reveal important truths about that society and to contribute to the freeing of the human consciousness from the limitations which class society has imposed upon it.'[11]

In the case of socialist realism, the convention is socialist consciousness and the correspondence is between the contents of the work and 'the point of view of the class-conscious working class'; for critical realism, Kettle offers us, respectively, a convention 'sufficiently critical of class society to reveal important truths about that society' and correspondence with 'the era of class society.'

A certain evident tautologousness about Kettle's distinctions in the relations postulated between types of realism and the social realities for which they serve as conventions, and with which works analysed critically according to their prescriptions are proposed as correspondentially interrelated, might suggest that realism is considerably less straightforward and extrinsic an approach than at first it appears. To say, as Kettle does, that socialist realist literature is written from the point of view of the socialist consciousness of the class-conscious working class, and that critical realist literature written in the era of class society is critical of class society, seems to propose no more than that socialists write socialism, critics criticism. Perhaps realising this himself, Kettle adds that 'the division between Critical Realism and Socialist Realism is a tricky business, which though basic is never clear cut.' The trickiness occurs, it seems, because:

> 'When we speak of point of view in relation to creative literature we are referring to something somewhat different from a man's consciously held, or fairly easily abstractable ideas . . . when we refer to the point of view of a writer and use the adjective "socialist" or "critical", we are using adjectives which, though valid and necessary, are normally used in contexts in which the texture of thought is rather more abstract and theoretical than the habitual processes of art . . . when in everyday life we refer to a man as "socialist" or "critical" we are usually referring to his formulated *opinions*, whereas the important thing about an artist is not his opinion (on that level) but his *sensibility*, his all-round apprehension and comprehension of things . . . when we refer to a writer's point of view in the artistic sense we are referring to his sensibility rather than to his opinions or intentions, though of course both of these are relevant factors.'[12]

At this point, not surprisingly, Kettle gives up the struggle to sustain a distinction between critical and socialist realism altogether, on the grounds that Dickens, who is his subject here, together with Hardy and Emily Bronte in,

> 'the view of the world they express, the feelings they generate, are not socialist but they are more than what is generally meant by critical . . . [they] write from a point of view which can be described not merely in somewhat negative terms as critical but in positive terms as popular, that is to say expressive of the sensibility of progressive sections of the people other than the petty-bourgeois intelligentsia.'[13]

What is nowhere abandoned, however, throughout this welter of distinctions that fail to distinguish, is the literary-critical aesthetic of realism itself. And it is this which is the trickiest business of all, for throughout Kettle's pursuit of the ultimately elusive differences between socialist and critical writing, he offers no challenge to the essentially mimetic character which he imputes to literature. Socialist realist literature *illuminates* a 'whole view of the nature of the world and of the potentialities of mankind'; critical realist literature can *reveal* 'important truths' about class society; and popular realists 'write from a point of view . . . *expressive* of the sensibility of progressive sections of the people.' In short, by illumination, revelation and expression, realists, of whichever of these three types, acquaint us, it seems, with what is *really* going on in the realities we share with them. If we now ask how it is that this acquaintanceship is supposed to be made, however, the fundamental issue begins more clearly to appear. It is that realism's conventions are didactic, and in this feature of them are to be found the roots of their extrinsic approaches. Marxism is clearly the source of socialist realism's didactic conventions: Kettle grants it autonomy as such when he informs us that it 'teaches us that reality is more basic than what we think about it.' And the source of those of critical realism are found, as David Caute has pointed out, together with those of naturalism, in the positivist philosophy of science.[14] Both sources are rooted in the rationalist philosophies of the enlightenment, and whilst they are not both articulated as a common socio-political philosophy, they do share what Caute terms 'the mimetic, mirror-of-life, representational philosophy of literature.'

Realism is an extrinsic approach to the analysis of works of literary art which renders them illustrative of what we know, or ought to know, already by providing us, through its resourceful conventions, with versions of reality from which the works are proposed as having emanated and which, in turn, their contents reflect. Essentially, the aesthetics of realism are technical, since they reside in two linked sets of artful practices: those of the artist, and those of the critic. The artful practices of the realist artist are directed towards persuading the members of his audience that the version offered in his work of the reality that he shares with them is the way it *really* is, or ought to, and thus eventually will, be. His practices are directed, that is, to disguising any difference between his and his audience's reality, and his representation of its appearance in his work – even to the point of attempting somehow to disguise the self-evident phenomenon that his work is a representation of the appearance of reality rather than a reality itself. The importance of (the conventions of) naturalism is obvious to such an enterprise. They are introduced through contrivances and devices of characterisation, narrative, depiction and exposition in order that the work shall present reality, apparently uncontrived and undevised, just as it is.[15] The artful practices of the realist critic, by contrast, are to expose those of the realist artist, in order to evaluate the adequacy of the latter's depiction of the appearance of reality, which he offers in and as his work, to reality itself. The critic is considering, that is to say, the adequacy of what Kettle has called the artist's 'sensibility, his all-round apprehension and comprehension of things' – and things stand here, of course, for the self-evident phemomena and events of reality. But the artfulness of the critic does not lie exclusively in exposing that of the artist's presentation of the appearance of reality; it is also a collaboration with the artist to interpret the character of the latter's sensibility in relation to it.[16] To quote Kettle again:

'Just because he is dealing with human material of a high degree of complexity, it is particularly possible for the artist to have very valuable specific insights without being able to transform them into general or theoretical ones.'[17]

In other words, the artist may need some help which, presumably, the critic can provide, in articulating the 'more general or theoretical' insights into reality which his work offers its audience. Hence, presumably, Kettle's judgement that Hardy, Emily Brontë and Dickens 'are not socialist but they are more than what is generally meant by critical . . . and . . . write from a point of view . . . expressive of the sensibility of progressive sections of the people other than the petty-bourgeois intelligentsia.' The details of the help that Kettle, as critic, offers both Emily Brontë and Dickens then follow in his contention that they,

'reflect, as it seems to me, that great popular alliance of working class and petty bourgeoisie which *might* – up to about 1848 – have succeeded in giving the bourgeois-democratic revolution in Britain a different and more revolutionary content and thereby in bringing the socialist revolution very much nearer.'[18]

Now the elements which constitute this reality, between which, and the works of Dickens and Brontë, Kettle is proposing a relation are, as he acknowledges,

'might-have-beens of history . . . mere speculation. To the literary critic and cultural historian, however, they have a certain reality, for he is concerned with the expression of forces which, though they may in the actual power struggle be for the time defeated, yet remain powerful and fruitful.'[19]

In making this acknowledgement, Kettle points to realism's own artifice, that of reality itself. The resourcefulness of realist criticism's conventions lies in its ability to provide us with versions of reality itself upon which we can depend in seeking to establish by critical analysis the degree and adequacy of a work of art's correspondential reflection of and relation to it. It is surely a mark of Kettle's integrity as a realist critic that he makes explicit the (version of) reality upon which his subsequent analytic evaluation of Dickens as a (popular) realist writer will depend. More usually, such versions of reality are implied rather than explicated, and this is especially the case with critical realism just because, perhaps, it grounds itself in positivist empiricism – a philosophy which conceptualises social and physical worlds, in a common way, as natural orders of events. Marxism, on the other hand, works in this respect from the sociologically important premise for its explanations of human action that men are conscious and creative participants in the human worlds that they inhabit socially. Positivist-empiricism predicates a passive sociology, Marxism an active one; yet both, when allied to realism in the analysis of literature, treat the engagement of literature with society – a process which occurs in and through the active practices of writing/reading – as if it were largely a passive correspondence, through the medium of the work and its language, between writer and audience. The realist approach begins with the creation of a version of social reality, conceived as either active or passive, proceeds to analyse and evaluate the adequacy with which it is reflected in the work under analysis, and then, perhaps, to draw conclusions about its effects for the version of social reality with which it commenced. Even the special mode of approach of popular realism, which Kettle proposes as necessary for adequate critical analysis of Dickens, Emily Brontë and Hardy, whose version of social reality is 'the point of view of the People seen not passively but actively' does not relinquish this passive reflectionist conceptualisation of the relationship between the work and its referent social reality. For,

> 'Such a literature will not, of course, except at its peril, gloss over the weaknesses, the corruptions, the unpleasantness or the degradation of the People: it will not, except at its peril, see life as it *wants* to see it . . . the essential characteristic of a popular tradition is not that it should be optimistic but that it should be true: and because it is true it will in fact be optimistic.'[20]

Work in the popular realist tradition, thus, must see reality in a way which reflects it as it is. It must record the truth – which is, as a matter of fact for Kettle, a particular and not a general truth. And lest we should baulk at the possibility of contradiction between connotations of absoluteness, or at least generality, that truth may have for us, and the particularity of optimism, Kettle suggests that,

> 'to use as a touchstone for the products of a popular tradition the question; is it true? may be in practice less helpful and have less to do with truth than the question: does it serve the People?'[21]

With this suggestion realism's circle of reflectionist correspondence is completed. Literature in a popular realist tradition emanates, by definition, from the people and is evaluated for adequacy according to the degree to which it reflects the truth of the point of view of the people; and this, in turn, may be seen as the degree to which it serves the people, from whom it has emanated.

Specifically what is being made explicit here is Kettle's earlier contention about Marxism, that it 'teaches us that reality is more basic than what we think about it,' as the articulation of the implicit 'might-have-beens of history' which he finds in Dickens's work. Whilst these are 'mere speculation' alongside the recorded empirical events of the social, political and economic history of Dickens's England, they have nevertheless, the 'certain reality' of incipiently enduring, 'powerful and fruitful' socio-historical forces. But this 'certain reality' is not an autonomous, natural reality; it is grounded in the naturalistic Marxism which teaches us that it is more basic than what we think about it: that is, in a system of thought which teaches us the product of its thinking – the thinking into existence of a version of reality as apparently autonomous. Yet apparently autonomous reality is by definition a phenomenon constructed according to conventions of (naturalistic) thought – whether positivist-empiricist or Marxist. And by making Marxism explicit as a set of didactic critical-aesthetic conventions in terms of which he proposes both to undertake analysis of Dickens's work as popular realism, and to construct the reality it reflects, Kettle shows in detail the practices by which this artifice of reality is accomplished as a conditional and necessary feature of his criticism. As such this cannot but be an adequately extrinsic formulation of the relationship between the creative work of Dickens and social reality, just because it is a self-fulfilling account of that relationship. The version of social reality between which and Dickens's work the relationship is formulated is constructed as a conditional and necessary feature of criticism of the work. But what it ignores in criticism of the work, like any predominantly extrinsic realist approach, is the social experience of literature.

I am not suggesting that there is anything about the process of constructing a circle of correspondence between social and literary realities that ignores the existence of the work, but rather that no attention is given to the detail of its contents which might suggest how, as a matter of practice, they may be read as being transformed by their author from the social reality from which they emanate into their coherent thematic unity as the work itself. For it is fundamentally by his

73

ability to offer his work for reading in this way that the collaboratively-creative social relationship that is writing/reading literature can be initiated by the author and sustained with his audience. The socio-literary relations thus formed constitute a central topic for the sociology of literature, since they are the point at which the active sociality of literature is locatable. But the relationship is only comprehensible in terms of its own practices, and they are in language. And so language, the crucial resource for creation and critical analysis – whether aesthetic or sociological – of the work must also be approached as the central topic in analysis of it. Critical analysis of works of literary art, that is to say, must be analysis of the language practices that are its contents and in active participation with which, as readers, we recover, and evaluate the adequacy of its meaningfulness for us.

Nor is it the case that realism as an approach circumscribes totally the languaged contents of literary art.[22] Rather, it is that its view of language is already pre-empted, as the medium of correspondence through which the reality expressed in the point of view of the writer is passed (communicated) to the audience with whom he shares it, by the conventions of naturalism within which realism is grounded. And since, for naturalism, reality is an inherent, pre-existing order of the things of the world, then all that writer and audience require are the appropriate tools for understanding it – the tools provided by the realist approach. On this issue, Caute has commented that,

> 'according to certain cultural conventions, naturalism sets up a series of signs and signals along one code (language) which we recognise as *equivalent to* the signs and signals of a different code (our sense perception of reality) . . . When the quintessential or typical truth about contemporary society is conceived with reference to a highly partial, partisan and problematical vision of a regenerated future . . . The writer's desire to convey to us a self-contained universe, with a claim to its own mimetic reality, is thwarted by our awareness of the author's manipulations and interventions. My complaint against the realists is of course not on account of these manipulations and interventions, which I consider to be necessary and inevitable, but rather on account of the attempted concealment, and the failure to make a dialectical appreciation of the relationship of literature to society.'[23]

What realism conceals, in both its literature and its criticism, is this dialectical relationship between literature and society, which is synthesised in and as the languaged contents of the literary work. For the socio-literary relationship is a dialectical one, in which society, as the audience, is involved with itself, as the writer, through the latter's 'highly partial, partisan and problematical vision of a regenerated future' for their actually or potentially common experience (reality). And this dialectical self-involvement is and can only be in the language of the work of literature. Literature, like all art, is not mimetic but, rather, is *transformative* of the reality from within which it emanates and to which it refers. Art's transformativeness is its active ability to re-direct in its own terms – the terms, that is, of the contents of its works – our experiences and understandings of our worlds. An understanding of the socio-literary relationship, then, is an understanding of the dialectics of transformation that are synthesised in and as the languaged contents of works of literary art.

III

I want to suggest how the process of understanding socio-literary relations might be undertaken with reference to some passages in *The Pickwick Papers*. Apart from the enormous pleasure I have derived from a number of readings of it over several years, three main and related reasons dictate its choice here. Firstly, compared with Dickens's later works, it has not attracted a great deal of serious literary critical attention.[24] Where it has been attended to, it has been for the most part regarded as an occasionally puzzling prologue to Dickens's later novels, which are widely considered to be his masterpieces.[25] *The Pickwick Papers* is typically regarded as the basis for Dickens's reputation as a popular entertainer, which has only fairly recently been challenged by the realisation of his greatness as a novelist.[26] A major exception to this view is found in the work of the American critic, Steven Marcus,[27] who reads the work as essentially about language itself, and the relation with language that he sees Dickens displaying in it as the writer's preparation of himself for the mature work to come. At a number of points in the course of *The Pickwick Papers* Marcus's analysis elicits a rich conjunction of 'society and social change on the one hand and language and writing on the other'[28] – that which, in other words, socio-literary relations are about.

Secondly, in the realist critical-aesthetic pantheon, Dickens occupies an important position: Kettle, as I have shown above, uses his work as an occasion for exploring distinctions within realist critical theory; Hauser takes the trouble to discuss at length his inadequacies as a socialist realist;[29] and even for Lukács he bears comparison with Tolstoy as one of 'the important realists.'[30] If it can be shown that such an acknowledged master of realist aesthetic practice offers, in his first literary work, a version of language diametrically opposed to that implied by realism, then strong grounds indeed should be established for the inadequacies of the latter to the analysis of socio-literary relations that I have attempted to adduce above.

Thirdly, the serial publication of *The Pickwick Papers* between April 1836 and November 1837 was arguably the most important literary harbinger of the major changes in British social structure and social consciousness which began to reach a decisive fruition in the 1840s, and to which Dickens's major works are such valuable imaginative responses. Marcus characterises it in this respect as 'the timely equivalent in written novelistic prose of the take-off into self-sustained growth.'[31] The circumstances surrounding and constituting the publication were themselves a part of the further changes in British society which they heralded.[32] The circulation increased during publication from 1,000 for the first of the twenty numbers to 40,000 for the last, discovering in the process a new, popular reading public with whom Dickens quickly established a strong and lasting relationship and for whom he had a strong and respectful sense of their humanity.[33] Moreover, the phenomenally successful methods of illustrated serial publication developed for *The Pickwick Papers* were those used for much major Victorian fiction up to 1870.

Let us begin with a passage from the work which offers a clear opportunity to introduce consideration of one of the wide range of devices and contrivances that Dickens employs to invite his readers into participation in a socio-literary relationship. It occurs well on in the narrative, soon after Pickwick has been committed to the Fleet prison. He begins to explore his surroundings, and Dickens brings this process to a climax with the following characterisation – almost Goffmanesque to us in retrospect – of what meets his eyes on the galleries and staircases:

> 'There were many classes of people here, from the labouring man in his fustian jacket, to the broken-down spendthrift in his shawl dressing-gown, most appropriately out at elbows; but there was the same air about them all – a listless jail-bird careless swagger, a vagabondish who's afraid sort of bearing, which is wholly indescribable in words, but which any man can understand in one moment if he wish, by setting foot in the nearest debtor's prison, and looking at the very first group of people he sees there, with the same interest as Mr. Pickwick did.'[34]

A possible contradiction is immediately apparent at the point at which Dickens asserts that the scene he has already constituted verbally as confronting Mr. Pickwick 'is wholly indescribable in words.' Taken literally, or as if referring to the reality of the situated practices that Dickens has displayed immediately prior to making it, this is a most extraordinary statement for a novelist to make in process – and a scarcely plausible one. The vivid human specifics, engendered in such sequences of words as 'the broken-down spendthrift in his shawl dressing-gown, most appropriately out at elbows' or 'a listless jail-bird careless swagger, a vagabondish who's afraid sort of bearing' is hardly the work of one who would seriously hold that the referents of such sequences are 'wholly indescribable in words.' On the contrary, such writing is testimony to the power of language to inscribe a sense of the experience it engenders upon human consciousness, even if it should fail to describe it to readers. Dickens tells us that we can understand the referents of his sequences of words if we wish to by doing as he has, perforce, made Pickwick do, and 'with the same interest'. The invitation into a socio-literary relation between writer and reader implicit in this passage can be placed there: do what Pickwick did, *and with the same interest.* Since Pickwick is well advanced on the adventures and experiences that constitute the narrative, the preceding events of the novel should provide us with a wealth of resources from which we may formulate an understanding of that interest.

Yet from the outset, Pickwick is something of an enigma. The opening, paragraph-long sentence of the first chapter speaks of 'that obscurity in which the earlier history of the public career of the immortal Pickwick would appear to be involved'; and, as Marcus points out,

> 'We later learn only that he "has retired from business, and is a gentleman of considerable independent property" (ch. 34) and that when he was a boy he used to slide in winter "on the gutters" (ch. 30). Quite literally Pickwick is a man without a history, created, as it were, entirely in the present: he exists only through his activity in the novel.'[35]

On the one occasion (ch. 19) on which Pickwick himself shows a concern with his own past, expressing 'a strong desire to recollect a song which he had heard in his infancy', he does so under the influence of an excess of milk-punch, becomes speechless and eventually passes out in the attempt.[36] Whatever, then, may be the interest with which Pickwick looked at the inmates of the Fleet, and which we must seek in order to understand that which Dickens has asserted to us is 'wholly indescribable in words' (though verbally constituted for us, nevertheless), we cannot infer it easily from any reference to a biography or characterisation of Pickwick prior to his activities in the novel. And even though to seek them there might be the most appropriate of the responses which a writer of fiction might be expected to want to encourage on the part of his readers, the very fact that a consequence of Pickwick's activities as important as his perception of the air about the inmates is verbally indescribable, implies that to do so will be difficult.

The difficulty is borne out by further reference to the opening of the novel, for what 'illumines the gloom, and converts into a dazzling brilliancy' the obscurity of Pickwick's earlier history is an,

> 'entry in the Transactions of the Pickwick Club, which the editor of these papers feels the highest pleasure in laying before his readers, as a proof of the careful attention, indefatigable assiduity, and nice discrimination, with which his search among the multifarious documents confided to him has been conducted.' (ch. 1).

The work of fiction is here presented as a work of non-fictional report, a set of 'Transactions' – albeit one that is being pseudonymously edited by 'Boz', who claims for himself the talent of a 'nice discrimination' in assembling it.[37] It is, at the outset, transformatively fictionalised into its opposite, and this dialectical illusion is reinforced recurrently through the early chapters. Pickwick is immediately presented as the author of a paper entitled 'Speculations of the Source of the Hampstead Ponds, with some Observations of the Theory of Tittlebats' – an hilariously incongruous title when set against the report that the 'Association has heard [it] read, with feelings of unmingled satisfaction and unqualified approval' and 'is deeply sensible of the advantages which must accrue to the cause of science from the production . . . no less than from the unwearied researches of Samuel Pickwick, Esq. G.C.M.P.C. in Hornsey, Highgate, Brixton, and Camberwell.' The Transactions proceed to report on the Association's view that 'inestimable benefits . . . must inevitably result from carrying the speculations of that learned man into a wider field, from extending his travels, and consequently enlarging his sphere of observation, to the advancement of knowledge, and the diffusion of learning,' by which point the illusion itself is made transparent through its own ludicrous exaggeration, though we are barely at the end of the fourth paragraph of the first chapter. For this is less a plausible characterisation of an Association concerned with the cause of science, the advancement of knowledge and the diffusion of learning than an hilarious oppositional caricature of one.

Dickens returns to the illusory characterisation of his narrative as a fictional non-fiction in the first two paragraphs of chapter 4 by presenting us with 'Boz's' extended re-affirmation of his editorial integrity. Apart from preserving and reinforcing the claim, again humorously flawed by exaggeration, with which the first chapter opened – that the work is realistic by virtue of being no more than his 'judicious arrangement and impartial narration', and not his authorship, of the adventures it contains, two further points of especial interest emerge in the following sentences, which occur in the middle of the passage:

> 'The Pickwick Papers are our New River Head; and we may be compared to the New River Company. The labours of others have raised for us an immense reservoir of important facts. We merely lay them on, and communicate them, in a clear and gentle stream, to a world thirsting for Pickwickian knowledge.'

Firstly, we are offered a metaphor for the editorial transmission ('the New River Company') of recorded reality ('our New River Head'), rather than just being told that we are literally reading no more than 'judicious arrangement and impartial narration' – though this insistence is interwoven with the statement of the metaphor. Yet the very enterprise of metaphorising the enterprise of editing reported reality seems to blur its apparently certain, literal and clear-cut correspondence with truth, in the assertion of a regard for which it is introduced. Secondly, we are offered here a new and, again, metaphorical formulation of the truth which is reported reality: as 'Pickwickian Knowledge.' Since it is in the name of science that Pickwick sets out into the world upon the adventures which are to constitute the work, we might reasonably infer that 'Pickwickian Knowledge' is no more than a synonym for it – ludicrously though science has already been presented to us through the instance of Pickwick's paper on the Hampstead ponds and tittlebats. But we have already been presented with a version of the adjective Pickwickian in the first chapter. When Pickwick makes his oration to the club accepting nomination to lead the corresponding members on their travels, he catalogues the troubles of the world which he proposes to observe, and report back upon to the club in the name of science and humanity, with such loquaciousness that he is called 'a humbug' by Blotton, one of his co-members. The altercation that ensues is only resolved when Blotton assures Pickwick that he had not used the expression 'in a common sense' but 'in its Pickwickian sense . . . he had merely considered him a humbug from a Pickwickian point of view.' Whereupon,

'Mr. PICKWICK felt much gratified by the fair, candid, and full
explanation of his honourable friend. He begged it to be understood,
that his own observations had been merely intended to bear a
Pickwickian construction.'

At this 'highly satisfactory and intelligible point' the debate ends:
and we are left with a sense of the Pickwickian that, when the word is
linked adjectivally with Knowledge in chapter four, suggests that if the
ensuing conjunction represents what the world is 'thirsting for', it is not
at all something which can be merely laid on in a *clear* stream – though it
may be gentle in the degree to which it is amusing and enjoyable. Just
as, in the name of realism, the fiction that is to be the novel is itself
fictionalised at the outset into its dialectical opposite, an edition of
reported events that have occurred in reality, so science, as Pickwickian
knowledge, is transformed into its opposite by having attributed to it the
Pickwickian sense, according to which a person insulted by being called
a humbug should not consider himself insulted when so called 'from a
Pickwickian point of view'. The activity of science, of observing and
reporting back upon, can hardly produce knowledge in any common
sense of 'careful attention, indefatigable assiduity, and nice
discrimination,' of 'judicious arrangement and impartial narration,' or
with 'a regard for truth' of its topics from such a point of view as the
Pickwickian here shows itself to be. And language, by this same token,
cannot be considered as in any but a highly problematical contextually
interpretive relation with its referent objects. Thus the very language in
and through which reality is to be objectively mediated and
communicated, the language of realism, appears from the outset to be
surreal and non-correspondential with it. A world thirsting for
Pickwickian Knowledge is one which will be quenched through
Pickwickian language – a language in which words do not have a taken-
for-granted common sense, whereby an insult is, more or less, an insult.
Instead, Pickwickian language creates its world and offers a version of
its sense which, though shared, is far from common in any sense that
may be taken for granted. It is a language of transformation of the
apparent, common, taken-for-granted senses of its referents into their
dialectical opposites.

Nor are these devices and contrivances, through which the surreality
of realism is shown so early in the work, themselves left untransformed
by Dickens as it proceeds. With decreasing frequency and insistence we
are reminded, for example, that 'the events recorded in these pages' are
not 'wholly imaginary' (ch. 15), and that 'we cannot state the precise
nature of the thoughts which passed through Mr. Trotter's mind,

because we don't know what they were' (ch. 16) until the fifty-seventh and final chapter, which is entitled: 'In which the Pickwick Club is finally dissolved, and everything concluded to the satisfaction of everybody.' This still, if rather tersely, preserves the re-fictionalising of the fictional narrative as a non-fictional, edited report with which the work began, and the club is dissolved within the first half of the chapter, as if to bear out the title of the whole work as its *posthumous* papers. But once this has been effected, and we have been offered 'our last parting look at the visionary companions of many solitary hours, when the brief sunshine of the world is blazing full upon them', we are presented with the following remarks:

> 'It is the fate of most men who mingle with the world, and attain even the prime of life, to make many real friends, and lose them in the course of nature. It is the fate of all authors or chroniclers to create imaginary friends, and lose them in the course of art. Nor is this the full extent of their misfortunes; for they are required to furnish an account of them besides.
> In compliance with this custom – unquestionably a bad one – we subjoin a few biographical words, in relation to the party at Mr. Pickwick's assembled.'

At this point the game of deception of the reader by devices and contrivances employed in the name of realist aesthetics, whose end is to render fiction as if it were identical with (a report upon) reality, is as nearly up as it is going to be. For the first time a clear implication is made that the preceding narrative has been 'the course of art' in which '*imaginary* friends' have been *created* (and lost) by their *authors* or chroniclers.[38] We may, perhaps, extend this implication to suggest that, during their course, the languaged contents of the work have become transformed from edited reports into art, imaginative creation. Or, to put it more accurately, the course of art – which is imaginative creation – has been an artful transformation of itself into its opposite, its self-negation, as an edited report of men mingling with the world and making and losing 'many real friends . . . in the course of nature.' And this accomplishment is now being as artfully asserted by the implied transformation of the work back into the disguised imaginative creation that must have been the originary grounds of the initial and long-sustained realist deception. The work, that is to say, is transformed by implication back into what it must always have been, even before its disguised appearance as an edited record of reality.[39]

Yet the game of disguise and deception is up only as nearly as it can be. Like all games, and especially language games, it has taken on its own life, for which such manipulations are necessary in order that a work of fiction, however picaresque, can offer a plausible version of its referent reality. Hence Dickens's further misfortune that he is also 'required to furnish an account of' the 'imaginary friends' that he has created and lost 'in the course of art.' For it is just because these imaginary friends, the characters of the novel, can be referred to as they are here that they cannot be solely the friends of their imaginative creator, the author. Although created by him in language, the language is not his language alone but one he shares in common with the readers of his work – without that shared-in-commonness of language, indeed, the work could not exist as such, because it could have no meanings. This sociality of language, therefore, means that he shares the imaginary friends whom he has created with his readers, and it is for the latter that 'he is required to furnish an account of them besides.' Dickens was undoubtedly made well aware of the strong demands for such an account, which made imperative his provision of it, by the circumstances of the serial monthly production of the work. He was in touch, as a result of this, with a continuing response from his readers as his work appeared, and whilst it was still in process of being created. Moreover, apart from the initial advertisement of the projected publication, Dickens addressed his readers directly on four separate occasions during the course of the appearance of *The Pickwick Papers*: before Parts II (ch. 3), III (ch. 6), X (ch. 27) and XV (ch. 41). And on the last two occasions, whilst still signing himself 'Boz', he abandoned the title Editor in favour of that of Author of them.[40] Hence his compliance with the custom of subjoining 'a few biographical words' on his major characters.

The biographical words are themselves quite unremarkable – even dull, as writing, by contrast with the rest of the novel; and they are brief indeed. But what is remarkable about them is their very presence, since it is precisely biography – most especially of Pickwick – that we have already noted as almost totally and significantly absent throughout the novel itself. It may be seen as significantly absent by the importance of the position *Pickwick Papers*, as the first of Dickens's works, occupies in the development of the novel form in English literature. By a detailed consideration of some of the opening passages, I have suggested that the Pickwickian sense or point of view is one which, in relation to language and knowledge of the world, is a highly interpretive and contextually-bound one. Marcus suggests that it is,

> 'language with the shackles removed from certain of its deeper creative powers, which henceforth becomes capable of a constant, rapid and

virtually limitless multiplication of its own effects and forms in new inventions and combinations and configurations . . . [a commitment] to something like pure writing, to language itself. No novelist had, I believe, ever quite done this in such measure before . . . In addition, the commitment was paradoxically ensured and enforced by the circumstances of compelled spontaneity in which Dickens wrote, by the necessity he accepted of turning it out every month, of being regularly spontaneous and self-generatingly creative on demand. Dickens was, if it may be said, undertaking to let the writing write the book.'[41]

This is achieved, according to Marcus, by Dickens's abandoning himself to 'the deep, nonlogical, the metaphoric and metonymic, processes of language . . . such an abandonment, successfully carried through, marks the opening up of a new dimension of freedom for the English novel, if not for the human mind in general.'[42] The abandonment to language is successfully carried through by Dickens's genius, which is not only imaginative in its transformative creation of narrative and character, but also technical in allowing language to have its way with him, whilst yet keeping it under a control strict enought to create a coherent work of fiction. This technical genius was hard-won by Dickens, through his self-training into the most accomplished legal and parliamentary shorthand writer of his day by the time he came to write *The Pickwick Papers*. Marcus suggests that,

'Dickens' prolonged experience as a shorthand writer had a significant effect on what for a writer must be the most important of relations, the relation between speech and writing. The brachygraphic characters, as he describes them in recollection, were themselves doodles – apparently random plays of the pen, out of which figures or partial figures would emerge and to which meaning could be ascribed. It was almost as if the nascent novelist had providentially been given or discovered another way of structurally relating himself to the language . . . This experience of an alternative, quasi-graphic way of representing speech had among other things the effect upon Dickens of loosening up the rigid relations between speech and writing that prevail in our linguistic and cultural system. By providing him with an experience of something that closely resembled a hieroglyphic means of preserving speech, it allowed the spoken language to enter into his writing with a parity it had never enjoyed before in English fictional prose. Speech here was not the traditional subordinate of its written representation; it could appear now in writing with a freedom and spontaneity that made it virtually, if momentarily, writing's equal. And yet whenever a development of this magnitude takes place in writing, in literature, the capacities and possibilities of that written art are themselves suddenly multiplied and enhanced.'[43]

The significance of such incorporation of speech into prose fiction for a still semi-literate population fast being concentrated into urban environments can hardly be over-estimated.[44] Together with Dickens's imaginative genius for narration and the creation of character, it accounts both for his phenomenal popularity as a writer[45] and for the subsequent effect that his work had on the development of English fiction. It is no understatement to say that he relates speech to prose in the novel as Shakespeare related it to verse in drama.[46]

Given Dickens's technical accomplishment and popular success – and the obvious enjoyment he took in both throughout his life – an interesting question becomes why it is that he presents the relatively brief subjoining of a few biographical words on Pickwick and company to the conclusion of the narrative as compliance with an unquestionably bad custom. An answer possibly emerges from the dialectical transformation that the work accomplishes for itself, through language, in its relations with its referent reality. The work has itself languaged this reality into existence, initially by postulating itself as a pseudonymously edited collection of the transactions of a now-defunct association of scientific amateurs. And the very success with which this has been accomplished in, and by extending the range of, language has brought its creator to the limits of language's autonomy within the form – narrative fiction – in which he has chosen to demonstrate his virtuosity. He has been able, for example, to claim that he has constituted in the words of his language that which is 'indescribable in words.' Dickens has recognised the autonomy of language and let it have its way with him to such an unparalleled extent that it has enabled him to tap 'that untapped resource of language in the near illiterate, and to get that speech and *its* genius into writing, into his writing . . . to be able *to write that as yet unwritten language.*'[47]

Yet there remains the responsibility to end the work by fracturing the illusion that has been essential for its accomplishment. *Pickwick Papers* is first an illusion as an edited record of reports upon reality, but it is also, and secondly, a much greater illusion; as well as being a written work, it is 'writing about writing,' 'writing [which] seems to be reflexively writing itself.'[48] And it is the fracturing of this second illusion that may be seen to occasion Dickens's remarks on the additional misfortune of the author, that he must furnish an account of the biographies of his principal characters after he has concluded the narrative. For to the degree in which he has successfully created and sustained the illusion of language's reflexively autonomous ability to write the work in and as itself, so have the characters that people the work, his 'imaginary friends', also taken on a life of their own. And part of Dickens's work in writing the novel has been to write in ways that sustain this illusion of their autonomous existences, by incorporating into the narrative remarks suggesting that what he has just described in words is 'wholly indescribable in words,' or reminding us that its contents are not 'wholly imaginary.' The illusion is that a surrender, such as that of Dickens in *Pickwick Papers*, to the reflexive autonomy of language is simultaneously a release into a total freedom to create an autonomous imaginary human world, populated with its own characters and in process to the rhythm of the events of its own narrative. But this is illusory precisely because of language's sociality. The creative freedom generated by Dickens's surrender to language's reflexive autonomy is tempered by his ultimate responsibility to his readers, those with whom he shares in common the language that makes such freedom possible, and who are as responsible, in their turn, for sustaining as he is for creating the illusion of an autonomous social world of the work.

Now, whilst it is clear, from his addresses to his readers, that Dickens was sensitive to his responsibilities to his audience in this sense, it may be that many of them were less well aware of their reciprocal responsibilities for sustaining this particular illusion which stemmed from the fact that they shared with him the language in which it was constituted. To subjoin biographies for Pickwick and company to the conclusion of the narrative, then, is to comply with an *unquestionably* bad custom in two senses: firstly, it is to comply with a custom which has developed because some, at least, amongst his audience were not prepared to accept that the creative freedom to produce an imaginary human world of the work, which is confined solely and exclusively to the work, is illusory. It is as if, perhaps, Coleridge's 'willing suspension of disbelief which constitutes poetic faith,' and which Dickens's genius engenders so brilliantly amongst his readers, has taken on a quasi-permanent form. The social worlds of the contents of novels exist, as empirical illusions, only within the confines of their form; but the wider social world of which, and because, they are a part precedes and succeeds them. For any creative artist, the realisation of his work in the social world in which it is produced and to which it refers is the degree to which it transforms that world by its active presence within it. Such realisation will hardly be assisted by sustaining whatever involution and encapsulation of the world into the work may have been necessary initially for its accomplishment. Our acquaintance with Pickwick, in and through the Papers, is an acquaintance with the Pickwickian sense or point of view only as it emerges and is transformed through the experiences which Pickwick encounters. We can know our world as Pickwick does his if we enter and look at it 'with the same interest' as he did that of the Fleet prison, for example. We cannot do so by sustaining the illusion of his existence, and that of his imaginary world as our own beyond its course as art. For Dickens, any custom which encourages such a practice cannot but be a bad one, since it is the passive acceptance of reportage as mimetic of reality.

Secondly, and relatedly, it is compliance with an unquestionably bad custom because it is an acknowledgement that Dickens has to make, however unwillingly, to the deceptiveness of that second, much greater illusion of the total creative freedom into which his surrender to the reflexive autonomy of language has projected him. At the level of reference to writing about writing itself, he may be seen here as summarising succinctly, but with a wealth of implication as extensive as the entire novel, the essence of the experiences through which he has put Pickwick during its course. For Pickwick is not the master of language that his creator is. Of the many incidents which befall him, those most important for the narrative's development – his compromising letters and utterances to Mrs. Bardell, his resulting trial and eventual imprisonment – all stem from and are accompanied by demonstration of his linguistic innocence in the form of an inability to appreciate the fact that everyday sequences of words invariably carry a multiplicity of different meanings. For all his competence as a natural language speaker, indeed, Pickwick might as well not have a biography prior to the commencement of the narrative. He is shown early on in it to be an easy mark for the linguistic confidence trickster, Jingle; and Mrs. Bardell is only able to capitalise on the implications of his words to her, innocent though he is of these himself, by the institutionalisation of linguistic confidence trickery that is the law, embodied in the personages and practices of Serjeant Snubbin, Messrs. Dodson and Fogg, and Mr. Justice Stareleigh. Only the interventions of Sam and Tony Weller, who are as masterly in the practices of natural language speakers as Pickwick is inadequate in them saves him from total misfortune – and even then not without many uncomfortable experiences which culminate in his term in the Fleet. It is in and through Pickwick's encounter with the law that the dialectical interrelation of language and social life which Dickens synthesises in his work undergoes its most significant transformation. As the trial takes its course in the novel, Marcus comments thus on the way Dickens writes it:

'that writing, which before was free, has become like Mr. Pickwick himself engaged and involved . . . with society. For in the person of the law Pickwick and Dickens have run into something which though it may seem at first to be an unalloyed linguistic universe is in fact much more than a world of words. It is and it represents society and its structures, in particular those structures known as property and money, both of them extralinguistic phenomena. Property and money are more than words, and words cannot make you free of them.'[49]

As the trial sobers us to this in the novel itself, so Dickens, referring to his writing of it, sobers us as readers to a concomitant realisation of its important implications for socio-literary relations by his reference to the bad custom, with which he has to comply, of sustaining the illusion beyond its conclusion. As words cannot make us free of the social structural phenomena that are other than words, so we cannot substitute the literary illusion and artifice of reality that is the realist novel for the wider and deeper realities of our ongoing social experiences, of which the novel, however significant for us its influence upon it, is only a part.

This final demonstration of literature as a synthesis of the dialectic between language and society points us back to the sociological inadequacies of realism as a creative and critical aesthetic. Far from representing a naturalist correspondence, a mimetic reflection, of the social reality from which it emanates and to which it refers, it is its dialectical opposite, an illusion. We can appreciate its implication for us only if we recognise the illusoriness of the version of the referent reality which we share with it, as Dickens encourages us recurrently to do throughout, and even after the artful course of *Pickwick Papers*. And we can do this, in turn, only if we attend to the ways in which we are able to share in sustaining the illusion of reality which Dickens has offered us as his work, through the language which we share in common with him and with each other. The work of art is in, of and about our common language; so that, far from being a neutral medium of naturalistic correspondence between it and reality, language constitutes the originary grounds of its existence and of whatever meanings – even realist, and whether popular, critical or socialist – it may have for us. Until this intrinsic feature of all works of art becomes a central topic for the sociology of art, it can have little of human relevance to say to us concerning the deeply social life that is art.

Goldsmiths' College, London

I want to acknowledge initially the valuable stimulus to the work in this paper that I have received in working collaboratively in the sociology of art over the past several years with Michael Phillipson at Goldsmiths' College. To the students there, and at the University of California at San Diego, with whom I have discussed *The Pickwick Papers* at considerable length, my thanks are also due. Valerie Somers gave me especially valuable encouragement whilst I was writing this paper; its shortcomings, though, are my responsibility alone.

1. An artist's understanding of his world is negotiated with others as a sharing of that world in and through his work — but not exclusively in this way. What Wellek and Warren have called 'extra-literary pronouncements and activities' to literature, and their correlates in the practice of the other arts, are also likely to be of considerable importance to the sociological analysis of art. See R. Wellek and A. Warren: *The Theory of Literature*, Penguin, Harmondsworth, 1963, Ch. 9.

2. Such primarily aesthetic critical analysis has rarely been cast in a sociological mode, for reasons that are suggested below. Some instances of work that is, nevertheless, especially valuable for its sociological insights may be found, for example in L. Goldmann: *The Hidden God*, Routledge and Kegan Paul, London, 1964, especially Ch. 1; F. R. Leavis and Q. D. Leavis: *Dickens The Novelist*, Chatto and Windus, London, 1970; E. H. Gombrich: *Art and Illusion*, Princeton University Press, New Jersey, 1961, especially Chs. II, VII, X; J. Berger: *Ways of Seeing*, B.B.C. and Penguin Books, Harmondsworth, 1972; R. Williams: *The English Novel From Dickens to Lawrence*, Chatto and Windus, London, 1970; R. Williams: *The Country and the City*, Chatto and Windus, London, 1973, especially Ch. 4.

3. E. H. Gombrich: *Art History and the Social Sciences*, Oxford University Press, London, 1975, p. 42.

4. See P. Filmer and D. Walsh: 'Sociology, Education and the Myth of Science' in *Meanings*, Guild of Pastoral Psychology, London, July 1976, where this issue is explicated in further detail.

5. For further consideration of these issues see Filmer and Walsh: op cit.; P. McHugh, S. Raffel, D. C. Foss and A. F. Blum: *On the Beginnings of Social Inquiry*, Routledge and Kegan Paul, London, 1974, Ch. 7; P. Filmer: 'Literary Study as Liberal Education and as Sociology in the Work of F. R. Leavis' in Chris Jenks (ed.): *Rationality, Education and the Social Organisation of Knowledge*, Routledge and Kegan Paul, London, 1977.

6. The editors of a recent anthology in the sociology of literature and drama have been led to remark with reference to this emphasis that sociologists in Britain and America,
    > 'where they have used literature at all, have treated
    > it as a kind of quarry for fossil specimens of classes
    > of events and stereo typed actions, performances, or
    > social roles.'
    See E. Burns and T. Burns (eds.): *Sociology of Literature and Drama*, Penguin, Harmondsworth, 1973, p. 10.

7. See e.g. L. A. Coser (ed.): *Sociology Through Literature*, Prentice-Hall, Englewood Cliffs, 1963; J. Dabaghian (ed.): *Mirror of Man*, Little Brown, Boston, 1970, and; R. Gliner and R. A. Raines (eds.): *Munching on Existence*, The Free Press, New York, 1971.

8. Coser: op. cit., p. 5.

9. Burns and Burns comment:
    > 'There has been, we should admit, a certain amount of
    > sociological research into the membership of audiences
    > and of reading publics over the past generation, but
    > we have to confess that none of the writings known to
    > us seemed to merit inclusion' (op cit., p. 28).

For work on the sociology of authorship, see D. Laurenson and A. Swingewood: *The Sociology of Literature*, Paladin, London, 1972, part II; R. D. Altick: 'The Sociology of Authorship: The Social Origins, Education and Occupation of 1,100 British Writers, 1800-1935' in *The Bulletin of the New York Public Library*, vol. 66, 1962; and, R. D. Altick: *The English Common Reader*, University of Chicago Press, Chicago, 1963. A selection of largely American work in this general area can be found in M. C. Albrecht, J. H. Barnett and M. Griff (eds.): *The Sociology of Art and Literature*, Praeger, New York, 1970, parts II, III, IV.

10. It is worth noting that, in general, the more sensitive insights into socio-literary relations developed within realist perspectives are found in work by literary critics rather than that of professional sociologists: cf. A. Kettle: 'Dickens and the Popular Tradition' in D. Craig (ed.): *Marxists on Literature*, Penguin, Harmondsworth, 1975; G. Lukács: *Studies in European Realism*, Grosset and Dunlap, New York, 1964; G. Lukács: *Writer and Critic and Other Essays*, Grosset and Dunlap, New York, 1971. A reasonable inference might be that it is past time that sociology began to attend to the aesthetic illiteracy of its students with the assiduity that its professional scientism has led it to attend to their statistical innumeracy.

11. Kettle: op. cit., p. 214.

12. ibid., pp. 215-6.

13. ibid., pp. 216-7

14. See D. Caute: *The Illusion*, Panther, London, 1972, pp. 88-91. On positivism in relation to literature, see S. J. Kahn: *Science and Aesthetic Judgement*, Greenwood Press, Westport, Con., 1970; Laurenson and Swingewood: op. cit.; G. D. Martin: *Language, Truth and Poetry*, The University Press, Edinburgh, 1975.

15. For instances of such practices in literary works, see Caute: op. cit., pp. 101-108.

16. For an extended discussion of the relation between writer and critic from a realist point of view, see Lukács: op. cit., 1971, pp. 189-226.

17. Kettle: op cit., p. 215.

18. ibid., p. 217.

19. ibid., p. 217.

20. ibid., pp. 229-30.

21. ibid.

22. Indeed Kettle: op. cit., pp. 230-238, for example, exemplifies his concept of popular realism by reference to Dickens's creation of character and his use of imagery, as well as to his point of view in relation to the law in *Bleak House.*

23. Caute: op. cit., pp. 101-2.

24. Important exceptions are the work of S. Marcus: *Dickens From Pickwick to Dombey*, Simon and Schuster, New York, 1968 and 'Language into Structure: Pickwick Revisited' in *Daedalus*, Winter, 1972, referred to in detail below, and E. Wilson: *The Wound and The Bow.*, Methuen, London, 1961.

25. The selection of Leavis and Leavis: op. cit. can stand as representative of the general view that the masterpieces are *Dombey and Son, David Copperfield, Bleak House, Hard Times, Little Dorrit* and *Great Expectations.*

26. Kettle: op. cit., pp. 217-8.

27. Marcus: op. cit., 1968 and 1972.

28. Marcus: op. cit., 1972, p. 199.

29. A. Hauser: *The Social History of Art, Vol. IV*, Routledge and Kegan Paul, London, 1962, pp. 114-120.

30. G. Lukacs: *The Historical Novel*, Penguin, Harmondsworth, 1969, p. 290.

31. Marcus: op. cit., 1972, p. 189. Marcus acknowledges annexing the term from Hobsbawm. Its appropriation can be seen with reference to the economic and social history of the period in which Dickens was writing. See, for example, Altick: op. cit., 1963 and J. L. Hammond and B. Hammond: *The Bleak Age*, Penguin, West Drayton and New York, 1947. R. Williams: *Culture and Society, 1780-1950*, Penguin, Hardmonsworth, 1958 is particularly valuable as a resource for setting this in a more long-term socio-cultural context.

32. Marcus: op cit., 1968, pp. 27-8, 44-51; R. L. Patten: 'Introduction' to Charles Dickens: *The Pickwick Papers*, Penguin, Harmondsworth, 1972.

33. Kettle: op. cit.; Wilson: op. cit.

34. Chapter 41. In the same chapter may be found another passage with similar implications:
    ' . . . each gentleman pointed with his right thumb over
    his left shoulder. This action, imperfectly described in
    words by the very feeble term of "over the left", when
    performed by any number of ladies or gentlemen who are
    accustomed to act in unison, has a very graceful and
    airy effect; its expression is one of light and playful
    sarcasm.'
    And so, I think, in the light of such perfect verbal constitutions of human action, is Dickens's use of phrases like 'wholly indescribable' or 'imperfectly described in words.'

35. Marcus: op. cit., 1968, p. 25.

36. ibid., pp. 38-9.

37. It is worth recalling here that the initial publication of the work was under the full title of *The Posthumous Papers of the Pickwick Club Containing a Faithful Record of the Perambulations, Perils, Travels, Adventures and Sporting Transactions of the Corresponding Members*, edited by 'Boz'. On the significance of this pseudonym for Dickens, see Marcus: op. cit., 1972, pp. 184, 199.

38. Even here, it may be argued, the game of deception is still being played: the *Shorter Oxford English Dictionary*, Third Edition, 1944 offers Chronicler as 'a writer of a chronicle, a recorder of events.' All that is missing from this formulation is the editing of the record that the narrative is purported to be.

39. Marcus: op cit., 1972, pp. 183-6, makes the interesting suggestion, and argues it thoroughly, that the beginning of the work was in the advertisement before the first number of its serial publication, and then in the two prefaces that Dickens wrote for subsequent collected editions.

40. Patten: op. cit., pp. 18-19, 899-903.

41. Marcus: op. cit., 1972, p. 189.

42. ibid., pp. 189-90.

43. ibid., p. 193.

44. See Q. D. Leavis: 'The Dickens Illustrations: Their Function' in Leavis and Leavis: op. cit., chapter 7, for an interesting discussion on Dickens's use of illustration as a way of relating to a semi-literate public.

45. Patten: op. cit., pp. 18-19.

46. On the relation between Dickens, Shakespeare and language, see F. R. Leavis: *Nor Shall My Sword* . . . , Chatto and Windus, London, 1972, ch. VI, especially p. 184.

47. Marcus: op. cit., 1972, p. 199.

48. ibid., pp. 195, 196.

49. Marcus: op. cit., 1972, p. 200.

Georg Lukács and the Novels of Emile Zola

Ian H. Birchall

The work of Georg Lukács represents one of the most ambitious attempts so far to construct a Marxist theory of literature, and no study of Marxism and literature can attempt to by-pass either its problematic or its achievements. At the same time it is impossible to ignore the striking limitations of Lukács's work. The inadequacy of his treatment of modernism, and in particular of Kafka, has been widely discussed. Another blind spot – in many ways more interesting for Marxists – is the work of Emile Zola.

On a purely empirical level, Lukács's judgements of Zola are so inadequate that they can be explained only by amazing ignorance on the part of one so erudite, or by a wilful misreading. Yet Zola – not simply as the author of some of the finest studies of working-class life in fictional form, but as one who lived and wrote on the uneasy margins between bourgeois and proletarian world-views – is a test-case for any Marxist.

How deep does the flaw go? Must Lukács's whole method be jettisoned? It is the contention of this article that there is no 'Marxist method' in abstraction from Marxist politics; and that if Lukács misread Zola, the explanation must be sought in the tortuous history of Lukács's involvement with Stalinist politics. Lukács got the wrong answers, but, unlike many, he was asking the right questions.

Lukács's judgement on Zola can be found scattered throughout three volumes of his works in English – *Studies in European Realism*,[1] *Writer and Critic*,[2] and *The Historical Novel*.[3] The main charges he levels at Zola can be collected under five headings.

(i) Zola is accused, because of his concern with heredity, of departing from realism in seeing 'the physiological aspects of self-preservation and procreation'[4] as dominant; this leads him into 'biological mysticism'.[5] This retreat from realism leads to a structural incoherence in his work; 'Thus the congenital drunkenness of Etienne Lantier in *Germinal* causes explosions and calamities with no organic connection to Etienne's character; nor does Zola seek any such connection.'[6]

Now it is true that Zola had some rather quaint ideas about the importance and nature of heredity. It is also true that these ideas have greater prominence in some of Zola's rather over-simplified 'theoretical' statements than in the actual fabric of the novels. But what is significant is not so much the quaint ideas as the project. Zola set out to achieve a materialist understanding of human behaviour. He did so

92

with the limitations of contemporary knowledge, and at a time when such contemporaries as Taine – horrified by the Commune – were rapidly retreating from their earlier materialism. Zola's insistence on 'tainted heredity' and his gallery of monster children can be seen as a firm rejection of the Romantic myth of 'natural goodness' with all its conservative implications. Zola may be misguided, sometimes grotesquely so, on questions of biology, but there is no 'mysticism' here.

This becomes abundantly clear if one rejects Lukács's approach of seeing Zola's work as a single block, and studies his development. As Zola's plans for the Rougon-Macquart cycle overspilled the original intentions, and Zola's investigation of contemporary society goes deeper, so fatalistic heredity fades and gives way to changeable *milieu* as the dominant theme. The one apparent exception, *La Bête Humaine*, must be placed in context. Zola's *ébauche* for the novel contains the phrase 'Reply to the Russian novel'.[7] Zola's study of the determinations that make Jacques Lantier a murderer are a materialist answer to Dostoievsky's *Crime and Punishment*, with its reactionary doctrine that 'progressive' ideas lead to crime.

Zola's flirtation with Darwin is likewise ambiguous. The reactionary potential of 'social Darwinism' is obvious; but for Zola Darwin's stress on struggle brings him closer than at any other point to accepting the necessity for revolutionary violence.[8]

As for Lukács's comments on *Germinal*, they are a ludicrous parody of the novel. Etienne's heredity has a minor part in the novel – so minor that a reader not familiar with Zola's theories would never notice it. The killing of Chaval is the *only* point at which Etienne's heredity (he is explicitly not drunk at the time) impinges on the narrative.[9] One might add that the conflict between political commitment and the temptations of drink has been a real one for many working-class militants. But one would hardly expect the aloof Lukács to notice that.

More importantly, what Lukács fails to point to is the struggle of ideas in Zola's work. There are bourgeois ideas, reactionary ideas – but there are also socialist ideas inextricably mingled with them. Lukács's schematism fails to grasp the ambiguity and sense of struggle.

(ii) Lukács's second set of charges concern the structure of Zola's novels. Zola is contrasted unfavourably with the great 'realists' of the nineteenth century, Balzac, Stendhal[10] and Tolstoy.[11] The key to the comparison is the concept of 'totality', a central theme in Lukács's work. By contrast with the greater realists, it is alleged, for Zola totality consists in the quantitative amassing of detail.

'Every reader will remember, for instance, Zola's markets, stock exchanges, underworld haunts, theatres, racetracks, etc. So far as the encyclopaedic character of his contents and the artistic quality of his descriptions is concerned, Zola, too, possessed this "totality of objects". But these objects have a being entirely independent of the fate of the characters. They form a mighty but indifferent background to human destinies with which they had no real connection; at best they are the more or less accidental scenery among which these human destinies are enacted.'[12]

From this failure to achieve 'totality' a whole range of defects is derived. Zola is said merely to 'describe' whereas Tolstoy 'narrates'[13]; Zola's account of the capitalist theatre in *Nana* merely presents 'social facts' whereas Balzac shows '*how* the theatre *becomes* prostituted under capitalism.'[14] Zola is preoccupied with 'things' and 'debases characters to the level of inanimate objects.'[15] Even where historical events are depicted, there is no effective integration of individual and social history.[16] The concern for facts leads Zola to portray the 'average' rather than the 'type'.[17] Lukács follows Paul Lafargue in arguing that in *L'Assommoir* and *L'Argent* Zola shows a failure to understand the workings of the capitalist system.[18]

To reply to these charges nothing less than a full-scale study of Zola would suffice. Such a study would stress Zola's grasp of the dynamics of capitalist society, the ruthless intrigues of the bourgeoisie and the internal problems of working-class organisation; it would point to Zola's awareness that most working people feel themselves totally estranged from what we normally call 'History', until it obtrudes itself upon them in devastating form; it would argue that if Zola subordinates men and women to things, he is telling no more than the truth about a society where the fetishism of commodities reigns.

But such an alternative reading would still, in a sense, be inadequate. For Lukács's judgements on Zola are in general highly schematic in nature. Apart from the one essay, *Narrate or Describe?*[19], where he does attempt a detailed if selective account of *Nana*, Lukács does not deign to argue his points. He simply appeals to what he takes to be commonly agreed assumptions – that Tolstoy and Balzac are universally acknowledged to be greater writers than Zola. That these assumptions coincide with the accepted canons of bourgeois taste does not seem to disturb him.

Lukács's treatment of Balzac is in general far more detailed and sensitive than that of Zola. But here too the desire to create a polemical stereotype often seems to triumph. A Balzac who always achieves 'totality' is as implausible as a Zola who never makes it. There are

94

certainly passages in Balzac that are guilty of all the charges levelled at Zola (for example, the description of Issoudun in *La Rabouilleuse)*. All too often in Lukács's work, Balzac and Zola cease to be real living authors of texts, and become disembodied Aunt Sallies acting out a dialectic through the corridors of his mind.

(iii) Lukács seeks to explain the gulf between Zola and earlier realists by a changed attitude to society. Earlier realists had been deeply involved in society – 'Balzac was a participant in and victim of the feverish speculations of emerging French capitalism; Goethe and Stendhal served as government officials'; while in the later period 'Flaubert and Zola had too much integrity. For them the only solution to the tragic contradiction in their situation was to stand aloof as observers and critics of capitalist society.'[20]

The proof of Zola's 'aloofness' as a mere 'observer' lies, not in Zola's works, but in his declared method. 'Zola's method, which hampered not only Zola himself but his whole generation, because it was the result of the writer's position as solitary observer, prevents any profoundly realistic representation of life. Zola's 'scientific' method always seeks the average, and this grey statistical mean, the point at which all internal contradictions are blunted, where the great and the petty, the noble and the base, the beautiful and the ugly are all mediocre 'products' together, spells the doom of great literature.'[21]

We can leave aside the more specious of Lukács's arguments. It is hard to see how participation in financial speculation or government administration enhances the qualities of a 'critical realist'. (Presumably on this criterion, Heidegger, who actively supported Hitler, should have grasped the totality of Nazi society better than Thomas Mann, who went into exile from it). Another piece of sleight of hand is the amalgam between Zola and Flaubert. If the two men were friends and admired each other's work, their concepts of literature always diverged sharply.

More fundamental is that Lukács completely distorts the trajectory of Zola's development. His claim that Zola was 'a mere observer and when at last he answered the call of life, it came too late to influence his development as a writer,'[22] is to misunderstand completely the place of the Dreyfus case in Zola's life. The Dreyfus intervention was not a late accident, but the logical outcome of Zola's development as an artist[23] and of the liberal, Republican values he had consistently fought for.

Zola's Republicanism is plain to see in his earliest novels. In *La Fortune des Rougon*, *Le Ventre de Paris* and *La Conquête de Plassans* there is no pretence of neutrality between the rapacious bourgeois and the heroic but defeated Republicans. Hippolyte Taine, who had a keen eye for leftists and subversives, did not fail to recognise this when he commented in a letter to Zola[24] that he objected to his 'parti pris politique'. 'An artist is above that, he never pleads for a camp.' And if Zola fell far short of supporting the Commune, either in 1871 or later, his honest reporting and revulsion at the repression set him at a very considerable distance from the reactionary hysteria of Taine, Goncourt, Flaubert and most of the intellectuals of the period.

There is a real development in Zola's work, a development from Republicanism to socialism, albeit of a Fourierist tinge; from the politics of bourgeois cliques to the economics of everyday survival; from inherited power-lust to socially-determined *milieu*. But it is an evolution within a profound commitment, a deep hatred of the powerful and the pampered. Whatever he may have been, Zola was never a 'mere observer'.

(iv) Lukács's fourth set of charges against Zola – once again linked to Flaubert – concern the trend to dehumanisation in modern literature. This trend is, of course, related to the 'dehumanising tendencies of capitalism'; but Zola and his contemporaries are seen as powerless to fight these. 'Flaubert, Baudelaire, Zola and even Nietzsche, suffer from this development and savagely oppose it; yet the manner of their opposition leads to an intensification in literature of capitalist dehumanisation in life.'[26]

But the charge is ambiguous. Discussing Flaubert's *Salammbô*, Lukács takes another side-swipe at Zola. 'In short, those brutal and animal features are emphasised and placed at the centre, which occur later in Zola as characteristics of the life of modern workers and peasants. Thus Flaubert's portrayal is 'prophetic'. Not, however, in the sense in which Balzac's works were prophetic, anticipating the actual, future development of social types, but merely in a literary-historical sense, anticipating the later distortion of modern life in the works of the Naturalists.'[27] What is Lukács implying here? That the life of modern workers and peasants is not brutalised? That Zola's portrayal is untruthful, that he would have done better to portray workers as idyllic cardboard figures, like George Sand, or ignore them altogether, like Balzac? It is hard to interpret the passage in any other way.

Likewise, Lukács refers to 'the eruption of mass cruelty in Zola's *Germinal*'.[28] Now it is just possible that the 'cruelty' referred to is that of the Army, but from the context it appears that Lukács means the accounts of workers in strike and demonstration. Now any careful reading of the passages dealing with mass action[29] shows clearly that (a) unlike such English novelists as Dickens, Disraeli, Eliot and Gaskell, Zola does not present the crowd as an irrational mass viewed from the outside, but rather shows it from the viewpoint of a participant; and (b) that he is keenly alive to the tensions and differentiations within the collective. Lukács's vituperations against Zola are sometimes almost reminiscent of one of Zola's own characters, Eugène Rougon, in his tirades against the indelicacy, lubricity, pornography and hysteria of contemporary fiction.[30]

More seriously, two main points can be made. Firstly, Zola is indeed sensitive to the dehumanisation inherent in capitalist society. One of the most striking features of his work is the use of imagery to capture this dehumanisation. In *Germinal* the image of the mine as a living beast swallowing human flesh recurs again and again; it is an unforgettable symbol of one of the central processes of the capitalist system – the way in which human creations acquire a life of their own, and turn those whose labour made them into victims. No amount of pontificating about Zola's ignorance of Marxism can obscure his grasp of this theme.

Secondly, and even more important, in *Germinal* above all, Zola portrays not merely dehumanisation, but also the active force that can destroy that dehumanisation, the working-class. Zola is one of the few nineteenth century novelists[31] who go beyond seeing the working-class as a mass deserving of pity, and who present it, not simply as a fighting force, but as a complex unity within which we perceive conflicts of ideas, tensions between individuals and changes of mood.

Even at times when he has been unfashionable with critics of left and right alike, Zola has always enjoyed a wide-working class readership, and the responses of such readers often show insights that escape academic Marxists. Thus a British metal-worker, reviewing *Germinal* between the two great miners' strikes of 1972 and 1974, points to the importance of flying pickets in the strike, underlining the fact that for Zola class struggle was not simply an abstraction, but very much a question of concrete realisations.[32] In her book *Les Maos en France*, Michèle Manceaux[33] reports the remarks of a young Maoist ex-student talking of the experience of going into a factory as an 'outsider': 'It's like *Germinal*; the bloke who lands in the Nord mines, ends up winning the confidence of the miners and unleashing their enthusiasm. Then, when the strike's failed, he's rejected, they don't believe in him any more, they distrust him. But slowly he'll get back the esteem of the workers . . . It's still like that today.' These brief comments are far more perceptive of the structure and meaning of *Germinal* than any of Lukács's peremptory judgements.

(v) Lukács is not wholly blind to Zola's merits. In some places, notably in the essay 'The Zola Centenary'[34] he pays tribute to his qualities both as a man and as an artist. But the tribute is always qualified, and in the last resort Lukács's most favourable judgement is that Zola was a tragic failure. His failure, apparently, derives from the epoch in which he was born. 'Balzac and Stendhal . . . had lived in a society in which the antagonism of bourgeoisie and working-class was not as yet the plainly visible hub around which social evolution moved forward. Hence Balzac and Stendhal could dig down to the very roots of the sharpest contradictions inherent in bourgeois society while the writers who lived after 1848 could not do so: such merciless candour, such sharp criticism would have necessarily driven them to break the link with their own class. Even the sincerely progressive Zola was incapable of such a rupture.'[35]

Capitalism is the villain which prevented Zola from fulfilling his 'talents' (where did this mysterious entity 'talent' come from? was it hereditary?): 'Hence Zola's fate is one of the literary tragedies of the nineteenth century. Zola is one of those outstanding personalities whose talents and human qualities destined them for the greatest things, but who have been prevented by capitalism from accomplishing their destiny and finding themselves in a truly realistic art.'[36] The whole argument is, of course, specious metaphysics. If Zola had lived at a time when the struggle between capital and labour was not at the centre of the stage, he would not have written *L'Assommoir* and *Germinal*, the manifestation and proof of his talent. Presumably his disembodied 'talent' ('What do you think talent is then? Mildew of the brain? A supernumerary bone?')[37] would have produced Petrarchian sonnets or tales of happy days in a Soviet factory.

In an essay on 'Pushkin's Place in World Literature' Lukács gives an even more startling twist to the tragedy of Zola: 'After the French Revolution two lines of development emerge in Europe: the first, the bourgeois, leads from the heroic illusions of the French Revolution to Balzac's Crevels and Popinots and to Flaubert's Homais and later to the baser types of our own day; the starting point of the second line of development is the Babeuf uprising: from it a road of heroic proletarian struggle leads to the Paris Commune and to the present. In Western Europe this line achieves no real victory and no real liberation.

'The road of Russian development is quite different: it leads from the Decembrists to the October Revolution and thence to the full, victorious emergence of socialist society.'

'Pushkin's unique position in world literature rests on the fact that he stands at the outset of this development. . . . The future victory of the liberation of the Russian people is the social basis of Pushkin's beauty.'[38] So Lukács actually seems to believe that the failure of the German Revolution and the triumph of 'socialism in one country' were *already inevitable* in the early nineteenth century!

But, whether it was his fault or not, Zola failed to 'break the link' with his own class. Unfortunately, Lukács is disappointingly vague as to what 'breaking the link' would involve. Could Zola have plunged straight over the barricades and become a 'socialist realist'? What would have been needed for the conversion? It could not be anything so simple as joining the Party – even if a Party to join had existed[39] – for many have done that and then slid back across the class lines.

In fact, Zola's work gains its strength precisely from the tension between bourgeois and socialist values. Time and again Zola, in disgust at the bourgeoisie and their society, groped towards an understanding of the socialist alternative. He met Jules Guesde, one of the leading socialist thinkers and activists in France, to discuss socialist ideas,[40] and in *L'Argent* he presents us with Sigismond Busch, a disciple and expounder of the ideas of Marx.[41] If Busch's ideas are in fact far too Utopian and gradualist for Marx, that is an indication that on certain key questions, the nature of the bourgeois state and the need for revolutionary violence (the two main lessons of the Paris Commune) Zola was still struggling against the limits of bourgeois ideology. But, as he wrote to Van Santen Kolff[42]: 'Every time I undertake a study now, I come up against socialism.'

Now that statement fits precisely the criteria laid down by Lukács for a 'critical realist': 'Not everyone who looks for a solution to the social and ideological crises of bourgeois society – and this is necessarily the subject-matter of contemporary bourgeois literature – will be a professed socialist. It is enough that a writer takes socialism into account and does not reject it out of hand. But if he rejects socialism – and this is the point I want to make – he closes his eyes to the future, gives up any chance of assessing the present correctly, and loses the ability to create other than purely static works of art.'[43] These comparatively lenient standards were enough to gain Thomas Mann his entry ticket into the Lukácsian Pantheon; but Zola falls short. We cannot help asking why double standards are being applied.

What reasons can be given for Lukács's blindspot on the question of Zola? Was he simply ignorant of Zola's work? Was he simply following established Marxist views? Is his whole method at fault? Or was he guided by political considerations? Let us examine each hypothesis in turn.

(i) A good case can be made out for arguing that Lukács did not have an extensive knowledge of Zola's novels. As has already been shown, most of his references are brief and cryptic, and rely excessively on Zola's stated intentions rather than his actual practice. In the essay on 'The Zola Centenary'[44] mentioned above, no novel by Zola is named at any point.

An interesting confirmation of this is provided by Lukács's book *The Theory of the Novel*, written in 1914-15 before Lukács became a Marxist. Here we find the statement: 'Zolaesque monumentality amounts only to monotonous emotion in face of the multiple yet simplified complexity of a sociological system of categories that claims to cover the whole of contemporary life.'[45] Despite the impenetrable language which characterises most of Lukács' early writings, this seems to be saying something very similar to that which Lukács was saying about Zola in his later works. This would suggest that Lukács's references to Zola are often to a reading remembered from his pre-Marxist days. This would account for the sweeping generality and impressionism of many of his judgements.

Ignorance, in itself, however, proves nothing. If Lukács had wanted to make an exhaustive study of Zola he could have done so. The fact that he did not, despite the fact that his judgements so often run up against the question of Zola, implies a prior value judgement.

(ii) 'Balzac, whom I consider a far greater master of realism than all the Zolas *passés, présents et à venir.*'[46] Thus wrote Friedrich Engels, and all of Lukács's writings on the Balzac-Zola dichotomy can be seen as an extended gloss on this phrase. Does this confirm that Lukács, whatever, his weaknesses, is in the main stream of Marxist orthodoxy when he summarily dismisses Zola?

Before coming to such a conclusion, we must examine the context of Engels's remarks. There are only two other references to Zola in Engels's correspondence – scarcely indicative of a deep or broad knowledge of Zola. In one Engels comments to Laura Lafargue somewhat ironically on a young doctor who claimed to have discovered a 'materialistic view of history' in Zola;[47] in the other he comments to Karl Kautsky that Paul Lafargue is the right man to write about Zola.[48]

We may therefore presume that Engels's views on Zola were largely derived from Paul Lafargue, who did take a keen interest in Zola's work. (Lukács too expresses his direct debt to Lafargue's work on Zola).[49]

Lafargue, like many others on the left, had reacted harshly to *L'Assommoir*, seeing it as a slander on the working class. 'Zola, straight after the terrible massacres of the week of blood, in order to spare the bourgeois conscience the slightest remorse, depicted in *L'Assommoir* the working class with the most repugnant features.'[50]

Lafargue's critique, then, was directly political rather than literary, seeing *L'Assemmoir* as a contribution to contemporary political discussion. Moreover, Lafargue was particularly concerned to draw the lines between socialists and the liberal-republican tradition in France – hence his violent attacks on Victor Hugo. Moreover, it should be remembered that Lafargue later came to take a more sympathetic position towards Zola; reviewing *L'Argent* in *Die Neue Zeit* he praised Zola's attempt to describe and analyse 'the giant organisms of the modern period.'[51]

Disapproval of Zola could hardly, therefore, be counted an article of Marxist faith. (If Lukács had really wanted an excuse to like Zola, he might have noted that Lenin is reputed to have liked the late Utopian novel *Travail*).[52] As Lukács himself had written: 'Let us assume for the sake of argument that recent research had disproved once and for all every one of Marx's individual theses. Even if this were to be proved, every serious 'orthodox' Marxist would still be able to accept all such modern findings without reservation and hence dismiss all of Marx's theses *in toto* – without having to renounce his orthodoxy for a single moment . . . orthodoxy refers exclusively to *method*.'[53] One does not need to go all the way with this position to be quite clear that an 'orthodox' Marxist is under no obligation to accept the literary tastes of Marx and Engels.

In this light it may be of interest to look again at the celebrated letter to Margaret Harkness where Engels takes his sideswipe at Zola, and see what substantive point he is making. Criticising Mr Harkness's own novel, he writes: 'In the *"City Girl"* the working class figures as a passive mass, unable to help itself and not even making any attempt at striving to help itself. All attempts to drag it out of its torpid misery come from without, from above. Now if this was a correct description about 1800 or 1810, in the days of Saint-Simon and Robert Owen, it cannot appear so in 1887 to a man who for nearly fifty years has had the honour of sharing in most of the fights of the militant proletariat. The rebellious reaction of the working-class against the oppressive medium which surrounds them, their attempts – convulsive, half-conscious or conscious – at recovering their status as human beings, belong to history and must therefore lay claim to a place in the domain of realism.'

It is clear from this passage that, while Engels's criticisms of *City Girl* could, to some extent, be addressed at *L'Assommoir*, *Germinal*, on the contrary, meets precisely Engels's requirements for 'realism'.

(iii) 'It is not the primacy of economic motives in historical explanation that constitutes the decisive difference between Marxism and bourgeois thought, but the point of view of totality. The category of totality, the all-pervasive supremacy of the whole over the parts is the essence of the method which Marx took over from Hegel and brilliantly transformed into the foundations of a wholly new science.'[54] It is this stress on totality which constitutes Lukács's significance as a Marxist thinker. Lukács does not revise or add to Marx, but he does make explicit an important theme in Marxism. It is the objective of grasping reality as a totality that ensures the ultimate superiority of the proletariat as a class. The bourgeoisie, not simply empirically, but by its historical nature, is incapable of achieving totality. 'The tragic dialectics of the bourgeoisie can be seen in the fact that it is not only desirable but essential for it to clarify its own class interests on *every particular issue*, while at the same time such a clear awareness becomes fatal when it is extended to *the question of the totality*.'[55]

After withdrawing from active politics in the late twenties, Lukács devoted his attention to the problem of totality in literature. This led him to develop two important emphases. Firstly, his approach to literature is essentially epistemological. Literature is of interest as a means by which mankind comprehends the world it lives in. The content and truth-value of literature are stressed, as against the formalism and aestheticism which characterise much bourgeois criticism. But, secondly, Lukács gives full importance to *form* as the means whereby totality is grasped. This counterbalances vulgar sociologism in literary criticism, which simply reduces the work to its content.

Whereas such critics as Barthes[56] and even Sartre[57] have stressed, in a rather negative way, the conservative elements of the nineteenth century realist novel, Lukács is able to give its full importance to realism. His account of realism in Balzac – even if we were to argue that empirically it is quite inapplicable to Balzac, or, conversely, that it is wholly applicable to some other individual such as Zola – is an important methodological contribution.

Equally important is Lukács's preoccupation with class consciousness. Here too his method could be fruitfully applied to Zola's work. In *Germinal* in particular the question of the limits of bourgeois class consciousness is posed. On the one hand Zola is determined to show that capitalism is a system independent of the will of individuals; it will not do to show the mine-owners and managers as morally responsible for the suffering of the miners. But on the other hand he is too deeply committed to the cause of social justice to allow any suggestion of impartiality between the conflicting forces. So Zola stresses the limits of bourgeois consciousness, the fact that the bourgeoisie are incapable of understanding either the depth of suffering or the nature of the miners' revolt.

It is true, however, that Lukács's account of the 'imputed' consciousness of a social class (the consciousness it is objectively capable of) is somewhat static. As Colin Sparks has argued:[58] 'What is at stake in any historical study is not the historical possibilities open at any given stage in history but the real, objective actions taken by classes. It is true that these can only be understood in the light of "imputed" consciousness, but this is only the beginning of comprehension. The real movement of history is located in the *relation* of the "imputed" consciousness of a class to its actual empirical consciousness.' Certainly this point would be highly relevant to an account of working class consciousness in *Germinal*, as the protagonists slowly grope their way out of bourgeois consciousness towards a socialist vision.

Nonetheless, it seems clear that Lukács offers an approach to totality, form and content and class consciousness that would permit a study of Zola far more illuminating than the psychologism and formalism which dominate most recent Zola criticism. For example, although much has been written about myth and symbol in Zola's novels, such accounts become abstract and formalistic unless they start from Zola's preoccupation with reification, from his realisation that capitalist society has distorted and inverted the relations between men and things. The flaw lies not in the method itself, but in the particular historical use that Lukács put it to.

(iv) Once he had abandoned the 'messianic sectarianism'[59] that characterised his work of the erly twenties, Lukács became a loyal follower of the Moscow line in the international Communist movement. On the surface, he went through all the turns and twists with perfect loyalty. He criticised Stalin – but only after the Twentieth Congress had given the green light. But as far as his literary criticism is concerned, it is from the rightward turns that Lukács derived his main inspiration.[60] The Popular Front of 1934-39, the anti-fascist war alliance of 1941-45, the peace movement of the early fifties – these were the movements for which Lukács tried to provide a sophisticated intellectual and cultural defence.

Gone is the 'sectarian' insistence that only the proletariat can be the bearer of totality. On the contrary, the common interest of bourgeoisie and proletariat are stressed. By 1955 Lukács was writing: 'The real dilemma of our age is not the opposition between capitalism and socialism, but the opposition between peace and war. The first duty of the bourgeois intellectual has become the rejection of an all-pervading fatalistic *angst*, implying a rescue operation for humanity rather than any breakthrough to Socialism.'[61]

In his study of Thomas Mann, Lukács is even more explicit in his abandonment of the working class as the agency of socialism. He tells us 'Thomas Mann was and remained a bourgeois. But as a great man and a great writer he realised that the contradictions of bourgeois society could only be solved by socialism; that only socialism could prevent mankind from sinking into barbarism.'[62] Mann, we are told, 'prescribed socialism as the future task of the bourgeois for whom he has been looking.'[63]

If we can manage to set on one side our amazement that anyone who calls himself a Marxist can make such statements, we can begin to get some clues as to why Lukács doesn't like Zola very much. To put it very crudely, Lukács isn't really interested in the working-class. For him, in the era of the Popular Front, the essential problem is internal to the bourgeoisie; to find that segment of the bourgeoisie that is true to 'progressive' bourgeois values, that will defend democracy against fascism and support peaceful coexistence with the Soviet Union. A man like Zola, who is so disgusted with bourgeois values that he turns increasingly to the working-class as potential destroyer of bourgeois society, can only be seen as ultra-left.

It may be noted that in 1949 J. Revai, the Hungarian Minister of Culture, made a long attack on Lukács[64] in which he declared that 'Comrade Lukács forgot, in the struggle against fascism, about the struggle against Capitalism.'[65] However Revai's critique is entirely of timing, not of principles; he concedes that Lukács was right in in the 1945-46 period;[66] he just failed to change line at the right time.

In his 1965 Preface to *Writer and Critic*, Lukács states that his analyses of such writers as Balzac and Tolstoy were in fact an implicit criticism of Stalin's requirement that 'literature provide tactical support to . . . current political policies.'[67] This is not a very convincing retrospective justification. It is more plausible to see Lukács's work as embodying the inevitable logic of the Popular Front, ever open to the right, but utterly intolerant on its left flank.[68] Lukács extends the hand of friendship to a non-socialist like Thomas Mann, but writers like Serge and Breton, critics within his own camp, are not even given a mention.

The same strategy is applied to the past. The outstretched hand to Catholic monarchist Balzac presents no problems. The categories of 'socialist realism' and 'critical realism' make everything clear. The former are in our camp, and follow the line; the latter in the bourgeois camp and we know what to expect of them.

Zola, however, is an awkward case, neither flesh nor fowl. Apart from anything else, it is hard to imagine the defender of Dreyfus being an uncritical supporter of the Moscow Trials. Zola had a penetrating eye for repression and bureaucracy that would have made him a very uneasy fellow-traveller. To take just one example, in *Son Excellence Eugène Rougon*, Rougon tells a departmental prefect that every department has been given a quota of arrests to fill. When the prefect timidly enquires *who* he should arrest, Rougon replies: 'Oh, arrest who you like! . . . I can't be bothered with details like that'.[69] Modern parallels would not be hard to find,[70] but a true supporter of the Popular Front would not be so indelicate as to point them out.

Lukács's abandonment of the struggle for socialism and the agency of the proletariat is a symptom of a whole era of defeat. While Lukács's deproletarianised Marxism is able to say much of interest and relevance about Balzac, Stendhal and Tolstoy, he finds Zola indigestible – a proof of the continued relevance of Zola. The class struggle, which a few years back was being pronounced obsolete, is reawakening around the world, and as it does Zola will be read with renewed understanding. History will show that the working men who chanted 'Germinal! Germinal!' at Zola's funeral had a deeper insight than the erudite Professor Lukács.

Middlesex Polytechnic.

Ian H. Birchall

1. Georg Lukács: *Studies in European Realism*, Merlin, 1972 (hereafter SER).

2. Georg Lukács: *Writer and Critic*, Merlin, 1970 (hereafter WC).

3. Georg Lukács: *The Historical Novel*, Penguin, 1969 (hereafter HN).

4. SER 7.

5. HN 216.

6. WC 123.

7. Cited E. W. J. Hemmings: *Emile Zola*, Oxford 1966, p. 242.

8. E. Zola: *Germinal*, Livre de Poche, p. 500.

9. *ibid.*, p. 481.

10. SER 130, etc.

11. WC 110ff.

12. SER 152.

13. WC 111.

14. WC 113-4.

15. WC 133-4.

16. HN 239.

17. WC 78.

18. WC 139-40.

19. WC 110-48.

20. WC 118-9.

21. SER 91.

22. SER 12.

23. As Henri Guillemin has shown (*Eclaircissements*, Gallimard, 1961, p. 271) Zola's notes on the Dreyfus case stress its *literary* qualities – 'Quel drame poignant!' 'Dressez donc cette figure-là romanciers.'

24. April 20, 1875.

25. Cf. Henri Mitterand: 'Zola devant la Commune', *Les Lettres Françaises*, July 3 1958.

26. HN 232.

27. HN 227.

28. HN 262.

29. e.g. E. Zola: *Germinal*, pp. 315-6.

30. E. Zola: *Son Excellence Eugène Rougon*, Livre de Poche, p. 131.

31. Another is Robert Tressell. Most critics see *The Ragged-Trousered Philanthropists* as a work of propaganda and ignore the sensitive portrayal of the tensions between a militant socialist and his non-socialist workmates.

32. Eddie Tomlinson in *Socialist Worker*, October 27, 1973.

33. Gallimard, 1972, p. 23.

34. SER 85-96.

35. SER 86.

36. SER 95.

37. J-P. Sartre: *Saint Genet*, Gallimard, 1952, p. 629.

38. WC 253.

39. The first united Socialist Party was established in France in 1905, after decades of splits and competing groups.

40. H. Barbusse: *Zola*, Gallimard, 1932, pp. 162-3.

41. E. Zola: *L'Argent*, Livre de Poche, pp. 45-52.

42. June 1886; cited in H. Guillemin: *Présentation des Rougon-Macquart*, Gallimard, 1964, p. 289.

43. Georg Lukács: *The Meaning of Contemporary Realism*, Merlin, 1963, p. 60.

44. SER 85-96.

45. Georg Lukács: *The Theory of the Novel*, Merlin, 1971, p. 49.

46. Draft of letter to Margaret Harkness, April 1888, published in *Documents on Marxist Aesthetics*, (ed. Baxandall), Vol. I. (New York, 1974), pp. 115-7. Letter written (largely) in English.

47. July 15, 1887 – Marx-Engels *Werke*, Dietz Verlag, Berlin, Vol. 36, p. 682.

48. April 30, 1891, – *ibid.*, Vol. 38, p. 88.

49. SER 90.

50. Quoted by André Wurmser in *Zola* (collection Génies et Réalités, Hachette, 1969), p. 222.

51. Quoted by Wurmser in *op.cit.*, pp. 212-3.

52. *op.cit.* p. 230.

53. Georg Lukács: History and Class Consciousness, Merlin, 1971, p. 1.

54. *ibid.*, p. 27.

55. *ibid.*, p. 65.

56. R. Barthes: *Writing Degree Zero*, Cape, 1967, p. 73.

57. J-P. Sartre: *Qu'est-ce que la Littérature?*, idées Gallimard, 1964, pp. 169-73.

58. 'Georg Lukács', *Working Papers in Cultural Studies 4*, Birmingham, 1973, p. 80.

59. The term is Lukács's own in the 1967 Preface to *History and Class Consciousness* p. xiii of the Merlin edition.

60. Lukács: *'Blue Theses'*, 1928-29, which were sharply criticised, in some ways anticipated the Popular Front line to be adopted in 1934.

61. Georg Lukács: *The Meaning of Contemporary Realism*, p. 92.

Ian H. Birchall

62. Georg Lukács: *Essays on Thomas Mann*, Merlin, 1964, p. 162.

63. *ibid.*, p. 43.

64. Published in English as *Lukács and Socialist Realism*, Fore Publications, 1950, with a sycophantic introduction by Eric Hobsbawm.

65. *ibid.*, p. 6.

66. *ibid.*, p. 4.

67. WC 7.

68. In political terms the clearest example is the Spanish Civil War. The Spanish Communist Party made endless concessions to openly bourgeois parties, but butchered the P.O.U.M. and any who dared call for socialist revolution.

69. Livre de Poche, pp. 287-8.

70. Thus Joseph Berger on conditions in Russian labour camps: 'When there were thousands of deaths each day it was obviously impossible to check the circumstances of each one. But a maximum permitted mortality rate was laid down; so long as mortality remained within these limits it was considered normal.' *Shipwreck of a Generation*, Harvill Press, London, 1971, p. 122.

Styles of Marxism; Styles of Criticism. Wuthering Heights: A Case Study

Ronald Frankenberg

Marxism as a theory has always been concerned with practice – revolutionary practice. Some misunderstanding of Althusser has led to an attempted evasion of this truth by intellectual withdrawal from a class struggle which has become too complex for easy comprehension – in the name of theoretical practice. This tendency, following self-criticism by Althusser and Balibar, has shown its barren nature both in theory and in practice. Marxist literary critics seem happy to reduce themselves to the social role of other academics – the subject and object of the final examinations and the neatly-bound gold-lettered and shelved thesis. Terry Eagleton, both aware of and sometimes victim to this danger, suggests a long term way out which is attractive despite its dangerous reflexivity – let us examine the historical determinants of the way we used to perceive and the way we now perceive our perceptions of our navel. He writes:

> 'The most valuable way of discussing Marxist criticism then, would be an historical survey of it from Marx and Engels to the present day, charting the ways in which that criticism changes as the history in which it is rooted changes.'[1]

I hope he may find time to do just that. In this paper, I am seeking to use a smaller time scale and a smaller canvas – what can be learned from examining changing analyses of Emily Brontë's *Wuthering Heights* from Caudwell's brief but extremely perceptive and revealing comments in his 1936 *Romance and Realism* (unpublished until 1970),[2] through the alleged reductionism of Wilson in *Modern Quarterly* 1947[3] and then Kettle 1951[4] whom it is now so fashionable to call black and Stalinist or pink and Liberal and on by way of the fascinating combination of vulgar Marxism and elite sensitivity which is Mrs. Q. D. Leavis[5] – she correctly preserves Brontë's unity of contraries but at the cost of shattering her own; to Raymond Williams's[6] projection of Lukács-Goldmann and his own relationships with his father and his semi-rural origins onto Catherine/Heathcliff, and finally to the slightly economically determinist sophistication of Eagleton[7] and the Lacanic Freudian sophistication of Musselwhite[8] set against the anglo-

* I am grateful to the late J. D. Stephenson who aroused my interest in literature; to Max Gluckman who taught me to dare to trespass; to Paul Lawford, who will probably be ashamed of his alleged mentor; to Charles Swann, Pauline Hunt, Margaret Whiteley and Gordon Fyfe who in their various ways encouraged; and to Terry Eagleton whom I hardly know but who presents a kind of challenge. Like everyone else I am indebted to Arnold Kettle and Raymond Williams who went bravely and rashly ahead.

structuralism of Kermode.[9]

It may clarify the problem of Marxist criticism as an introduction to refer to Lenin's obituary of Tolstoy.

> 'Tolstoy is dead and the pre-revolutionary Russia whose weakness and impotence found their expression in the philosophy and are depicted in the works of the great artist has become a thing of the past. But the heritage which he has left includes that which has not become a thing of the past, but belongs to the future. This heritage is accepted and is being worked upon by the Russian proletariat. The Russian proletariat will explain to the masses of the toilers and the exploited the meaning of Tolstoy's criticism of the state, the church, private property in land – not in order that the masses should confine themselves to self-perfection and yearning for godly life, but in order that they should rise to strike a new blow at the Tsarist monarchy and landlordism, which were but slightly damaged in 1905, and which must be destroyed. The Russian proletariat will explain to the masses Tolstoy's criticism of capitalism – not in order that the masses should confine themselves to hurling imprecations at capital and the rule of money, but in order that they should learn to utilise at every step in their life and in their struggle the technical and social achievements of capitalism, that they should learn to weld themselves into a united army of millions of socialist fighters who will overthrow capitalism and create a new society in which people will not be doomed to poverty, in which there will be no exploitation of man by man.'[10]

Lenin, then, saw the bearers of Marxism, the proletariat, as explaining and creating the current significance of the great artist to the masses in the context of class struggle and revolutionary change.

Mao[11] takes up this point which he calls *stand* but later adds –

> 'Our writers and artists have their literary and art work to do but their primary task is to understand people and know them well.'

He presents this in the context of Yenan and the revolutionary society which existed there in the late thirties and the forties, and he is speaking of the people both as an audience and as a subject.

In the light of these two statements, is there anything for Marxists to say about Brontë at all? Unlike Tolstoy, she produces no analysis of the state, of capitalism, of class relations in the countryside, nor would Charlotte's descriptions of her sister's relationships to the people have endeared her to Mao:

> 'I am bound to avow that she had scarcely more practical knowledge of the peasantry amongst whom she lived, than a nun has of the country people who sometimes pass her convent gates . . . My sister's disposition was not naturally gregarious; circumstances favoured and

fostered her tendency to seclusion; except to go to church or take a walk on the hills, she rarely crossed the threshold of home. Though her feeling for the people round was benevolent, intercourse with them she never sought; nor with very few exceptions, ever experienced. And yet she knew them; knew their ways, their language, their family histories; she could hear of them with interest and talk of them with detail, minute, graphic, and accurate; but *with* them she rarely exchanged a word. Hence it ensued that what her mind had gathered of the real concerning them, was too exclusively confined to those tragic and terrible traits of which, in listening to the secret annals of every rude vicinage, the memory is sometimes compelled to receive the impress:'[12]

There is some evidence that Marx himself was indeed closely familiar with at least some of the Brontë's work although Prawer[13] regrets and wonders that he made no use especially of Emily's in his writings. We cannot then start from Marx, we can however begin to trace the perceptions of revolutionary relevance of *Wuthering Heights* in the last 40 years, in the hopes of revealing the way in which the bare-bones of the politician's precepts have been fleshed by the critical specialists. Class, gender and commitment as preoccupations of the thirties, give way to essence, alienation and totality of the fifties – and now?

We can furthermore, move beyond Lenin and Mao, by ceasing to think of the novel as a determinate, finished thing.

As Barthes has written,

'Our literature is characterized by the pitiless divorce which the literary institution maintains between the producer of the text and its user, between its owner and its customer, between its author and its reader. This reader is thereby plunged into a kind of idleness – he is intransitive; he is, in short, *serious:* instead of functioning himself, instead of gaining access to the magic of the signifier, to the pleasure of writing, he is left with no more than the poor freedom either to accept or reject the text: reading is nothing more than a *referendum.*'[14]

Lenin and Mao were in one sense both addressing what they saw as the producers of literature – professional writers – although Mao at least, like William Morris, in this as in other fields held out the long term perspective of devaluing the professional; on the one hand by transferring the craft to the amateur and on the other by imposing the knowledge of life on the professional, thereby abolishing the contradiction.

We can now see each reader as his/her own producer. If the text has sufficient power (plurality – Barthes) to start with, each reader produces his or her own text from it. The aim of Marxist criticism then becomes to enable the working-class collectively or individually to produce its own text, and in doing so to move a step nearer to producing the revolution. Such criticism does not define or categorise; it multiplies. The referendum always reduces.

Eagleton accuses Caudwell (at least in *Studies in a Dying Culture*)[15] of both seeing the world in terms of a contradiction between social being and consciousness on the one hand (undeniable – RF); and on the other seeing forms (of consciousness) as inherently restrictive, while social being is dynamic, chaotic, progressive and formless. A view, as Eagleton points out that has more in common with Shelley than with Stalin. At the same time he sees the artist as a store and liberator of social energy. Too simple a view, in Eagleton's assessment (and in mine), of the relations of form and content and of the artist and society. It results in the kind of humanism which leads Eagleton to end his book by categorising Marxist criticism in the humanist terms of liberation from oppression rather than revolution. Caudwell, however, died young in Spain leaving the contradictions of his work unresolved. In *Romance and Realism*, he provides us with a brief but important clue to a non-reductionist reading of *Wuthering Heights*, and to an understanding of how the dynamics of social being, far from formless, might be structured. He writes in the early thirties:

'The Brontës are characteristic of the final phase of bourgeois culture, in which woman revolts against her subjection. Bourgeois development has made possible her emancipation. On the one hand it has produced an economy in which it is no longer necessary for woman to play a non-cognitive domestic role; on the other hand it has drawn up a charter for itself – no domination, equal rights – which woman cannot fail to utilise. But the woman revolts *within* the categories of bourgeois culture. Like the Brontës, like George Sand, she asserts her right and ability to play the role of a man, and to create masculine values. *Wuthering Heights*, the most Brontëesque of the Bell novels, has a wild virility, a kind of quintessence of masculinity as seen by woman, of which Emily's demon lover, Heathcliff, is the incarnation.'

'Of course this revolt is bound to fail, because it asserts woman's right to be man, in other words to enslave herself to masculine values. It is like those pseudo-socialisms in which the proletariat is given bourgeois rights. The suffragette movement is another stage. Woman is to be given democracy, and thus she is fooled in just the same way as the proletarian and given the shadow of power without the substance. Later still, in the person of authors, such as Virginia Woolf, she asserts her right to build up a feminine culture inside the masculine, as a kind of critical moderating influence. None of these revolutions gains real equality because they are ultimately parasitic on male values. This

equality can be achieved only in a culture whose values are
contributed jointly by men and women.'[16]

This position is neither profound nor adequately thought out, but it
points to the central contradiction between the Macro Marxist
conclusions of Eagleton to which I shall later turn[17] and social reality.
In the end the dynamic of the social formation and the novel as a whole
depends on the class struggle. There is a reality which unites literature
and revolution and divides them from sociology and unsuccessful
revolutionary parties – namely that the specificity of the parts depends
on gender and generation. The absence of this realisation in the
Marxists gives what strength it has to the false 'real novel vs. sociological
novel' antithesis of Mrs. Leavis.

Another Marxist critic of the thirties who like Caudwell died in
Spain, Ralph Fox, is as explicit on the point as Caudwell, but less
analytic.

'Wuthering Heights is certainly the novel become poetry, it is beyond
all doubt one of the most extraordinary books which human genius
has ever produced, yet it is these things only because it is a cry of
despairing agony wrung from Emily by life itself. The life of mid-
Victorian England, experienced by a girl of passion and imagination
imprisoned in the windswept parsonage on the moors of the West
Riding, produced this book. Charlotte expressed the thwarted, lonely
lives of these girls in the sublimated love of Rochester and Jane Eyre,
in the burning story of Lucy Snowe in *Vilette* (sic). Emily could not be
satisfied with this. Her love must triumph, and in the violent, horror-
laden atmosphere of the stone farmhouse on the moors, it did triumph.
Catherine and Heathcliffe are the revenge of love against the
nineteenth century.'[18]

He goes on to quote Lockwood's nightmare and to comment

'It is the most terrible passage in English literature in the nineteenth
century, but it is not, even in the intensity which gives it such life,
outside of space and time. For the words of agony are wrung from
Emily by her own time and no other age could have tortured her so
sharply, twisted the words of aching, awful suffering out of her in
accents of such terrifying force. Through the book, with the grotesque
and horrid echo of a chorus, runs the complaint of the farm-hand
Joseph, the canting, joyless, hating and hateful symbol of the obscene
morality of his age, as though the prison walls themselves are endowed
with voice to mock and spurn the prisoner.'[19]

Ralph Fox continues to claim that the Haworth of his own childhood
was little different to that of the Brontës and to conclude by repeating
that 'It is the most violent and frightful cry of human suffering which

even Victorian England ever tore from a human being.'[20]

It is clearly a reductionist view – more so than Caudwell's because period is euphemistically substituted for class relations, because he fails to see the crucial difference between *Jane Eyre* and *Wuthering Heights*, between Charlotte and Emily. Charlotte does not transcend her period. For her, as we shall see, when love wins it is a triumph. Emily knows that even when it triumphs it is a defeat. She helps us to see that while relations of gender and generation are the stuff of experienced reality, there is still a determining last instance. However, the romanticism of place and person which is the symptom of Ralph Fox's humanist Marxism, is characteristic of the Marxism of the thirties; after the war Wilson and to some extent Kettle are to be one-sided in a differently reductionist way.

Two Quarterly writers looked again at *Wuthering Heights* in 1947, on the eve of its centenary, Klingopoulos in *Scrutiny*[21] and Wilson in the Marxist *Modern Quarterly*.[22] David Wilson at once looks to the future and to the past; he sees Emily Brontë as the precursor of the proletarian novel, although he is uncertain of the form the latter should take. On the other hand his main thrust is justifying his view that Emily Brontë had an intellectual consciousness of the proletarian struggles of her time, a consciousness that prissy Charlotte sought to hide from the world because in so far as she understood it, she rejected it. He first seeks to establish, successfully in my view, and in that of most of his successors, that Haworth was no Elizabethan backwater as Lord David Cecil had averred,[23] but in the heart of an industrial area swept over by the class struggles of Luddism, Chartism and the plug riots. By referring to Emily's poems, he seeks, not entirely convincingly, to show her awareness and identification with the downtrodden. Some he quotes seem to me perhaps merely to show a familiarity with Blake. When he turns to *Wuthering Heights* itself, he notes first Charlotte's 'genteelising' of part of Emily's prose, and uses it to distinguish the sisters from each other. He next considers Lockwood's dream in Chapter 3 as evidence in its 'satire and symbolism' . . . 'of how Emily Brontë identified herself with the people in suffering and oppression.'[24] He continues

> 'Mark the preacher, with his exhortations to violence, with his excommunications, and his congregation who carried cudgels for pilgrim's staves. Do they not represent official Methodism as it then addressed itself to the turbulent people; its pharisaism, its authoritarianism, its clerical violence? Is it possible not to connect the Rev. Jabes Branderham of the novel with that High Tory of Methodism, the Rev. Jabez Bunting? [now a commonplace connection

– RF]. And is there not an echo of a personal connection in
Lockwood's words: "I'm not going to endure the persecution of your
honourable ancestors again. Was not the Reverend Jabes Branderham
akin to you on the mother's side?" We recall that the mother of the
Brontës was a Methodist in circles closely associated with Bunting.'

The key passage of Wilson, however, which many now refer to, is that
in which he compares Heathcliff to the proletariat. He precedes this
with the kind of Marxist humanist approach which Kettle, Williams,
and others are to make familiar. In this, mankind is seen as persisting in
essence through time and the social structure.

'The book has an atmosphere that is wild and elemental. Its hints of
witchcraft, its suggestions of kinship and the tribal blood feud, its
uncouth roughness, undoubtedly reflect the traditional Pennine
character. Within this atmosphere the story of Heathcliff and
Catherine Earnshaw works itself out as a metaphor of the social
struggle of her own time, with all its cruelty and hatred. It is replete
with problems, not of the relations between the individual men and
women, but of the relations between all men, and between mankind
and nature. Yet the narration of the story by the sophisticated
Lockwood, and the common-sense, matter-of-fact Nelly Dean, sets the
picture in a frame of gentle irony and reason which relate its savagery
to the mood of quieter and more stable times.'
'Whether Emily Brontë was fully conscious of it or not, we can see in
the character of Heathcliff a true representation of the working men of
her time, after enduring suffering and degradation at the hands of
their "betters" turning to defiance and destruction and to the violent
movement for the People's Charter. Heathcliff comes into the family
circle without name, nationality or ancestry "dark as from the devil".
He is at first treated by old Earnshaw with fatherly benevolence; but
the son Hindley brings him low, and deprives him of the tuition of the
curate. From his new masters he receives nothing but cuffs and kicks,
insults and degradation. He replies at first with outbursts as when he
flings the tureen of hot soup in young Linton's face; but gradually he
comes to delight in the disgust he creates, and eventually turns with
devilish energy and intelligence to bring down the houses of his
enemies to ruin.'[25]

Charlotte's reaction to this, like her reaction to the 'mob' in 1848,
says Wilson, is a genteel one, characteristic of

'the old order to the people whenever they take independent violent
action: dark, uncouth, and brutal, moved by a hateful will and guided
by an intelligence that seems of the Devil. So seemed the Luddists, the
Chartists, and the devotees of the "Sacred Month" in the Brontë days.
So seemed the Bolsheviks of the 1917 Revolution in our own time.'[26]

Emily however treats Heathcliff with sympathy as well as unsoftened clarity. She not only shows him as hateful, cruel and destructive; she shows also how he became so. She relates men's lives to their environment, says Wilson. This is undoubtedly true but the examples he gives are partly metaphor with more complex meaning, and partly examples of how trees are moulded by *their* environment.[27] He then quotes the *sine qua non* passage of *Wuthering Heights* criticism, as we shall see, Catherine's 'great betrayal' of Heathcliff for Linton – culminating in 'I *am* Heathcliff' and the article takes a downhill drift into vulgarisation – for example 'and when he returns to ruin Hindley, he unintentionally brings Catherine herself to her death by the way.'[28]

As we shall see Kettle later conflating ruling classes; so Wilson conflates the ruled – when he recounts the kitchen/dining room dilemna of where the returned Heathcliff shall be received at the Grange.

He sees this, and Catherine's sarcastic solution of separate tables as suggesting that Emily Brontë was conscious of 'Heathcliff as representing the rebellious working men, and of Catherine as that part of the educated class which feels compelled to identify itself with their cause.'[29] The subtler social distinctions of Heights and Grange seem to have escaped him. Nor is his straight identification of Emily Brontë, Catherine Earnshaw and *Hamlet* any more convincing.

Wilson then (to some extent consciously – he claims only to contribute a new facet to our view of Emily and her book) supplies an over-simple view which derives mainly from an economistic view of Marxism. 'Evitez La Femme et Cherchez la Classe Ouvriere' is his first motto. And 'Look she was one of us really, *she* understood!' is his second. Nevertheless, like Caudwell he correctly situates his criticism in the present and the future, at least in his title *Emily Brontë: First of the Moderns* and in his peroration. If proletarian literature is a thing to be expected in our time:—

> 'The label has been attached indiscriminately to literature written by workers, or written about workers, or addressed specifically to the working class. Surely all this is beside the point. If there is to be a proletarian literature, it can be so only by virtue of whether life is seen from a new point of view, a point of view growing out of the working class in society, not as a dependent and subsidiary thing, but as a living and independent force.'
> 'If that be so, then the proletarian novel may find its roots and the beginning of its tradition one hundred years ago in Emily Brontë's *Wuthering Heights;* born amid the flowering of the great Victorian period in literature – in it, but not of it, the new germinating in the soil of the old.'[30]

As we saw, Fox ended his chapter (on *Wuthering Heights*, *Jude the Obscure* and *The Way of All Flesh)* by saying the three books are a long way from Dickens –

> ' . . . they belong indeed to another world from that of Dickens, and they are, in a sense, only mighty fragments, mutilated statues. In them, however, the real tradition of the novel is kept alive, and the writer of the future will acknowledge them as his inspiration when he attempts the task of conquering reality, that ceaseless creative way in which Dickens hauled down the battle flag to replace it by a blameless white flag of sentimental compromise.'[31]

Ironically Arnold Kettle begins his analysis by identifying Emily Brontë and Dickens.

The central unspoken contradiction of Kettle's argument seems to me to be not the unity of opposites – concrete and general which he sees in *Wuthering Heights* but the antagonism between his praise for the concreteness of the novel and the reason for his praise – that the concreteness enables the reader to perceive what appear to be the essence of womanhood in Catherine and manhood in Heathcliff. He appears to be suggesting – no less than Mrs. Leavis – that the social conditions in which Heathcliff and Catherine find themselves distort some inner being which Emily perceives and allows to rise triumphant in the moment of their deaths. As he writes in conclusion to his chapter.

> '*Wuthering Heights* then is an expression in the imaginative terms of art of the stresses and tensions and conflicts, personal and spiritual, of nineteenth-century capitalist society. It is a novel without idealism, without false comforts, without any implication that power over their destinies rests outside the struggles and actions of human beings themselves. Its powerful evocation of nature, of moorland and storm, of the stars and the seasons is an essential part of its revelation of the very movement of life itself. The men and women of *Wuthering Heights* are not the prisoners of nature; they live in the world and strive to change it, sometimes successfully, always painfully, with almost infinite difficulty and error:'
> 'This unending struggle, of which the struggle to advance from class society to the higher humanity of a classless world is but an episode, is conveyed to us in *Wuthering Heights* precisely because the novel is conceived in actual, concrete, particular terms, because the quality of oppression revealed in the novel is not abstract but concrete, not vague but particular.'
> 'And that is why Emily Brontë's novel is at the same time a statement about the life she knew, the life of Victorian England, and a statement about life as such.'

For Kettle in 1951, as for Mrs. Leavis, human life is an absolute which exists outside and transcends specific social reality. There is an existentialist even petty bourgeois ring about these characters struggling to realise themselves in a hostile world of nature and ruling class nastiness. One is reduced to memories of H. G. Wells. Heathcliff, who is seen by Kettle as *born* in a Liverpool slum (Brontë does not say this, merely that he was found there), is the working-class boy who makes good, an unsentimental Oliver Twist – the comparison is Kettle's.

He specifically describes *Wuthering Heights* as a symbolic novel put in a real context by the narrators Lockwood and Nelly Dean who grow like the characters in the novel, as they learn from experience.[32] What they narrate in Kettle's view is the stages in a relationship between a man and a woman whose affinity is forged in a series of concrete rebellions against the tyranny of Hindley and his sentimental love-relationship with Frances, against the moral religious tyranny symbolised by Joseph, against the false values of the opulent [unproductive] Grange. United in their rebellion, Catherine chooses a [reformist] path of succumbing to compromise from within. Her integrity is itself compromised and her fate sealed – only in death will she be buried outside in the Churchyard with the yeomen, not under the Chapel roof with the squires. Heathcliff as an outsider, sees the true nature of total bourgeois society, learns their predatory skills and turns them back on his oppressors. He undergoes in Brontë's words a moral teething. As Kettle explicates, Heathcliff's revenge is not merely pathological it is moral.

> 'For what Heathcliff does is to use against his enemies with complete ruthlessness their own weapons, to turn on them (stripped of their romantic veils) their own standards, to beat them at their own game. The weapons he uses against the Earnshaws and the Lintons are their own weapons of money and arranged marriages. He gets power over them by the classic methods of the ruling class, expropriation and property deals. He buys out Hindley and reduces him to drunken impotency, he marries Isabella and then organises the marriage of his son to Catherine Linton, so that the entire property of the two families shall be controlled by himself. He systematically degrades Hareton Earnshaw to servility and illiteracy. "I want the triumph of seeing *my* descendant fairly lord of *their* estates: My child hiring their children to till their father's land for wages;" . . . And what particularly tickles Heathcliff's fancy is his achievement of the supreme ruling-class triumph of making Hareton, the boy he degrades, feel a deep and even passionate attachment towards himself.'[33]

Just as Kettle identifies the class struggle, as an episode in the struggle for existence, so he here conflates both Heights class, and Grange class, and ruling classes of all periods and times, (compare Barthes distinction in *S/Z* between the ruling class of the title deed and that of the ledger entry).[34]

His analysis is further weakened by his limited view of a sexual relationship – the feeling that binds Catherine and Heathcliff he states 'is not primarily a sexual relationship' – but above all by his search for the hidden asocial essence – a humanity which transcends not only class but gender. In this his achievement is characteristically less than Caudwell's.

Heathcliff's refusal to repent (at Nelly Dean's request – is she less of a 'real' woman for suggesting it?) and his desire simply 'to be carried to the Churchyard in the evening' enables him to face the full horror of his betrayal as Catherine had done before.

> 'And once he has faced it he can die, not nobly or triumphantly, but at least as a man, leaving with Cathy and Hareton the possibility of carrying on the struggle he has begun, and in his death he will achieve again human dignity, "to be carried to the Churchyard in the evening". 'It is this reachievement of manhood by Heathcliff, an understanding reached with no help from the world he despises, which, together with the developing relationship of Cathy and Hareton and the sense of continuity of life in nature, gives to the last pages of *Wuthering Heights* a sense of positive and unsentimental hope.'[35]

In Barthes's words perhaps – 'a statement general enough to include the truth, but too general in fact, to designate it.'[36]

Kettle emphasises one area of petty bourgeois concern, the struggle of the individual to find his essential self, (is Heathcliff the English Peer Gynt?), Raymond Williams emphasises another, characteristic of his lifetime dialogue with his rural past and his father's ghost. In *The Country and the City*, he writes,

> 'Emily Brontë's *Wuthering Heights* is remarkable because it takes the crises of inheritance at its full human value, without displacement to the external and representative attitudes of disembodied classes. There is a formal contrast of values between the exposed and working Heights, and the sheltered and renting Grange, and the complicated relations between their families are consistently determined by the power and endurance of the Heights. Yet the creation is so total that the social mechanism of inheritance is transcended.'[37]

He seems to me to undervalue the plurality of Brontë's writing when ignoring the interplay of gender, sibship and affinal genealogy he continues:

> 'It is class and property that divide Heathcliff and Cathy, and it is in the positive alteration of these relationships that a resolution is arrived at in the second generation. But it is not in social alteration that the human solution is at any point conceived. What is created and held to is a kind of human intensity and connection which is the ground of continuing life. Unaffected by settlements, it survives them and, in a familiar tragic emphasis, survives and is learned again through death. The tragic separation between human intensity and any available social settlement is accepted from the beginning in the whole design and idiom of the novel. The complication of the plot is then sustained by a single feeling, which is the act of transcendence.'

This brief reference, foreshadows or reflects, Williams's concern with *Wuthering Heights* not merely as a novel of the human essence, but more frankly than Kettle with alienation, which is fully spelled out in *The English Novel*. Again Caudwell is not transcended; if 'human intensity' is replaced by 'women's position' in the last but one sentence quoted – alienation ought to become an unnecessary hypothesis and the comparison which follows with George Eliot even more apt. Despite Williams's concern with gender, alienation survives.

If Fox provides an anti-Dickensian thesis and Kettle a Dickensian antithesis; Williams provides a synthesis albeit divided against itself. At first sight, he argues, nothing could be more different than Dickens and Gaskell on one side and the Brontës on the other, except perhaps *Jane Eyre* and *Wuthering Heights*. *Wuthering Heights* has an intensity of feeling, a passion which is a psychological approach to the intensities and difficulties of love and growth, 'in the moving earth, the unprecedented disturbance of those English years'. Dickens and Gaskell respond through a social criticism to poverty and oppression.

> 'On that later projection, the interests of the Brontë sisters and the interests of Dickens and Elizabeth Gaskell are in different continents, the East and West of society and personality. But in experience and in these novels it is not like that. The world we need to remember if we are to see these connections of the 1840s is the world of Blake: a world of desire and hunger, of rebellion and of pallid convention: the terms of desire and fulfilment and the terms of oppression and deprivation profoundly connected in a single dimension of experience.'[38]

Kettle[39] also notes a connection with Blake but in terms of *moral* emotion. The words 'duty' and 'humanity' 'pity' and 'charity' have precisely the kind of force Blake gives such words in his poetry. Williams makes it the centre of his analysis at a different level. 'Intensity of desire' is as much a response to the 'human crises of that time' as the 'more obviously recognisable political radicalism.' He ties in its appearance in the novel of the time with what he calls the masculinisation of society – that is what became seen as manly – especially at public schools, the removal of feeling, the assertion that men don't cry. Women (albeit using male pseudonyms) kept humanity alive – and they reacted to their repression as women and as people. In Williams's words, they ' . . . knew directly a whole structure of repression in their time; knew it and in their own ways broke it with a strength and a courage that puts us all in their debt.'[40]

Wuthering Heights says Williams, contains a struggle, a dialectic – but it contains it in every sense. This revelation of intensity of feeling against repression and restraint is more important than the mere reductionist identification of Heathcliff with the proletariat, or the social dialectic of rentier Grange vs. farming Heights.

> ' . . . there is no convincing way in which the context – the real social description – can be made to override the direct and pre-occupying relation between persons. What we have again to say is that social experience is a whole experience. Its decriptive or analytic features have no priority over its direct realisation in quite physical and specific personal feelings and actions.'[41]

Irreducibility is not merely asserted, it is proclaimed for the critic as well as for the author. The demand for analysis is thrust aside by the synthesis – the whole.

Williams's argument continues by calling attention to the identification by herself of Catherine to Heathcliff. As Wilson and Kettle did more fully he quotes –

> 'If all else persisted and *he* remained, *I* should still continue to be; and if all else remained, and he were annihilated, the universe would turn to a mighty stranger: I would not seem a part of it. My love for Linton is like the foliage in the woods: time will change it, I'm well aware, as winter changes the trees. My love for Heathcliff resembles the eternal rocks beneath; a source of little visible delight, but necessary.'[42]

She continues unquoted by Williams – 'Nelly , I *am* Heathcliff.' In Williams's view, Catherine affirms not desire *for* but desire *in* another; 'a depth of relationship around which an idea of oneself and literally then of the universe forms – is both stated and taken for granted: and the taking for granted is the profound, the dislocating error'.

The taking of her profound identity with Heathcliff for granted, leads

Cathy to succumb to her shallower, but nevertheless real feeling for Linton and the convenience of his position. She betrays herself, Heathcliff and a place – the novel is after all called *Wuthering Heights.* Williams maintains that far from being strange, this is a common betrayal (*Border Country* is after all a novel about the tension between his being *in* his father and *in* Pandy; and his existence with his wife and 'at' London).[43]

Wuthering Heights is 'quite central' to its time (an interesting adverb?) not because of its documentary element or what can be called its symbolism, (is he reacting to Kettle?) but because its experience is so direct it does not have to be translated

> 'It is the positive experience which has elsewhere been given a negative translation – a negative term – as alienation, and the process beyond that catchword is undoubtedly real. And because this is so, the organizing experience of the novel is a more than personal desire, a more than personal longing. Indeed the intensity of persons has to be seen being displaced and then qualified, observed, interpreted; there and yet seen at a distance, seen in other modes; convincing and yet unnecessary opposition with other persuasive versions of reality. And this is its critical difference from the ordinary related fiction of intense and personal feeling.'[44]

In this and in his later characterisation of *Wuthering Heights* as deriving not only its power but also its narrative structure from the contrast: desire *for* another, desire *in* another, Williams is at once falling victim to and failing to perceive the nature of the dilemma for the Marxist – he shows how the specific can be seen as general; but the tension between early relationship, – achieved but preconscious and therefore seen as ascribed, and the inevitable betrayal of origin for destination is (at least) as old as Oedipus. What and why the Marxist wants to know, is its historical specificity produced in the text initially by Emily Brontë, and reproduced as a series of new texts by each reader and set of readers in their social and historical place.

Brontë-Fox-Caudwell is the text of class struggle and Virginia Woolf gender consciousness of the thirties, Brontë-Wilson is pure class struggle, Brontë-Kettle is Hegelian-Marx – the eternal quest for essence, Brontë-Williams is the agonised left outsider of the fifties – half realised Freud in Marx's clothing. In Musselwhite, Freud bursts out and Marx is engulfed. I shall proceed to the Eagleton seventies by way of Marx-rejecting Leavis and on to non-Marxist Kermode.

If Kettle represents one side of the dialectic social/personal and Williams the other; Leavis is the disunited dyad of opposites. For her the sociological (Marxist) novel is trivial but there, and important as a frame for the real novel; the real novel is timeless and deals with the ultimates of reality – for Mrs. Leavis the rhetorical question is 'How can we fail to see that the novel is based on an interest in, concern for, and knowledge of, real life?'[45] It belongs with *Women in Love,* (surprisingly) *Jules et Jim, Anna Karenina* and *Great Expectations.*

> 'The human truths, *Wuthering Heights* is intended to establish are, it is necessary to admit, obscured in places and to varying degrees by discordant trimmings or leftovers from earlier writings or stages of its conception; for these stylistic and other evidence exists in the text. Nor could we expect such complexity and such technical skill to have been achieved in a first novel otherwise; it is necessary to distinguish what is genuine complexity from what is mere confusion. That there is the complexity of accomplished art we must feel in the ending, ambiguous impersonal, disquieting but final. And when we compare the genius devoted to creating Nelly Dean, Joseph, Zillah, Frances, Lockwood, the two Catherines and to setting them in significant action, with the very perfunctory attention given to Heathcliff and Hareton as wholes (attention directed only when these two are wheeled out to perform necessary parts at certain points in the exposition of the theme to which – like Isabella and Edgar Linton – they are subsidiary) then we can surely not misinterpret the intention and the nature of the achievement of *Wuthering Heights.*'[46]

It is significant, as we shall see, that the active men are shadowy obstacles; the narrative and commenting men Joseph and Lockwood are the ones who seem alive.

Clearly for Mrs. Leavis – Leavis-Brontë is *the* text and it is about (romanticised) real women and real men and their transcendent relationships.

Nelly Dean, for example, is the normal woman 'whose truly feminine nature satisfies itself in nurturing all the children in the book in turn'[47] who understands and shares with Mrs. Leavis the basic truth 'that the identification of interests in marriage is the only way of getting over the conflict of egos.'[48] A more convincing reading of Nelly and her language than Musselwhite's pre-shadowing of Arnold [and Lord Reith]. As Nelly herself is made to say ' . . . it is as much as you can expect of a poor man's daughter.'[49] Leavis sees Catherine as 'the wife [who] therefore never becomes integrated or truly mature'[50] – and her daughter as reliving and rehabilitating her wayward mother.[51]

> 'Emily Brontë is as far as possible from admiring Catherine; being a woman, Emily Brontë has none of [the author of *Jules et Jim*] Roché's fascinated respect for his Kate as a force of nature. The woman

novelist does not believe that all women share these characteristics more or less and are unfeminine without them, in fact, she takes pains to show that these characteristics are incompatible with what is required of a wife and mother.'[52]

I do not accept Mrs. Leavis's apparent conviction that Emily's achievement in this regard puts the text alongside the moral views of herself and Barbara Cartland. It clearly can be read that way, but it is not necessary so to do.

Mrs. Leavis begins her critique by ground-clearing. She accepts Klingopoulos's[53] view that the problems of the book are clarifying Catherine's relationships with Heathcliff and Edgar; the Cathy-Hareton relationships are a modified reprise. But she rejects Catherine as a heroine. Indeed the second part of the book demonstrates this

> 'through Cathy, who, inheriting her mother's name and likenesses both physical and psychological, is shown by deliberate choice and trial and error, developing the maturity and therefore achieving the happiness, that the mother failed in, whereas we have seen the mother hardening into a fatal immaturity which destroys herself and those (Heathcliff and Edgar principally) involved with her.'[54]

It is difficult to follow Mrs. Leavis's article in detail and to do its stimulating texture justice. She sees reflected in the novel the confusions of her own eclectic erudition, and her apparent feeling that, classic though it is, the sources of *Wuthering Heights* have not joined into a single stream, is reflected in turn in light-scattering insights rather than sustained argument. Thus she starts from a comparison with *King Lear* – Heathcliff is Edmund, and Edgar *is* Edgar, moves rapidly to Wordsworth and the romantic poet's image of childhood. She identifies Heathcliff as originally 'the illegitimate son and Catherine's half-brother, which would explain why . . . Catherine never really thinks of him as a possible lover either before or after marriage.'[55] This leads into a footnote explanation that the first part of Catherine's speech to Nelly, about not marrying Heathcliff 'on social grounds – belongs to the sociological novel'. She then suggests that Emily Brontë was originally going to write about incest – asserts as Kettle does that Catherine's feelings about Heathcliff are never sexual 'while Heathcliff's for her are always those of a lover.'[56] She then goes off on *Beauty and the Beast* and Hoffman and then back to the romantic image of childhood and Wordsworth. A footnote provides much needed rehabilitation to Joseph 'the indispensable Joseph who survives the whole action to go on farming the Heights and who is made the vehicle of several central judgements, as well as of many disagreeable Calvinist attitudes'[57] *and* an insightful characterisation of Lockwood 'as the town visitor continually exposing his ignorance of country life and farming' again at least as convincing as Musselwhite's.'disturbing word of his [Lockwood's] own unconscious'. The same page contains a comparison with Estelle's treatment of Pip in *Great Expectations* and so breathlessly on through references to *Peggotty*, to Lord Shaftesbury's nurse, to Dora in *David Copperfield*, Dolly in *Anna Karenina* and Dostoievski's Stavrogin and Iago. Heathcliff we are told, like Stavrogin, an unsatisfactory composite, is an enigmatic figure only by reason of his creator's indecision.

> 'There is nothing enigmatic about either Catherine, we note, and this points to the novelist's distribution of her interest.'[58]

Mrs. Leavis sees Emily Brontë, no doubt correctly, as taking up the romantic poets' theme of 'the corruption of the child's native goodness by society'. This is pointed to by Lockwood's reading of Catherine's childhood journal as well as by Heathcliff's account of the broken-in Linton children seen through the Grange window by the '*Noble Savage*'. But Emily Brontë adds to this 'naive and commonplace subject' a new insight based on personal experience and 'also a specific and informed sociological content'[59]

> 'The theme is here very firmly rooted in time and place and richly documented: we cannot forget that Gimmerton and the neighbourhood are so bleak that the oats are always green there three weeks later than anywhere else, and that old Joseph's Puritan preachings accompany his "overlaying his large Bible with dirty bank-notes, the produce of the day's transactions at market," and we have a thoroughly realistic account of the life indoors and outdoors at Wuthering Heights as well as at the gentleman's residence at the Grange. In fact, there would be some excuse for taking this, the pervasive and carefully maintained sociological theme which fleshes the skeleton for the real novel. This novel, which could be extracted by cutting away the rest, was deliberately built, to advance a thesis, on the opposition between Wuthering Heights and Thrushcross Grange, two different cultures of which the latter supersedes the former.'[60]

Mrs. Leavis continues to argue that the date in which the novel is set, it ends in 1801, is deliberately chosen to enable a meticulously worked out antithesis between natural patriarchal family life and unnatural gentility. The theme was derived from on the one hand the Brontës' direct observation and on the other from the novels of Sir Walter Scott. Emily does not merely tell a story, she thinks herself into the meaning of historical changes for the actors. She uses the contradictions; moor as against gentleman's park to point up romantic freedom versus restraint. But she also recognises the complication farmland versus moor – as in the conflict fruit bushes versus flowers towards the end of the novel – resolved on the one hand by restoring the fruit bushes at the Heights and on the other by the gentry moving to the Grange – leaving Joseph the survivor, puritan, mercenary and manually hard working, to tend them.

Mrs. Leavis sees these materialist elements of the novel more clearly than most, as she also sees, albeit with anti-feminist values, the significance of gender, generation, and the changing definition of childhood.

> 'But' she writes 'if we were to take the sociological novel as the real novel and relegate the Heathcliff-Catherine-Edgar relationship and the corresponding Cathy-Linton-Hareton one, as exciting but ex-centric dramatic episodes, we should be misconceiving the novel and slighting it, for it is surely these relationships and their working out that give all the meaning to the rest.'[61]

Do we have to make so stark a choice? *Surely*, we can echo, the two aspects of the novel give meaning to each other. Are not interpersonal relations within a wider social context not also sociological in Mrs. Leavis's sense? Why are the wars of classes and of sexes less real than the clash of personality and the battles of individuals? Do not wars generate battles; and battles, duels? Do not duels generate battles in turn, and battles wars?

What Mrs. Leavis presents, as timeless, essential and real, merely extends across a greater period of time and a smaller scale of space. For her, in life perhaps as in art, the family is real, it can be seen; the class, mere sociology. In her attempt to assert timelessness and enduring anthropological value, Mrs. Leavis makes a comparison with Roché's novel and Truffaut's film, *Jules et Jim* (the director is put in his place by the publisher if not the author describing him as Truffaud. Mrs. Leavis's footnote characterising the film is of interest.

> 'In general, the film wipes out inessentials and makes the theme inescapable; it telescopes with advantage, translates intellectual elements successfully into dramatic forms while wherever possible exactly reproducing the original, and interpolates very little.'

A rare tribute by the literary to the filmic which is counter-balanced by no doubt justified attacks on *Saturday Night and Sunday Morning* and *The Heiress)*

The outline of the Roché novel is very similar to the first part of

Wuthering Heights but is apparently based on the early life of an author at the time ignorant of both it and *Women in Love*. Two friends, one French and Catholic, Jim; one German and Jewish, Jules, become involved with Kate. She loves both; the gentle bookish Jules, and the passionate hard violent Jim. She marries the former; elopes with and destroys the latter leaving Jules to foster their surviving children.

Mrs. Leavis suggests that Roché's (and Truffaut's) case study is presented psychologically and clinically and with the anguish of experience. Catherine in *Wuthering Heights* therefore needs no mystical explanation. She has reality but is outside Emily Brontë's personally involved experience. She is presented in a social context, but artistically and with insight (Dickens presented similar characters; Rosa Dartle in *David Copperfield* and Miss Wade in *Little Dorritt*. Mrs. Gaskell nearly put one in *North and South.*)[62]

Kate in *Jules et Jim* is presented 'as WOMAN in essence, a menace to masculine stability and man's achievement of a civilized code, and yet indispensable to any life worth living'; in fact in terms of the old nature versus culture division. Catherine in *Wuthering Heights* is similar – like Kate she is anti-literary – and sees Edgar's bookishness as the source of his weakness. Even when she thinks she is on her death bed 'she envisages him with great bitterness as "offering prayers of thanks to God for restoring peace to his home, and going back to his *books.*'"[63]

Mrs. Leavis does not believe that Emily, who kneaded the dough with a German book propped up before her, endorses Catherine's hostility to learning; nor does she necessarily speak directly through Nelly Dean.

> 'But she is as far as possible from admiring Catherine; being a woman, Emily Brontë has none of Roché's fascinated respect for his Kate as a force of nature. The woman novelist does not believe that all women share these characteristics more or less and are unfeminine without them, in fact she takes pains to show that these characteristics are incompatible with what is required of a wife and mother. On the other hand, Roché's strength lies in being able to evoke a civilization made by the efforts of men which is indestructible by Woman'.

So near and yet so far, in her anxiety to reveal the essence of transhistorical reality, Mrs. Leavis once more overlooks the unity of the contradiction – a unity so marked that even Durkheim could see it. The indestructible civilisation created by men depends on the kneading of the dough by wives and mothers. The role of wife and mother, the vocation of love for son or lover, cut women off from the outside culture and professional vocations. Even the Brontës wrote under male names as we have already remarked. Women are cut off from culture in the broadest sense and its production; they are confined within the apparently non-social world of nature, and in the case of Catherine and Kate, driven to a hatred of the social outside. The hatred is itself complicated by the different social worlds to be rejected – Moor and Farm, Farm and Park, Heights and Grange. Emily Brontë – German Book and Dough, Poetry and care for drunken brother – lived this contradiction in the parsonage – she did not have to go out beyond the gate to seek it. She reveals it artistically in her work, as in their separate ways Roché suppresses it in his – the male fantasy of woman as witch; and Mrs. Leavis in hers. In Mrs. Leavis's reading *Wuthering Heights* is in the last analysis a novel about maturity. She points the way to a sophisticated reading on class and gender – but in the end she fails to achieve her promise. There is a sad failure of nerve revealed in the passage read onto Emily Brontë through Nelly Dean. 'This is a basic truth, that the identification of interests in marriage is the only way of getting over the conflict of egos.'[64] If the most that *Wuthering Heights* could present to the modern reader was the identification of passive submission with maturity, then it would deserve the label of sentimental mystical romance rather than novel and justify the banal films made in its name.

Eagleton writes at greater length than the other critics we have discussed. He is more class conscious than Kettle; better organised but less aware of gender than Leavis. His statement that Charlotte's *Villette* 'smooths the edge of a social criticism by transmuting it into sexual conflict – a move which leaves orthodox society intact, yet turns from it to a more fertile centre of commitment'[65] reveals at once his perception, his economistic tendency in analysis, (sexual conflict pushed to extreme is to all except a biological determinist, social criticism) and in 'fertile' his conscious/unconscious command of metaphor. He helpfully sets Emily in contrast with Charlotte and develops Charlotte's own efforts in that field already partially quoted. I have not space here to quote in full what seems to me the key passage of Eagleton's analysis of Charlotte in his chapter 'on the structure of Charlotte Brontë's fiction' – the reader needs perhaps to know the disclaimers and definitions which lead up to this quotation

> 'The structure of Charlotte's fiction then, must achieve an appropriate balance between nostalgic reaction and forward looking enterprise – or, conversely between Romantic *panache* and realist prudence. In searching out the point of balance, the novels, as I have argued, are attuned to a real history: their ideological interplay has its source in a

pattern of conflicts and alignments between contemporary social classes.'[66]

It is because he does not add – genders and generation and even perhaps national consciousness that I accuse him of over-reductionism. If *The Professor*, for example, is read with this in mind the point becomes clear.

His general contrast however I accept. Schematically speaking Charlotte is an 'if-only' writer with an almost Hegelian devotion to resolvable contradictions. Eagleton points out the 'horizontal' structure of her novels which begin in domestic settlement and arrive at reintegration through a break to isolation and independence. At the same time each 'moment' is dominated by one of the structural roles he identifies – conservative authority – protagonist – Romantic Radical. For Emily, however, contradictions are antagonistic. *Wuthering Heights* is a story of their impact and painful non-resolution. In Eagleton's words –

> ' . . . the paradoxical truth that *Wuthering Heights* achieves its coherence of vision from an exhausting confrontation of contending forces, whereas Charlotte's kind of totality depends on a pragmatic integration of them. Both forms of consciousness are ideological but in so far as Emily's represents a more penetrative, radical and honest enterprise, it provides the basis for a fine artistic achievement'[67]

Could one perhaps rephrase it yet again by saying that Emily's characters and situations are overdetermined and hence realist?

Interestingly, as Eagleton points out, Charlotte sees the difference between herself and her sister in terms of Emily being a 'theorist'. 'Now and then' she wrote 'she broaches ideas which strike my sense as much more daring and original than practical'. In Eagleton's words . . . 'the cautious empiricist greets the totalising visionary with a mixture of respect and reservation'. Thus in Charlotte, spite, violence, and bigotry are transposed to the narration. In Emily they are firmly entrenched in the narrative.[68]

The clarity – almost black and whiteness – of Charlotte's characters are in sharp contrast to the deliberately maintained ambivalences of *Wuthering Heights*. Is Heathcliff hero or demon? Does he represent capitalism's unacceptable face – unmasked Thrushcross Grange or the rising Proletariat. Is Catherine tragic heroine or spoilt brat? Is Nelly Dean shrewd or stupid? or even evil? Is Lockwood a mere cypher or as Musselwhite suggests – the central character of the novel?

Eagleton does not seek to deny the contradictions, but to order them in classical Mao Tse Tung style by identifying the principal.

> 'The primary contradiction I have in mind is the choice posed for
> Catherine between Heathcliff and Edgar Linton. That choice seems to
> me the pivotal event of the novel, the decisive catalyst of the tragedy;
> and if this is so, then the crux of *Wuthering Heights* must be conceded
> by even the most remorselessly mythological and mythical critics to be
> a social one. In a crucial act of self betrayal and bad faith, Catherine
> rejects Heathcliff as a suitor because he is socially inferior to Linton;
> and it is from this that the train of destruction follows.'[69]

Catherine, he says, trades her 'authentic selfhood' (shades of Kettle
and Williams) for social privilege. Heathcliff in Eagleton's view rightly
denounces her spiritual suicide and murder. He quotes[70]

> '*Why* did you betray your own heart, Cathy? I have not one word of
> comfort. You deserve this. You have killed yourself. Yes you may kiss
> me, and cry; and ring out my kisses and tears: they'll blight you –
> they'll damn you. You loved me – then what *right* had you to leave
> me? What right – answer me – for the poor fancy you felt for Linton?
> Because misery and degradation, and death, and nothing that God or
> Satan could inflict would have parted us, *you* of your own will, did it.
> I have not broken your heart – *you* have broken it; and in breaking it,
> you have broken mine.'

Cathy, however, has a different view, which Eagleton's over-simple
Marxism and surface dialectic leads him to overlook. To him, she has
betrayed her authentic self (her Hegelian Essence?) by *choosing* the
wrong side in the class struggle. A feminist, an early Victorian woman
writer's, or even a woman's reading, might recognise that the major
social system created a situation in which women had no choice or
irreconcilable choices – as Eagleton praises Emily for recognising while
he provides a male reductionism to her realism

> 'you and Edgar have broken my heart, Heathcliff! And you both
> come to bewail the deed to me, as if you were the people to be pitied!
> I shall not pity you, not I. You have killed me and thriven on it, I
> think. How strong you are! How many years do you mean to live after
> I am gone'[71]

In the light of this reading we can appreciate Mrs. Leavis's insight on
the relations of Cat and Mouse.[72] In a scene in which Cathy has shown
her 'power' by hitting a child (Hareton), lying to Edgar Linton and
then striking him in turn, Nelly Dean sends him away and significantly
reveals the latent situation in an apparently twice-reversed metaphor.

> 'the soft thing [Edgar] looked askance through the window – he

> possessed the power to depart, ·as much as a cat possesses the power to leave a mouse half killed, or a bird half eaten.
> 'Ah I thought, there will be no saving him – he's doomed, and flies to his fate.'

Eagleton thus makes Cathy the subject author of the novel whose actions are free and directed towards authenticity. He at once displaces Emily Brontë and the determinism of the historical moment,

> ' . . . she [Cathy] hopes to square authenticity with social convention, running in harness an ontological commitment to Heathcliff with a phenomenal relationship to Linton. "I *am* Heathcliff" is dramatically arresting, but it is also a way of keeping the outcast at arm's length, evading the challenge he offers.'[73]

For Williams, the *I am Heathcliff* is the core of the novel's exploration of contradictions between desire in and desire for; for Eagleton it is a distancing device; for Musselwhite a distraction from the real identiy – Lockwood and Heathcliff. Perhaps it is a dramatically overstated part of the common parlance of romantically illicit love – 'I shall stay with James but you will always be part of me and I shall always be part of you' could well be a dialogue line from *Brief Encounter*. Mrs. Leavis notes the shadowiness of Heathcliff's portrayal; Eagleton takes it further.

> 'Stripped as he is of determinate social relations, of a given function within the family, Heathcliff's presence is radically gratuitous.'[74]

He goes on to argue that he provides the other characters with a chance to break out of restrictive social relations without representing in himself a clear social position or class. He is proletarian in appearance and swarthy but as Nelly Dean tells him – he might equally be a prince.[75] In short he is but a 'touchstone for responses'.

> 'Heathcliff is a purely atomised individual, free of generational ties in a novel where genealogical relations are of crucial thematic and structural importance.'[76]

As a stranger, in the sense that Simmel uses it, and that I have used it in earlier work[77] he can take the blame for unavoidable structural change. He can also be linked, if only marginally, with the marginal Catherine, *daughter* (my italics, Eagleton's half made point) of the family,

> 'Heathcliff offers Catherine a friendship which opens fresh possibilities of freedom within the internal system of the Heights: in a situation where social determinants are insistent, freedom can mean only a relative independence of given blood ties . . .'[78]

In the analysis that follows Eagleton is at his most convincing. Whereas Charlotte's protagonists find freedom moving upwards – Catherine's potentiality is downward and out – back to external nature and the moor. But surrender to the moor and denial of class and lineage is the ultimate threat to the Heights – so unwittingly Heathcliff by merely existing brings out the hidden violence. He is simultaneously (like Orlando in *As you like it*) disciplined as a servant and deprived of the discipline of cultural education.

> 'It is a contradiction which encapsulates a crucial truth about bourgeois society. If there is no genuine liberty on its "inside" – Heathcliff is oppressed by work and the familial structure – neither is there more than a caricature of liberty on the "outside", since the release of running wild is thereby a function of cultural impoverishment.'[79]

When Heathcliff goes off, it is to collect culture as a weapon and as capital the investment of which will turn the tables on his oppressors. The use of culture as capital is an unsurprisingly recurring theme of the Brontë novels in *Jane Eyre*, in *Villette*, and in *The Professor*, for example. For men, it may bring real victories; for women always hollow ones. For women must turn their culture inwards and expressively to their family; men can turn it outwards and instrumentally on society. Eagleton's analysis recognises that *Wuthering Heights* is able

> 'ruthlessly to demystify the Victorian notion of the family as a pious, pacific space within social conflict'

but he stops short at realising that the conflict in the family arises from the depersonalisation of women that is necessary to free the men as individuals and members of a class. I show this by representing Eagleton's argument with my own commentary added,

> 'Throughout *Wuthering Heights*, labour and culture, bondage and freedom, nature and artifice appear at once as each other's dialectical negations and as subtly matched, mutually reflected. Culture – gentility – is the opposite of labour for young Heathcliff and Hareton; but it is also a crucial economic weapon, as well as a product of work itself. The delicate spiritless Lintons in their crimson-carpeted drawing-room are radically severed from the labour which sustains them; gentility grows from the production of others, detaches itself from that work (as the Grange is separate from the Heights), and then comes to dominate the labour on which it is parasitic. In doing so, it becomes a form of self-bondage; if work is servitude, so in a subtler sense is civilisation.'[89]

So it is indeed, and for all the women of the class the subtle servitude of civilisation is their fate. The crucial economic weapon is culture from outside; internal culture is a unity with conventional feminine nature. It carries no sustained power. It is this reality that Nelly and Zillah accept and Cathy rejects. It is this contradiction that is ideologically resolved when the second Cathy first educates and then marries Hareton. There lies the danger (as Lenin long ago reminded Bukharin) of reducing contradictions to dichotomies, nature/labour is but one pair: nature/culture, field labour/house labour others.

> 'To some extent, these polarities are held together in the yeoman-farming structure of the Heights. Here labour and culture, freedom and necessity, nature and society are roughly complementary. The Earnshaws are gentlemen yet they work the land; they enjoy the freedom of being their own masters, but that freedom moves within the tough discipline of labour; and because the social unit of the Heights – the family – is both "natural" (biological) and an economic system, it acts to some degree as a mediation between nature and artifice, naturalising property relations and socialising blood ties. Relationships in this isolated world are turbulently face-to-face, but they are also impersonally mediated through a working relation with nature'

I will not labour the point but the abstract family is, for a time at least, real, but of course fictitious, women.

Eagleton's next two points are less convincing. First he takes issue with Mrs. Leavis about Joseph and his wholesomeness. Once again, I am reminded of *As You Like It* – Joseph is loyal and persisting as well as grim – Adam in *As You Like It* is the optimistically romanticised loyal servant; Joseph is perhaps his puritan pessimistic counterpart. Adam worked for a landowner; Joseph for capitalist farmers. Times change and so do romantic ideals. Similarly his view of Heathcliff as a catalyst rather than cause of violence involves what seems to me a rare careless reading.

> 'Heathcliff disturbs the Heights because he is simply superfluous: he has no defined place within its biological and economic system . . . The superfluity he embodies is that of a sheerly human demand for recognition; but since there is no space for such surplus within the terse economy of the Heights, it proves destructive rather than creative in effect, straining and overloading already taut relationships. Heathcliff catalyses on aggression intrinsic to Heights society; that sound blow Hindley hands out to Catherine on the evening of Heathcliff's first appearance is slight but significant evidence against the case that conflict starts only with Heathcliff's arrival.'[81]

Ronald Frankenburg

In one reading of the novel which I shall spell out in detail elsewhere I argue that Heathcliff does represent a 'sheerly human demand for recognition' – but that he symbolises woman's demand to be a person and this indeed is a destructive force to the Heights and to Victorian capitalist society both at a societal and at a local level, as Emily well knew. It is only if we give him real life as novels tempt us to do (and as Brecht tries to teach us not to) that we cannot make this reading. Emily did her best to convince us it was a story – Lockwood tells us what Nelly told him the characters told her. As Goodridge points out this is an involving device.[82] But it is also a distancing one. The substantive point is however answered unequivocally by the text itself

> ' . . . and Cathy, when she learnt the master had lost her whip in attending on the stranger [the infant Heathcliff], showed her humour by grinning and spitting at the stupid little thing, earning for her pains a sound blow from her father to teach her cleaner manners.'[83]

In the rest of his analysis, Eagleton seems to me to retreat into Romanticism himself, led there by his personalisation of Heathcliff, his failure to recognise any but large-scale social conflict, and his search for the authentic.

> 'Their relationship articulates a depth inexpressible in routine social practice, transcendent of available social languages. Its impersonality suggests both a savage depersonalising and a paradigmatic significance; and in neither sense is the relationship wholly within their conscious control. What Heathcliff offers Cathy is a non- or pre-social relationship, as the only authentic form of living in a world of exploitation and inequality, a world where one must refuse to measure oneself by the criteria of the class-structure and so must appear inevitably subversive. Whereas in Charlotte's novels the love-relationship takes you into society, in *Wuthering Heights* it drives you out of it. The love between Heathcliff and Catherine is an intuitive intimacy raised to cosmic status, bypassing the mediation of the "social"; and this indeed, is both its strength and its limit. Its non-sociality is on the one hand a revolutionary refusal of the given language of social roles and values; and if the relationship is to remain unabsorbed by society it must therefore appear as natural rather than social, since Nature is on the "outside" of society. On the other hand, the novel cannot realise the meaning of that revolutionary refusal in social terms, the most it can do is to *universalise* that meaning by intimating the mysteriously impersonal energies from which the relationship springs.'[84]

and later,

'Their love remains an unhistorical essence which fails to enter into
concrete existence and can do so, ironically only in death. Death,
indeed, as the ultimate outer limit of consciousness and society is the
locus of Catherine and Heathcliff's love, the horizon on which it
moves.'[85]

Here is insight and sophisticated analysis; but here also is ideology
situated in the practices of humanistic Hegelian neo-romantic search
for authenticity, in a Durkheimian division of pre-social nature and
post-cultural society, in a Marxist sectarianism which sees society at
large as the site of class struggle and the family as merely personal. A
reversal of Leavis's values but not their rejection. Above all despite its
sophistication; it lacks Caudwell's awareness of gender (confusedly
echoed in Leavis); as well as Williams's consciousness of generation. It
slips back as it steps forward.

An adequate reading for Marxists in the sense I laid down at the
outset requires a theoretical realisation that while the dynamic of the
capitalist mode of production (and social formations based on it as a
whole) depends on class struggle – in this case according to Eagleton –
bourgeoisie versus landed gentry; the dynamics of the parts and their
articulation depends on gender and generation. The specificity of the
social formation is historically unique as Charlotte explores in her
treatment of nationality elsewhere.

To complete my survey, however, two opposing structuralisms
remain – the brief but revolutionary (or radical?) Musselwhite and the
Kermode *Tel-Quelism* which he denounces.

Kermode is interesting to me because he represents (like Leach
elsewhere) an English structuralism and perhaps the partial failure of
the promise which structuralism in general and Levi-Strauss in
particular seemed to offer to New Left Review Marxism in the sixties.
We are all post-structuralists now and bear the telegonic impress of the
theory that violated our historicist, economic-determinist, humanist
virginity. Musselwhite and others may reject the parenthood of Sartre
and Levi-Strauss – even their infant hubris cannot escape the hybrid
vigour they inherit.

Kermode's overt problem is anti-Marxist – what is a classic? – and his
answer deceptively simple. It is a work that the competent reader free of
institutional restraint is still reading a hundred years or more after the
death of both its writer, and its original reader. Why is the reader still
reading it? – because he/she is still writing it. He rejects (as do we all?
but Williams, Kettle?) Charlotte's apparent view that, at least as far as
Emily is concerned there is but one answer to the enigma of *Wuthering*

Heights which one perceptive critic straightway perceived.

> 'Few would believe that such an interpretation exists, however
> frequently the critics produce new "keys". For we don't think of the
> novel as a code, or a nut, that can be broken; which contains or refers
> to a meaning all will agree upon if it can once be presented *en clair*.
> We need little persuasion to believe that a good novel is not a message
> at all.'[86]

His way into a novel is a self-consciously literary one, it is to look at its
key inscriptions – Hareton Earnshaw 1500 inscribed over the door at
Wuthering Heights – and Catherine Earnshaw-Catherine Heathcliff-
Catherine Linton carved on the panels of the room within a room, the
enclosed bed in which Catherine Earnshaw slept and in which (even
more significantly for my reading than for his) Heathcliff is going to die.

> 'All of them [novels] contain the equivalent of such inscriptions;
> indeed all writing is a sort of inscription, cut memorably into the
> uncaused flux of event; and inscriptions of the kind I am talking about
> are interesting secondary clues about the nature of the writing in
> which they occur. They draw attention to the literariness of what we
> are reading, indicate the story is a story, perhaps with beneficial effects
> on our normal powers of perception; above all they distinguish a
> literary system which has no constant relation to readers with interests
> and expectations altered by long passages of time.'[87]

A reading of Lockwood's experience in the nightmare of Chapter
three is only possible when the book is completed. Then the reader can
see that Earnshaw-Heathcliff-Linton is the story of the first Catherine;
Linton-Heathcliff-Earnshaw is the story of the second. In this reading,
Catherine's 'I *am* Heathcliff' is the most crucial statement in the book.
All movement is through Heathcliff. It is not necessary for this reading
that Emily should have been conscious of presenting this paradigm for
'A narrative is not a transcription of something pre-existent.'

Since all movement is through Heathcliff – what is the significance of
Heathcliff for Kermode? First of all – he is 'between names, between
families'. Second he is between houses and culture. Third he is a
mediator of barbarism to the civil or civilised. Fourth he is a mediator of
dreams. Finally he is created by the reader. In Barthes's words 'The
work proposes, man (sic) disposes.'

Some quotation from Kermode will spell out this sequence.

> 'Heathcliff is then as it were between names, as between families (he is
> the door through which Earnshaw passes into Linton, and out again to
> Earnshaw). He is often introduced, as if characteristically, standing
> outside, or entering, or leaving, a door. He is in and out of the

Earnshaw family simultaneously; servant and child of the family . . .
His origins are equally betwixt and between: the gutter or the royal
origin imagined for him by Nelly; prince or pauper, American or
Lascar, Child of God or devil. This betweenness persists, I think:
Heathcliff, for instance fluctuates between poverty and riches; also
between virility and impotence. To Catherine he is between brother
and lover; he slept with her as a child, and again in death, but not
between latency and extinction. He has much force, yet fathers an
exceptionally puny child. Domestic yet savage like the dogs, bleak yet
full of fire like the house, he bestrides the great opposites: love and
death (the necrophiliac confession), culture and nature ("half-civilised
ferocity") in a posture that certainly cannot be explained by any
generic formula ("Byronic" or "Gothic").'[88]

He goes on to explicate that Heathcliff stands and mediates between
north and south, past and future, Heights and Grange, and then to a
long analysis of the dreams in *Wuthering Heights* to which I refer the
reader in the original.

The second part of Kermode's analysis refers back to Mrs. Leavis's
essay of which, while he appears at first to reject its central point he
writes 'in its mature authority it dwarfs all the others.'

As we have done already, he accepts Mrs. Leavis's division but rejects
her rejection both of Heathcliff and of sociology. He feels he can do this
because of the existence, in Levi-Strauss's term, of a 'surplus of signifier'
– it is this that allows a science of the text – which is produced not by the
author in her time alone, but by the text and the reader. However, he
finally reminds us that in Barthes's saying – man has been replaced by
the literary work and God by man. This is a truth that can be taken
holistically in a Durkheimian – God is Society direction or in terms of
class as Musselwhite and Barker[89] in their way and I, in mine, try to do.
I pause only to note that Kermode despite his disclaimer that narrative
is not a description of a real pre-existing past treats Heathcliff as a real
pre-existing man. Leavis sees the character as an ill-delineated shadow;
Eagleton as a touchstone; Musselwhite as a dialectical opposite, a
Freud/Lacan mirror to Lockwood. I would wish, as I have said, to
analyse the texts labelled Heathcliff as an ideology, concealing and
revealing, perhaps to Emily as to us, her own potential rebellion against
a situated femininity – situated in time, in place, and at a moment in
class struggle.

Like much structuralism, Kermode seeks the hidden, but in a limbo
between the text and society, like a virtual image in a mirror.
Musselwhite seeks it in the Freudian unconsciousness; Barker in '*both*
the specificity of literature and its [socially] *determinate* status.'[90]

Musselwhite argues, following Balibar and Macherey,[91] that Marxist criticism is not just the substitution of Marxist terms for liberal ones. *Wuthering Heights* to him is a text unacceptable to bourgeois ideology. Not only does it direct attention from its own dominant themes – especially the identity of Heathcliff and Lockwood; but editors have conspired(?) to direct our attention away from the key structural figures – Joseph, Nelly and Lockwood by presenting a genealogy in which they do not, indeed cannot, figure. Critics have failed to bring out the sexual undertones – as an example to follow the implications of C. P. Sanger's famous genealogy further.[92]

> 'But the tree contains two *italicised* places; those of Heathcliff and Frances Hindley. We have already commented on the potential identity of Heathcliff and Lockwood. In other words there is a place available for Lockwood in the family tree: It is his tragedy that he never occupies that place. More remarkable though is the place held open for Nelly by the italicised figure of Frances, Hindley's wife. Throughout the novel there are suggestions that the relationship between Nelly and Hindley is a highly charged one, not to say a highly sexual relationship. Again we have noted that it is she who removes the shot from his fowling piece. There is too the extraordinary scene in which Hindley forces a knife between Nelly's lips (p. 114). Nelly seems to regard Hareton as *her* child and there is the further disturbing episode where Nelly has a vision of Hindley as he had been as a child *twenty years earlier* (p. 147) the same period of time that the child Cathy has been wandering on the moors. It is as if the whole story might have been otherwise – as if indeed, it might have been "told . . . in half a dozen words" (p.101) as if, in fact, Emily Brontë is alerting us to the fact that she is not writing an "everyday story of country folk" but is contributing a highly complex and consciously sophisticated piece of work the mechanisms of which deserve prolonged attention.'[93]

Yes, indeed, but by whom, and what for? There are clearly many readings including a deeper oedipal/oral one than even Williams allows to surface and which Musselwhite (apparently) finds attractive. To Marxists however deep penetration is not enough – it needs a social, more a class, context. Barker answered Musselwhite in the following issue of *Red Letters*. For him *Wuthering Heights* is not a knowledge. What needs to be explained now is, is it possible, within the ideological and historical conjuncture of 1848, for the textual operations of the book which challenge and criticise bourgeois ideology to take place. It is necessary to provide a knowledge, which is of course something *produced* and distinctly different from its object – the book under analysis – of the complex system of determinations that bring it into existence at odds with dominant ideology.

I here want to interrupt and add 'and keep it in existence' for unless we are going to produce a new text, it is the continual re-reading/rewriting of the old in class terms which is important (and clearly I include more in class than Eagleton).

Barker seems to follow with a formula for historical reconstruction albeit combined with close attention to the text.

> 'Resting ultimately on the economic infrastructure, these determinants – class ideology, the state of the class struggle and its forms, the history of literary forms and techniques, the ideological project of the author and so on must be elucidated to make intelligible the book's inner workings.'
>
> 'Admittedly, the distance between an anti-reductionist attention to the text rather than to something else which is *substituted* for it – history, ideology, etc., and a pure formalism which pays no more than lip-service to the real conditions of the production of literature in a given society, can often seem small. But it is, in fact, infinite, Musselwhite's insistence that the analysis of literature should elucidate literature is timely and correct, but his attempt to achieve this by making the text's "real conditions" its own self-constitution, without sociological explanation, falls sharply away from an authentically Marxist emphasis on both the specificity of literature, and its *determinate* status.'

So we are left where we began – after ranging from the mature opinions of the arrived, to the struggles to think literature of recent research students – what is an authentically Marxist emphasis?

For Caudwell, Wilson, Fox, Kettle, and Williams, the principal aspect of the contradiction context/text is the context. The context suggests to all but the first two of them that historical materialism is about the past in which they see reflected their own present (encapsulating their own past). For Fox, *Wuthering Heights* is the search for self and love frustrated by 19th century capitalism. Catherine/Heathcliff are the heartcry (ideological) revenge of love against their century and, in Joseph, puritanical religion. Look on this, see how nasty capitalism was! – it still is, fight against it. Kettle and Williams in their separate ways see men and women seeking to find their natures by means of the struggle against nature and achieving victory through death – perhaps an appropriate image for the generation which participated and returned from global war, Nature and place provide continuity for both. Williams, more than Kettle, influenced by Hegel through Lukács, seeks and finds in literature an ordered totality which life lacks.

Kettle, Wilson, Leavis and Eagleton seem to share a

characteristically English puritanism which consciously puts sex outside society, and unconsciously, with Durkheim, banishes women to the limbo of nature and maternal instincts from which her socially unacceptable other face occasionally emerges to tempt men to destruction. Caudwell and Williams have greater understanding – but for Musselwhite perhaps sex is over socialised.

Alone among the contextualists Caudwell situates his history *firmly* in the future. The ideology of female emancipation through becoming masculine he sees as being resolved not in present literature but in ongoing and future class struggle.

With Leavis, Eagleton and Kermode, as well as their would-be successors – it is the text that dominates – for Leavis the context is splintered – she is within the ideology and seeks to reinforce it. Her view of *Wuthering Heights* as a moral text is safe not merely for Roedean but for Holland Park. For Kermode the context disappears altogether, his humanity hides beneath the structure of both the text and of his own erudition and conceals his class practice.

Even Eagleton is trapped between a past seeking authenticity, and a future of grand cataclysmic class struggle. The daily struggles of personal life, undisguised in Emily Brontë and papered over in Charlotte, he sees: but he does not, in this work, yet see their overdetermination and their relevance for making the social cataclysm come alive.

The emphasis on text and theoretical understanding make carrying Caudwell further possible; the grand contextual focus makes immediate progress unlikely. The dialectic of Musselwhite and Barker, unsituated Freud against textual sophistication and old basis/superstructure Marx offers some hope.

In my view Marxist criticism of literature must not primarily be concerned with origin, although what we know of Emily's life *does* in fact suggest she might have been concerned with gender within class struggle, but with the process of production of the text.[94] Criticism is in fact an intervention in the actual process of that production as it still goes on each time the book is read.

As Musselwhite and Balibar and Macherey have suggested, official critics and the schools and colleges treat the work as having been produced; the ideology is retailed, old class struggles indulgently sympathised with. New class struggles are conveniently ignored.

Marxists need continually to reproduce, to reveal the contradictions unresolved and unresovable in the text and in their actual specificity as they are now. The function of literature is to reflect light on the present not the distant glow of the past. If people still like to read *Wuthering Heights* and find it enjoyable and relevant; the Marxist critic should be able to tell them why. If, as I think there is, there is a sense in which the text of *Wuthering Heights* produces a description of reality 'more intense, more concentrated, more typical, nearer the ideal, and therefore more universal than actual everyday life'[95] we should be able to demonstrate how it does so, and use it to forward a movement in which life successfully competes with art; and then art again with life. To achieve such criticism it is necessary to remember with Brecht, that even a realist novel is an interplay of ideas and concepts not of real people. To accept realism at its face-value is to accept ideology rather to analyse it. It is a demonstration of the control of language of Emily Brontë that despite the complexities of the narrative and the carefully organised structure of the novel, even her Marxist critics seem so far to have failed to suspend belief in the 'authentic' characters for long enough to think about what the text is saying. Perhaps as academics rather than intellectuals they would rather see their own reflections than those of the present or future. This is not to impugn their personal good faith; merely to recognise the generative strength of the structures in which they, like us, are embedded. Only theoretical clarity combined with practice – critical and political – can break this persistent reproductive chain.

University of Keele

1. Terry Eagleton: *Criticism and Ideology*, New Left Books, London, 1976, p. vii.

2. Christopher Caudwell: *Romance and Realism*, Princeton University Press, Princeton, N.J., 1970.

3. D. Wilson: *Modern Quarterly Miscellany*, *No. 1.*, Lawrence and Wishart, London, 1947.

4. Arnold Kettle: *An Introduction to the English Novel*, Arrow Books, London, 1962.

5. Q. D. Leavis: 'A Fresh Approach to Wuthering Heights', in Q. D. and F. R. Leavis: *Lectures in America*, Chatto and Windus, London, 1969.

6. Raymond Williams: *The Country and the City*, Chatto and Windus, London, 1973; also, *The English Novel: From Dickens to Lawrence*, Paladin, London, 1974.

7. Terry Eagleton: *Myths of Power: A Marxist Study of the Brontës*, Macmillan, London, 1975.

8. David Musselwhite: 'Wuthering Heights: The unacceptable Text', *Red Letters*, 2, Summer, 1976.

9. Frank Kermode: *The Classic*, Faber and Faber, London, 1975.

10. V. I. Lenin: 'L. N. Tolstoy' (1910), in *On Literature and Art*, Progress, Moscow, 1970, p. 52.

11. Mao Tse Tung: 'Talks at the Yenan Forum on Literature and Art' (1942), in *Selected Works*, Vol. III, Peking, 1965, p. 70.

12. Charlotte Brontë: 'Editors Preface to the New (1850) edition of Wuthering Heights' in Emily Brontë: *Wuthering Heights*, Penguin Books, Harmondsworth, 1965, p. 39.

13. S. S. Prawer: *Karl Marx and World Literature*, Oxford University Press, London, 1976, p. 396.

14. Roland Barthes: *The Pleasure of the Text*, Jonathan Cape, London, 1975a, p. 4.

15. Eagleton: op.cit., 1976, pp. 23-24. Christopher Caudwell: *Studies in a Dying Culture*, Martin Lawrence, London, 1947.

16. Caudwell: op.cit., 1970, p. 72.

17. Eagleton: op.cit., 1975, p. 115.

18. Ralph Fox: *The Novel and the People*, Cobbet, London, 1944, pp. 72-73.

19. ibid., pp. 73-74.

20. ibid., p. 74.

21. E. D. Klingopolous in *Scrutiny*, 1947.

22. Wilson: op. cit.

23. cf. Leavis and Leavis: op.cit., p. 87 – Mrs. Leavis describes Lord David Cecil as woolly.

24. Wilson: op.cit., p. 105.

25. ibid., pp. 110-111.

26. ibid., p. 111.

27. ibid., p. 112.

28. ibid., p. 113.

29. ibid., p. 113.

30. ibid., p. 115.

31. Fox: op.cit., p. 74.

32. cf. Sarrasine in Roland Barthes: *S/Z*, Jonathan Cape, London, 1975a.

33. Kettle: op.cit., pp. 164-165.

34. Barthes: op.cit., 1975b, pp. 39-40.

35. Kettle: op.cit., p. 168.

36. Barthes: op.cit., 1975b, p. 162.

37. Williams: op.cit., 1973, p. 176.

38. Williams: op.cit., 1974, p. 50.

39. Kettle: op.cit., p. 161.

40. Williams: op.cit., 1974, p. 52, but compare Caudwell above and Musslewhite on Nelly Dean below.

41. ibid., p. 51.

42. ibid., p. 55; Kettle: op.cit., p. 157; E. Brontë: op.cit., p. 122; Leavis and Leavis: op.cit., p. 106 – characterises it as 'not very impressive rhetoric.'

43. Raymond Williams: *Border Country*, Chatto and Windus, 1960.

44. Williams: op.cit., 1974, p. 57.

45. Leavis and Leavis: op.cit., p. 137.

46. ibid., p. 138.

47. ibid., p. 93.

48. ibid., p. 114.

49. E. Brontë: op.cit., p. 103.

50. Leavis and Leavis: op.cit., p. 126.

51. ibid., p. 88.

52. ibid., p. 112.

53. Klingopolous: op.cit.

54. Leavis and Leavis: op.cit., p. 88.

55. ibid., p. 89.

56. ibid., p. 90.

57. ibid., p. 92.

58. ibid., p. 96

59. ibid., p. 98.

60. ibid., pp. 98-99.

61. ibid., p. 101.

62. ibid., p. 109, footnote.

63. ibid., pp. 111-112.

64. ibid., p. 114.

65. Eagleton: op.cit., 1975, p. 82.

66. ibid., p. 76.

67. ibid., p. 98.

68. ibid., p. 99.

69. ibid., p. 101.

70. ibid., p. 101.

71. E. Brontë: op.cit., p. 195.

72. ibid., p. 112; Leavis and Leavis: op.cit., p. 197.

73. Eagleton: op.cit., 1975, p. 101.

74. ibid., p. 102.

75. E. Brontë: op.cit., p. 98.

76. Eagleton: op.cit., 1975, p. 103; cf. Musselwhite: op.cit.

77. Georg Simmel: *The Sociology of Georg Simmel*, edited by Kurt Wolff, Free Press, New York, 1950; Ronald Frankenberg: *Village on the Border*, Cohen and West, London, 1957; Ronald Frankenberg: 'The Carpet of Agamemnon' in Max Gluckman: *The Allocation of Responsibility*, Manchester University Press, Manchester, 1972.

78. Eagleton: op.cit., 1975, p. 103.

79. ibid., p. 101.

80. ibid., p. 105.

81. ibid., p. 106.

82. Frank Goodridge: *Emily Brontë: Wuthering Heights*, Studies in English Literature No. 20, Arnold, London.

83. E. Brontë: op.cit., p. 78.

84. Eagleton: op.cit., 1975, p. 108.

85. ibid., p. 109.

86. Kermode: op.cit., p. 119.

87. ibid., pp. 120-121.

88. ibid., pp. 123-124.

89. Musselwhite: op.cit.; Francis Barker: 'Wuthering Heights and the Real Conditions', *Red Letter*, no. 3, Autumn 1976.

90. Barker: op.cit.

91. E. Balibar and P. Macherey: 'Sur La Litterature Comme Forme Ideologique: Quelques Hypotheses Marxistes', *Litterature*, 13, February, 1974, pp. 29-48.

92. C. P. Sanger: *The Structure of Wuthering Heights*, Hogarth Press, London, 1926.

93. Musselwhite: op.cit., p. 4.

94. As Eagleton: op.cit., 1976, has also since written.

95. Mao Tse Tung: op cit., p. 82.

Towards a Virginia Woolf Criticism

Michèle Barrett

The critical literature on Virginia Woolf contains not only paeons of overstated praise but also a good deal of dismissiveness and contempt. Any serious attempt to denigrate a writer starts off well with a slur on originality, such as the one made by Leon Edel when he says 'The influence of James Joyce upon her is much more profound than is generally believed.'[1] In particular he claims that '*Mrs Dalloway's* structure seems largely to be modelled on the multiple-scened chapter in *Ulysses*',[2] and that '. . . the painting of the sensibility tends to be Proustian.'[3] John Rosenberg is equally at pains to establish Virginia Woolf as an inferior and derivative novelist, for he asserts that 'She followed Dorothy Richardson not only in her mode of writing, but also in the feminism of her novels . . . she never adequately expressed her debt to Dorothy Richardson.'[4]

Joyce, Proust and Richardson are alleged to be the models from whom Virginia Woolf acquired her techniques, although Guiguet has refuted these claims with definitive chronological evidence.[5] Guiguet himself prefers to relate both Virginia Woolf and this other group of writers to a 'common participation in an attitude of mind, a stock of ideas.'[6] In this he endorses Auerbach's brilliant historical interpretation of Woolf's work[7] – a work of criticism which soars above the petty and inadequate examples which I shall be discussing here. Before attempting to explain why Virginia Woolf criticism is so unsatisfactory, I shall try to describe some common aspects of the secondary literature on this writer.

As well as being unoriginal Virginia Woolf is thought by some of her critics to be severely constrained by her class and gender. Her work is said to be élitist, trivial, narrowly feminine in scope, and she is held not to have understood its technical significance. The charge of élitism, although equally applicable to the novels of E. M. Forster and Aldous Huxley, is frequently levelled at Virginia Woolf in her capacity as a member of 'Bloomsbury', with the implication that such membership by definition explains the texts. Elizabeth Hardwick states that 'The arrangements of Bloomsbury, shored up by stout logs of self-regard, are insular in the extreme', from which premise she follows through to the conclusion that Virginia Woolf is 'awful' (as are Forster and James) because '. . . it is bad taste for authors to come down so heavily on the lacks of the luckless and deprived.'[8] Walter Allen similarly introduces into his critical evaluation his knowledge of Virginia Woolf's life and opinions, for he pronounces that 'Virginia Woolf is a novelist of very narrow limits . . . (Her characters) tend to think and feel alike, to be the aesthetes of one set of sensations; they think and feel and express their thoughts and feelings, in fact, exactly as Virginia Woolf herself does in such non-fiction works as *Mr Bennett and Mrs Brown* and *A Room of One's Own*. They are distinguished by a discriminating intelligence and an acute self-conciousness which weave a close sieve through which the greater part of the common experiences of life will not pass.'[9]

Although it is well known that Virginia Woolf was born into an established upper middle class literary intelligentsia,[10] other writers of similar or wealthier background escape censure on these grounds. Indeed with Virginia Woolf this particular line of attack almost serves instead of a discussion of the text, as when Bradbury, in his *The Social Context of Modern English Literature* refers under the index entry for Virginia Woolf more frequently to 'Bloomsbury' than to the novels.[11] Judgements of this kind, in which the class position of an author is used as a means of establishing the supposedly self-evident limitations of his or her work, are merely a crude and inadequate response from conventional criticism to the challenge from a Marxist aesthetic.

References to Virginia Woolf's feminine limitations of mind are even more common, and are by definition, it would seem, pejorative. Bradbury writes that '. . . no one single novel of Virginia Woolf's seems to get beyond the feminine fragility of her sensibility . . .'[12] and he concludes that '. . . she not only tends to poeticise modernism, but also to feminise and domesticate it. . . . . . the essential form of her novels, whatever the complexities of their pattern, is always finally the domestic novel of sensibility; and hence, I think, there is something inescapably limited about the matter of consciousness with which she deals . . .'[13]

Bradbury then turns with relief to Ford Madox Ford, whose 'panoramic' work he can wholeheartedly praise in contrast to that of Virginia Woolf. The judgement of her work as essentially *limited* (in Edel's words 'a scaling down of Joycean architectonics'),[14] is again linked with her situation as a *woman* by the French critic Floris Delattre. After stating rather baldly that Woolf 'directly borrowed' her technique from James Joyce, Delattre mobilises a little charm to soften the blow: 'She also created monologue, she also created a "slice of interior life", but she reduced it to delicate proportions, more sharp and cursory, to which her feminine subtlety gave the tone.'[15]

It is no coincidence that charges of derivativeness and unoriginality are coupled with references to the fact that the author in question was a woman, and the extension of these prejudices is simply that Virginia Woolf did not fully understand what she was doing in her work. A mindless, whimsical, eccentric female is conjured up in Walter Allen's remark that '. . . when one thinks in the abstract of a typical Virginia Woolf character one seems to see a tiny figure on tiptoe eagerly grasping a butterfly net alert to snare the significant, the transcending moment as it flies.'[16] This tiny figure has a tiny mind to match, and G. S. Fraser goes so far as to say that 'I doubt, from her own writings whether Mrs Woolf was any more capable of following an abstract philosophical argument than Clarissa Dalloway.'[17] Even Daiches, in many respects an admirer of Woolf, writes in the same vein that 'Joyce went the whole way in rejecting the normative and involved himself in an immense paradox; Virginia Woolf went only halfway (probably without being concious that she was going in that direction at all) and stopped at subtilisation.'[18]

In addition to this it has been argued that the work itself has no real content. Woolf's novels are held to lack any grip on the concrete, historical, fabric of society – indeed A. J. P. Taylor has pronounced that they are 'irrelevant for the historian.'[19] The combination of her class position and gender have resulted in a fatal distance from the processes of social life and production. Bradbury comments that '. . . for Virginia Woolf conciousness is intuitive and poetic rather than subterranean and mythopoeic; it is the creative energy of the self . . .The flux has no marked social origin.'[20] This view of Woolf as an ahistorical writer is put forward very clearly (and perhaps misleadingly, since the author purports to recognise Woolf as a feminist) by Elizabeth Hardwick in a recent essay.[21] Hardwick declares that 'Exegesis about Virginia Woolf is a trap; the fictions are circular and the critic spins in a drum of tautology. The novels are beautiful. . . And yet in a sense her novels aren't interesting. . . I was immensely moved by (*The Waves*) when I read it recently and yet I cannot think of anything to say about it except that it is wonderful. The people are not characters, there is no plot in the usual sense. What can you bring to bear: verisimilitude – to what? You can merely say over and over that it is very good, very beautiful, that when you were reading it you were happy.'[22]

Although tribute of a kind, Hardwick's response is not what Woolf would have wanted or deserves, and the inarticulateness demonstrated in this passage may tell us more about the critic than the novelist. For *The Waves* is not merely 'wonderful'; it contains a sustained critique of patriarchy, of social stratification, of the family and relationships between men and women, of our conception of personality, as well as discussion of the role and function of the artist in society. In this respect it is comparable with Virginia Woolf's other novels, many of which, as I shall outline below, deal with similar themes. Far from these books having no social historical content, in their subject matter they correspond with the works of Forster, Huxley, Eliot and other contemporaries.

There are however certain inconsistencies and contradictions in Virginia Woolf's thought, and to some extent these are the source of the critical attitudes to which I have pointed. Such contradictions are certainly evident in the critical literature, as in the following examples. Malcolm Bradbury, in his essay on Virginia Woolf,[23] appears at times to contradict his dismissive approach to his subject. Although grudging in tone and qualified by riders, he lets the occasional acknowledgement through – that '(*Mr Bennett and Mrs Brown* and *Modern Fiction*) add up to an important general plea for a new timbre in the novel.'[24] More importantly he admits that 'After reading Auerbach's chapter on her, it would be impossible not to grant that she was deeply and seriously involved in a revolution in the novel. . .'[25] In his closing words he ignores this admission, and concludes '. . . a fiction that refines the tradition but does not *make* a tradition on which successors can draw.'[26]

Hardwick contradicts herself in the reverse manner, for having charged Woolf with a-historicity in the body of her essay she concludes by claiming for her precisely this quality. Indeed she even asserts that '. . . only a great conception could have made history out of the pageant on the lawn in *Between the Acts*. This novel and *The Waste Land* are the most powerful literary images we have of the movements of life and cultures, the dying of the past in the dying of a day, the shift from one order to another in an overheard conversation.'[27] A simple explanation may exist for such inconsistencies, and particularly in Bradbury's case it is not difficult to point to possible motivations (an evident sexism, some rather crude class prejudice, and the awkward fact that Woolf's novels stand as chronological refutation of his theory about the rise and fall of modernism,) for his attitudes. Nevertheless it is interesting to note that the same writer has generated a very wide range of interpretations of her work, with aesthetes, feminists, literary critics and Marxists all presenting totally different pictures of one subject. This difference lies only partly in the inevitably partisan accounts of such groups, and is partly to be found in the internal contradictions within the subject itself. In order to illustrate this I shall now turn to the themes and subject matter of Virginia Woolf's novels and the world view expressed in them.

In common with other writers of the period Virginia Woolf expressed in her work a very hostile reaction to the World War. Three of her characters are killed by the war, and in the case of Septimus Warren Smith she demonstrates a bitter perceptiveness of the psychological damage caused by the war. Septimus was innocent, brave and friendly at the beginning of the war, but at the end of the war he realises that he has survived (indeed, has been promoted), at the expense of his natural human feeling. His death is the outcome of this train of events, and we are given no doubt that it was the inhumanity of the war which was responsible for it.[28] This indictment is to be found explicitly stated by an earlier, and very sympathetic, Woolf character – Mrs Ambrose in *The Voyage Out* – in the following remark: '. . . it seemed to her as wrong to keep sailors as to keep a Zoo, and that as for dying on a battlefield, surely it was time we ceased to praise courage.'[29] This pacifism is part of Woolf's hostility to patriarchy, and to many of its component institutions.

One such institution was religion, which is criticised both implicitly and explicitly in Virginia Woolf's novels. In *The Waves* Neville disliked the school chapel service, and said 'The brute menaces my liberty, when he prays. Unwarmed by imagination, his words fall cold on my head like paving-stones, while the gilt cross heaves on his waistcoat. The words of authority are corrupted by those who speak them . . .'[30] Similar examples of a dislike of religion could be found in any Woolf novel, and in *Mrs Dalloway* there is a particularly strong animosity which is revealed in the hostile characterisation of the religious Miss Kilman. This novel also stresses the connections between religion and other oppressive patriarchal institutions, and it does this through the use of significant juxtaposition and metaphor. Hence an account of the crowd's reaction to possible proximity to a member of the Royal Family leads the author to add 'The spirit of religion was abroad with her eyes bandaged tight and her lips gaping wide.'[31] Religion is of course hierarchical and inhuman for Virginia Woolf, and is portrayed as the cloak under which crimes of selfishness are committed. Later in the same novel she attacks the sense of 'proportion' advocated by the complacent, middle class psychiatrist, and moves imperceptibly into anti-religious imagery: '. . . Proportion has a sister, less smiling, more formidable . . . Conversion is her name and she feasts on the wills of the weakly . . . shrouds herself in white and walks penitently disguised as brotherly love through factories and parliaments; offers help, but desires power; smites out of her way roughly the dissentient, or dissatisfied . . .'[32] In a more humorous way she frequently conveys her opinions about religion, as when Mrs Ambrose in *The Voyage Out* says of her children that 'So far, owing to enormous care on my part, they think of God as a kind of walrus . . .'[33] We should note here that Virginia Woolf's objection was to the specific type of religion (patriarchal Christianity) found in her society, and that she was to some degree amenable to mystical and neo-religious ideas.

Woolf was equally hostile to the hierarchical system of academic institutions, and considered these to be serving predominantly male interests. The portrait of Mr Ramsay in *To the Lighthouse* shows a man whose distinguished intellectual efforts are won at the expense of his wife's independence; nor is the sacrifice justified, since his philosophy does not finally make sense of the world. Woolf says of his intellect that 'It was a splendid mind. For if thought is like the keyboard of a piano, divided into so many notes, or like the alphabet is ranged in twenty-six letters all in order, then his splendid mind had no sort of difficulty in running over those letters one by one, firmly and accurately, until it had reached, say, the letter Q. He reached Q. Very few people in the whole of England ever reach Q. . . . But after Q? What comes next? After Q there are a number of letters the last of which is scarcely visible to mortal eyes, but glimmers red in the distance. Z is only reached once by one man in a generation. Still, if he could reach R it would be something.'[34] Virginia Woolf points out that he never does reach R, and concludes drily that he is like the leader of a splendid but doomed expedition whom no-one would blame when '. . . having ventured to the uttermost, and used his strength wholly to the last ounce and fallen asleep not much caring if he wakes or not, he now perceives by some pricking in his toes that he lives, and does not on the whole object to live, but requires sympathy, and whisky, and someone to tell the story of his suffering to at once.'[35]

The light tone in which the subject of academic life is treated here belies a more profound hostility on the author's part. She wrote to Lytton Strachey that she had just visited Cambridge – 'that detestable place . . . perhaps not as bad as I imagine. But when I think of it, I vomit – that's all – a green vomit, which gets into the ink and blisters the paper.'[36] This bile is not as intrusive in her work as she suspected, and indeed is often well disguised in her novels. Nevertheless she felt very strongly that the public schools and universities served patriarchal interests, and felt bitter that her own education had been so much less rigorous than that of her brothers.

Virginia Woolf's novels display an impressive awareness of the inter-relations between the different institutions of patriarchal society. I have already mentioned her hostility to war, to established religion and to the elitist educational a system of her time. In addition to this she perceived the exploitative nature of marriage and the family, and the extent to which women's domestic roles precluded their independence. This theme runs consistently through her books, from *The Voyage Out* (1915) to *Between the Acts* (1941), and is particularly strong in *Mrs Dalloway*, *To the Lighthouse* and *The Years*. Indeed in the last named novel one character expresses a total hostility – '. . . it was an abominable system, he thought; family life.'[37] It is in the novel *Mrs Dalloway* that we find the clearest exposition of the inherent corruption of patriarchal capitalist society. The assumption is made that men obtain and secure for themselves influential positions and material assets through the systematic exploitation of women and working class men. Hugh Whitbread, a symbol of conventional middle class values and masculine ideology is attacked on precisely these grounds when 'Sally suddenly lost her temper, flared up, and told Hugh that he represented all that was most detestable in British middle class life. She told him that she considered him responsible for the state of "those poor girls in Piccadilly" – Hugh, the perfect gentleman, poor Hugh! – never did a man look more horrified!'[38] Recent feminist sociology has confirmed[39] that the accusation is a just one and that working class prostitution functions to protect the bourgeois family. Similarly Woolf points very perceptively to the oppression suffered by the working class at the hands of upper middle class professional people – a good example being Septimus Warren Smith (in the same novel), whose death indicts the rich uncaring psychiatrist who neglected him.

Virginia Woolf's novels contain a fundamental criticism of bourgeois patriarchal society, and although the attack is launched mainly from a feminist perspective it encompasses to some degree a left wing critique of the class system. As I demonstrated above, this criticism has not been taken seriously by Woolf's literary critics, despite its continued oblique presence in her novels. In addition to the novels there is the non-fiction writing, in which the author states her position very clearly. Both·*A Room of One's Own* and *Three Guineas* provide us with clear accounts of the depth of her hostility to patriarchy, and of her understanding of the exploitative processes by which it is maintained. In *Three Guineas* she explicitly links together the institutions of patriarchal society, moving from war and militarism, through academic, judicial, religious and political hierarchies to an analysis of how such institutions display their power in social ritual.

Primitive though Woolf's sociology may be in comparison with current work, it is none the less impressive for the period in which she was writing. This is also true for her insight into psychological processes, and her rather cynical view of relationships between individuals. This applies especially to her treatment of relationships between the sexes, but is not restricted to these. E. M. Forster observed of the main character in *The Voyage Out* that 'Rachel has lost everything – but she has not swerved from the course honesty marked, she has not jabbered or pretended that human relationships are satisfactory'[40] – a comment which could well be applied to most of Woolf's characters. One of the major problems of relationships between individuals is simple lack of communication, as is portrayed in an incident in *The Years*. Peggy, at a party, asks a rather deaf man a question which he mishears. In response to what he thought to be her question he begins to tell some amusing stories. Peggy laughs at the absurdity of the situation, and by a fortunate coincidence her laughter occurs when he has just made a joke. She has not been listening to him. 'How many people, she wondered, listen? This "sharing", then, is a bit of a farce. She made herself attend.'[41] This cynicism becomes very much more apparent when Woolf is treating relationships between the sexes, and is present from her earliest work *The Voyage Out* in which one character remarks 'Even the Ambroses whom he admired and respected profoundly – in spite of all the love between them, was not their marriage too a compromise? She gave way to him; she spoilt him; she arranged things for him; she who was all truth to others was not true to her husband, was not true to her friends if they came in conflict with her husband. It was a strange and piteous flaw in her nature.'[42] Quentin Bell has pointed to an experience of Virginia Woolf's which may have contributed to this cynicism, as he comments of her father that 'With men his conduct was invariably gentle, considerate and rational . . . . . . But he needed and expected feminine sympathy' and to obtain it he would create the most dreadful scenes.[43]

The same theme recurs in more depth in *To the Lighthouse*, where Mrs Ramsay comments to herself that 'human relations, how flawed they are, how despicable, how self-seeking at their best.'[44] Her train of thought is continued by Lily Briscoe, who adds that '. . . the worst . . . were between men and women. Inevitably these were extremely insincere.'[45] It is clear that this criticism of relationships between the sexes rests on an aversion to traditional definitions of sex roles. Relatively frequently in Virginia Woolf's work we find examples of characters whose sexual identity is ambiguous. In *The Voyage Out* Evelyn approves of Terence because 'there's something of a woman in him', and Mrs Dalloway says of her husband 'He's a man and woman as well.'[46] The most extreme example of this is found in *Orlando*, where the protagonist flouts all the conventions of sexual characterisation by changing sex and engaging in bi-sexual conduct. Woolf's characters do not as a rule observe the conventions in these matters, for men cry, women learn mathematics, and both sexes admit attraction to others of their sex.

Woolf herself wrote that '. . . the public and the private worlds are inseparably connected; . . . the tyrannies and servilities of the one are the tyrannies and servilities of the other,'[47] and in her non-fiction work she demonstrated her hostility to the patriarchal structure which determined and corrupted relationships between men and women. The argument of *A Room of One's Own* (that women need financial independence if they are to write fiction) is pushed much further in her later work *Three Guineas*, where Woolf outlines the militaristic and hierarchical nature of patriarchal society. In this book she presents a radical feminist case, despite her own reluctance to use the word.[48] Running through the ideas in this book we find them to be strikingly radical. Woolf argues that women have a right to earn their own living, and that this is consistently denied them in practice and only recently permissable in theory. The entire educational and scientific systems militate against their being able to exercise this right. The concept of indirect power or influence, as held to apply to the case of women, reduces them to a prostitution relationship with men. Women have no capital and no power, are discriminated against in employment, and in the home are unwaged workers. They should, Woolf argues demand wages for domestic and childrearing work, and should reject the ritual (decorations, degrees, etc.) of a society from which they have gained nothing. It is very hard to reconcile this stated political position, which as I have argued above is clearly implied in the content of the novels, with the critical literature described at the outset of this discussion. It seems hardly possible that Leavis can write, influencing a generation of critics, that Virginia Woolf's writing '. . . seems to shut out all the ranges of experience accompanying those kinds of preoccupation, volitional and moral, with an external world which are not felt primarily as preoccupation with one's conciousness of it.'[49]

It is with relief, therefore, that we turn to the more recent work on Virginia Woolf in which her feminism and radical social criticism is explored. In this context we may note that Kaplan, in her *Feminine Conciousness in the Modern British Novel*, stresses the radical and anti-authoritarian attitudes that Woolf shared with other women writers from Dorothy Richardson to Doris Lessing.[50] Leaska's study of *To the Lighthouse*[51] first raised the possibility that the figure of Mrs Ramsay was not one that Virginia Woolf admired, and the point is pressed home in Heilbrun's important work on androgyny in Woolf's fiction:- '. . . it is only in groping our way through the clouds of sentiment and misplaced biographical information that we are able to discover Mrs Ramsay, far from androgynous or complete, to be as one-sided and as life-denying as her husband. Readers have seldom been clear as to whether her son and daughter reach the lighthouse because her spirit has survived her death, or because her death has liberated her children.'[52]

Heilbrun argues, after Millett, that Woolf's reputation as a feminist has suffered from the repressive sexual counter-revolution of the period following 1930 and continuing until around 1960. Certainly it is interesting to look at the production of Woolf criticism in these terms, since if we take works specifically concerned with the theme of feminism and sexual politics we find that for every one Heilbrun published there will be a large batch of hostile or misguided interpretations. Batchelor, for example, claims that Virginia Woolf found feminism 'aesthetically unacceptable' and that it is hardly ever present in her work; instead she is concerned with 'womanhood', which the writer obviously finds more acceptable himself.[53] In different ways Marder, Naremore and Bazin, in recent works on Woolf[54] all reduce her world view to a sexual polarisation which she herself explicitly opposed. On the theme of feminism in Virginia Woolf we are left with a very small number of works which provide illuminating discussion – such as Holtby(1934) and Heilbrun – and a great deal of prejudice. Not all of this prejudice is anti-feminist in origin, as can be seen from Hennig's virulent attack on the male members of Virginia Woolf's family,[55] which she makes in order to establish Woolf as a feminist lesbian. It is relatively rarely that one comes across an interpretation of Virginia Woolf, such as the one offered by Richter,[56] in which a balanced discussion of these topics occurs in the general context of the work.

Virginia Woolf's interest in feminism and bi-sexuality has perhaps led to a rather simple view of her life and work (as with Sylvia Plath, she is held to be one of the women's movement's 'martyrs'). How then can we reconcile the two views of Virginia Woolf propounded by the critics (upper class twit versus radical feminist) with each other and the works themselves? The answer to this problem lies partly in an account of the ideological factors influencing the judgements of literary critics at various historical periods, and partly in the inconsistencies to be found in Virginia Woolf's work. Taking the first item it is important to observe the way sex and class prejudices are played off against each other. As an example I could quote an article about Woolf which appeared in *Scrutiny* in 1932, written by a female English Literature don, M. C. Bradbrook. The writer complains that Woolf's heroines are too dependent and ingenous, and that they do not engage in intelligent thinking – which they regard as a masculine activity. Also she objects to the structure and tone of *A Room of One's Own*, as she feels '. . . it prevents Mrs Woolf from committing the indelicacy of putting a case or the possibility of her being accused of waving any kind of banner.' She concludes that 'To demand "thinking" from Mrs Woolf is clearly illegitimate: but such a deliberate repudiation of it and such a smoke screen of feminine charm is surely to be deprecated. Mrs Woolf has preserved her extraordinary fineness and delicacy of perception at the cost of some cerebral etiolation.'[57] This accusation stems directly from the ideological position found among *Scrutiny* contributors, to which Virginia Woolf was opposed. Not only were they anti-feminist (for example Q. D. Leavis reviewed *Three Guineas* in *Scrutiny*, suggesting that 'The position then with regard to further female emancipation seems to be that the onus is on women to prove that they are going to be able to justify it, and that it will not vitally dislocate (what it has already seriously disturbed – and no responsible person can regard that without uneasiness) the framework of our culture. . . Certainly there is no longer any use in this field of speculation for the non-specialist like Mrs Woolf';[58] they were opposed to Woolf on more general artistic and political grounds.

Scrutiny propounded a cultural elitism and conservatism which was to be disseminated hierarchically from English Literature departments in universities (preferably Cambridge). It took the form of supporting the great tradition of bourgeois realism, and condemning other types of writing. In this it is clear that Woolf was totally antipathetic in both her literary technique and her political views to the Scrutiny view of literature. Empson sums up the objection to Woolf by quoting her view that '. . . the great revelation perhaps never did come. Instead there were little daily miracles, illuminations, matches struck unexpectedly in the dark.' To which his own response is that '. . . it is the business of art to provide candelabra, to aggregate its matches into a light house of many candlepower.'[59] In this he asks Woolf to be a realist writer, which she clearly could never be, and it is a combination of her radical politics and modernist style which makes her so unacceptable to the highly influential *Scrutiny* stream of criticism. Many of the quotations given at the beginning of this article reiterate the objections of the Scrutineers.

Marxist literary critics have in a parallel manner written off Virginia Woolf's work as decadent, bourgeois, introspective and limited in historical materialist understanding. Again Woolf has suffered particularly in not espousing a realist style, since the early English Marxists were impressed by socialist realism and critical judgements were handed down with little re-evaluation (prior to recent developments in the theory of ideology and discourse). The decade in which Virginia Woolf's reputation might have been thoroughly consolidated (the 30s) saw an upsurge of interest, through *Left Review* and the publication of much Marxist writing, in the experience of ordinary working class people as the legitimate subject matter of fiction. Despite the fact that Woolf identifies in her writing with the underprivileged and uneducated of her characters (such as Septimus Warren Smith), rather than with the successful bourgeoisie, there is sufficient surface concern with middle class intellectual life for a negative judgement to have been made. This, I would argue, results mainly from a superficial reading which pays little attention to the profound social criticism in her work and over-emphasises the bourgeois life style which is ironically presented in them. In this context Michelene Wandor has pointed out[60] that for the English Marxists a critical breakthrough was achieved when the importance of 'being determines conciousness' was realised. The recognition that conciousness was not autonomous (as Scrutiny and the tradition of conservative criticism had always assumed), but was shaped and determined by material conditions, was a crucial one. It is one, as I have tried to show above, that Virginia Woolf made in both her fiction and non-fiction writing from her earliest works.

It may be argued that Woolf was in many respects a writer of great interest to Marxists of the period, but that the value of her ideas was not realised by them. This is partly because she adopted the anti-realist, modernist style which Lukács and other Marxist critics objected to, and partly because her political Radicalism is implied rather than belaboured in the novels themselves. Also one may suspect that her strong feminism was the reason for her work being systematically denigrated from a Marxist point of view. The possibility of a socialist feminism has only arisen since theoretical advances in our understanding of the position of women in the capitalist economy were made, and until then there was a distinct tendency to polarise and stress the differences between Marxist and feminist points of view.

Thus it would appear that for different reasons Virginia Woolf has been denigrated from both the right and the left of the literary critical spectrum. In both cases we can observe a hostility to her modernist style, and it is worth noting that the true radical nature of modernism has only been appreciated outside England.[61] Also in a general sense it can be said that Virginia Woolf has suffered from the anti-feminism of the male critical establishment (as well as of male left wing critics), and that her reputation has suffered from allegations of triviality, domesticatedness and so on. There are, however, other reasons why Virginia Woolf's critical reputation is an ambiguous one, and these lie within the author herself. In her work we find reflected the contradictions which she experienced within herself, and which she never satisfactorily resolved. Thus if we look again at the characterisation of Mrs Ramsay in *To the Lighthouse* we can see that she was a compelling figure, that she comanded love and admiration from the author; nevertheless her values were pernicious. It is of course generally true that no individual can by sheer force of intellect and will power totally emancipate him or herself from the emotional make-up which upbringing and enviroment have inculcated. To a degree Virginia Woolf, like many of us, had to accept that her personality and emotions had been formed by ideologies which she deplored. The resultant conflict is not resolved in her work, as I have demonstrated elsewhere.[62]

One could make a case here for the particular difficulties attached to the position of women. Virginia Woolf, in company with Simone de Beauvoir and others, commented on the difficulties encountered in trying to free her writing from the inhibitions created by a sexually repressive childhood. In *Three Guineas* she digresses from her argument that women should eschew patriotism, in order to say:- 'And if, when reason has had its say, still some obstinate emotion remains, some love of England dropped into a child's ears by the cawing of rooks in an elm tree, by the splash of waves on a beach, or by English voices murmuring nursery rhymes, this drop of pure, if irrational, emotion she will make serve her to give England first what she desires of peace and freedom for the whole world.'[63] Obstinate, irrational emotion was to infiltrate Virginia Woolf's work at the expense of consistency in her literary and political theories. In her novels she failed to achieve her androgynous ideal, and we find many elements of mysticism and privatisation which are discordant with the political feminism underlying the books. This obstinate, irrational emotion was her own, although by no means her worst, enemy.

University of Hull

1. L. Edel; *The Psychological Novel, 1900-1950*, Hart Davis, London, 1961. p127

2. ibid. p. 131

3. ibid. p. 133

4. J. Rosenberg; *Dorothy Richardson, The Genius They Forgot* Duckworth, London, 1973. p. 168-9

5. J. Guiguet; *Virginia Woolf and her Works*, Hogarth, London, 1965. p. 244

6. ibid.

7. E. Auerbach; *Mimesis The Representation of Reality in Western Literature*, Princeton U.P., 1971.

8. E. Hardwick; *Seduction and Betrayal, Women and Literature*, Weidenfeld, London, 1974. p. 134

9. W. Allen; *The English Novel*, Penguin, Harmondsworth, 1965. p. 347-351

10. See N. Annan; 'The Intellectual Aristocracy', *in* Plumb, J. H. (ed) *Studies in Social History*, Longman, London, 1955. p. 243-287

11. M. Bradbury; *The Social Context of Modern English Literature*, Blackwell, Oxford, 1971.

12. M. Bradbury; 'The Novel in the 1920s' *in* Bergonzi, B (ed) *The Twentieth Century*, (Vol 7, Sphere History of English Literature), Sphere, London, 1970. p. 191

13. ibid. p.201

14. Edel; op. cit. p.133

15. F. Delattre; *Le Roman Psychologique de Virginia Woolf*, Librairie Philosophique, Paris, 1932. p. 226-7 (Trans. MB)

16. Allen; op. cit. p. 347ff

17. G. S. Fraser; *The Modern Writer and His World*, Penguin, Harmondsworth, 1970. p. 117

18. D. Daiches; *The Novel and the Modern World*, Chicago U. P., 1960, p. 199-200

19. A. J. P. Taylor; *English History 1914-1945*, Clarendon, Oxford, 1966. p. 311

20. Bradbury; *in* Bergonzi (ed): op. cit. p. 199

21. E. Hardwick; 'Bloomsbury and Virginia Woolf',*in* Hardwick, op. cit.

22. ibid. p. 136

23. Bradbury *in* Bergonzi; op. cit.

24. ibid. p. 198

25. ibid. p. 196

26. ibid. p. 203

27. Hardwick; op. cit. p. 139

28. V. Woolf; *Mrs Dalloway*, Penguin, Harmondsworth, 1973, p. 203

29. V. Woolf; *The Voyage Out*, Hogarth Press, London, p. 75

30. V. Woolf; *The Waves*, Penguin, Harmondsworth, 1972, p 29

31. V. Woolf; *Mrs Dalloway*, p. 17

32. V. Woolf; *Mrs Dalloway*, p. 111

33. V. Woolf; *The Voyage Out*, p. 23

34. V. Woolf; *To the Lighthouse*, p. 29

35. V. Woolf; *To the Lighthouse* p. 43

36. V. Woolf; to L. Strachey; *Letters*, Hogarth, London, 1956, p. 38

37. V. Woolf; *The Years*, Hogarth, London, p. 239

38. V. Woolf; *Mrs Dalloway*, p. 81

39. See for example M. McIntosh; unpublished work on the sociology of prostitution, (University of Essex).

40. E. M. Forster; 'The Early Novels of Virginia Woolf' repr. *in* Majumdar, R & McLaurin, A. (eds.); *Virginia Woolf, The Critical Heritage*, RKP, London, 1975, p.172

41. V. Woolf; *The Years*, p. 283

42. V. Woolf; *The Voyage Out*, Hogarth, London, p. 242

43. Q. Bell; *Virginia Woolf, A Biography*, Hogarth, London, 1972, Vol 1, p. 63

44. V. Woolf; *To the Lighthouse*, Hogarth, London. p. 69

45. V. Woolf; *To the Lighthouse*, p. 144

46. V. Woolf; *The Voyage Out*, Hogarth, London, p. 302 & 65

47. V. Woolf; *Three Guineas*, Hogarth, London, p. 258

48. V. Woolf; *Three Guineas*, p. 184. Woolf claims that the feminist struggle is part of a larger struggle for justice, equality and liberty.

49. F. R. Leavis; 'After *To the Lighthouse*',*in Scrutiny* Vol. 10, 1942.

50. S. J. Kaplan; *Feminine Conciousness in the Modern British Novel*, Urbana, Illinois U.P., 1975.

51. M. A. Leaska; *Virginia Woolf's Lighthouse: a study in critical method.* Hogarth, London, 1970.

52. C. Heilbrun; *Towards Androgyny*, Gollancz, London, 1973, p. 155

53. J. B. Batchelor; 'Feminism in Virginia Woolf *in* C. Sprague, (ed): *Virginia Woolf*, Prentice-Hall, New Jersey, 1971.

54. H. Marder; *Feminism and Art: a study of Virginia Woolf*, Chicago U.P., 1968.
J. Naremore; *The World Without a Self: Virginia Woolf and the Novel*, Yale U.P., 1973.
N. Bazin; *Virginia Woolf and the Androgynous Vision*, Rutgers U.P., New Jersey, 1973.

55. S. Hennig; Review of *Virginia Woolf: A Biography* by Q. Bell *in Virginia Woolf Quarterly*, California State University Press, San Diego (School of Literature), 1972.

56. H. Richter; *Virginia Woolf, The Inward Voyage*, Princeton, U.P., 1970.

57. M. C. Bradbrook; 'Notes on the Style of Mrs Woolf', *Scrutiny* May 1932, pp 33-8

58. Q. D. Leavis; Review of *Three Guineas, Scrutiny*, Sept. 1938, pp 212-14

59. W. Empson; 'Virginia Woolf' in E. Rickword, (ed): *Scrutinies by Various Writers*, London, 1931, p. 216

60. M. Wandor; *Literary Theory and Literary Criticism in Britain in the 1930s*, Unpublished MA dissertation, University of Essex, p. 67

61. Bradbury deals rather inadequately with this question in his *The Social Context of Modern English Literature*; otherwise we are left with the Marxists' accounts, from which not only Woolf but other English writers are invariably left out. See for example G. Lukács: 'The Ideology of Modernism' in *The Meaning of Contemporary Realism*, Merlin, London, 1972.

62. M. V. Barrett; *A Theory of Modernism and English Society Between the Wars, With Particular Reference to Virginia Woolf*, Unpublished D. Phil. Thesis, University of Sussex.

63. V. Woolf; *Three Guineas*, op. cit. p. 197-8

Propaganda and Ideology in Women's Fiction

Helen Roberts

> ' . . . what had happened to me, that I, who had seemed cut out for
> some extremity or other, should be here now bending over a washing
> machine to pick out a button or two and some bits of soggy wet
> cotton? They would not think much of me now, I thought, if they
> could see me; those Marxists in Rome, those historians and
> photographers in Hampstead, those undergraduates in two
> universities.[1]

The above question from Margaret Drabble's novel *The Garrick Year*
highlights in an acute form one of the problems raised by Arnold Hauser
in his recent essay on propaganda, ideology and art.[2] In this essay,
Hauser argues very cogently for a distinction between ideology and
propaganda in relation to works of art. Propaganda, he claims, is less
efficient than ideology in convincing the reader as it is more explicit and
can therefore be criticised at a conscious level. He makes the distinction
as follows:

> 'Art contains propaganda, assertion and intent if the artist expresses
> his political views in such a way that they remain distinguishable and
> separable from the strictly aesthetic factors of his work. In art with an
> ideological content on the other hand, the philosophic and
> corresponding political motifs form an inseparable unity with the
> work's other components: the universal intent – the ideology –
> interlocks with the aesthetic structure and is completely integrated into
> the totality of the artistic creation.[3]

He goes on, however, to make the important point that,

> ' . . . the artist's position in both is equally partisan and is in
> furtherance of certain interests, no matter whether this expresses itself
> through overt propaganda or hidden ideology. The difference is
> merely tactical . . . and does not affect the aesthetic stature or the
> artistic validity and suitability of the means employed.'[4]

It is clear that a great deal of fiction – and not only the fiction
produced by writers with a stated and explicit political commitment – is
a vehicle for propaganda and ideology of different types. In what ways
are propaganda and ideology evident in fiction written by and for
women? And how far is a stated political position compatible with
subtlety and smoothness of style?

Clearly, it is by no means only in fiction such as the example quoted
above that a challenge is posed to the traditional romanticized view of
childbirth and maternity. Margaret Drabble in *The Millstone* writes:

'One hears much, though mostly from the interested male, about the beauty of a woman with child, ships in full sail, and all that kind of metaphorical euphemism, and I suppose that from time to time on the faces of well-fed, well-bred young ladies I have seen a certain peaceful glow, but the weight of evidence is overwhelmingly on the other side. Anaemia and exhaustion were written on most countenances: the clothes were dreadful, the legs swollen, the bodies heavy and unbalanced . . .'[5]

Like Drabble, Fay Weldon is concerned with housewives and mothers and she describes the limitation of their lives. 'We are the cleaners', Weldon writes.

'We empty ashtrays which tomorrow will be filled again. We sweep the floors which tomorrow will be dusty . . . When she dies it will be said of her, she was a wonderful wife and mother. She cooked a hundred thousand meals, swept a million floors, washed a billion dishes, went through the cupboards and searched for missing buttons.'
' . . . Down among the women, we don't like chaos. We will crawl from our sickbeds to tidy and define. We live at floor level, washing and wiping. If we look upward, it's not toward the stars or the ineffable, it's to dust the tops of the windows. We have only ourselves to blame.'[6]

These extracts raise in an exploratory way the problems of stating social or political problems in an *explicit* manner in literature. The attitudes expressed challenge not only accepted views of women, but also the conventional definition of suitable subject matter for the novel, and so intrude harshly on the reader's consciousness. It is legitimate to examine the degree to which such challenges succeed in their object. Before examining in some detail ways in which it might be possible to analyse social change in women's literature, we may ask what can be said of the other side of the coin – the vast amount of literature for women which does not raise the conflicts and problems experienced daily by many of its women readers?

I shall be arguing below that there is a considerable body of literature read by women, and to a considerable extent written particularly *for* women, which seems to be deliberately lagging behind changes which are taking place in the 'real' world, and which rejects outside pressure for women to play new roles. This literature not only reflects but also endorses the dominant ideology so that readers are presented with a clear, if simplified view of the world and of a woman's place within it. Foremost among such fiction is that to be found in the high circulation women's magazines. Although women's magazines have in the past been ignored by the sociologists of literature, presumably on the grounds that they are ephemeral and thus unworthy of his (her) attention, they are not only remarkably enduring as a market but the content and themes of the stories published in them have been anything but transitory.

The imaginary world of women's magazine fiction knows of no illnesses or accidents which do not add to rather than detract from the allure of the hero or heroine; it knows of no real poverty, and politics are ignored. War, even in wartime issues of the magazines, tends to be discussed only as a rather glamorous background to love stories; marriages only very exceptionally break up, and then only so that a more suitable partner may immediately be found to restore faith in the power of love. It need scarcely be said that the children of this imaginary world, even if occasionally naughty, never become juvenile delinquents. Pregnancy, like sex, is never examined critically in women's magazines fiction, but is described obliquely in terms of the tender emotions it calls forth and the sentimental images of childhood which it provokes. A young man selling nursery furniture in one 1968 issue of *Woman* experiences the mystique which surrounds pregnant women: 'Expectant mothers were a breed apart . . . creatures of secret wisdom.'[7] Two years later, a *Woman* heroine looking round the garden of a new house reflects: 'It was a place . . . for little children in faded shorts with scratched knees; a place for a swing under the cherry tree. A place she would love.'[8] It is not only the shortness of stories appearing in women's magazines that dictates the stereotyped images of women presented in them and the type of sentiments offered, as can be seen if one turns to those full-length romantic novels written by women largely for women's consumption. It is interesting to note that the most popular type of romantic fiction is the historical novel – a genre automatically favouring traditional roles for its heroines. To take an example, Georgette Heyer's novel *Powder and Patch* provides numerous instances of a traditional and stereotyped view of woman. The heroine is of course traditionally beautiful: 'She had thick gold curls, eyes of cornflower blue, and a pair of red lips that pouted or smiled in equal fascination. She was just eighteen and the joy and despair of all the young men of the countryside.'[9] But however beautiful, women are seen as both cunning and stupid: 'You should know by now that no woman means what she says when it's to a man.'[10] Even more alarmingly, one of Heyer's characters in this book asserts that: 'Women don't want gentle politeness! . . . They like a man to be brutal.'[11] Cartland, writing in a similar vein, has a male admirer of her heroine make an engaging analogy between women and horses – drawing on the fact that both have to be 'broken in': 'And damn it all, I like looking at you. As I have told you already, you are a beautiful creature – but rather like an unbroken filly at the moment. Sooner or later, a filly learns to obey her master's hand.'[12]

The foregoing merely serve to indicate the well-worn view of women current in some contemporary literature written by and for women. Between the literature of this type, and the literature which might be said to be ahead of its time, and sensitive to the very beginnings of social change, I would suggest that there is a third very important and highly interesting intermediate category.

This intermediate category consists of a literature of acceptance which comments on the changes taking place and explores their implications. This literature examines the consequences of oppressive ideologies without actually questioning them. This is the type of fiction in which a backlog of ideas about romantic love are in a state of friction with those ideas of independence for women which are embodied in political, social and economic changes. One method useful in analysing the way in which literature reflects cultural, social and political changes is to pick out certain salient themes and examine the ways in which these appear (or fail to appear) in different types of literature over a historical period. In order to analyse changes in the situation of women as portrayed in literature, I looked at three themes which encapsulate the sociological dimension of changes in women's situation between 1900 and 1970.

Ideologies of romantic love are used to legitimate marriage and the family as such, not merely the position of the woman in the family. Any challenge to such ideologies is a challenge to the family as a key institution of modern industrial society, and not just to the role of women within it. Secondly, *role conflict* and *role distance* arise when women's traditional roles are challenged, and wider opportunities offered. A discussion of role conflict in literature underlines women's increasing contact with secondary roles and with agencies outside domestic life. Thirdly, themes of *fate and chance* are often employed to convey an implicit view of the social system. A malign fate indicates its constraints and inequalities, a benign fate its 'openness'.

Thus in these three themes we can obtain insight into a writer's assumptions about social mobility, the function of the family and the possible roles open to women, all of which are key factors in a sociological account of their changing position.

Before looking at general fiction, it might be useful to recall the sort of changes which were taking place in the position of women at the turn of the century. The Married Woman's Property Act of 1870 meant that women could keep their own earnings whilst still living with their husbands and, in 1875, a law was passed enabling women to go to university. The 1882 Married Women's Property Act gave a wife the right to own property and dispose of it whatever way she wished, and the 1907 Qualification of Women Act allowed women to become councillors. To what extent did these and other changes affect the work of contemporary women novelists?

Two enormously popular writers at the turn of the century were Marie Corelli and Mrs. Humphrey Ward. The sort of romantic love ideologies later to appear in women's magazine fiction appear in Corelli's work, but are not altogether subscribed to. David, in *The Treasure of Heaven* speaks of his first marriage: 'Then I "fell" in love – and married on the faith of that emotion, which is always a mistake. "Falling in love" is not loving.'[13] While a friend, speaking of the old man's search for love says: 'A fit of romance has seized him late in life – and he wants to be loved for himself alone – which, of course, at his age is absurd! No-one loves old people, except perhaps (in very rare cases) their children . . .'[14]

It is, of course, part of the traditional love ideology of women's magazines and popular literature that in order to be loved one has to be young and beautiful, but the sort of unpalatable sentiments expressed above concerning those who do not have these valuable qualities are never specifically articulated in these same magazines. It might well be suggested, without subscribing to any conspiracy theory of the media, that the extent to which women's magazines subscribe to ideologies concerning romantic love is not unrelated to the economic interests of these magazines and the way in which advertisers in womens magazines (and even more in magazines for teenage girls) sell their products through implicit or explicit statements that these will make the woman look more beautiful, look younger (if a woman's magazine) or more mature (if a teenage magazine) and therefore be more lovable.

Much comes through from the image of women in *The Treasure of Heaven* which supports Corelli's own stated feelings concerning women. Notwithstanding the rather critical approach to romantic love quoted above, the bulk of Corelli's work endorses traditional attitudes. David talking to a young woman, says: 'Many good, many beautiful, many delicate women "do something" as you put it, for a living . . . But the fight is always fierce, and the end is sometimes bitter. It is better for a woman that she should be safeguarded by a husband's care and tenderness, than that she should attempt to face the world alone.'[15] The women's magazine tradition of regarding learning among women with suspicion, is similarly approved. David, talking to the same young woman says, 'You are not clever, and I am glad you are not. You are good and pure and true, these graces outweigh all cleverness.'[16]

Later the suffrage is referred to directly: 'Women are doing a great deal of mischief just now. Look at them fussing about female suffrage. Female suffrage quotha! Let them govern their homes properly, wisely, reasonably, faithfully, and they will govern the nation!'[17] Ruskin's ideas[18] on the influence of women, later to be found too in Mrs. Humphrey Ward's work, can be seen in the following: 'A woman who really loves a man . . . governs him, unconsciously to herself, by the twin powers of sex and instinct. She was intended for his helpmate, to guide him in the right way by her finer forces . . .'[19]

Mrs. Humphrey Ward, like Corelli, was a popular and prolific writer, although while any propaganda in Corelli's work tends to be in the religious field, Ward's work is very much concerned with social and political themes. A contemporary critic comments: 'When we think of the number of women of the rebellious type whom Mrs. Ward has drawn, and drawn too with no small amount of sympathy and insight . . . we should almost expect to find her among the feminists; but she is not to be found in that camp.'[20] Indeed, Ward was very active in the anti-suffrage campaign between 1908 and 1914; her daughter wrote that her mother was 'practically the only speaker of rank on her own side.'[21] Although an anti-suffragist, Mrs. Ward made her heroines on the whole strong, independent and intelligent women – an apparent paradox which reveals in this instance an interesting relationship between the author's ideological position and the views implicit in her fiction. Such a paradox may be resolved by a more careful analysis of the assumptions made by this author.

When in *Lady Rose's Daughter*, Julie has the opportunity to live on a relative's money rather than work, she declares: 'It is more amusing to earn one's own living'[22] and more acutely (recalling Virginia Woolf's argument in *A Room of One's Own*[23] that economic independence is necessary for psychological independence),' '. . . Besides, if Lord Lackington gives me money, he will want to give me advice, and I would rather advise myself.'[24] At the same time, however, housework is extolled in this novel in much the same terms as in women's magazines: 'As she washed and tidied and dusted, a true housewife's love growing up in her for the little house and its charming old world appointments – a sort of mute relation between her and it, as though it accepted her for mistress, and she on her side vowed it a delicate and prudent care.'[25]

Romantic love ideologies are firmly scotched in *Lady Rose's Daughter* where Julie, as a Frenchwoman, is not horrified at the idea of a dowry, although since settling in England, this has been mingled with: '. . . the more English idea of "falling in love".'[26] – the idea which puts personal choice first in marriage and makes the matter of dowry subordinate to that mysterious election and affinity which the Englishman calls 'love'. Nor does Julie subscribe to the enthusiasm of many of Barbara Cartland's heroines for assertive, almost brutal men. Indeed, like other of Mrs. Ward's heroines, she has a horror of sacrificing her independence to a domineering husband. Even while in the depths of infatuation for a man, she exclaims: 'No! She would show him that she was *not* his chattel, to be taken or left on his own terms.'[27]

It can be seen from the above that Mrs. Ward's work was in many respects ahead of its time in considering the conflicts facing women once they step outside the orbit of the home and family. Nevertheless, the contradictions in her work are resolved in favour of traditional attitudes. Her heroines may be strong, yet they still capitulate at the end to some degree. Role conflict is never severe, and the sanctity of the patriarchal family is not seriously questioned.

Moving forward to the twenties, thirties and forties, we may note several social changes as background information. After the First World War women over the age of thirty gained the vote, although there was not universal suffrage until 1928. The numerical preponderance of women over men was at its height in 1921 and in 1923 the birthrate fell to 20 per thousand for the first time. The Sex Disqualification Removal Act did away with some of the erstwhile barriers to women; higher education was increasingly open to them and between the wars equal pay was achieved in most of the professions, although not in the Civil Service and teaching. As for cultural life A. J. P. Taylor writes: 'The cinema changed the pattern of English life, particularly for the lower middle class. It took people from their homes; spread romantic, but by no means trivial values. Women joined their husbands in enjoyment, as they had never done at football matches or other public pleasures.'[28]

One well-known author of this period was E. M. Delafield, whose *Provincial Lady* series was particularly popular. The books are based on the diary of a middle-class Devonshire woman. To what extent the Provincial Lady's observations should be interpreted in terms of role conflict is arguable, but certainly she constantly assesses and reassesses herself and questions her thoughts, actions and assumptions. Having tactlessly said in front of her husband that the most wonderful thing in the world must be to be a childless widow, she reflects: 'Should often be very very sorry to say what exactly it is I *do* mean, and am in fact conscious of deliberately avoiding self-analysis on many occasions. Do not propose, however, to go into this now or at any other time.'[29] Later, she is conscious of avoiding the truth when she is talking to a female friend:

> 'Barbara says it is sometimes very difficult to know which way Duty lies, that she has always thought a true woman's highest vocation was homemaking, and that the love of a Good Man is the Crown of Life. I say Yes Yes to all of this. (Discover on thinking it over, that I do not agree with any of it, and am shocked at my own extraordinary duplicity).'[30]

This sort of duplicity has been discussed by Simone de Beauvoir, and more recently, by Trevor Pateman. De Beauvoir speaks of the passive acceptance of women in being defined as the Other, and explains this irresponsibility and bad faith in the following terms: ' . . . along with the ethical urge of each individual to affirm his subjective existence, there is also the temptation to forgo liberty and become a thing. . . . When man makes of woman the Other, he may then expect her to manifest deep-seated tendencies towards complicity.' Pateman notes the conservatism consequent on such duplicity: '. . . such evasions sustain, in practice, all existing social institutions, since they stand in the way of any critical (reflective) consciousness.'[31]

As a housewife, a writer and a mother, the Provincial Lady is all too well aware of the problems involved in running a home, albeit with the cook and two servants customary in an upper middle class home at the time. As a housewife, she asks a question only very recently to have been seriously tackled by sociologists: 'Query, mainly rhetorical: Why are non-professional women, if married and with children, so frequently refered to as "leisured"? Answer comes there none.'[32]

As far as love ideologies and the themes of fate and chance are concerned, the Provincial Lady has no need of either, being too sensible to subscribe to the former and too well organised for the intervention of fate and chance to be necessary in her life. She provides a very good example of developing role conflicts in her determined attempts to pursue her career as a writer at the same time as being a competent wife and mother. Winifred Holtby and Dorothy Sayers, both of whom were writing novels during this period, are perhaps more interesting than the case of E. M. Delafield. In their novels they explore in some detail the arguments put forward by the new independent woman and examine the social consequences of her emancipation.

Winifred Holtby was a WAAC in the First World War and a student at Somerville. Among her critical works was a volume on Virginia Woolf, whom she greatly admired, and a book on women and social change.[33] Perhaps her best known novel is *South Riding*, a study of local government and politics, which was written in 1936. The most recent edition selects the following passage for a preface, thus preparing the reader for a traditional romantic novel:

> 'As they danced together in the hotel ballroom, Sarah kept reminding herself of all the things she detested about Carne: but it was no use. His arm was round her, his hand held her hand, she could feel the hard uneven thumping of his heart. With her body pressed to his, she thought, I know what movement he will make before he does it, but I know nothing of his mind, and I can never learn his heart. But she knew her own heart, and suddenly, this contact of her body with his, which she desired so hungrily, became unbearable.'[34]

However, the above quotation misrepresents the tone of the story. For this novel, far more than those already considered, contains a great deal of pertinent comment and argument on the position of women and particularly on the conflict facing professional women in reconciling their work lives with their emotional needs. The central character of *South Riding* is Sarah, the headmistress of a prestigious Yorkshire High School, a character who looks 'with disfavour' at one of her mistresses who suggests:

> 'What I always say is, – the really important thing is to equip these girls for life. And most of them will go into shops or become nursemaids, or help their mothers run lodging houses till they marry. So really, so long as they've *been* to the High School and can count as high school girls, I don't see it matters so much what they *do* here. Speaking honestly as a woman if you know what I mean.'[35]

Sarah's own point of view becomes clear sometime later when she explains: '. . . my trouble is to persuade my girls that membership of my profession need not imply complete indifference to all other sides of life.'[36] She goes on to explain why she does not feel that teaching and an interest in one's appearance are incompatible. This is a far cry from the stereotype of the ugly 'bluestocking' found in most romantic fiction. Sarah makes the point: ' . . . I regard lipstick as a symbol of self-respect, of interest in one's appearance, of a hopeful and self-assured attitude towards life.'[37]

Winifred Holtby's anger about the position of women in society is made clear when she writes, describing the bric-à-brac cluttering the drawers of one of her female character's homes: 'The indictment of a whole social system lay in those drawers if they but knew it – a system which overworks eight-tenths of its female population, and gives the remaining two-tenths so little to do that they must clutter the world with useless objects.'[38]

Sarah's wish to sleep with one of the school governors is examined in some detail: '"He's drunk", she thought. "And he takes me now for a little tart. That's the kind of man he is. That's the kind of way he thinks of women – all but his wife. I'm a little tart."' And later, 'Her mind was quite cold. "He is drunk" she thought. "He has forgotten who I am or who he is; he thinks – I am a little tart. Well? I am Sarah Burton. I have Kiplington High School; he is a governor. This may destroy me. I will be his little tart, I will comfort him for one night."'[39]

This situation however is solved (in one sense) by Carne, the governor, having a heart attack as soon as he reaches Sarah's room. The virtue of the headmistress is threatened but saved. The important point here however, is that Sarah does make a choice. She sees the possibilities open to her, sees the dangers, but is able to make a deliberate decision. A manipulation of the plot in the manner described above so that Carne suffers a heart attack before the virtue of a respectable woman is lost may well indicate that Holtby's views on such relationships were ambivalent. Certainly as it stands there is an inconsistency between the arguments propounded ('propaganda') by Holtby's heroine, and the working of the plot in a more traditional romantic framework. From a historical point of view Holtby's case might be an interesting one to examine in detail as an indicator of the ideological complexities and contradictions in women's thought at this period. It is not clear whether this example is an intentional or unintentional illustration of the author's attitudes.

Writing in a different genre at this time was Dorothy L. Sayers, whose work provides interesting examples of the conflicts facing professional women and also of the dilemma facing an author in deciding her career. Her biographer writes:

> 'With cold calculation, she wrote what she knew would sell, but she was too much of a scholar, and had too much feeling for her creations, to write "cheap thillers", and whatever she wrote, she could not resist the urge to educate.'[40]

The two novels in the Peter Wimsey series which deal most fully with his romance with Harriet Vane are worth looking at in some detail. At a college reception at the beginning of *Gaudy Night*, Harriet's reaction to a brash American scholar's views on eugenics and marriage throw some light on her views of marriage: 'Harriet agreed that intellectual women should marry and reproduce their kind; but she pointed out that the English husband had something to say in the matter and that, very often, he did not care for an intellectual wife.'[41]

Harriet herself had been reflecting only a few pages earlier on her relationship with Wimsey: '. . . I could have liked him so much if I could have met him on an equal footing.'[42] Later, however, she is to find that possibly she can meet him on this equal footing. Knowing that she is in quite considerable danger, Wimsey has written to her and she considers his letters:

> ' . . . he had deliberately acknowledged that she had the right to run her own risks. "Do be careful of yourself", "I hate to think of your being exposed to unpleasantness"; "If only I could be there to protect you"; any such phrase would express the normal male reaction. Not one man in ten thousand would say to the woman he loved, or to any woman; "Disagreeableness and danger will not turn you back, and God forbid they should." That was an admission of equality, and she had not expected it of him. If he conceived of marriage along those lines, then the whole position would have to be reviewed in that new light.'[43]

It is not only marriage with which this novel is concerned however. Comment is also made on more general matters, as when one of the women dons says:

> ' . . . look at this university. All the men have been amazingly kind and sympathetic about the women's colleges. Certainly. But you won't find them appointing women to big university posts. That would never do. The women might perform their work in a way beyond criticism. But they are quite pleased to see us playing with our little toys.'[44]

Although there is little expression of the ideologies of romantic love in *Gaudy Night* there is satire on this subject. Wimsey has been teaching Harriet how to defend herself – an operation which involved a certain amount of manhandling – and Harriet sits smoking afterwards: ' . . . mentally turning the incidents of the last hour into a scene in a book . . . and thinking how, with a little vulgarity on both sides, it could be worked up into a nice piece of exhibitionism for the male and provocation for the female concerned.'[45] Dorothy Sayers professed herself not to care for love interest in a detective story, but in fact *Busman's Honeymoon* while ostensibly a detective novel, is based on the honeymoon following Harriet's marriage to Peter Wimsey. One question to arise concerns the distribution of income after marriage, and the way in which this affects a wife's independence. It is significant that although Wimsey *claims* to be aware of the difficulties experienced by

Harriet in accepting his enormous wealth, he argues: 'Either your pride or mine will have to be sacrificed – I can only appeal to your generosity to let it be yours.'[46]

From the point of view of a study of women writers, Dorothy L. Sayers is an interesting case. Highly intelligent and with a writing career of great potential, she nevertheless spent the greater part of her career writing in a genre which traditionally is not taken very seriously. It was not until she had earned enough from her detective writing to secure her independence that she turned to more serious areas. Nevertheless, it is clear from the extracts given above that even in her detective novels she goes into the problems facing women in some depth, although offering no real solutions. In spite of an intelligent and independent heroine, Harriet, Wimsey is always the leader, Harriet always one step behind. As his great brain hits on the solution in *Gaudy Night:* 'Harriet said nothing. Peter's intelligence could always make rings round her own more slow-moving wits.'[47] It is interesting that in this way, the question of a woman's autonomy and independence is raised, but is finally resolved in favour of traditional attitudes. A certain amount of feminist argument is put forward, but endings belie these and endorse a more traditional view.

More recently in the 'sixties and 'seventies, the Women's Movement has been given quite a large amount of media coverage (albeit to a large extent trivialising) and changes are taking place in both the law and in general attitudes towards women. How are these changes manifested in contemporary novels?

Bergonzi has written that Edna O'Brien is an 'exponent of the woman problem',[48] and certainly O'Brien's heroines Kate and Baba in *The Country Girls* series show problems of role conflict after their move to Dublin in search of fun and a rich husband. In *Girls in their Married Bliss*, Kate repents an affair and plans to return to her husband: 'She lay awake and planned a new heroic role for herself. She would expiate all by sinking into domesticity. She would buy buttons and spools of thread other than just black and white.'[49] There is some similarity here between the work of Edna O'Brien and that of Margaret Drabble. The heroines of both these novelists have a preoccupation with the way in which 'normal' women spend their lives. On meeting another woman taking her child to the nursery, Jane in *The Waterfall* wonders about her domestic life. 'Oh God she thought with a sudden shock, her faith shaken, perhaps all the world's as bad as me, perhaps none of them get up and clean their houses.'[50]

Edna O'Brien's work tends to satirise the effects which the love ideologies of popular romantic fiction have on young girls. In *Girls in Their Married Bliss* for instance, Kate reflects: 'I sat on the chair . . . thinking of all the men I'd met, and the exhaustion of keeping my heels mended and my skin fresh for the Mr. Right that was supposed to come along.'[51] Baba claims a similar indifference to how she 'ought' to feel: When her builder husband telephones and unexpectedly invites her to dinner at a restaurant, she says: 'I wrote down the details and told him to take care, which was strange coming from me. Normally, I'm praying he'll fall off a scaffold.'[52]

Kate and Baba have no need of fate and chance to help them catch their men; they have their own cunning and determination for that, although one very poignant comment is made on the workings of fate and chance after Baba has given birth to the child which is not her husband's. She comments: 'Don't ask me to say that crime doesn't pay, because I'll say it, but I'll also say virtue doesn't pay, it is all pure fluke, and our lives prove it.'[53] There is again a similarity here with Drabble's work, where her heroines have a similarly pessimistic view of the workings of fate and chance, and where Jane comments in *The Waterfall:* 'If I were drowning, I couldn't reach out a hand to save myself, so unwilling am I to set myself up against fate.'[54]

In the foregoing, I have attempted to look at what I consider to be a very important category of general fiction written by and for women this century. I would argue that it is literature of *this* type which reflects ideological ambiguities – stating a new view while implicitly endorsing the old one. Much the same could be said of the soi-disant 'liberated' women's magazines such as *Nova* and *Cosmopolitan* which may well present the new view of women in the form of *explicit* propaganda, while an implicit and much more pervausive *ideological* content contradicts this. Thus, it is not seen as paradoxical that photographs of painstakingly coiffured and made up women and articles on how to undress sexily in front of your husband/myriad lovers appears side by side with articles on women's rights and the Women's Movement.

While it would appear to me that there *are* one or two contemporary novelists – among them Fay Weldon and Margaret Drabble, whose work I have discussed elsewhere – who explicitly challenge conventions and offer alternative possibilities for women, the vast majority do not. Notwithstanding explicit arguments for a new view, the impression left is one which does little to challenge the status quo.

Consequently we may agree with Hauser on the two ranks mentioned at the beginning of this case study. The difference between 'propaganda' and 'ideology' is a merely tactical one, and the use of propaganda does not necessarily detract from the aesthetic impact of a novel. Nevertheless it is the ideological assumptions – the conclusions drawn from the workings of plot and characters – which leave the most lasting impression with the reader. The literature discussed above may raise the question of women's independence, may challenge conventional sterotypes of women but, by failing to provide an alternative, merely contains protest and results in an endorsement of the status quo.

University of Bradford.

1. M. Drabble: *The Garrick Year*, Weidenfeld and Nicolson, London, 1964, p. 108.

2. Arnold Hauser: 'Propaganda and Ideology in Art' in Istvan Meszaros (ed.): *Aspects of History and Class Consciousness*, Routledge and Kegan Paul, London, 1971, pp. 128-151.

3. ibid., p. 129.

4. ibid., pp. 129-130.

5. M. Drabble: *The Millstone*, Weidenfeld and Nicolson, London, 1965 p. 57.

6. Fay Weldon: *Down Among the Women*, Penguin, Harmondsworth, 1973, p. 83 (first published by Heinemann, 1971).

7. *Woman*, April 6th 1968, 'Girl in a Million' by Barbara Robinson.

8. *Woman*, July 4th 1970, 'A Place to Grow' by Hilda Rothell.

9. Georgette Heyer: *Powder and Patch*, Heinemann, London, 1930, p. 16.

10. ibid., p. 135.

11. ibid., p. 137.

12. Barbara Cartland: *The Fire of Love*, Pan, London, 1964, p. 63.

13. Marie Corelli: *The Treasure of Heaven*, Constable, London, 1906, p. 16.

14. ibid., p. 71.

15. ibid., p. 47

16. ibid., p. 52.

17. ibid., p. 404.

18. J. Ruskin: *Sesame and Lilies*, George Allen, London, 1865, pp. 90-91. 'We hear of the "mission" and of the "rights" of Women, as if these could ever be separate from the mission and rights of Man – as if she and her lord were creatures of the independent kind, and of irreconcilable claim. This, at least, is wrong. And not less wrong . . . is the idea that the woman is only the shadow and attendant image of her lord, owing him a thoughtless and servile obedience, and supported altogether in her weakness by the pre-eminence of his fortitude. This, I say, is the most foolish of all errors respecting her who has been made to be the helpmate of man. As if he could be helped effectively by a shadow, or worthily by a slave!'

19. T. Coates and R. S. Warren Bell: *Marie Corelli: The Writer and the Woman*, Hutchinson, London, 1903, p.153.

20. J. Stuart Walters: *Mrs. Humphrey Ward: Her Work and Influence*, Kegan Paul, Trench, Trubner and Co., London, 1912, p. 177.

21. Mrs. G. M. Trevelyan: *Mrs. Humphrey Ward*, Constable, London, 1923, p. 233.

22. Mrs. H. Ward: *Lady Rose's Daughter*, Smith Elder and Co., London, 1903, p. 281.

23. Virginia Woolf: *A Room of One's Own*, Hogarth Press, London, 1928.

24. Ward: op.cit., p. 281.

25. ibid., p. 277.

26. ibid., p. 269.

27. ibid., p. 264.

28. A. J. P. Taylor: *English History 1914-1945*, Clarendon Press, Oxford, 1965, p. 181.

29. E. M. Delafield: *Diary of a Provincial Lady*, Macmillan, London, 1934, pp. 198-199.

30. ibid., p. 129.

31. Trevor Pateman: *Language Truth and Politics*, Pateman and Stroud, Sidmouth, 1975, p. 47.

32. Delafield: op.cit., p. 244.

33. Winifred Holtby: *Virginia Woolf*, John Lane, 1932 and *Women and a Changing Civilisation*, Wishart, London, 1934.

34. Winifred Holtby: *South Riding*, Collins Fontana, London, 1974, preface. (The first edition of this novel was published in 1936).

35. ibid., p. 79.

36. ibid., p. 202.

37. ibid., p. 202.

38. ibid., p. 380.

39. ibid., p. 369.

40. Janet Hitchman: *Such a Strange Lady: An Introduction to Dorothy L. Sayers (1893-1957)*, New English Library, London, 1975, p. 85.

41. Dorothy L. Sayers: *Gaudy Night*, New English Library Edition, London, 1974, p. 46. (First published by Gollancz, 1935).

42. ibid., p. 31.

43. ibid., p. 210.

44. ibid., p. 55.

45. ibid., p. 365.

46. Dorothy L. Sayers: *Busman's Honeymoon*, New English Library Edition, London, 1975, p. 21. (First published by Gollancz, 1938).

47. Sayers: op.cit., 1935, p. 278.

48. Bernard Bergonzi: *The Situation of the Novel*, Pelican, London, p. 238.

49. Edna O'Brien: *Girls in Their Married Bliss*, Penguin, Harmondsworth, 1964, p. 31.

50. Margaret Drabble: *The Waterfall*, Weidenfeld and Nicolson, London, 1969.

51. O'Brien: op.cit., 1964, p. 11.

52. ibid., p. 45.

53. ibid., p. 120.

54. Drabble: op.cit., 1964, p. 7.

The Image of the Homosexual in Contemporary English and American Fiction

Mike Brake

'What it looks like depends upon where you are'
An early experience that homosexuals have in terms of their relationship to heterosexual culture, is that they learn they do not exist. They are invisible in the world of fiction, plays, films and the mass media. When they are presented, they are depicted not as ordinary people, but someone to be ridiculed or pitied. The homosexual is rarely presented seriously in English or American literature[1] and is usually relegated to a minor tragic, maladjusted, degenerate or perverted role.[2] It is the purpose of this article to discuss the change in the image and treatment of homosexuals in fiction, and the ways in which this reflects and interacts with the changing image of homosexuals and their consciousness in contemporary society. The absence of homosexuals in mainstream culture increases the young homosexual's alienation. He or she, like any young person, seeks a figure to identify with (besides the opposite gender), and finds a conspiracy of silence concerning his or her sexual preference, or else a figure presented as a maladjusted creature struggling through an unhappy unloved life. This reinforces the fear of abnormality, and increases the sense of isolation of the homosexual. This was particularly true in the nineteenth century and the early twentieth century when heterosexual prejudice banned the homosexual from fiction, and frightened most gay writers into never writing about their homosexuality. Consequently homosexuals appeared as stereotypes which *bore little or no relation* to how homosexual readers actually thought or behaved, especially the working class ones. As Tax[3] says, art is not neutral, it serves someone's interest. Heterosexual hegemony was supported by this bias. It offered no cultural support to those perceived as deviants, to assist them resist the stigma of perversion. It thus redefined as normal, heterosexual sexuality, explaining away any challenge to this as outside any normative categories. A homosexual, presented as a serious character would pose a major problem in terms of heterosexual hegemony, and would certainly increase the heterosexual fear that one of its cherished institutions, the family would be challenged. The distortion of the homosexual world was partially this, and partially the ignorance of worlds outside the mainstream which caused writers to misrepresent the homosexual life. Consequently homosexuality was ignored, and hence it culturally ceased to exist.[4]

In the early nineteenth century there was emphasis on Byronic wickedness among an élite of upper class homosexuals, but there was no real artistic movement important to homosexuality until the Aesthetic Movement at the end of the century. This argued for a conviction that the pursuit and employment of beauty can give meaning and value to life. It was a reaction favouring the autonomy of art outside a moral context, and against the materialist Philistinism of English Victorian capitalism. Its anti-didactic mood considered the moral sentiments assisting in the production of art as of little relevance. Art was for art's sake, art did not, as Ruskin argued, possess a moral or religious value, only an artistic one. This influence is traceable to France. After the 1830 revolution and the rise of Louis Phillipe to the throne Romanticism became popular. One aspect of this, supported by many artists including Hugo, was concerned with social issues. There was some dissent with this 'Mouvement utilitaire', in particular from Baudelaire who reacting against the Rousseauan idea that nature is the source of all that is good and beautiful, emphasised the cult of the artificial and the effect of shocking. Gautier also insisted on 'l'art pour l'art' and its amorality, which he combined with a desire to 'epater les bourgeois.' From them developed the Decadent Movement with its central theme of the importance of art over nature.[5] They desired to transcend the natural, and used drugs and alchohol to increase sensation and create inspiration. Homosexuality was important to them because of its attack upon nature (heterosexuality). However, their view of homosexuality was still heterosexual. Homosexuality was celebrated for its wickedness and its perversity, not welcomed as a joyous and natural sexual expression. The Decadent idea of the autonomy of the artist, and his or her freedom from social and moral consideration was introduced into England by Swinburne. Walter Pater also contributed by stressing relativism as a concept not only in art but also in morality (which caused him to defend the homosexuality of the eighteenth century German poet Wincklemann). Pater's support of the Decadents' search for 'exquisite passions' and ecstasy was interpreted as sanction of ultimate hedonism by any means, including drug use and sexuality.[6]

Male homosexuals, as a result of the Aesthetic Movement were given a precious, sensitive and artistic image, which was essentially non-masculine. It was this feminine aspect of homosexuality as well as its 'unnaturalness' which was to escalate English prejudice against homosexuality. Whilst artists were defended for their homosexuality in the sense that they were not like ordinary men, ordinary homosexuals (especially if they were not precious or artistic) received no support from the public or from the artistic community. They had no creativity to justify their existence. However the artistic community provided something of value for homosexuals, and that is the Bohemian subculture. Subcultures are of important significance to deviant and minority groups.

> 'Subcultures are the meaning system and modes of expression developed by groups in particular parts of the social structure in the course of their collective attempt to come to terms with the contradictions in their shared social situation. More particularly subcultures represent the accumulated meanings and means of expression through which groups in subordinate structural positions have attempted to negotiate or oppose the dominant meaning system. They therefore provide a pool of available symbolic resources which particular individuals or groups can draw on in their attempt to make sense of their own specific situation and construct a viable identity.[7]

Historically the artistic Bohemian subculture had its roots in the Latin Quarter of the medieval University of Paris, and in the eighteenth century English coffee houses, as well as Henri Murger's artistic ghetto.[8] The literature market of the nineteenth century freed the artist from the last vestiges of aristocratic patronage. He or she became a worker in the creative arts who was set apart from the materialism of nineteenth century commercialism and Philistinism. As such the artist was not only a skilled worker with a unique relationship to society, but also a myth to live by.[9] Artistic bohemianism was a category which offered a refuge to deviant and outcast groups. The Bohemian ghetto with its emphasis on subjectivity and non conformity was to provide a geographical and existential location to minority groups such as criminals, prostitutes and immigrants. The homosexuals could live in the Bohemian quarter as tolerated eccentrics whose isolation and unconformity reflected the Bohemian values of the artistic community. Respectable values failed to apply in this subculture, and so with the encouragement of Aestheticism's flamboyance and amorality homosexuals were able to live a life style more sympathetic to their values and outlook. The gay ghetto grew up in the Bohemian subculture. This was to end with the Wilde trial in 1895.

Wilde carried aestheticism not only into his art, but also his appearance. The long hair, velvet jackets and the demeanour and exquisite appearance of the artist were set off by the carrying of a lily or some other flower.[10] Wilde specialised in the dying of carnations to an unnatural green. This was a recognised symbol of homosexuality which outraged bourgeois morality,[11] and indicated not only the improvement of art over nature, but also symbolised homosexuality as an improvement on 'natural' or biological sexuality. An extravagant mode of dress, artistic sensitivity and a precious attitude were all equated in the public mind with homosexuality. This was the contribution of Aestheticism to homosexuality. Victorian sexism and Philistinism was to respond to dandyism and creativity as unmanly effeminacy. There was, as Brigid Brophy correctly indicates,[12] a confusion in the public mind between Aestheticism and homosexuality. Sexual and moral prejudice against femininity and homosexuality combined with philistine prejudice against artiness and affectation as a result of the 1895 trial of Oscar Wilde. This stereotype of effeminate decadence is resurrected even today to attack male homosexuals. Philistinism gained a great victory with the conviction which killed Wilde and destroyed Aestheticism. Such was the backlash that Beardsley was dismissed from the *Yellow Book*, and his appointment with other Aesthetes to the '*Savoy*' magazine ended with W. H. Smiths' refusal to distribute it in 1896.

After the Wilde trial Aestheticism faded, showing its influence only in the Bloomsbury group's advocacy of free love and struggle against sexual possession.[13] Only in Wilde's disciple, Firbank, did outrageousness show itself as homosexual protest against Philistinism (and even Firbank allows himself only homosexual women in his novels). For many years writers who were themselves homosexual, Maugham, James, Forster and Hugh Walpole for example, all wrote heterosexual novels, or thinly disguised the homosexuality.[14]

Women fared somewhat better. Female friendships have been discussed with more seriousness, especially by women writers, and with varying degrees of sympathy by men. Dickens for example, recognises an erotic element to Miss Wade's friendship with Tatty Coram in '*Little Dorrit*'. Miss Wade's interest in Tatty relates also to her close friendship with another girl whilst at school, where they spent nights in each other's arms.[15] Dickens disapproves of this friendship and of Miss Wade's bitterness and independence from male patronage. When treated by men, this kind of erotic friendship is subject to the type of voyeurism that all lesbians are familiar with. The erotic element although there, is permitted because at any public level, attitudes tended to be that women were emotional but devoid of any sexuality of an autonomous nature, outside that defined by men.[16] Women of course, were more understanding. Gertrude Stein discussed her own early lesbian love affair in '*Fernhurst*', and in '*Q. E. D.*' Based on her student days at Bryn Mawr, it analyses her own apprenticeship in sexual power, and in love. She goes beyond emotions into sexual initiation. Her main character (the Stein character), declares

'I could undertake to be an efficient pupil, if it were possible to find an efficient teacher'

and later with confidence says to her lover

'Am I not a promising pupil?'

Her lover sardonically replies

'Not so good a pupil as so excellent teacher as I deserve'.

This actually happened to Stein and had a lasting effect on her. Vulnerability had to be replaced by power, and yet to be generous though powerful was significant in her own maturity. Stein describes her own disgust and self hatred in her awakening homosexuality. Unfortunately the novel's publication was delayed until 1950. Indeed the only early homosexual novels are lesbian, Djuna Barnes '*Nightwood*', (1936), which is a compelling and strange study of the intermingling of destiny and temperament but which reveals little about the nature of lesbianism. More important to homosexuals is the lesbian classic, Radclyffe Hall's, '*The Well of Loneliness*', (1928, J. Cape) the only novel really to 'come out'. The book reflects the values of the upper class of the time, honour, patriotism, self sacrifice, and these are applied unthinkingly to the gay world. Homosexuals are called upon to show their finer side

'Have courage – do the best with your burden – but above all be honourable. Cling to your honour for the sake of those others who share the same burden. For their sake show the world that people like you can be quite selfless and fine as the rest of mankind.'[17]

The homosexual attitude is, to present oneself as a nobler form of human being than the heterosexual. The heroine, more transsexual than lesbian, takes up masculine values and role-play, tempered with a woman's tenderness and sensitivity. She feels herself to be in the wrong body. Her loneliness is acute and for the first time the isolation of homosexuality is presented honestly in a novel.

'An immense desolation swept down upon her, an immense need to cry out and claim understanding – for herself an immense need to find an answer to the riddle of her unwanted being.'[18]

The end of the novel is melodramatic in the best tear-jerker sense. The heroine Stephen, sacrifices her relationship with her lover, so that her lover can marry and live a normal life. Despite the over writing, and the self-sacrificing values which in fact betray a guilt and deep self-hatred, the novel was important because it was popular and easily read.

It's very popularity was to make it a subject of legal attack. Its sincerity is undoubted, and Hall was prepared to sacrifice her literary career, (indeed only fear for the peace of mind of her lover, Una, raised any doubts in Hall's mind) to write an honest account of lesbianism. The publication caused a public outcry, Wilde's persecutors were still powerful. A *Sunday Express* article of the time stated

> 'I would rather give a healthy boy or a healthy girl a phial of prussic acid than this book.'

thereby putting its finger firmly on the pulse of the nation. At the obscenity trial, 57 defence witnesses, including Arnold Bennett and Havelock Ellis were refused.[19] The book was banned in England for years. However it remained very popular. The Paris and American editions were still selling 100,000 copies annually 14 years after publication. The book was translated into 11 languages, and sold over 1 million copies. None of the traditional English values of the middle class are challenged, there is no attempt to discover new roles for women, or new modes of woman-centred behaviour and values. Stephen accepts heterosexuality as 'normal' and marriage as destiny for women. Traditional roles are not challenged, merely interchanged. The analysis is strictly that of the middle class straight gay, who unable to conceptualise new models of behaviour, instead takes up the stereotyped behaviour of the opposite gender. As such the novel is more transsexual than 'lesberated'. However, as an American journalist of the time, May Lamberton Becker put it, the book had 'torpedoed the Ark'. Hall lived most of the rest of her life in exile as Wilde had done, in Paris.

What could have been the male equivalent, Forster's '*Maurice*' had a different fate. Completed in 1914, the book was published posthumously at Forster's insistence in 1971. He once stated he feared it would destroy the public image created by his other writing. The book has a strange origin. Forster on a visit to Edward Carpenter in 1913, whom he describes as 'a socialist who ignored industrialism, and a simple-lifer with an independent income', was touched on the buttocks by Carpenter's lover Merrill.

> 'The sensation was unusual and I still remember it . . . It was as much psychological as physical. It seemed to go straight through the small of my back into my ideas, without involving my thoughts.'[20]

Forster returned home and wrote '*Maurice*'.
It was to be a homosexual love story and;

> 'A happy ending was imperative. I shouldn't have bothered to write
> otherwise. I was determined that in fiction anyway two men should
> fall in love, and remain in it for the ever and ever that fiction allows,
> and in this sense Maurice and Alec still roam the greenwood. I
> dedicated it "To a Happier Year."'[21]

The importance of a happy ending was not lost on Forster. He
realised that it would increase the fury of those who were anti-
homosexual, and that it would at the same time give hope to
homosexuals, tired of seeing their relationships doomed to tragedy in
fiction. The novel itself is based on the relationships of a young man,
utterly dull 'By 23 he was a promising suburban tyrant', except for his
homosexuality. He has an intense but platonic relationship with Clive
an aristocratic undergraduate at Cambridge. After being sent down,
there is a horrofic interview with a G.P. which reveals the lack of
medical sympathy which so many gay people are familiar with. As
Forster says in a letter to Forrest Reid,

> 'The man in my book is, roughly speaking, good, but Society nearly
> destroys him, he nearly slinks through his life furtive and afraid and
> burdened with a sense of sin.'[22]

He feels also that homosexual love should sometimes express itself
physically. Maurice does this with a young gamekeeper whom he meets
in a rather unconvincing ending to the book. The lusty Alec, climbs into
Maurice's window, and after much doubt the two decide to make a life
together. Forster's insight, and indeed his understanding of social
persecution can be observed from the last sentence of his terminal note
to the novel

> ' . . . police prosecutions will continue, and Clive on the bench will
> continue to sentence Alec in the Dock. Maurice may get off.'[23]

It is a great pity that the book was not published on completion.
Forster has been greatly criticised by the Gay Liberation Front for this
moral cowardice.[24] The aftermath of the Wilde trials, left homosexual
men in particular, atomised, open to prosecution, contempt and
ridicule. Prison and assault faced them.[25] The nineteen twenties and
thirties were the continuing of the dark ages for homosexuals. No serious
homosexual novel was published about men. Whilst wit and bitterness
were the weapons of Coward and Novello, homosexuality was never
discussed as a serious social issue. The legitimacy of homosexual love
was dismissed, and the only defence of the open homosexual was
outrageous camp. Firbank is a typical example, his work is plainly that
of a homosexual, but he is a butterfly, describing the lives of the rich and

the decadent against a background of traditional culture. His wit, his idiosyncratic style, and complex technique are used to evade rather than develop the position of homosexuals, the gays in his work are women.

Socially there was no consolidated homophile movement in England at the time. The forms of consciousness that showed themselves in the late 1960s had not yet developed. Homosexual attitudes were either to form an inverted elite, which drew upon great figures of history to explain that really everyone who was important was homosexual, (thus denying the existence of 'ordinary' homosexuals, and adding a dimension of class oppression to one of sexist oppression for working-class homosexuals). This often took the form, as with Aestheticism, of an artistic elite, sensitive and sophisticated. Homosexual literature where it existed, was full of guilt, self-searching agonies, peaks of fleeting happiness and a final unhappy reckoning. This reinforced the guilt of the homosexual readers, who were not encouraged to combat the result of that guilt – self hatred. The homosexual remained isolated, atomised and guilty.

In the work of Isherwood, we see developments in the literary attitude to homosexuality. In the Berlin stories,[26] homosexuals are set figures in the decadent atmosphere of pre-war Berlin during the rise of the Nazis. Isherwood describes them as 'the Lost'. Typical is Otto, a bisexual indolent prostitute, incapable of love, and Peter, the unhappy neurotic ex-patriate homosexual, typical of the '30s. In the post-war work, Isherwood explores extensions of 'the Lost'.[27]

Ambrose, whose very commitment to a way of life related to sexual freedom suggests a sort of asceticism, Waldemar, in fact another Otto, and Paul 'the most expensive male prostitute in the world', and the most interesting of characters. Paul is a debauchee, camp, brittle and sophisticated, struggling in a pilgrimage towards a form of Vedantic asceticism and purity – a theme which runs through Isherwood's later work. Paul, sophisticated, cynical, wild and cruel has the capacity to become a form of holy sinner. However the Isherwood of the sixties writes one of the best popular novels about homosexual men, '*A Single Man*'. The 'down there' of '*Down there on a visit*' is the isolation within the individual, and '*A single man*' further explores the loneliness of that isolation. Isherwood looks at several things, firstly homosexuals as a minority

> 'I have never in my life written specifically about homosexuality . . . what I have done in this novel is to write among many other things about minorities, and the homosexuals are used as a sort of metaphor for minorities in general.'[28]

and secondly the way in which homosexuals relate to the straight world. George the 'single man', is a middle aged ex-patriate English professor in Southern California, whose lover has recently been killed. Bitterness, irony and amused contempt make up George's sensibility. George's suburban neighbours regard him with pity.

'New tolerance – technique of annihilation by blandness . . . no reason for disgust – no cause for condemnation. Nothing here that is wilfully vicious. All is due to heredity, early environment, (shame on all those possessive mothers, those sex segregated British schools!) arrested development at puberty, and/or glands. Here we have a misfit, debarred forever from the best things of life, to be pitied not blamed.'[29]

He is aware of how the straight world sees gay affairs

' . . . this kind of relationship can sometimes be almost beautiful – particularly if one of the parties is already dead – or better yet, both.'[30]

Their desire to categorise his dead lover is resisted

'Your book is wrong Mr. Strut, says George – if it tells you Jim is the substitute for a real kid brother, a real husband, a real wife. Jim wasn't a substitute for anything.'[31]

He concludes triumphantly.

'The unspeakable is still here, right in your midst.'[32] George is aware of his isolation, he is a stranger, an outsider. He is aware that he has fooled the straight world every time they accept his I.D. or stamp his passport. His bitterness is deep. In a lecture he states

'A minority has its own kind of aggression. It absolutely dares the majority to attack it. It hates the majority . . .'.[33]

His bitterness increases after Jim's death, and his fantasies about the mass murder of heterosexuals is one of the most honest accounts of gay alienation.

'All (heterosexuals) are in the last analysis responsible for Jim's death – their words, their thoughts, their whole way of life willed it, even though they never knew he existed.'[34]

his relations with his heterosexual colleagues take place in the neutral trivia of small talk, or man-to-man talks,

'Does he know about me, George wonders, do any of them? Oh yes, probably. It would not interest them. They don't want to know about my feelings or my glands or anything below my neck.'[35]

He is conscious, as are all homosexuals in heterosexual company, of play acting. He accepts his homosexuality with amused despair, and finds little solace in the heterosexual world. It is a novel of a form of coming out, as was '*The Well of Loneliness*'. Isherwood describes his feelings of outsideness even in his political interests.

> 'I am sure that it was my queerness that kept me from being a communist in the thirties. The attitude of the Russian communists towards homosexuals disgusted me so much that I could not join the Communist Party, though I agreed at that time with some of its other attitudes.'

In order to understand this shift in Isherwood, it is necessary to look at some of the literary and social movements that led up to this state of consciousness.

Until the mid-sixties, the United States experienced no real challenge to sexist hegemony. Because class barriers in the United States are blurred, consciousness can develop along different lines of oppression. In America two things assist this. There has been no real development of a class conscious political struggle because in an immigrant society, ethnicity has created a hierarchy which creates a myth that the unskilled working class are minority groups. Culturally, because of its geographical size, it is harder to rank someone in the social scale by for example accent or similar cultural measurement. This combined with an affluent semi-skilled working class meant that oppression could be experienced and recognised in other ways. Racism created the Civil Rights movement, black power and black consciousness, Sexism created a very strong sense of consciousness among women. An off-shoot of this was the development of the gay liberation. This was assisted by the development of the alternative counter-culture. All these challenged American hegemony. Gramsci has described hegemony as a situation where one concept of reality is diffused, so that the interpretation of reality, and the norms supporting it have been internalised by all classes.[36] Firstly blacks challenged it, they were economically oppressed and had their basic legal civil rights witheld for them. The counter-culture developed a sense of immediate joyousness, a desire to experience hedonism now, and to eroticise everyday experiences.[37] Finally women challenged patriarchy and demanded the end of anti-feminine attitudes, which by definition encompassed anti-homosexuality. This debate was also felt in literature.

The fifties emphasised the cult of the hipster. The values of the delinquent were working class, and highly masculine, completely unlike the ambisexual appearance of the hippy of the sixties. Millet[38] has brilliantly analysed the sexist base of much literature of the time. Mailer in particular summed up the traditional masculine attitude to homosexuals. Fiedler argued[39] that for 10 years after the Second World War, middle class, middle brow attitudes to homosexuality softened, which permitted the publication of such works as Gore Vidal's '*The City and the Pillar*', and Baldwin's '*Giovanni's Room*'. However on examination Vidal writes of a homosexual who retreats into a common defence,[50] that his homosexual feelings for his school friend are not like the crude feelings of more run-of-the-mill homosexuals, while Baldwin writes of bisexuals more than total gays – Capote, Vidal, Tennessee Williams wrote of homosexuality, but only Ginsberg lived as an open political gay. The main defence was being respectable and respected. The only form of coming out was being camp. Camp has a contradictory relationship in the gay world. Isherwood first speaks of it as a concept in literature. In '*The world in the evening*' camp is when

> 'You're expressing something that's basically serious to you in terms of fun and artifice.'[40]

Susan Sontag discovering the phrase in the novel, altered it to describe play acting in a particular way, exaggerated into a form of style (as in High Camp). To camp is to involve oneself in a form of anticipatory socialisation by imitating the stereotyped behaviour of homosexuals and thus identify publicly with them. In a sense it can integrate, argues Sontag, homosexuals into a wider society

> 'Homosexuals have pinned their integration into society on promoting the aesthetic sense. Camp is a solvent of morality. It neutralises moral indignation, sponsors playfulness.'[41]

It is of course very easy for camp humour to pass over the boundaries into self oppression and overt hatred of women, especially when performed for straights. Camp when it degenerates into the minstrelisation of women or gays loses its political edge. Campness can conceal sexism. Camp however does emphasise the play acting that most homosexuals feel they have to perform. As de Mott[42] has argued, the homosexual has repeatedly to justify his difference, he cannot not relax into unthinking self acceptance.

For the other side, masculine machismo literature, Mailer summed up the common attitude, 'queers' were 'humans-with-phalluses who choose to be female'. If you suppress your homosexuality then you are not homosexual, and you should be congratulated. Mailer describes male bonding as a form of non-sexual love. (Fiedler reminds us this is a major theme in the American novel). For Mailer, you love your friends and fuck your mistress.[43] As Millett point out, in Mailer to renounce virility is tantamount to renouncing masculinity, hence identity and even self.

> 'I think there may be more homosexuals today than there were fifty years ago. If so the basic reason might have to do with a general loss of faith in the country, faith in the meaning of one's self as a man. When a man can't find dignity in his work he loses virility. Masculinity is not something given to you, something you're born with, but something you gain. And you gain it by winning small battles with honour. Because there is very little honour left in American life.'[44]

He goes on in another work to say that a man is someone who resists homosexuality. He may get into fights in bars every night, and women will wonder why he doesn't just get on with it and become homosexual. He is protected by other men, who realise that he has chosen not to be homosexual and is entitled to the dignity of his right to pay his price. Even in his semi-apology, 'The homosexual villain' he states

> 'there was an intrinsic relation between homosexuality and evil'[45]

and apparently he still believes it.[46]

Mailer's attitude is sadly often found amongst American men of all races. Among black novelists, only Baldwin in the late fifties began to explore the relations between sexism and racism. It is interesting to note that most literary critics see Baldwin's homosexuality as irrelevant, even when major figures in his novel are gay. Homosexuality in Baldwin is explained away as a literary device used to deal with more abstract treatments of general sexuality. Baldwin's homosexuals are gay in a relativistic rather than an absolute sense. In '*Giovanni's Room*',[47] David and Giovanni's love is the love of two boys who were originally heterosexual. Giovanni, (the more homosexual boy) is deserted by David who is almost totally heterosexual, abdicating all responsibility towards his homosexuality. Giovanni is abandoned to the sordid rent boy underworld he fears and loathes. In a superior work '*Another Country*', Baldwin explores the inability to love, because of the hatred fostered by an oppressive world. This occurs not only between the homosexual and bisexual characters, but also between the black and white.

> 'People don't take the relations between boys seriously you know that. We will never know many people who believe we love each other.

> They do not think there can be tears between men. They think that
> we are only playing a game, and that we do it to shock them.'[48]

Black Rufus cannot love his white mistress, but in guilt torments her
into insanity. Rufus's sister Ida cannot forgive Vivaldo whom she
genuinely loves, for being white. Eric, a white Southerner flees in exile
in Paris after a brief affair with Rufus, where he has an idyllic love affair
with Yves, a street boy. It is a novel about the perversion of love by
social oppression. Baldwin explores power in relationships, especially
when the powerful are endorsed by social pressure. The straights can't
love the gays,

> 'American males are the only people I've ever encountered in the
> world who are willing to go on the needle before they'll go to bed
> with each other'[49]

the blacks and whites cannot love each other, men and women fear each
other. Yet he recognised that blacks and the whites must free each
other, and by extension the straights and the gays. The blacks and the
gays strike at the heart of America's fear of and repression of sexuality.
The link between race and sex is distinct. Baldwin's self hatred as a
black is programmed into him by racism, but his self hatred as a
homosexual is programmed by both black and white sexism. The
evidence of this is Cleaver's attack on him for his honest account of his
self hatred, and for his homosexuality. Cleaver as Altman[50] argues, sees
like Mailer, masculinity as demanding a renunciation of
homosexuality, which is part of 'racial death wish'.

> 'The case of James Baldwin aside for a moment, it seems that many
> Negro homosexuals, acquiescing in this racial death wish are outraged
> and frustrated because in their sickness they are unable to have a baby
> by a white man.'[51]

For Cleaver and many blacks, to be homosexual is to opt out of being
black. Heterosexual Superstud is one stereotype that black males cling
to in their revenge on whites, only too often using white women as
instruments of revenge. A black homosexual then is doubly despised.
LeRoy Jones also attacks Baldwin[52], and it was Huey Newton, Supreme
Commander of the Black Panthers who took the courageous step of
rebuking black militants for rejecting the women's movement and gay
liberation. He argued that blacks feared homosexuals because they
feared their own homosexuality, and feared liberated women in case
they were castrated, but that these may potentially be the most
revolutionary groups of all. In fact in his autobiography[53], Newton says
he has always been interested in sexual freedom, and had he not been a

black radical, he would have founded a movement for sexual liberation.

An important writer who influenced sexual politics was Genet. Millet, who was herself to come out and to discuss this in her book '*Flying*',[54] argues that he is one of the few male writers to understand sexism. Genet analyses the position of the lowest form of gay life, the 'maricone', the despised female role playing drag queen prostitute who was to develop by age, fame and wealth into male from slave to master. Drag queens challenge more than homosexual oppression they 'uncover the fact that sex role is sex rank'. The world of the rent boy is also explored in Rechy's '*City of Night*', and '*Numbers*'. Rechy's anonymous hero is a compulsive hustler, who wanders through the rent world of Los Angeles, New York and San Fransisco. In the first book the theme is trade, and the transvestite prostitutes have a Genet-like atmosphere. Miss Thing is near to Genet's Divine. In '*Numbers*', the cash relationship is replaced by cruising, another form of sex without commitment. Sex is a means of escape from commitment. The hustler subculture is not confined, despite Jones's and Cleaver's contempt, to white rent boys. Wright describes the similar world of the black hustler, where blackness has the added commercial value of allowing white punters to act out their racist fantasies.[55]

Lesbianism in literature has been treated with one or two notable exceptions, rather like male homosexuality. Even Millet hardly mentions lesbianism. In pornography a pseudo-lesbianism has always been popular for the voyeuristic elements of male sexuality. The absence of lesbianism as a serious element, Brophy's '*The finishing touch*' is typical of works which refuse to take women's sexuality seriously even when written by women can be explained as a result of the invisibility of the lesbian social life. Lesbians since the late sixties have identified less with male homosexuals in the gay liberation movements, and more with the women's movement. Lesbians have felt excluded by gay men's sexism, which tolerates them as a form of inferior gay man, and have allied themselves with other women. They have raised important issues in the movement, assisting women to develop autonomy from male dominance, and assisting previously heterosexual sisters to come out. They have led the vanguard which demands that women's sexuality is not seen merely as an aspect of biological functionalism; that it is women defined and taken seriously. The Norman Mailers and the Henry Millers have no place in the new sexuality. We can look forward to serious novels concerning women's sexuality as a result, concerning isolation, class (Maureen Duffy's '*The microsm*' suggests the lesbian world is also stratified)[56] and also fulfilment and happiness.

Intellectually some of the best writing on lesbianism has been produced by Monique Wittig.[57] In '*The guerillères*' she presents a triumphant epic about a military caste of women, whilst in '*The lesbian body*' she attempts something unique. She writes of a mythical country of women, in a style whose syntax attempts to eliminate male culture, and whose mythical universe uses language to extend the female body to a wider human context. It is an important work about women, but it is difficult and will have a restricted but appreciative public. There is not a comparable male novel, because there is no comparable male consciousness.

Even in the popular fiction market, the writing of women is superior. Isabel Miller's '*Patience and Sarah*'[58] is a pastoral romance about two women falling in love in a Connecticut farming community in 1816. The historical setting is bereft of oppression, and is used to create a distanced, idyll about the women's purchase and development of a farm. The atmosphere is of strong, tranquil optimism, instead of the frenetic sturm und drang usually found in gay romances. It's a pleasant relief to know she gets her woman, and they live happily ever after.[59] It has a justifiable popularity among gay women. Rita Mae Brown's '*Rubyfruit Jungle*'[60] (the title is an allegory for women's genitals) is a more raunchy study of the lesbian struggle. Molly is a poor white, illegitimate Southern woman, whose intelligence and cheerfulness help her to forget her identity in America as a woman and as a lesbian. She is a courageous iconoclast whose earthy lack of hypocrisy help her to see through the myth of womanhood as described in American small town life. She faces up to the contradictions of sexual love with straight brainwashed American women with gutsy good humour. She has a brief scene in junior high with a prom queen. ('I'm an all American queer'), who when challenged fears the taint of homosexuality will sully her feminine image 'We are not queer, how can you say that? I'm very feminine, how can you call me a queer? Maybe Molly, after all she plays tennis and can throw a football as far as Clark, but not me . . . You know lesbians are boyish and athletic. I mean Molly's pretty and all that, but she's a better athlete than most of the boys that go to this school, and besides she doesn't act like a girl you know? I'm not like that at all. I just love Molly. That doesn't make me queer.'

She goes to college where she starts an affair with her room mate which scandalises the other members of her sorority, who react with the usual heterosexual dread of homosexual rape. Molly's lover reacts with courage

'Why Karen, are you afraid I might sleep with you, are you afraid I might sneak over in the middle of the night and attack you . . . If you were the last woman on earth I'd go back to men – you're a simpering, pimply-faced cretin.'

Expelled, Molly leaves for New York to study film. She lives at first in an old car with a young male gay hustler who introduces her to the New York gay bar scene. She is flabbergasted at the role playing 'A lot of these chicks divided into butch and femme, male-female . . . That's the craziest, dumb-ass thing I ever heard tell of. What's the point of being a lesbian if a woman is going to look and act like an imitation man? Hell, if I want a man, I'll get the real thing not one of those chippies. I mean, the whole point of being gay is because you love women.'

She resists men

'. . . men get kind of boring, I'm not trying to put them down. I mean I like them as people, but sexually they're dull.'

She resists hustling older wealthier women (the book tends to ageism) 'But its more than poor pride. If that woman loved me it'd be different or if I loved her I'd take anything she gave me, but she don't give a flying fuck about me. She buys me the way she goes and buys a winter coat . . .'

She argues with close friends shocked at her declaration of lesbianism, 'Molly don't be silly, you can't be a lesbian. You're joking, I'd know if you were such a thing.

'Madam, I am a full-blooded bona fide lesbian. As for the way I look most lesbians I know look like any other woman . . . the big pigs use heterosexuality and women's bodies to sell everything in this country – even violence. Damn, you people are so bad off you got to have computers to match you off these days.'

At film school, despite chauvinist jokes and opposition to her using the hardware, she graduates, the only woman in a class of men, phi betta kappa and cum laude. She does not win, she is still a woman and from the poor South, she has earned the right to write copy for movies or to be a secretary in a film office, whilst her men classmates are taken on as assistant directors. She ends the book with a challenge

'Damn, I wished the world would let me be myself . . . I wish I could make my films. That wish I can work for. One way or another I'll make those movies and I don't feel like having to fight until I am fifty. But if it does take that long then watch out world, because I'm going to be the hottest fifty year old this side of the Mississippi.'

Compare this with '*Frost*', Richard Amory's gay thriller.[61] The plot is irrelevant, and the book describes a relationship between a college professor and a delivery man. The whole context is masculine, there is no discussion of sexual politics, and women do not exist. At least Molly always urges men who are leaving women to make sure that their children receive proper child support. There is a brief discussion in '*Frost*' that brotherhood is love,

'. . . being queer's a real bag of shit unless you got somethin going like the two of us got, and I'll tell you something else, I love you like the fires of hell, but hellfire ain't got no fence around it, and never did.'

That is the level of political discussion. The book is enormously popular but that is probably because every other page is full of descriptions of tangle-haired penises quivering between white buttocks. It is interesting that women have managed to publish the most courageous and politically important books. This is probably because they have always had at some level a sense of their gender oppression. There is no novel which actually attempts to overcome male sexism written by men. For homosexual men, the sexist contradictions of relations with women does not exist, or is substituted by sexist relations with other men which seem to escape the analysis of the writer. There has been of course since the late sixties a considerable amount of political and social analysis of sexism, but this has come from the women's movement on the whole. Men have always tended to confuse pornography and unloving promiscuity with sexual liberation. This relates directly in the heterosexual world to their sexual power. Heterosexual pornography objectifies women, who are seen as the receptacles and instruments of male lust. Lesbianism is closely allied to the feminist demand for an autonomous and aggressive sexuality for women. It is the total logical extension of women's love for women. The gay male world has not yet learned this lesson, because the roots of the lesson are not based on the sexual exploitation of women. A gay male relationship can ignore women, or despise them. Only by linking itself with a counter-sexist analysis can it hope to succeed as a political movement of force. It has to widen its analysis and its vision of the future. When that occurs we may see the development of homosexual male novels of considerable stature, aimed at all levels of popularity.

University of Kent

1. R. F. Smith: *The Cumulated Fiction Index*, Association of Assistant Librarians, London, lists 46 novels with homosexual male characters and 18 with lesbian characters published between 1960-74.

2. Even novels written by gay authors fall into this trap. For example, Robin Maugham: *The Wrong People*, Heinemann, London, 1971 – the degeneracy of Tangiers rich homosexuals, and their ruling class attitudes is illustrated in Cyril Connoly's introduction which nostalgically remembers Tangiers as containing 'above all excellent servants'.

3. Meredith Tax: 'Culture is not neutral, whom does it serve?' in Lee Baxandall (ed.): *Radical Perspectives in the Arts*, Penguin, Harmondsworth, 1972.

4. French literature, on the other hand, has a long history of the serious treatment of erotica, but this is obviously outside the scope of this paper.

5. The effects of the Decadents on the Symbolists in France can be seen in the work of Rimbaud and Verlaine, themselves two important homosexual poets.

6. Rossetti and Swinburne were both attacked by Robert Buchanan for their celebration of sensuality. See Robert Buchanan: *The fleshly school of Poetry and Other Phenomena of the Day*, Strahan, 1872. It is worth noting that Gilbert and Sullivan lampoon Aestheticism in 'Patience', in which Wilde appears thinly disguised as a 'fleshly Poet'.

7. G. Murdock: 'Mass communication and the construction of meaning' in N. Armistead (ed.): *Reconstructing social psychology*, Penguin, Harmondsworth, 1974.

8. See Henri Murger: *Scenes of Bohemian Life*, 1849.

9. This is illustrated by the character of Stephen in James Joyce: *Portrait of the Artist*, 1966.

10. Floral symbols were important to the Decadents not only in Baudelaire, but also in J. K. Huysen: *A. Rebours*, 1884; Firbank was also to use them as symbols of aestheticism and homosexuality.

11. See Robert Hitchens: *The Green Carnation*, 1894, published anonymously but withdrawn during Wilde's trial.

12. Brigid Brophy: *Prancing Novelist*, Macmillan, London, 1973.

13. Homosexuality was a latent theme in Lytton Strachey. Virginia Woolf also examines Vita Sackville-West's bisexuality in the strange androgynous *Orlando*. Dorothy Bussy also wrote an anonymous account of an adolescent's lesbian feelings for her teacher in *Olivia*.

14. Even Proust, although openly creating homosexual characters, leaves Baron de Charlus a solitary figure, and conceals the gender of Marcel's lover.

15. I am grateful to Roz Carne for drawing my attention to this and other female friendships in nineteenth century writers such as Charlotte Brontë and Mrs. Gaskill.

16. This at least protected them from legal persecution for lesbianism. They were open to social ostracism (as indeed they were for adultery). Compare with Wilde's prosecution, the fate of Renee Vivien (nee Pauline Tarn), who rebelled against her middle class debutante life, and after a homosexual scandal fled to Paris where she wrote poetry and translated Sappho. See Jeannette H. Foster: *Sex variant women in literature*, Muller, London, 1958.

17. R. Hall: *The Well of Loneliness*, J. Cape, London, 1928, p. 154.

18. ibid., p. 206.

19. Lady Una Troubridge: *The Life and Death of Radclyffe Hall*, Hammond and Hammond, London, 1961.

20. E. M. Forster: *Maurice*, E. Arnold, London, 1971, p. 235.

21. ibid., p. 236.

22. ibid., p. vii.

23. ibid., p. 241.

24. A. Hodges and D. Hutter: *With downcast gays*, Pomegranate Press, London, 1974.

25. See Quentin Crisp: *The Naked Civil Servant*, 1967.

26. C. Isherwood: *Mr. Norris changes trains* and *Goodbye to Berlin*, New Directions, New York, 1935 and 1939 respectively.

27. C. Isherwood: *Down there on a visit*, Simon and Schuster, New York, 1962.

28. See an interview in H. Breit: *The Writer Observed*, Collier, New York, 1961.

29. C. Isherwood: *A single man*, Simon and Schuster, New York, 1964.

30. ibid.

31. ibid.

32. ibid.

33. ibid.

34. ibid.

35. ibid.

36. The argument is developed in A. Gramsci: *Selections from the prison notebooks*, Lawrence and Wishart, London, 1971.

37. Obviously I am not doing justice to the counter-culture, nor am I subjecting it to a substantive criticism. For a brief analysis of this nature see J. Young: 'The hippie solution – an essay in the politics of leisure' in L. and I. Taylor: *Politics and Deviance*, Penguin, Harmondsworth, 1973; see also my own comments in 'Cultural Revolution or Alternative Delinquency' in R. Bailey and J. Young: *Social Problems in Contemporary Britain*, Saxon House, Farnborough, 1974.

38. Kate Millet: *Sexual Politics*, Abacus, London, 1971.

39. Leslie Fiedler: *Love and Death in the American novel*, Criterion, New York, 1960. Fiedler in fact suggests that this paved the way for Capote and McCullers, but it is more valid to suggest the overt homosexual novels of Baldwin and Vidal.

40. See C. Isherwood: *The world in the evening*, Random House, New York, 1954, p. 111.

41. Susan Sontag: *Against Interpretation*, Farrar, Strauss and Giroux, New York, 1966.

42. Benjamin de Mott: 'But he's a homosexual . . .', *New American Review*, September 1967.

43. See in particular N. Mailer: *Why we are in Vietnam*, Putnam, New York, 1967; also, N. Mailer: 'The Armies of the Night', *New American Library*, New York, 1968.

44. N. Mailer: *Cannibals and Christians*, Dial, New York, 1966, p. 112.

45. N. Mailer: 'The homosexual villain', *Advertisements for Myself*, Putnam, New York, 1959.

46. Contrast this with Leroi Jones's view that 'all white American men are trained to be fags', see his 'American sexual reference – blackmale' in *Home – Social Essays*, McGibbon and Kee, New York, 1968.

47. James Baldwin: *Giovanni's Room*, Dial, New York, 1956.

48. James Baldwin: *Another Country*, M. Joseph, London, 1962, p. 216.

49. James Baldwin: 'Disturber of the Peace', an interview, *Mademoiselle*, May 1963.

50. Dennis Altman: *Homosexuality, oppression and liberation*, Discus Avon, New York, 1971.

51. Eldridge Cleaver: *Soul on Ice*, McGraw Hill, New York, 1968.

52. See Leroi Jones: *Brief reflections on 2 hot shots*, 1963.

53. Huey Newton: *Revolutionary Suicide*.

54. Kate Millet: *Flying*, Hart-Davis, London, 1974.

55. The hustler theme is in John Rechy: *City of Night*, Grove Press, New York, 1963, and his *Numbers*, Grove Press, New York, 1963; also Charles Wright: *The Messenger*, Farrar, Strauss and Giroux, New York, 1963.

56. Maureen Duffy: *The Microsm*, Hutchinson, London, 1966.

57. Monique Wittig: *The Guerillères*, Paladin, London, 1972 and *The Lesbian Body*, Peter Owen, London, 1976.

58. Isabel Miller: *Patience and Sarah*, R. Hart Davis, London, 1972, in which the author feels it necessary still to use a pseudonym.

59. The lesson of the happy ending seems to be gaining ground. Iris Murdoch in *A Fairly Honourable Defeat*, Viking, New York, 1970 has happier endings for the gays than the hets.

60. Rita Mae Brown: *Rubyfruit Jungle*, Daughters Inc., Vermond, 1973.

61. Richard Amory: *Frost*, Freeway, New York, 1973.

The Literature of Alienation

Mary Horton

Introduction

The first question is – who are the writers of the literature of alienation? A review of some of those literary critics and thinkers who have written on the alienation theme shows that literary alienation is seen to be primarily a twentieth century phenomenon, but with roots going back to the nineteenth century and earlier. It is also seen, unlike the closely-knit literary movements of the symbolists, surrealists or dada, which preceded or were contemporaneous with it, as a broad grouping of poets, dramatists and novelists with a similar outlook on life but differing in both content and style. Another, and most important difference between the literature of alienation and other movements is that it is a label not chosen by the writers themselves, but imposed by outsiders; these being not even literary critics, but mere social scientists. In this sense, the literature of alienation is a bastard categorisation, and should be treated with care. A further examination shows that it overlaps to a large extent with that genre called the literature of the absurd, and also with the writers called 'existentialist'. The three categories are being considered together, but the point must be made that alienation is not a literary genre, it is a literary theme.

The first step in this investigation was an analysis of some critical writers on the alienation theme who have attempted to label certain creative writers as alienated, and some of whom have tried to define the literature of alienation.[1] This was followed by an attempt at a synthesis, and a deeper look at the portrayal of the theme itself in a number of works.[2] The twentieth century writers whose names have most often been linked with alienation themes are Camus and Kafka, followed by Sartre and Genet. Then come Beckett, Ionesco and the théatre of the absurd generally. Eliot, and to a lesser extent Joyce, have also been linked to the alienation theme. Also mentioned have been the names of Barbusse, Gide, Hesse and Robbe-Grillet; the novelists Hemingway, Graham Greene and Nathaneal West; and the playwrights Arthur Miller, Eugene O'Neill and Tennessee Williams. The major nineteenth century precursors of the literature of alienation are seen to be primarily the existentialist writers Dostoevsky and Rilke, and the symbolist poets, Baudelaire and Rimbaud. Numerous other names were mentioned two or three times only, among them being, in the twentieth century, Conrad, Faulkner, Thomas Mann and Proust; and in the nineteenth century or earlier, Blake, Goethe, Melville, Poe and De Sade. What, if anything, can these writers have in common?

But first we must consider on precisely what level we are looking at alienation in literature. Four levels of approach can be distinguished. In the first place we could look at the objective situation of the writer in relation to the society within which he is writing. In the second place, we could look at what he conceives the role of the writer to be, that is, at his image of his own function. In the third place, we could look, from biographical and other records, at the psychological state of the writer, and make some estimate of his level of self-alienation. And finally, we can look at the expression of alienated states and feeling in literature. It is obvious that all these levels are closely linked, and will influence each other, but they are clearly distinct in terms of the sources from which their data are drawn. My interest is in the last level – the expression of alienated states and feelings in literature, but it is clear that these states are part (but not all) of the psychology of the writer.

Themes of alienation

It is difficult to find any coherent theme in a group of writers so disparate. The attempt made here is based on intuition. The one point where one can start is that they are all trying to express the incoherent and the incommunicable. However, all creative literature, all art in fact, is the expression of the incoherent, in the sense of the unformed or the unknown. It is the reader, the public, the critic, the academic, who demands reasons and intentions. As Robbe-Grillet says:

> 'Mais le public, qui est habitué a ce qu'on lui mache la besogne . . . nous demande alors 'Qu'est ce que tout cela signifie? Qu'est ce que vous avez voulu dire avec *L'annee Derniere a Marienbad?'* Et la, nous sommes obligés de repondre: eh bien, nous ne savons pas encore.'[3]

This attempt, then, is an attempt to impose a meaning on and a relationship between a group of writers, disparate in both origin and style, and who would probably themselves deny the structure I am trying to enclose them in. My only excuse is that it seems to be there.

The way I am approaching the task is to look simply at the meaning of what is written. When the medium is words, it seems to me that their meaning is the important thing, and the art lies in the manipulation of meaning. Further, it is my profound belief that what a work of art is trying to say, is precisely (but not simply or obviously) the way it is trying to say it. That is to say, form and content are inseparable, they exist in symbiosis. And this is the distinguishing character of art. The public's question to Robbe-Grillet therefore – 'What were you trying to say *with Last Year at Marienbad?'* – is simply the wrong question. The form is not the channel for the content, any more than the content is the channel for the form.

THEMES OF ALIENATION

1) *The Insider*
   – the overconformist
   – the universal salesman
   (Eliot, Kafka, Sinclair Lewis,
   Arthur Miller)

2) *The Outsider*
   – the homeless
   – the uncommitted
   (Camus, Hesse, Mann, Sartre)

3) *The Detached Man*
   – the camera man
   – the shadow man
   (Arnold, Camus, Mann, Robbe-
   Grillet)

4) *The Hollow Man*
   – the inauthentic
   – the underground man
   (Camus, Dostoevsky, Eliot,
   Rilke)

5) *The Waste-Land*
   – Absurdity
   – Nothingness

   (Beckett, Conrad, Eliot, Sitwell)

6) *The Possessed*
   (a) *The Escape*
   – the romantic
   – the retreat or search
   (Conrad, Genet, Hemingway,
   Hesse, Rimbaud)

   (b) *The Metamorphoses*
   – internal change only
   – external change only
   – the splitting
   (Blake, Dostoevsky, Kafka,
   Melville, Thomson)

   (c) *The Embracing*
   – the challenge or the alliance
   (Baudelaire, Camus, Goethe,
   Kafka, Melville) – the sacrifice

Starting from the works themselves, six distinct but related themes can be seen. However, the diagrammatic sketch was designed only as a starting-point. According to the Oxford Dictionary, the words 'alien' and 'alienation' are derived from the Latin 'alienus' meaning 'belonging to another'. This phrase can be thought of as containing the dual ideas of being both 'dispossessed' – of freedom, territory, autonomy, identity, and 'possessed' – by masters, gods, devils, knowledge or power. Both these ideas, sometimes complementary and sometimes apparently contradictory, seem to have attached themselves to the concept of alienation in literature. The first five themes on the diagram relate mainly to the concept of dispossession, and the last, to that of possession. Secondly, the first three themes can be thought of as social alienation, in the sense that they have slightly more to do with the outside world than the last three, which can be called 'individual alienation'. Finally the six themes are very roughly arranged in order of increasing portrayal of sickness or disorder. However, these so-called types that I have detached from one another and dwindled to a diagram, are, in reality, as you will see, intricately interwoven.

1) *The Insider*

Being alienated has in the first place, simply a legal connotation. To alienate is to give or to sell. This first 'insider' theme is directly related to the connotation of buying and selling. It is the theme of the over-conformist, the individual who can only decide what he wants to do in terms of the expectations of others, with the accompanying loss of feelings of spontaneity and authenticity. The condition is described clearly in Eliot's *Love song of J. Walter Prufrock*:

> Shall I part my hair behind? Do I dare to eat a peach?
> I shall wear white flannel trousers, and walk upon the beach.
> I have heard the mermaids singing each to each.
> I do not think that they will sing to me.[4]

It is interesting that the symbol of the salesman has been used to portray this aspect of alienated man. Sinclair Lewis's *Babbitt* is the epitome of the other-directed man, so also is Willy Lomas in *Death of a Salesman*, and both, in the end, in their different ways, are betrayed by their conformities. At Willy's graveside Charles says:

> You don't understand; Willy was a salesman. And for a salesman
> there is no rock bottom to the life . . . He's a man way out there in
> the blue, riding on a smile and a shoe-shine. And when they start not
> smiling back – that's an earthquake . . . A salesman has got to dream
> boy. It comes with the territory.[5]

Perhaps the most terrifying picture of the over-conformist is that given in Kafka's *Trial*. At the end, the two anonymous executioners take K to a stone quarry, lay him on the ground and begin to pass a knife backwards and forwards across him:

> K now perceived clearly that he was supposed to seize the knife himself . . . and plunge it into his own breast. But he did not do so . . . He could not relieve the officials of all their tasks; the responsibility for this last failure of his lay with him who had not left him the remnant of strength necessary for the deed.[6]

There are many layers of meaning to Kafka's *Trial*, but the important point here is K's complete other-direction. He tries his best to conform to the expectations of the executioners, and it does not occur to him to question either their right to hold those expectations, or the requirement that he should try to fulfill them. Finally, in the ultimate negation of self, even the responsibility for failing to live up to what he conceives to be the expectations of his destroyers, cannot belong to K.

2) *The Outsider*

The sense in which alienation implies being separated from the tribe, being homeless and outcast, goes deep in the tradition of literature and myth. For instance, in Anglo-Saxon verse *The Seafarer* shows loneliness as an inner hunger (and hunger from within tore the sea-weary spirit) and very much dependent on the absence of the patron or lord ('no patron had I there who might have soothed/my desolate spirit'). The point however, must be made that the theme of loneliness in itself is not alienation. (Carson McCullers *The Heart is a Lonely Hunter*, is a novel of loneliness but not of alienation). It begins to be alienation when the feeling of isolation becomes reflected in a sense of inner or outer desolation. The following translation from the fifteenth century French poet Eustace Dèschamps, definitely shows feelings of alienation:

> Why are the times so dark
> Men know each other not at all
> But Governments quite clearly change
> From bad to worse
> Days dead and gone were more worthwhile
> Now what holds sway? Deep gloom and boredom
> Justice and law is nowhere to be found.
> I know no more where I belong.[7]

But again, it should be made clear, that mere intellectual awareness of the state of purposelessness is not alienation. Hardy's *New Year's Eve* is an example of the former. What is important is the sense of confusion, and of impending chaos as described by Dèschamps.

Very closely related to the 'homelessness' aspect of the alien of the tribe, is the idea of the alien as having mixed, opposing or unknown roots. Some of the characters of the literature of alienation are the victims of divided roots, as are their authors. Meursault (of The *Outsider*) like Camus, was a white Algerian. Both Tonio Kroger and his creator Thomas Mann had Italian mothers and German fathers. At the end of *Tonio Kroger*, Mann says:

> I stand between two worlds. I am at home in neither, and I suffer in consequence.[8]

The two worlds were those of the bourgeoisie (or Germany) and the Bohemian (or Italy). Hesse, who seems to mirror Mann in a curious way, creates the same problem for his Steppenwolf, but with a difference. The Steppenwolf is trapped in one world (the bourgeois) but belongs to the other (the artistic). His problem is one of integrity or compromise.

Apart from the malaise of the uncommitted or the compromised intellectual, another malaise is epitomised in Sartre's *Nausea*. It is that of the intellectual separated from self-awareness by his own intellect. In *Nausea*, Roquentin is a lonely scholar with a casual friendship with a clerk he calls the Autodidact who is a homosexual. Roquentin finds himself suffering from attacks of an odd kind of nausea and begins to feel he is losing his mind, which in a way is true. The attacks become worse until one day in the park:

> I flop onto a bench between the great black trunks . . . I should so like to let myself go . . . But I can't, I'm suffocating: existence is penetrating me all over, through the eyes, through the nose, through the mouth . . . And suddenly . . . the veil is torn away, I have understood, I have *seen.*[9]

What Roquentin has seen is that the Nausea is 'no longer an illness or a passing fit, it is *me*.'[10] In an effort to understand this 'feeling' part of himself, this 'existence', the philiosopher-Roquentin struggles with words. He finds the word Absurdity:—

> The essential thing is contingency. I mean that, by definition,
> existence is not necessity. To exist is simply to be there; what exists
> appears . . . but you can never deduce it.[11]

One begins to wonder who is *really* winning this battle – the thinker or the feeler; and then one realises that the feeler *is* the autodidact. By the end of the novel, Roquentin himself has become aware of this aspect of his personality.

3) *The Detached Man*

The third theme is the retreat from the split condition of the outsider by the denial of reciprocity – or, in the mirror-world of art, the awareness and expression of the denial of reciprocity. The condition is aptly summarised in the motto of Peer Gynt's trolls 'to thyself be sufficient'. In its more gentle form, it is the world of Horney's detached neurotic. One of the clearest expressions of the detached man on this level is given by Arnold in *The Buried Life*, in which he anticipates both Horney and Winnicott:

> Fate, which foresaw
> How frivolous a baby man would be —
> . . . . . .
> That it might keep from his capricious play
> His genuine self, and force him to obey
> Even in his own despite, his being's law,
> Bade through the deep recesses of our breast
> The unregarded river of our life
> Pursue with indiscernable flow it's way;[12]

'The unregarded river of our life' seems a deeply intuitive description of the unconscious in a basically integrated if somewhat detached personality. The poem ends:

> Only – but this is rare –
> When a beloved hand is laid in ours,
> . . . . . .
> A lost pulse of feeling stirs again.
> The eye sinks inward and the heart lies plain
> And what we mean we say, and what we would, we know,
> A man become's aware of his life's flow.[13]

Perhaps Arnold is only a semi-detached man.

To both Hesse and Thomas Mann the condition of detachment is seen as closely connected to the creative temperament itself. Veraguth, at the end of Hesse's *Rosshalde*, sees this after the death of his son, but he sees it as a consolation – 'The consolation of the outsider, to whom it is not given to drain the cup of life'. It is Mann who sees the necessity. Tonio Kroger explains it to his friend Lisabeta:

> For so it is, Lisabeta . . . The artist must be unhuman, extrahuman
> . . . The very gift of style, of form and expression, is nothing else than
> this cool and fastidious attitude towards humanity; you might say
> there has to be this impoverishment and devastation as a preliminary
> condition.[14]

The surface life of the spectator is shown most strongly in Camus's *Outsider* where all the events are described as though the protagonist were not involved. The atmosphere is set in the opening line of the book, where Meursault describes his mother's death:

> Mother died today. Or maybe, yesterday; I can't be sure.[15]

Meursault's total detachment, which is far deeper than a facade, persists throughout the book until the very end when a sudden gush of explosive rage overcomes him during the exchange with the prison chaplain. But what has been disclosed by that eruption of feeling is no long repressed hunger for life, merely another and deeper level of detachment:

> It was as if that great rush of anger had swept me clean, emptied me of hope, and gazing up at the dark sky spangled with its signs and stars, for the first time, the first, I laid my heart open to the benign indifference of the universe.[16]

However, it is perhaps Robbe-Grillet who is the supreme master of alienated writing at this level, showing the relationship between form and content in its most truly symbiotic form, particularly in *Instantanes*. In these snapshots of precise and sharply-coloured detail, the main attribute of the camera makes itself felt – that of indiscrimination. The camera takes a picture of everything within its range with equal clarity, be it children playing on a beach, or the murdered body of a woman – and so does Robbe-Grillet; but as a consummate artist he selects his indiscriminations with fastidious care. Robbe-Grillet pursues the spectator theme of alienation on another level – that of Peer Gynt's onion – in *Last Year at Marienbad*. Here the defensive posture of this strand in the alienation theme is clearly shown – if clearly is the right word. The audience is taken from ambiguity to ambiguity. Did they meet last year at Marienbad? Was there a last year at Marienbad? Is, perhaps, this year, last year? – or rather, last year, this year? – or perhaps . . . ? or perhaps . . . ? The impression that the film leaves is that no escape into dreams or into illusion has been portrayed, but an escape into evasion itself.

This third level of alienation is escape from reciprocity to the clearer world of the observer. The problem is (as the film *Blow-Up* showed) that although the camera may not lie – precisely what truth is it telling?

4) *The Hollow Man*

The next strand in the alienation theme is that of the hollow man. It is a more extreme state than that of detached man. The idea of evasion remains, but it is altogether more brittle, more shrill. Eliot's *The Hollow*

Men is obviously the paradigm. The extract below shows the main strands of avoidance and disguise:

> Let me be no nearer
> In death's dream kingdom
> Let me also wear
> Such deliberate disguises
> Rat's coat, crowskin, crossed staves
> in a field
> Behaving as the wind behaves
> No nearer —[17]

Eliot can only be understood through his literary allusions. It is an oblique and evasive technique that at the same time so clearly points the alienation theme, that it can be seen as one of the greatest artistry. It is significant, therefore, that the quotation at the beginning of *The Hollow Men* 'Mistah Kurtz – he dead' comes from Conrad's *Heart of Darkness*, the story of the inner dissolution of a man:

> Anything approaching the change that came over his features I have never seen before, and hope never to see again . . . It was as though a veil had been rent. I saw on that ivory face the expression of sombre pride, of ruthless power, of craven terror – of an intense and hopeless despair. Did he live his life again in every detail of desire, temptation and surrender during that supreme moment of complete knowledge? – he cried out twice . . .
> 'The horror! the horror!'
> I . . . left the cabin . . . suddenly the manager's boy put his . . . head in the doorway, and said in a tone of scathing contempt – 'Mistah Kurtz – he dead!'[18]

Perhaps the difference between the Hollow Man and the Detached Man can be seen in the difference between Arnold's 'And what we would we know' and Eliot's 'Let me be no nearer'.

The original hollow man is Dostoevsky's Underground Man. He is a hollow man who knows he is a hollow man and projects his self-contempt outwards. Spite and vindictiveness are the major emotions he is given by Dostoevsky. Of himself, the underground man says:

> I missed life through decaying morally in a corner, not having sufficient means, losing the habit of living, and carefully cultivating my anger underground.[19]

Above all the underground man is aware that underground *is* underground:

> And so hurrah for underground! . . . the underground life is more

advantageous. There at any rate one can . . . Oh but even now I am
lying! I am lying because I know myself that it is not underground
that is better, but something different, quite different, for which I am
thirsting, but which I cannot find. Damn underground.[20]

This self-awareness gives a curious nuance of self-torment to his
situation. The underground man is the self-labelled first anti-hero.
There are two sorts of anti-hero – the ridiculous and the contemptible,
but they perform the same function, that of the mockery or imitation of
sacrifice – and sacrifice is a major theme of the literature of alienation.

Clamence, the 'I' of Camus's *The Fall* is an underground man of
exquisite talent. An ex-Paris lawyer who has fled to Amsterdam unable
to face the self-contempt he feels at having failed even to attempt to
rescue a girl drowned in the Seine, he succeeds at every turn, in facing
himself with his own self-contempt. He accosts a hapless visitor and tells
him the story of his life down to every contemptible detail. But even the
sudden frankness at the end has a false ring to it. What we see uncovered
is yet another layer of self-contempt. He asks for a second chance to
rescue the drowning girl:

> A second time eh, what a risky suggestion! Just suppose . . . that we
> should be taken literally? We'd have to go through with it and the
> water's so cold. But lets not worry! It's too late now. It'll always be
> too late. Fortunately![21]

The most important attribute of the Hollow Man is that of
inauthenticity itself – even inauthenticity in being inauthentic. The
point is made by Rilke:

> We discover that we do not know our role; we look for a mirror; we
> want to remove our make-up and take off what is false and be real.
> But somewhere a piece of disguise that we forgot still sticks to us. A
> trace of exaggeration remains in our eyebrows; we do not notice that
> the corners of our mouth are bent. And so we walk around, a mockery
> and a mere half: neither having achieved being nor actors.[22]

The achievement of the status of 'actor' is the final condition of
alienation that I have called 'the possessed'. However first we must go
through the 'wasteland'.

5) *The Wasteland*

This is the fifth theme in the journey through the literature of
alienation. We have come from the inauthentic to the arid; the
wasteland is the land of accidie. Perhaps the defining attribute of the
condition is that of incommunicability. Whereas the detached man
performs a voluntary act of separation, in the Wasteland, the condition
is thought to be inherent.

The theme of incommunicability has its greatest expression in the theatre of the absurd. But, and here is one of the clearest demonstrations of the symbiosis of form and content in art, it is at one and the same time an expression of the state of incommunicability, and a technique for communicating what lies underneath it. The dramatists of the Absurd are using the meaningless to express the terrible. The main exponent is of course Beckett and *Waiting for Godot* with Vladimir and Estragon 'waiting for messages out of the dark'. They are trapped by their hope, as this dialogue between Vladimir and the messenger boy shows:

> V You have a message from Mr Godot,
> B Yes sir
> V He won't come this evening
> B No sir
> V But he'll come tomorrow
> B Yes sir
> V Without fail
> B Yes sir[23]

It is important to note here that Vladimir's remarks are statements – they are not questions. The boy is merely the mirror for Vladimir's own hopes, or delusions. The point is made throughout, but particularly at the end:

> V We'll hang ourselves tomorrow – unless Godot comes
> B And if he comes?
> V We'll be saved.[24]

One is reminded of Eliot in 'What the Thunder said'

> We think of the key, each in his prison
> Thinking of the key, each confirms a prison.[25]

The use of the meaningless to express the terrible, as an artistic technique, is usually thought of in relation to drama only. But it is just as usable, though less used, in poetry. Kenneth Patchen's work is an example, and a poet who belongs to the wasteland in both form and content is Edith Sitwell in *Facade*. These surfacely gay nonsense poems were designed to be chanted or sung as a 'piece' for a musical evening – thus heightening their macabre quality. The 'message' of *Facade* is given in the frontispiece:

> This modern world is but a thin matchboard flooring spread over a shallow hell. For Dante's hell has faded, is dead. Hell is no vastness; there are no more devils who laugh or who weep – only the maimed dwarfs of this life, terrible straining mechanisms, crouching in trivial sands and laughing at the giants crumbling.[26]

What precisely is the message of the waste-land, that so much effort seems to be spent in communicating or miscommunicating? Eliot gives a clue at the beginning of the *Waste-Land* in 'The burial of the dead':

> That corpse you planted last year in your garden,
> Has it begun to sprout? Will it bloom this year?
> Or has the sudden frost disturbed its bed?
> Oh keep the Dog far hence that's friend to men,
> Or with his nails he'll dig it up again!
> You! hypocrite lecteur – mon semblable – mon frere.[27]

The reference leads directly to the first poem in Baudelaire's *Fleurs du Mal* 'Au Lecteur':

> C'est L'Ennui' – l'oeil chargé d'un pleur involontaire,
> Il rêve d'échafauds en fumant son houka.
> Tu le connais, lecteur, ce monstre délicat
> Hypocrite lecteur, – mon semblable – mon frère![28]

(The french 'ennui' is a stronger word than the english boredom. Ennui, in this context is a boredom of the soul.)

The Waste-lander knows (or sometimes prefers not to know) what the Hollow-Man cannot know as he is busy avoiding another knowledge, and the detached man cannot know as he is using 'ennui' (in its weaker sense) as a defensive weapon. 'Ennui' is quite simply, the state of no horror – 'Dante's hell is dead'. The point is made by Conrad in *Heart of Darkness* a few lines farther on from 'Mistah Kurtz – he dead':

> I have wrestled with death. It is the most unexciting contest you can imagine. It takes place in an impalable grayness . . . without spectators . . . without glory . . . in a sickly atmosphere of tepid scepticism . . . I was within a hair's breadth of the last opportunity for pronouncement, and I found with humiliation that probably I would have nothing to say. This is why I affirm that Kurtz was a remarkable man. He had something to say . . .' 'the horror' . . . this was the expression of some sort of belief.[29]

The wasteland experience of despair can be a valuable encounter, as, for example, and in different ways, Kierkegaard and Heidegger have shown, but, it is extremely important at this point to distinguish between true and false despair. False despair can lead to the condition of alienation that I have called 'the possessed'. Milton's temporary encounter with the wasteland in *Paradise Lost* was a false despair, as he was clearly aware: (the words are spoken by Belial)

> Thus repulsed, our final hope
> Is flat despair. We must exasperate,

> The almighty victor to spend all his rage,
> And that must end us, that must be our cure,
> To be no more; (Book II p. 142-146)[30]

But Milton's Satan, like all good Satans, was no lover of the nihil for himself. It is interesting in this context to note that Nietzsche, having killed God, took great care not to do the same thing to Satan; though the relationship between the two, as Blake saw, was such that one might have expected Satan's death to have been as inevitable as Dorian Gray's. Instead Nietzsche wrote *The Anti-Christ.* It is apparent that Satan is more necessary than God. As Nietzsche said 'Man will wish for Nothing, rather than not wish at all.'[31]

6) *The Possessed*

This is the true state of alienation in the sense of 'belonging to another'. Three strands can be distinguished: the escape, the metamorphosis, which is another, more desperate form of escape; and the embracing or acceptance (on some level) of the state of being possessed.

a) *the escape*

The escape motif shows itself all through the literature of alienation, but always up to now in the form of defence or evasion. Here, it is in the form of flight. The first form of flight is that of the romantic and the archetype of the romantic escaper is Rimbaud, who used his life as his exit, and escaped from literature altogether. His rejection of the Paris literary society who had rejected him is too well-known to elaborate; but perhaps Auden's conclusion in his poem *Rimbaud* is an intuitively more correct interpretation of Rimbaud's motives than is Edmund Wilson's panegyric in *Axel's Castle.* Auden ends:

> Integrity was not enough; that seemed
> The hell of childhood: he must try again.
>
> Now, galloping through Africa, he dreamed
> Of a new self, a son, an engineer,
> His truth acceptable to lying men.[32]

A Season in Hell which was Rimbaud's last work and describes his rejection of the role of the poet, is an obscure poem, but there is one key to it – given by Rimbaud himself: "Charity is that key – this inspiration proves that I have dreamed." What charity symbolises for Rimbaud is again difficult to interpret, but it seems a direct disavowal of the famous letter of May 1870 to Bretagne, when he describes the role of the poet as that of being 'intolerant'. The rejection of poetry is shown clearly at the end:

J'ai créé toutes les fêtes, tous les triomphes, tous les drames. J'ai essayé d'inventer de nouvelles fleurs, de nouveaux astres, de nouvelles chairs, de nouvelles langues. J'ai cru acquerir des pouvoirs surnaturels. Eh bien! je dois enterrer mon imagination et mes souvenirs! Une belle gloire d'artiste et de conteur emporté.[33]

And then a few lines later there is the curious and significant sentence:

'Suis-je trompé? La charité serait-elle soeur de la mort pour moi?'[34]

It is obvious from reading *A Season in Hell* that a sense of disgust at his association with Verlaine, was one of the motivating factors in Rimbaud's repudiation of art. But the important point here, is the loss of integrity itself.

Hesse in *Steppenwolf* has been depicted as a romantic escaper, but the ending is ambiguous and we are left uncertain as to whether Haller (the 'I' of the story) is going forward into illusion or reality. The book ends:

'Pablo' I cried . . .' where are we?'
'We are in my Magic Theatre' he said with a smile, 'and if you wish at any time to learn the Tango or to be a General or to have a talk with Alexander the Great it is always at your service. . . .'
I understood it all . . . I knew that all the hundred thousand pieces of life's game were in my pocket. And I was determined to begin the game afresh. I would traverse not once more but often, the hell of my own inner being.
One day I would be a better hand at the game . . . Pablo was waiting for me . . .[35]

My own interpretation of *Steppenwolf* is that Haller was going forward into a deeper hell than that of Rimbaud – that of playing the game of being authentic. However this is directly contradicted by the author's own foreword to the 1961 edition:

I would be happy if many (readers) were to realise that the story of Steppenwolf pictures a disease and crisis – but not one leading to death and destruction, on the contrary; to healing.[36]

A more savage 'Magic Theatre' is that of Genet in *The Balcony*. Not content with playing the game of being real, Genet turns reality itself into a game. This faculty comes out clearly in his 'magical' autobiography *The Thief's Journal*. The message, I think, shows itself most clearly (as do most messages) at the end of the book, when Genet, doing another of the double-twists he has been performing throughout the work, describes his relationship to the book itself:—

Heroicised, my book, which has become my Genesis, contains . . . the commandments which I cannot transgress. If I am worthy of it, it will reserve for me the infamous glory of which it is the great master, for to what shall I refer if not to it? And . . . would it not be logical for this book to draw my body on and lure me to prison . . . by means of a fatality contained within it, which I have put there, and which, as I have intended, keeps me as witness, field of experimentation and living proof of its virtue and my responsibility.[37]

By an act of reification, Genet has at the same time both accepted and abnegated responsibility for his own life – 'for to what shall I refer, if not to it'? Genet is truly one of the possessed.

The second form of flight is that of the retreat, which sometimes comes under the guise of the search. In literature it is associated with the symbols of water, of whiteness and of coldness. One of its clearest expressions is in the words of Stein, the butterfly-hunter in Conrad's *Lord Jim.'*

There is only one remedy! One thing alone can us from being ourselves cure . . . A man that is born falls into a dream like a man who falls into the sea. If he tries to climb out into the air as inexperienced people do, he drowns . . . No, I tell you. The way is, to the destructive element submit yourself, and with the exertions of your hands and feet in the water, make the deep, deep sea keep you up . . .[38]

Hemingway's short story *The Snows of Kilimanjaro* is an example of the 'retreat as search' theme. The symbol of the story is the leopard:

Close to the western summit (of Kilimanjaro) is the dried and frozen carcase of a leopard. No one has explained what the leopard was seeking at that altitude.[39]

The mountaineer hero with the gangrenous leg is waiting with his party for a rescue plane. In his dying delerium he thinks the plane has arrived and he is put in it:

And then instead of going on to Arusha they turned left . . . Then they began to climb . . . and then it darkened and they were in a storm . . . and then they were out . . . and there ahead, all he could see, as wide as all the world, great, high, and unbelievably white in the sun, was the square top of Kilimanjaro. And then he knew that there was where he was going.[40]

One of the most terrifying descriptions of the retreat is given in Conrad Aiken's short story *Silent Snow, Secret Snow*. It describes a psychotic condition in a child in the form of a growing blanket of snow that the child sees as separating him from the rest of the world. His family become worried at his strange behaviour and try to question him. He runs away into his bedroom:

> Not a moment too soon. The darkness was coming in long white waves . . . The snow was laughing, it spoke from all sides at once . . .
> 'Listen to us' it said, Listen . . .
> But then a gash of horrible light fell . . . across the room from the opening door – the snow drew back hissing – . . . It was as if he had to reach up a hand toward another world for any understanding . . . but of that other world he remembered just enough to know the exorcising words . . .
> 'Mother. mother, go away, I hate you'
> And with that effort, everything was solved . . . The seamless hiss advanced once more . . .
> 'Listen' it said 'We'll tell you the last, the most beautiful and secret story . . . a story that gets smaller and smaller – it comes inward instead of opening like a flower – it is a flower becoming a seed – a little cold seed – do you hear? . . .[41]

b) *metamorphosis*

The position I have labelled 'metamorphosis' is that where, in literature, the condition of 'possession' is expressed fairly directly in terms of metaphors connoting the taking over of the body (or soul) by something alien. There are three distinct conditions. The first is where the body remains outwardly intact, but is inwardly consumed. The metaphor of the worm seems often to be used. It is, for instance used by Eluard in *From the depth of the Abyss*. Blake's poem 'O rose thou art sick' is perhaps the most well-known, and it is used by Laing in *The Self and Others* to describe the psychosis of one of his patients. The description of Captain Ahab in *Moby Dick* is particularly apposite:

> . . . the tormented spirit that glared out of bodily eyes when what seemed Ahab rushed from his room, was, but a vacated thing, a ray of living light to be sure, but without an object to colour, and therefore a blankness in itself. God help thee old man, thy thoughts have created a creature in thee; and he whose intense thinking thus makes him a Prometheus; a vulture feeds upon that heart for ever; that vulture the very creature he creates.[42]

The second condition is that where the identity, the 'I', remains intact (to begin with at any rate) but is enclosed in a different casing. The obvious example is Dante's wood of suicides. It is interesting that all the shades in Dante's Hell retain their own form except that of the suicides. The tree-transformation is apparently a symbol of self-hate. The other main example of this type of transformation is, of course,

Kafka's curious short story *The Metamorphosis.* The story of the man transmuted into a giant insect has many interpretations, but perhaps the strongest thread of meaning, as Kaufmann suggests, leads back to Dostoevsky's *Underground Man* who is so full of self-loathing that he cannot even become an insect.

The third condition of metamorphosis, is that of alienation in the strictest sense, that is, the experience of splitting itself. One example is Hesse's *Steppenwolf*. Harry Heller feels himself to be half-wolf and half-man. But it is made very clear, early in the book, that it is no dreamlike or psychotic condition Hesse is describing, it is merely a convenient metaphor for Harry's predicament. Dostoevsky's *The Double*, on the other hand is a description of a true psychotic condition. It is the story of a man, driven into a breakdown by the appearance of his own double which follows him everywhere, in spite of his efforts to escape it; until at last he is taken to the asylum, where the double cannot follow. There is some initial ambiguity as to whether the double really exists or not, but it is clear by the end that it is a creation of Golyadkin's mind.

Perhaps the most terrifying description of the experience of splitting itself is given in James Thomson's *City of Dreadful Night:*

> As I came through the desert thus it was,
> As I came through the desert: I was twain,
> Two selves distinct that cannot join again;
> One stood apart and knew but could not stir
> And watched the other stark in swoon and her;
> And she came on and never turned aside,
> Between such sun and moon and roaring tides;
> And as she came more near
> My soul grew mad with fear.

The final couplet has a particularly sharp impact as the previous seven stanzas had ended:

> But I strode on austere
> No hope could have no fear.[43]

It seems that beyond this level, no description is possible, for there can be no "I" to describe what is happening to the 'I'. However, Laing in *The Divided Self* has succeeded in giving vivid portrayals of the divided condition, and the writings of psychotics themselves, with which I am not familiar, may also do so.

c) *the embracing*

The last level of the possessed I have called 'the embracing'. There are two ways of embracing death: one is that collection of gambits, variously known as the game, the challenge, or the alliance; and the other is the sacrifice. The motive for them both is hope – the cure unto death.

First, the devices of the game, challenge or alliance. They are really all the same, but can be distinguished on the manifest level. The 'game' technique is shown in Nietzsche's advice to his 'preparatory men':

> For believe me, the secret of the greatest fruitfulness and the greatest enjoyment of existence is: *to live dangerously!* Build your cities under Vesuvius! Send your ships into uncharted seas! Live at war with your peers and yourselves! Be robbers and conquerors, as long as you cannot be rulers and owners, you lovers of knowledge.[44]

The prototype of the challenge is, of course, the pursuit of the White Whale in Melville's *Moby Dick*, but perhaps the most strikingly direct example can be found in a poem by Sylvia Plath, about a suicide attempt, called *Lady Lazarus*

> I have done it again
> One year in every ten
> I manage it
> . . . . . .
> Dying
> Is an art, like everything else.
> I do it exceptionally well.
> . . . . . .
> Herr God, Herr Lucifer
> Beware
> Beware
> I shall rise from the dead
> With my red hair
> And I eat men like air.[45]

The alliance technique is epitomised in *Faust*, but again, the more direct expressions come from poetry. Baudelaire's *Fleurs du Mal*, are almost all variations on the theme. In the poem called "*le possède*" he says:

> Tout de toi m'est plaisir, morbide ou pétulante;
> Sois, ce que tu voudras, nuit noire, rouge aurore;
> Il n'est pas un fibre en tout mon corps, tremblant
> Qui ne crie: *mon cher Belzebath, je t'âdore.*[46]

And again in a different mood in *le gout du Néant:*

> Je contemple d'en haut la globe en sa rondeur,
> Et je n'y cherche plus l'abri d'une cahute.
>
> Avalanche, veux-tu m'emporter dans ta chute?[47]

Finally, referring to his fighting at the barricades in 1848, Baudelaire says:

> Moi, quand je consens à être republicain, je fais le mal le sachant . . .
> Je dis Vive la Révolution! comme je dirais: Vive la Destruction! Vive
> La Mort![48]

The sacrificial or scapegoat theme is particularly evident in the work of Camus and Kafka, and I will concentrate on *The Trial* and *The Outsider*. In both books it is obvious that a ritual is being played out in the sense that the end is already known. In both books the theme of guilt is dominant, but mainly in the symbol of external justice – the two trials. Both men consistently deny their own guilt. Both trials are, in fact, caricatures of justice. K is not even told what he is accused of, and Meursault is convicted of shooting an Arab primarily on evidence that he showed no emotion at his mother's funeral. Meursault's lawyer asks 'Is my client on trial for having buried his mother or for killing a man?':

> . . . the prosecutor . . . said he was amazed at his friend's
> ingenuousness in failing to see that between these two elements of the
> case there was a vital link. They hung together psychologically . . .
> 'in short' he concluded . . . 'I accuse the prisoner of behaving at his
> mother's funeral in a way that showed he was already a criminal at
> heart.'[49]

The same theme, of both denial of guilt, and on another level of guilt, is shown in K's conversation with the priest:

> 'But I am not guilty' said K 'it's all a misunderstanding. And if it
> comes to that, how can any man be called guilty? We are all simply
> men here, one as much as the other.' 'That is true' said the priest 'but
> that is how all guilty men talk.'[50]

In both books the theme of unconscious self-destruction is very strong. In *The Trial*, it is shown in K's persistent refusal to see the true nature of the Court, in spite of the priest's help. The Parable of the Door, although it has been given many meanings, for it has the opaque quality of the true mirror, is basically, as the priest himself states, describing a delusion about the nature of the Court. 'The Court' the priest says very plainly at one point 'Makes no claim upon you. It receives you when you come and it relinquishes you when you go.' But K does not understand. There is also a clear indication in *The Trial* that Fraulein Burstner, who plays the main female role, has a significant part to play in K's self-immolation; just as Meursault's mother plays a leading part in his destruction. At the very end of *The Trial* K is being led through the town by his executioners, but he is holding back:

> And then before them Fraulein Burstner appeared . . . (K) suddenly
> realised the futility of resistence. He set himself in motion . . . (His
> warders) suffered him now to lead the way, and he followed the
> direction taken by the Fraulein . . .[51]

In *The Outsider*, the theme of unconscious self-destruction makes itself
felt in a way more directly relating to the myth of the scapegoat. In the
final talk with the chaplain there is an indication that Meursault is
perceiving himself in the role of Christ. The chaplain and Meursault
have been arguing about sin. Meursault maintains that he was guilty of
a criminal offence for which he was paying the penalty, but of no sin,
and no-one had the right to ask more of him. The priest replies:

> You're mistaken my son . . . These stone walls are steeped in human
> suffering . . . and yet . . . I *know* that even the wretchedest among
> you have sometimes seen, taking form upon that greyness, a divine
> face. It's that face you are asked to see.'[52]

Meursault is not impressed.

> The chaplain gazed at me mournfully. I know I had my back to the
> wall and the light was flowing over my forehead, He muttered some
> words I didn't catch; then abruptly asked if he might kiss me. I said
> No.[53]

The implication is here that the priest is seeing Meursault in the role
of Christ. Camus himself confirms this impression of the Christ-role, but
somewhat obliquely:

> I have sometimes said, and always paradoxically, that I have tried to
> portray in this character, the only Christ we deserved.[54]

The ends of both books emphasise the sacrificial, and at the same
time, theatrical elements in the two deaths. In *The Trial* K is laid down
in a stone quarry (almost, but not quite, on the sacrificial stone) and a
ritualistic pantomime is conducted with the knives. In both books also,
the sense of shame – of being bad in the eyes of the other – is manifest,
but not guilt. In both deaths, it is the audience that is important. *The
Outsider* ends

> For all to be accomplished, for me to feel less lonely, all that remained
> was to hope that on the day of my execution there should be a huge
> crowd of spectators and that they should greet me with howls of
> execration.[55]

The Trial ends

But the hands of one of the partners were already at K's throat, while the other thrust the knife into his heart and turned it there twice. With failing eyes he could see the two of them, cheek leaning against cheek, watching the final act. 'Like a dog' he said: it was as if he meant the shame of it to outlive him.[56]

There is one very useful attribute of the *agnus dei*. Although he may carry all the sins of the world, he remains *within himself* an innocent lamb.

Conclusion

The theme of alienation, of Man Possessed, is as old as man, and the artists have always told the same stories, in one form or another. At this direct level, the artist has always been aware. What has happened since Freud is that the artist has become reflectively aware – aware of being aware – and with reflection has come what Heidegger calls 'Legein', the need to know. Whereas, before Freud, the artist could speak innocently, direct from the myth, now he must speak knowingly. The knowingness brings both the need to probe – one can no longer merely repeat the myth, one must ask why – and the need to hide one's knowledge, both from the audience and perhaps sometimes from oneself. For there is yet a further stage of reflection. The artist is aware that the audience is aware, and the audience is aware that the artist is aware. I think it is for this reason that much of the art of the twentieth century can truly be described as alienated in a particular way. It is art 'after the fall'. It has become no deeper – a work of art is always as deep as the artist – but it has become more self-conscious and therefore more oblique, more condensed, more hidden. The literature of alienation is a glass through which one sees darkly.

Hatfield Polytechnic

1. B. Van S. Bark: 'The Alienated Person in Literature', *American Journal of Psychoanalysis*, Vol 21, no. 2, 1961. p. 183.
   M. Eckhardt: 'Alienation and the Secret Self', *American Journal of Pyschoanalysis*, Vol. 21, no. 2, 1961, p. 219.
   F. S. Finkelstein: 'The Artistic Expression of Alienation', in H. Aptheker (ed.): *Marxism and Alienation. A symposium*, Humanities Press, New York, 1965.
   B. H. Gelfont: 'The Imagery of Estrangement: Alienation in Modern American Fiction.', in F. Johnson (ed.): *Alienation: Concept, Term and Meanings*, Seminar Press, New York and London, 1973.
   E. and M. Josephson: *Man Alone: Alienation in Modern Society*, Dell Publishing Co. Inc., New York, 1962.
   H. D. Langford: 'The Imagery of Alienation', *in* Aptheker (ed.): op.cit.
   D. T. Laurenson and A. Swingewood: *The Sociology of Literature*, McGibbon & Kee, London, 1971, pp. 207-248.
   F. Pappenheim: *The Alienation of Modern Man*, Modern Reader Paperbacks, New York, 1968.
   S. Reichart: 'A greater Space in which to Breathe: What Art and Drama tell us about Alienation', *The Journal of Social Issues*, Vol. xxv, no. 2, 1969, pp. 137-146.
   G. Victor: *Invisible Men: Faces of Alienation*, Prentice-Hall, New Jersey, 1973.

2. M. Esslin: *The Theatre of the Absurd*, Garden City, New York, 1961.
   E. Heller: *The Disinherited Mind*, Penguin, London, 1961.
   W. Kaufmann (ed.): *Existentialism from Dostoevsky to Sartre*, Meridian Books, Cleveland & New York, 1970.
   R. D. Laing: *The Divided Self*, Tavistock, London, 1960.
   H. M. Lynd: *On Shame and the Search for Identity*, Harcourt Brace & World Inc., New York, 1958.
   R. Poggioli: *The Theory of the Avant-Garde*, translated from the italian by Gerald Fitzgerald, Harvard University Press, Cambridge, Mass., 1968.
   S. Spender: *The Destructive Element*, Jonathan Cape, London, 1935.
   E. Stone: *Voices of Despair: Four Motifs in American Literature*, Ohio University Press, Ohio, 1966.
   C. Wilson: *The Outsider*, Gollancz, London, 1956.

3. A. Robbe-Grillet: *Revue de L'Institut de Sociologie*, 1963, pp. 446.

4. T. S. Eliot: *Selected Poems*, Penguin, London, 1948, pp. 13-14.

5. A. Miller: *Death of Salesman*, Penguin, London, 1961, p. 111.

6. F. Kafka: *The Trial*, Penguin, London, 1953, p. 250.

7. Josephson: op.cit., p. 17.

8. T. Mann: *Death in Venice, Tristran, Tonio Kroger*, Penguin, London, 1972, p. 190.

9. J. -P. Satre: *Nausea*, Penguin, London, 1967, p. 181.

10. ibid., p. 181.

11. ibid., p. 188.

12. M. Arnold: 'The Buried Life', in J. Stephens *et al:* (eds.): *Victorian and Later English Poets*, American Book Company, New York, 1937, p. 524.

13. ibid., p. 525.

14. Mann: op.cit., p. 152.

15. A. Camus: *The Outsider*, Hamish Hamilton, London, 1958, p. 11.

16. ibid., p. 126.

17. Eliot: op.cit., p. 76.

18. J. Conrad: *Three Short Novels*, Bantam Books, New York, 1960, p. 84.

19. F. Dostoevsky: 'Notes from Underground', in Kaufmann (ed.): op.cit., p. 63.

20. ibid., p. 80.

21. A. Camus: *The Fall*, Penguin, London, 1963, p. 108.

22. R. M. Rilke: 'The Notes of the Malte Lauride Brigge', in Kaufmann (ed.): op.cit., p. 120.

23. S. Beckett: *Waiting for Godot*, Faber & Faber, London, 1959, p. 91.

24. ibid., p. 94.

25. Eliot: op.cit., p. 65.

26. E. Sitwell: *Bucolic Comedies*, Duckworth, London, 1928, p. 51.

27. Eliot: op.cit., p. 51.

28. C. Baudelaire: *Les Fleurs du Mal*, Librairie Armand Colin, Paris, 1958, p. 4.

29. Conrad: op.cit., p. 85.

30. H. F. Fletcher (ed.): *The Complete Poetical Works of John Milton*, Houghton Mifflin Co., New York, 1941, p. 177.

31. F. Nietzsche: *The Anti-Christ*.

32. W. H. Auden: *A Selection by the Author*, Penguin, London, 1958, p. 63.

33. A. Rimbaud: *A Season in Hell and the Drunken Boat*, New Directions Paperbacks, New York, 1961, p. 86.

34. ibid., p. 86.

35. H. Hesse: *Steppenwolf*, Penguin, London. 1972.

37. J. Genet: *The Thief's Journal*, Penguin, London, 1965, p. 224.

38. J. Conrad: *Lord Jim*, Penguin, London, 1972, p. 162.

39. E. Hemingway: 'The Snows of Kilimanjaro', in C. Fadiman (ed.): *Reading I've Liked*, Hamish Hamilton, London, 1947, p. 414.

40. ibid., p. 416.

41. C. Aitken: 'Silent Snow, Secret Snow', in Fadiman: op.cit., p. 720.

42. H. Melville: *Moby Dick*, Dent, London, 1969, p. 176.

43. J. Thompson: 'The City of Dreadful Night', in Stephens *et al*: op.cit., p. 1094.

44. F. Nietsche: 'Live Dangerously', in Kaufman: op.cit., p. 106.

45. S. Plath: 'Lady Lazarus', *Ariel*, Faber & Faber, London, 1965, p. 16.

46. Baudelaire: op.cit., p. 40.

47. ibid., p. 81.

48. Caudwell: *Illusion and Reality: A Study of the Sources of Poetry*, Macmillan, London, 1937, p. 320.

49. Camus: *The Outsider*, op.cit., p. 102.

50. F. Kafka: op.cit., p. 232.

51. ibid., p. 247.

52. Camus: op.cit., p. 123.

53. ibid., p. 123.

54. A. Camus: in C. C. O'Brien: *Camus*, Fontana Modern Masters, London, 1970, p. 20.

55. Camus: *The Outsider*, op.cit., p. 127.

56. Kafka: op.cit., p. 251.

The Semiology of 'La Chinoise'

Michael Rustin

The Semiology of 'La Chinoise'

The sociology of literature or film is far from being an unambiguous or clearly established mode of work at this time. On the one hand literary or cultural criticism seeks to explicate the effects, intentions, and formal mechanisms of a cultural work, and to evaluate works against some moral or aesthetic standards. Such work seems inherently concerned with individual expression, and with judgements of quality,[1] rather than with analysis of the social or with theoretical generalisation. On the other hand, the assertion of typicality in cultural work, related to some presumed 'given' of social reality to which works of art are held to correspond, risks a woeful reductionism, found in many sociological and Marxist treatments of the subject.

The central problems are to characterise both cultural phenomena, and the social, in ways which allow some theoretically intelligible relations to be established between them. Clearly current debates about both the nature of society and sociological method, and the nature of works of art, are critical to the problems of a sociology of culture.

In recent years, crucial intellectual developments have been taking place that are now transforming the field of the sociology of culture. A burgeoning interest in the cultural and phenomenological dimensions of the social, in sociology, has substantially overthrown an unconsidered and unreflective determinism.[2] The empiricist climate in British sociology in the period up to the mid-sixties barely had a concept for the cultural at all. The change of focus in recent years in the sociology of education[3] and the sociology of deviance[4] are sufficient examples of a general switch of interest from differential rates of behaviour and their correlates, to cultural and sub-cultural formations and their interaction. The idea of the inherent subjective meaningfulness of social phenomena, and an interest in ethnographic and interpretive methods has been central to this change. This subjectivist tradition tends however to lead to the individualisation of social phenomena,[5] to the idea of their natural idiosyncrasy and difference, and thus to a merely descriptive or typifying method. Symbolic interactionism exemplifies this tendency, its central idea of self-created meanings continually undermining any wider determining idea of the social without which sociology seems empty as a project.

Now of equal importance to the study of culture is the growing influence of structuralist approaches. Whereas phenomenological and interactionist approaches have the effect of defining the social in terms of subjectively created meanings, the structuralists adopt the converse approach, of characterising subjective meanings as attributes, products or illusions of the social. But their concept of the social, though in principle deterministic, is resolutely cultural. Thus they recommend an objective, scientific analysis of cultural forms, modelled on the science of linguistics and extending to analogous and derived kinds of discourse, conceived as matrices of the social. The antithesis which was formerly so fatal for a sociology of culture, namely between a positivistic approach which reduced culture to something else, and a cultural approach which rejected as reductionist all ideas of social relation or dependency, can thus in principle at last be resolved. The question of the autonomy of art becomes merely a special case of the wider problem of individual and collective agency, the cultural level being established in both of the above schools as constitutive of the social order, one among other forms of practice.

The third and of course integrally related area of intellectual development has been in Marxism. The cultural and voluntarist dimensions of the social have been forcefully demonstrated by historians such as E. P. Thompson,[6] and the reductionism of received Marxist treatments of culture have been criticised notably by Raymond Williams,[7] in terms of an emphasis on the creative and created dimensions of the cultural and the social, and of the irreducibility of aesthetic work to other definitions. While this represents the most important English contribution to the Marxist study of culture to date, structuralist contributions have informed Althusserian work, reconnecting the ideas of cultural modes of determination with a more general Marxist theory in which ideological transmission is given a crucial weight.[8] Thus the divergent subjectivist and structuralist approaches to culture have both been effective tendencies within the Marxist tradition in recent years. We must note also a quite general emphasis on culture as a mode of class domination which as Perry Anderson[9] has recently pointed out has been so central a theme in recent Western Marxism, of almost all schools, and which has been a major influence on the sociological study of culture. (I use the term sociological in the most inclusive and general sense here, though cultural studies might be more appropriate. While the discipline of sociology has made its important contribution, the field now in no way coincides with academic sociology's boundaries.)

The aim of this study of *La Chinoise* is to explore firstly the language of films, since only if the character of films as objects of study and the methods appropriate to this are clarified can any useful sociological discussion of them take place. The paper, whose initial writing ante-dates some of the important recent theoretical writings and translation in this area, is influenced by Peter Wollen's seminal *Signs and Meaning in the Cinema*[10] which set out an initial programme for the applications of semiology to film. The paper also suggests an implicit view, which unfortunately it is not possible to develop here at length, on the question of how films relate to the social formation in which they are generated. This view asserts a film like *La Chinoise* to be a source as much as an object of knowledge. A source not in the sense of 'evidence' for some otherwise-derived propositions about society, but rather as an act of discovery or realisation of its chosen subject-matter. On the polarity of science versus ideology,[11] this paper looks upon a film like *La Chinoise* as being nearer to a mode of science. Clearly these are the wrong terms, since the ordering structures of art are different in kind from the ordering structures of the sciences. Yet it is argued that the arts must be seen as capable of rational and truthful realisation, and not merely of distrusted and partial statement, or, at any rate, that some of the epistemological privilege conferred on scientific modes of discourse must also be accorded to aesthetic ones.

La Chinoise clearly goes out of its way to establish a method of clarifying its own function, of forcing on its audiences a recognition of its own artifice, and of alternative ways of perceiving and valuing the phenomena it presents. It would be difficult to regard a film so contradictory in the definition of reality it offers in any simple way as an ideological representation, especially given its own forceful repudiation, through the words of its characters and its own techniques, of representation as a form.

The film has a prescience, made a year before the events of 1968, not least in the concluding summation of the students' somewhat nihilistic political summer as 'a start', recognising as serious this somewhat desperate and apparently hopeless striving for real political connection by these young bourgeois. Its acuteness, like others of Godard's films, to the ubiquity of cultural bombardment and control in contemporary capitalism and the need to contest this in cultural terms, may be seen as an aesthetic parallel of the theoretical position of Western Marxists, notably the Frankfurt School[12] referred to above, itself of course influential through Marcuse's work in the political events of that time. The pressures of finding an integrity of political response in this time of intense moral crises for Western radicals (the Vietnam War) are eloquently caught in their many contradictions through the experience of this particular student group. Godard is attempting to work out an aesthetic which could provide a form for revolutionary work in these cultural conditions. Such a film asserts itself as definitive of social realities, not as a representation or ideological reflection of them.

No doubt in the light of subsequent knowledge a work formerly thought of as a unique act of discovery can come to be seen as representative, expressive of and able to be connected in a determinative way with the society it seeks to explore and expose.

Even in such cases, however, determinations are hard to trace. Works of art have their own determining force, their relative autonomy within a larger totality, as well as being themselves products. We may think we can see a work as reflective of its social context, while its contributions to defining the meanings and values of that context for its time may in fact make it constitutive of that context and of our social knowledge. A mistake often implicit in the sociology of culture is to assume a knowledge of the social structure in which works are placed which in reality may be more conjectural and subjective than our understanding of the cultural object itself, and in any case is derived from other cultural objects of scientific and artistic kinds.

Other forms of artistic work may be never more than ideological reflections, that is replications of existing social definitions, typifications with no power of discovery or knowledge at any point. For such typifications we may be able to forget interactive relationships between art and its generative society, and 'explain' works largely as derivatives of known patterns of meanings, themselves with an understood role in social reproduction. Sociologists may find such typified, routine works more amenable for their forms of analysis, since they are more readily seen as determined products, subject to generalisation like other social phenomena.

The view taken here is that the analysis of forms of language and code as constitutive of both the formally aesthetic and social worlds will be increasingly important and helpful. The restoration of the cultural dimension of Durkheim's conception of the social is a substantial advance on empiricism. But the thoroughgoing structuralist attack on the idea of the active subject is here opposed. It implies a kind of omniscience, in face of all creative work, a prior totalisation to which all works can be related as pre-determined components, when in fact our conception of such totalisations depends on the very works, both artistic and scientific, that they seek to explain. For these reasons Godard's film is seen less as a reflection of its moment than as a realisation of it, a constituting element of its political time rather than a fully determined one, a creation and communication of knowledge rather than merely of ideology. Its partiality is to be understood not in terms of some anterior scientific perfection, against whose standard it can be judged, but as an incompleteness inseparable from any actual history in which outcomes cannot be known in advance of attempts,[13] in which experiments have to be made in order that knowledge can be won. Godard's kindness to his fictional subjects in virtue of both their youth and the political predicament they share with their creator, depends on the actual impossibility of finding scientific solutions to the problems posed in this film, of how to live the whole political and cultural life of a socialist at this time.

Semiology is the science of signs.[14] It seeks to understand the codes or languages of gestures, images, colours, cultural artifacts like fashion and furniture, as well as verbal languages, on the assumption that virtually all deliberate human creations make communications, have meanings, as well as and as part of their use.

Cinema, combining images, sounds, music, words, colours, gestures with the body and expressions of the face, photographed objects, decor, is clearly the case study par excellence for the justification of this science. To a greater degree than theatre, films cannot be understood as the representation of a text. To know and evaluate what is going on in a film we need to 'read' many languages besides those of words. The case for a semiology of cinema has been made explicitly (for example by Peter Wollen),[15] and has lately become the subject of an elaborated theoretical discourse.[16] All film criticism perhaps makes an attempt at a semiology for specific works and directors.

Films raise a critical problem for semiological method. They use not an arbitrary language of signs (like verbal languages) but images from nature. Films can get nearer than any other art to pure naturalism; a film of a kind can be made by pointing a camera at a scene and screening any ensuing action. Even this, however, entails the selection of what appears within the frame, both spatially – the camera's field of vision – and in the texture of the screen image, which itself constitutes a kind of simplification and stylisation of our 'natural' vision. Naturalistic cinema maintains the illusion of reproduced reality, while in fact departing from literal actuality. Time is compressed, by cutting and juxtaposing scenes. Actuality is contrived by actors and sets. The film 'sees' different locations, and from different spatial and human points of view. The 'unities' of the camera pointing at a sequence of action are abandoned, and a more complex 'unity' of an imagined 'ideal' sequence replaces it – what 'might have happened' – as if reconstructed by a human memory, or as lived by a human observer or participant. What such films work for is an illusion of life as it is, and the problem of maintaining the consistency of this illusion controls many of the decisions in making a film. What happens on the screen must be as it might have happened to the characters. This is, of course, an ordering of experience, but of a self-negating kind: the more successful the ordering, the less the audience will notice it. The conventions of narrative realism seek an illusion which makes them invisible – that the film reflects life itself.

But there is an opposite pole of cinematic method, which emphasises rather than conceals the ordering and formalisation of experience. The cinema, by this canon, becomes a way of restructuring our sense of reality, rather than merely bringing out its latent pattern. Eisenstein belongs to this pole, as Rossellini to the other. As the cinema of naturalism works diachronically, through the flow of time within the film and 'real time' that it stands for, formalist cinema works synchronically, through metaphoric rather than temporal relationship. The dimension of time is one constraint holding films to the story-telling, diachronic method. It is harder to sustain metaphoric connections across a lengthy flow of material; as narrative poetry is less resonant and intense in its synchronic associations than lyric poetry. But consideration of poetic drama shows us that it isn't narrative sequence in time that explains this lack of metaphoric density in film. The difficulty lies in the nature of the language of cinema: the inferiority, for purposes of poetry, of images taken from nature compared with the complexity and multi-dimensionality of verbal language. What can be conveyed with one is perhaps just less complex than can be achieved with the other.

Nevertheless, cinematic languages have been created, through which individual communications can be made. We have discussed above how these languages can be naturalistic, presenting a recognisable version of the experience which the director and his audience share. This may seem like a representation of 'nature', but on inspection, especially when the context of expectations changes, will be shown to be a stylisation. This cinema aims at a congruence of the various 'channels' through which communications are made in film – sound, image, etc. Or languages may arise from specific genres, like the Western, coding and mythologising experience, and increasing the specific significance of each image through a focussed context of relevance. Within a known genre, much can be taken for granted; the film's 'reality' being established by familiar conventions, the director can concentrate on the achievement of a personal inflection and meaning within them. Again, congruence is sought, between the various 'channels' of a film, but within a selected frame of a reference – a 'restricted code'. Or thirdly, languages may be developed by specific directors, establishing a universe of meaning shared with the audience by repetition and association through various films. The 'auteur' theory draws attention to this cumulative quality of directors' work, while to my mind confusing 'language' and 'speech' in its transfer of critical emphasis from the individual film to the *oevre* of films of a given director. We may need the whole body of work to understand a director's language, but the primary focus of criticism and evaluation must nevertheless be the individual film. There is much that can be said about a director's whole development, and about themes common to his work. But the most decisive experience must be of the individual film, or 'speech'. The temporal quality of films, the impossibility of reference back, of taking it all in at once, already makes difficulties enough in creating a criticism. Critical response is all the harder over a director's life-work.

The creation of specific languages, through genres like the musical, or by the 'auteur', provides the context for greater complexity of meaning. Each 'channel' of meaning can acquire an autonomous significance for the audience. The channels can be separated, no longer aiming at a congruence sustaining the unity of an illusion, but counterpointing each other. The complexity of words, through their multiplicity of associations and combinations, can be more nearly reached.

This introduces a discussion of the semiology of Godard's *La Chinoise* (Ou Plutôt à la Chinoise). This is a film far towards the pole of formalism. There is only one real 'action' in the film, the murder of the Minister of Culture and the political quarrel that precedes it; much of the film is 'documentary', not specifically related to this, though a 'documentary' paradoxically 'remote from naturalistic method. *La Chinoise* sets out specifically to avoid the 'illusion' of narrative. We watch a 'film in the making', actors acting, stepping in and out of their roles as characters in the film. Belief in what is happening on the screen, as we immerse ourselves in a story, cannot carry us through this film. The film is fragmented, composed of episodes, punctuated by graphics. It switches through many conventions: mime, wall-posters, graphics, interviews to a camera, lectures by the cast, life-like action, music, lengthy two-person dialogue. Many of these modes of expression have become familiar to us from Godard's other films. In this sense, Godard has created his own 'language'; this film uses the resources of a director's highly individual and achieved style. Yet it has a consistency and intensity greater than much of Godard's work; it quite lacks the arbitrariness and casualness that we find elsewhere. It is highly formal. The action is almost all within one flat, explicitly the 'set'. The members of the cell each lecture and are interviewed. The repetitions reinforce the basic theme, place differences between the individuals in the central context of a group experience. Other 'languages', to be discussed below – colour, lighting, illustration etc. – have their own re-iterative consistency. The most important connections in this film are not sequential and linear, but metaphorical, associative, logical. Most brilliantly, holding this formalist film in its own unity, are the connections and movements between one language and another.

La Chinoise is so good a case-study for semiology in the cinema because it controls and links its many 'codes' with such precision and relevance. Godard has dismembered the language of naturalism, in which images count only in the 'gestalt' of the moving present, and in which the relevance of immediate action and intention diminishes other relevances to a mere background, or to incongruous intrusions like 'symbolism' in a naturalistic context. He has reconstructed a language, with homologies and themes transcending story and recurring in patterns throughout the film. The subject-matter of *La Chinoise* is specifically appropriate for this treatment. An iconographic consistency lies behind this film, in the Chinese Cultural Revolution and the political response to it, as well as being achieved *in* the film. Nevertheless, *La Chinoise* persuades us of the value of its method beyond its particular occasion. This 'formalist' synthesis of the languages of cinema, in this as in Godard's other work, extends cinema's resources, and the poetic density and force of what a film can say.

La Chinoise declares its own aesthetic. Kirilov, who has been lecturing on the theory of art to a little group of young revolutionaries in their borrowed Paris flat, declaims that ideolgical correctness in a work of art is useless if it lacks artistic force. War on two fronts is necessary, the political and the artistic. This explains why it is that so much of the great quality of this most political of films is in its form, in the cinematic language that Godard invents. Art, says Kirilov, is in a dialectical relation to reality. This is why there can be a *cultural* revolution – why cultural forms break through and change a social reality. *La Chinoise* embodies its own dialectic, in its serious theme of French students making themselves revolutionaries, and in a continously paradoxical quality. Truth comes through contradiction and paradox – we see the importance of argument between the comrades, recurring ambiguity and the unexpected on the screen, the paradox of Lumière and Meliés used by Guillaume – such a model teacher – to instruct the others. The film declares itself against ideological reductionism, for the autonomy of the cultural within the political moment.

This is a film of total, explicit contrivance. The first title tells us it is a 'film in the making'. Throughout we see reminders that it *is* a film – the camera from the actor's point of view, clapboards starting scenes, actors ready to move before the beginning of a take. It is made clear that the rooms in which the young people are living are a set. Yvonne gives her interview, about her life in the country and in Paris, against a wall which has a poster about the French Peasant Today pinned beside her. When Kirilov talks about fashion, Veronique is seen under a group of art nouveau fashion pictures. As the camera moves around the flat, we recognise these separate backdrops from episodes of the film, consistent with the whole decor yet each with its specific filmic purpose.

Kirilov, who declares that art should be the reality of reflection, not the reflection of reality, citing Eisenstein, and Guillaume, who cites Brecht, both proclaim the function of art as teacher, as the mode of rational enlightenment, as dialectical, as the discovery of truth beneath surfaces. Both in these doctrines, and in its practice, *La Chinoise* is against naturalism, against illusion, and against unthinking emotion. The film makes its contrivances explicit, and when it moves us requires us to understand how and why we are being moved.

Guillaume explains and illustrates this. His story of the Chinese who demonstrated in Moscow, bandaging his face the day after there had been a beating from the Russian police, and then when he removed his bandage in front of the summoned photographers, annoying them as there was nothing for them to photograph, illustrates the use of theatre. 'Who do these Chinese think they are, comedians?'. Yes, Guillaume implies, actors. Mime can make a point better than pictures of the real. Guillaume illustrates his own lectures, contrived with props of spectacles and mimes all ready. He can bring material to life, as the others can't. Naturalism isn't the only way of making a point.

Most beautifully, the artifice and deliberatness of Godard's cinema is conveyed in the scene where Veronique, to teach him a lesson, tells Guillaume she doesn't love him. She no longer loves his eyes, his mouth, the colour of his sweaters, reminding us of how carefully the colour of his sweaters, like everything else, has been chosen in this film. War on two fronts is too complicated, Guillaume has said in disagreement with the departing Kirilov, wanting her attention and agreement. Politics and art, music and work, how can you do it? I don't love you, she says, because you interfere with my work, it's too complicated. And she

switches the record player from what sounds like Jelly Roll Morton to
Chopin, conveying the pathos to him of what she is saying. Two fronts,
her actions invoke, words and music. She mimes the effect of film music
behind action and dialogue, consciously within the film. The history of
the cinema, one might say, is summed up in this visible but no less
powerful manipulation of our feelings. The metaphor of the two fronts,
in words, music and mime, grows in this complex and concentrated
scene, denoting in turn politics and art, work and music, music and
words, politics and love, all of which must be held in their relations to
each other.

The stress on theatre, on art, on culture, is integral of course to the
film's inspiration, the Chinese Proletarian Cultural Revolution. The
film is about the Cultural Revolution. Or at least, about a group of
young French people who try to live it out in the summer of 1967.
Through this imagined group, Godard expresses his response to this
event. There is a specific meaning, force and relevance to Godard in
cultural revolution. The film is built from his profound sense of his own
culture, and conveys the doctrine and practice of being a cultural
revolutionary. Guillaume, of the group, is an actor, a disciple of Brecht
and Artaud. *La Chinoise* combines elements of the aesthetic of each.
Kirilov is a painter. His references to Mayakovsky and Eisenstein assert
the film's allegiance to revolutionary art, as well as to revolutionary
politics. That is, to the formalist pole in revolutionary art, consistent
with the aesthetic of the film itself, not the social-realist. Veronique is a
philosophy student, oppressed by the authoritarianism and class basis of
French culture, opposed to the existing university. Even Henri, who
disagrees with Veronique's application of cultural theory to politics and
is expelled from the cell for opposing terrorism, makes it a point against
the Maoists that they have attacked *Johnny Guitar.* His cultural work,
chemistry – significantly physical science – takes him in a different
ideological direction. The fifth member Yvonne, responds only to
images, experiences, feelings, not at all to ideas. But she, the nearest to
being a peasant, is the most moved by the cell's progress: she mimes the
Vietnamese peasant and guerilla in the film.

This film in the making is itself, we understand, a political act. The
cell about which it is made models itself on the Cultural Revolution in
China, whose progress it monitors in radio bulletins. The members are
Red Guards. The Little Red Book is read aloud, sung about, made into
gun emplacements, thrown at toy American tanks, given out in the
street, read from as a mode of drawing lots, bookcases are full of them,
and in lectures they are heaped on a bed. The activity of the Cultural

revolution is followed, in the morning exercises on the verandah, timed with shouted revolutionary slogans; in the use of toys for political theatre; in the display in the flat, and the shots in the film of posters and slogans; the use of masks – Johnson as paper-tiger; in the playing of mimes. The recent documentary film from China, *The Little Red Book*, made by a French camera crew on an official trip, remind us how closely Godard has followed the dramaturgy and iconography of the Chinese.

Later, it is a Minister of Culture who is assassinated, after a plan for terrorism in the university is dropped. Francis Jeanson, who disagrees with Veronique's project of terrorism, is himself working on a cultural action. Revolutionary culture is this film's whole preoccupation.

Politics has often been a resistant subject for film, so wholly has it seemed a matter of words, and so wordy are ideological men. Yet Godard has made a political film of images, as well as words. How has this been done? We must attempt to understand the various 'codes' through which the meanings of *La Chinoise* are expressed.

The semiology of film has suffered from the difficulty that languages, other than words, through which speech can take place, seem so subjective and elusive. Is there an established language, in the cinema, to which different directors can give an individual expression? Is there a vocabulary and syntax of colour, lighting, cutting, camera-movement, sound?

I want to suggest that *La Chinoise* uses such language with extraordinary force and clarity. One of the principal reasons why it does so, with such complete control of each frame, is because of the subordination of narrative line. Normally, getting an intelligible action and persuasive performances on the screen must be the primary problem of the director. This accounts for so much 'inert' screen material, on second and third viewings: interest is sustained only by the suspense of the story – what happens next. When this is known, there is nothing else. In this film, each frame is a problem in its own right, and the connections within the film are as much analogical and metaphorical as they are sequential and linear. It is because the film is operating on a plane of associations, as much as in narrative form, that its many levels of language can be juxtaposed without distraction. The substantial element of verbal, conceptual thought in the film doesn't negate this, for the thinking too has an autonomous life, linked to image as much as to plot. The plot runs parallel to the development of the argument, and then is held up, qualified by it, in Jeanson and Veronique's dialogue, and in Henri's interview. What we do not have is that familiar pattern in which thought and image merely fill out, casually, illustratively, or still worse, symbolically, an already-conceived story.

It is a film of associated, cumulative, visual and verbal signs. The tiger, springing on Yvonne from a petrol tank named Napalm, associates to the tiger's head on Johnson, while we see atom bomb = paper tiger on the blackboard and hear this sung in the rock-number. As Jeanson tells Veronique she'll be arrested in a week the camera moves for the first time to another passenger behind her in the carriage. Some metaphors are explicit dramaturgy within the film – Yvonne in black sacking. Others the characters discover in conversation – France is like dirty dishes, as Yvonne washes up.

In this sense, of its escape from the constraint of a narrative structure, and the consequent emancipation of its other modes of expression, *La Chinoise* is closer to poetry than to prose. The captions – first movement, of film, second movement of film, suggests that Godard thinks of it, as closest to music.

Godard creates, in *La Chinoise*, visual and aural correlatives of an ideological universe. This is the central key to the semiology of this film, the basis for its concentration of meanings.

Ideological thinking, especially perhaps among adolescents, is simplifying, dichotomising, all-embracing. Everything must be interpreted within the same systematised, ideological categories. In a sense it is a process of reduction of complexity to a single scheme. We are familiar with this process, perhaps, as a matter of ideas (if we have had an 'ideological' experience). It is represented, in words, in this film. Arguments about what films can count, denunciation of bourgeois romantic fiction in the PCF women's magazine. The extension of the concept of class struggle by Veronique, linking the university at Nanterre with the Algerians working outside: 'my class is Philosophy'. And by Guillaume, who announces himself as a worker in the industry of theoretical production.

But this ideological mode of thinking also dominates the visual style of *La Chinoise*. The flat in which the young people live, both a working and a living space and a set, becomes a projection of the mental universe of the young comrades. Through colour, lighting, camera-position, and by visual and verbal reference, Godard conveys what it means to try to live out a Cultural Revolution, to transform oneself and one's culture in ideological terms. It is an illustration of the force of McLuhan's propositions, about the saliency, given electric media, of non-linear, imagistic channels of communication, especially for the young, that an ideological universe can now be represented most forcefully in these terms. And indeed perhaps of the saliency of communications as a 'structure in dominance' of late capitalism.

The film shows a consciousness not only of the graphic and pictorial formation of consciousness, but as so often in Godard's films the pervasiveness of the mass media as primary modes of experience. Radio, tape-recorder, record-player, travel advert for Russian tourism, magazine story, are all important to the young people. All this justifies the centrality of a cultural revolution. Formulas do oppress.

There is even a further, physical correlate of this mode of power in the opening and closing of hotel doors and gates by photo-electric beam, when Veronique goes to assassinate the Soviet Minister. We see the gate close behind her car, by remote control. Yet the car itself operated the mechanism (we have already seen the doors open before Veronique). Are they trapped, or will those bars roll back as unexpectedly and silently as they came?

Two striking convergences occur in the relationship between the Chinese Cultural Revolution and the West. Firstly, the mobilisation simultaneously in underdeveloped, peasant China and in the decadent, urbanised West, of adolescents as the major force in revolutionary upheaval. Secondly, the common pre-eminence of culture in the revolutionary process – the remaking of the thoughts and imagination – the product of the specific traditions of the Chinese, and of a certain state of communications and marketing technology in the West. An authentic spark of energy flashes across between these two experiences, a specific affinity amidst so much else that is alien between the two stages of development. This connection is given its richest exploration in Godard's film. The May Events of 1968, the year after *La Chinoise*, a cultural explosion and the mobilisation of a Western Red Guard, unmistakably demonstrated this convergence. There is the third, weaker connection, specific to France, in the peasant, agricultural character of the two countries, expressed through Yvonne, the country girl.

Colour is perhaps the most important of the 'languages' used by Godard to establish this ideological universe. Red is the most important of these colours. Its several associations are powerful and unmistakable enough for us to recognise here a language – objective and interpersonal – put to the use of individual speech.

The flat is painted red and blue, unfinished, with the mouldings left white, as if to convey that it is being lived in for a short time, that it is a set, that it must not be too bourgeois. Upholstered chairs are a deep, rich red, as are the lampshades on ornate stands. These convey to us the opulence of the flat's bourgeois owners, and the plushness and decadence of their surroundings. The reminder, in this deep, luxurious colour, of the brighter, revolutionary blood-red so prominent in the film visually associates revolutionaries and the bourgeois, in a premonition of bloodshed.

Henri comes into the flat, his face covered in blood. Kirilov shoots himself, and bleeds. Yvonne plays the Vietnamese peasant, attacked by American aeroplanes. At the second shot, she is covered in blood, though this is pretend-blood, illustrating Guillaume's lecture. Later, crying 'Victory to the N.L.F.' she fires a toy gun which folds into a transistor radio from behind a barricade of Little Red Books. Again she is covered in blood. The association of the Little Red Book and revolutionary blood could not be clearer.

The posters to which the film continually cuts are splashed with red-Stalin's eyes, for example, and Alice's apron as she looks down the rabbit-hole to illustrate Veronique's interview. Sometimes, in pictures of red flags from Peking or Moscow in 1917, the red belongs in the originals, but often it has been daubed on, adding point in this most red of colour-films, in these photographic evocations of a Communist tradition.

There are red shells in a toy gun. Guillaume gestures with a red plastic felt pen. The handlebars, to which a saddle and a mirror are grotesquely wired by Kirilov in a metaphor of bodily confusion and deadlock, have red grips. When Veronique and Yvonne play toreadors with it, there is the unspoken allusion to the reds of the bullring.

Yvonne begins the film in a pale blue, pink-edged housecoat, and graduates, as her political education proceeds to a bright red Chinese shirt, which she wears when her boy friend walks out of a meeting, and she stays with the majority.

The second important colour is blue. The red, white and blue of the walls of the flat are also the colours of the Tricolour. This waves behind the train in which Jeanson and Veronique have their conversation, and perhaps less coincidentally, appears on Guillaume's sash and hat when he demonstrates in revolutionary costume of 1789. The demonstration is double-theatre – Guillaume, the actor, dressed as a revolutionary, in a theatre; the audience in the boxes dressed like aristocrats. Kirilov carries a tape recorder through a bedroom, playing the Marseillaise as a reveille. The revolutionary bulletins and ordinances captioned on the screen between scenes ('Imperialism still lives . . .' etc.) are in bright red and blue, tricolour colours. Veronique wears a long blue dress, a blue Chinese shirt (the converse of Yvonne's red) a dark blue cap. Though she wears other colours too, perhaps her fondness for blue emphasises her coldness, and her social distance from the proletarian cause; her family are bankers.

There are of course other colours in the film. It is not a strip-cartoon, and however much it breaks up into fragments, displays its own mechanics, interrupts its actions with slogans and stills, the audience must nevertheless accept the reality of these young people's summer. An element of naturalism remains necessary, though within this non-naturalistic convention. Naturalism as a method contradicts the selection and concentration of this style of cinema. 'Art should be the reality of reflection, not the reflection of reality'.

There is a little green paint in the flat. Veronique has a yellow jumper, beige jeans, the furniture has dark brown wood, etc. But the predominance of red, blue and white, and of primary colours in general, is such that we notice other colour complexes as dissonant with the revolutionary setting. The still of the Club Mediterranee, for example, in Guillaume's interview; the fashion pictures above Veronique in Kirilov's talk; the stills from classical art illustrating what he says; Guillaume's experiences as an actor after the cell has dispersed, selling and being pelted with fruit. The view from the railway carriage as Jeanson and Veronique talk of revolution in an intractable context. Here we see browns, yellows, purples, greens – there is nothing in common with the colour-motifs of the revolution. There are scenes of the country, as Yvonne talks of her earlier life. Isn't a social contradiction suggested (certainly it's talked about) as we see, alive to the meaning of reds in this film, the red combs of the lines of chickens running to be fed?

A second 'code' used by Godard, reinforcing the effect of the primary colours, is the lighting. Most of the scenes in the flat are shot in a flat, shadowless light, giving a two-dimensional impression. The bold primary colours, without shadows, remind one of comics, and their effect, like the boldness of the colours, is to simplify. There are comic strip pictures in the film, illustrating Superman-style American violence. Sometimes the group behave like comic strip characters, as Veronique grabs a toy gun and fires at Guillaume, in rebellion against the cell-decision to put Novalis's picture in the collage of class enemies. Guillaume vociferously protests – the Party controls the gun, not the gun the Party! And in the questions to the beaten-up Henri, which are like balloons in the characters' mouths, losing all pretence to naturalism.

The implication of these primary colours, the two dimensional lighting, and the pictorial and live comic strips is to enforce the simplified universe of the young people. There are, literally, no shades of meaning in these episodes, but only reds and blues (*La Chinoise's* equivalent of black and white). And as with the use of contrasting colours, the occasions when there is shadow and depth to the frames add point to the majority of scenes when there isn't. The evening talks between Guillaume and Veronique have a depth of intimacy, and a visual depth of shadow. The shadow is cast, aptly, by the table lamps, so conspicuously the relics of the flat's bourgeois occupancy. It is appropriate that shadows should be the property of the bourgeois world. And in Veronique's interview with Jeanson, in the railway carriage, there is again the appropriate, more intimate shading of a two-person conversation. Among the cell-members, intimacy is limited, and comradeship primary. Though there are two couples, the men do not dominate – Veronique is the strongest, Yvonne refuses to follow Henri out of the group. There is play, affection, and shared work, but little sexual contact.

The simplicity of the camera positions and the sparseness of its movements has the same effect. We know where we are looking from. There is little redundant complexity of different vantage points, changes of position, uncertainty of situation. When the camera moves, in Kirilov and Henri's lectures to the group, it moves on runners back and forth. The camera-movement is formal and predictable, not breaking the formality of the classroom situation. Godard achieves here not simplicity – there is too allusive a plot, and too much happening visually and aurally in each successive, often rapidly switching scene for that. But rather, a highly sophisticated transparency. Within any single scene, there is an unequivocal force. It is like watching a succession of episodes of agitprop, and at the same time a film about agitprop in the making.

The simplification and dichotomisation following from this use of colour, lighting and stationary camera has an implication of the childlike which *La Chinoise* makes conscious in many ways. In the dialogue with Yvonne, what is appealing about her is her innocence and transparency of expression. When she is asked to define Marxism-Leninism, her eyes open wide, she puts her fingers to her lips, purses her mouth, and shrugs her shoulders in a mime of ingenuousness and self-consciousness before the camera. She cuddles up in bed to Henri, sucking her thumb. When Veronique gives a first ideological lecture to Yvonne, who has complained at being deserted by Henri, and talks in empty tautologies, the poster behind her is of Chinese children. The blackboards around the flat remind us of a schoolroom. When the first lecture is given, by the visiting African from the Nanterre Philosophy Faculty, Veronique introduces him nervously, and told to speak up makes a face to Guillaume and she sits down – 'is that loud enough?'. The visitor is a bit dull, like a young schoolteacher (his sweater is a duller red), and the class misbehaves. We see them nudging and grimacing at each other, more preoccupied with each other than with the lecture. Again, we see Yvonne's ingenuous ignorance of ideology, when the class is asked 'where do ideas come from?' and she volunteers 'they fall from the skies?' The play-acting with toys, the element of make-believe, the illustration from Alice and the association to the rabbit cages and little rabbits of the Algerian workers of Nanterre, the magical Little Red Book – all these recall childhood. In the rock-number, with its chorus of Mao Mao, the lines about the Little Red Book which will make everything alright are sung in a childish falsetto, magically dissolving the nihilism of the rest of the song.

There are serious references by the group, to the question of relations between generations. Veronique gives it as a reason for finding inspiration so far away in Peking that Merleau and Nizam are dead, Sartre has taken refuge in Flaubert and Aragon in maths. Her conversation with Jeanson, her teacher, whom she admires, is an attempt to maintain a relationship, though she gets angry and is tempted to write him off as past-it, knowing nothing. When Guillaume demonstrates at the theatre, it is Hamlet he interrupts. 'We are sick of this analysis' he cries from the parapet of the box, meaning (perhaps) that Hamlet should get on with his oedipal murder and quasi-parricide, and stop thinking about it. It seems to be a problem for Veronique, as well as for her respectable friends, what is to be said to her friends' parents about the revolutionaries' use of the flat over the summer.

The film is about learning. The cell members are learning to be revolutionaries. It is genuinely moving and impressive how they work together, practising, teaching themselves and each other, without older teachers. At least what they learn, in this way, is theirs, fought for, questioned, tested out in public utterance and argument, in the way that what is taught in universities is often not felt to be taken into the personality of students. Guillaume is learning to act. When he is described as a fanatic, Henri means that he is a fanatic about acting ('his father worked with Antonin Artaud') not ideology, though later Henri says the cell members were all too fanatical. And at the end, when Veronique thinks back over the summer, and admits it was a fiction, her final sense of the experience is that it was a beginning, the start of a Long March. The film ends with the title, 'The End of a Beginning'.

The mixture of being at times like children, yet also playing with total seriousness the role of adults, is a dramatisation of adolescence. The Cultural Revolution, led by the Red Guards, was a movement of adolescents. Veronique replies, full of feeling when Jeanson tells her she doesn't care what would happen after her act of terrorism, that they care everything for the revolution, they *live* it. The cell searches for the simplicities of childhood, while developing the resources and capabilities of adults. The group believes in certainty, of feelings and ideas. They believe there is a reality beneath 'reflections', waiting to be discovered. Wouldn't it be good, say Guillaume and Veronique, if meanings could change their words instead of words their meaning. But for that to be possible, we would all have to know the meanings, independently of and preceding the mere words and appearances. There is a beautiful example of this creation of a form for a meaning in Guillaume and Veronique's game of word association. 'Nicholas' says Veronique and draws at her cigarette, 'Ray' 'Rock' says Guillaume, taking a sip of coffee, 'and Roll'. The separation of the paired words, which emphasises their connection is a metaphor for the connection of Guillaume and Veronique as a couple, and later in fact in the dialogue Guillaume tells Veronique he loves her. The young people believe in total commitment of themselves, they simplify in order to create a pure identity. It is simultaneously what is admirable about them, and the respect in which, by refusing complexity, they fail to be adult.

We have written of this film's multiple consistencies, its reinforcement by colour, lecture, slogans, lighting, mime, poster, cartoon, caption, action, of the total project of living the Chinese Cultural Revolution one summer in a Paris flat. This consistency, though dazzling, by no means exhausts the complexity of *La Chinoise*.

We do not, after all, forget that the young people in this film are in Paris, living in a bourgeois flat. Four of them are the intelligentsia – scientist, philosophy student, actor, painter. The fifth has been – and still is from time to time – a prostitute; she smiles as she remembers the car she bought with her money. There is a dialectic in this film between the willed project of the Cultural Revolution and the given reality to the young people of bourgeois feeling. The leaning of the young people is towards nihilism, terrorism. Sergei Dimitri Kirilov, with his Dostoyevskian name, evoking Kirillov in *The Possessed*, American-French accent, Pepsi-Cola bottle, and tape-recorder playing the Marseillaise is a parody of a nihilist, in looks and in words. 'A revolutionary without a bomb is not a revolutionary. Give me a bomb.' Veronique cites to Jeanson the example of the Russian terrorists in the 1890s, after whom came the October Revolution. Their rock-number, Mao Mao, is an orgy of destruction, of burning, screaming, bombing, magically transformed into utopia by the Little Red Book. The young people belong to French culture as much as they belong to anything. Nowhere else could a film be as rich in references to philosophy, cinema, linguistics, theatre, aesthetics, intellectual life, without falseness or pretension. The meaning of the bursts of what sound like a Bach Violin Concerto behind various parts of the young people's doings is to confer on them a dignity and lyricism, and to situate their remaking of a culture within their own culture's historical and continuing presence. Whereas another recurring interruption, the red and blue bulletins flashing up the continuing spread of imperialism, reinforces the urgency and compulsion of the revolutionary effort.

Guillaume's acting is situated in a culture, by the reference to his father's work with Artaud, and by the caption, as Guillaume continues his training after the cell had dispersed, the Theatrical Vocation of Guillaume Meister, recalling Goethe.

One critic has described Jeanson's moving dialogue with Veronique as anticipating the line taken by the French Communist Party against the students in the May Events of 1968. Nothing could be further from Godard's (or Jeanson's) intention. What is pertinent is that Jeanson represents a position much more consistent with that of the Chinese than Veronique herself. His political reasoning to her, that revolutions are made by masses, not by individuals; that one can participate in, not *create*, a revolution; that one must know in advance of one's actions what one intends of them, expects of them, distinguishes revolutionary politics from mere *actes gratuits*. Veronique is shown, by her confrontation with Jeanson, to be individualist, existentialist, whereas Jeanson speaks for the discipline of the collective action, based 'in a community, a class'. But of course Veronique expresses an important truth of the situation of intellectual revolutionaries in a bourgeois society, where violence can seem the only sufficient response to impotence and despair. This dialogue must be the best thing of its kind in cinema, so much does it grow from its own dialectic, with such a sense of the finality of the human issue, and such intellectual force, does Jeanson press his point. Veronique has admirable qualities, which the middle-aged Jeanson, so aware of complexity and the intractability of reality, himself responds to. Yet, in the end, she is wrong.

This is the dialectic of the film, and what makes it in the end the statement of a situation, not a propagandist tract. How can one respond, as an intellectual and artist, to the imperatives of being a revolutionary? How can one be young in this political and social situation, and avoid madness, nihilism and terror on the one hand, or 'slow death under de Gaulle, Wilson, Johnson, Garaudy' on the other. Only, Godard seems to say, through art, and through continuing to learn, the Long March which Veronique has begun.

The issue of violence and ruthlessness in the film stands poised, seen alternately as the necessary disposition for a revolutionary, but on the other hand as a sickness of nihilism and irresponsibility. *La Chinoise* can be seen in part as exploration of the meaning of violence.

Guillaume has an Artaudian doctrine, that violence is part of us and should be expressed for our own health. Sincerity and VIOLENCE (shouted) are his watchwords as an actor. But for him, there is theatre and reality, and the one is to illuminate, not reflect the other. Guillaume is the gentlest and freest of the group. We remember the actor, Jean-Pierre Leaud from the softer-textured humanistic Truffaut films, Les Quatres-Cents Coups (as a boy) and Baisers Volés. We may think that his capacity to express violent feelings frees him from compulsion by them, and that expression in art is the most satisfactory mode of resolution of violence the film offers.

Whereas Sergei 'is mad, he wants to kill himself'. And Veronique's ruthlessness, so beautifully expressed in the sequence in which she tells Guillaume that she no longer loves him, leads her to terror. She has an upper-class coldness, under a girlish appeal. She turns down Kirilov's offer to kill the Minister, and is chosen herself by lot. But we learn that Kirilov still has his place in the plan of action. He is to sign a paper claiming the assassination as his own. Godard, through ambiguity, plants in the audience the mixture and conflict of feelings present in the scene, ruthless calculation for the cause overruling compassion for the friend. 'Has he given up the revolver?' Veronique asks. We think she is expressing concern. No, says Guillaume, only when he kills himself can we have the revolver (to assassinate the Minister) and the paper (incriminating Kirilov). Veronique sits and waits, while Guillaume, more moved than she, asks Sergei for the paper and rushes back to him at the sound of the shot. His sacrifice has already been anticipated, in mime, and we realise that they count on his suicide.

Sergei's self-destructiveness is exploited by the revolutionaries. He is a creative person, driven to daubing paint; his death is a loss. Veronique's nihilism is attacked by Jeanson. 'All you know is that you hate the system, you don't care what comes afterwards', he says. But hard as she is, we feel that her capacity for violence is part of what a revolutionary will need. There is an ambivalence here, between the feelings and dispositions that the revolution will need, and the actual costs of those feelings in the here and now. And also an interweaving of the *existential* importance of violence and risk, and its political value. 'A revolution is not a dinner-party,' Guillaume quotes (the phrase recurs), and magnanimity and gentleness are out of place in it. When Guillaume tells Veronique, you scared me, she says 'I'm scared too sometimes'. She has to be, for to risk oneself is everything. It is a test of one's commitment how much pain one will endure for it. Henri comes in bleeding and Guillaume says it's a good thing, it divides the revolutionaries from their enemies. They discuss the flat they have been lent, and the parents who have lent it are denounced as the most dangerous class of people, humanitarian liberals. In the film, there are three deaths, a suicide, a beating up, an expulsion, and while exhilarating, what is being evoked in us is the excitement of destruction.

Whereas, on the other hand, Henri, who is expelled from the group, saying that what frightens him is not the 'silence of infinite spaces' but fury and frenzy, is too peaceable, too dull, too out of contact with the intense feelings around him. His lecture is the most halting, the least coherent of the group, despite his reiteration of key words. Whereas the cell appears not to sleep proper nights, and to live on coffee, Henri is pictured after his expulsion eating his breakfast, beneath a kitchen geyser, with repeated shots of his thick bread and coffee, as if he is now eating to recover. Veronique had argued that the P.C.F. might defend the living standard of the workers, but not Marxism. The group lives on ideas and action, not food, and now Henri, who defends the P.C.F., eats. Henri, unlike Guillaume, Yvonne and Veronique, has unchanged clothes, another restriction of expression. (Another judgement on the implications of clothes is made when Veronique's friends come back, looking schoolgirlish, buttoned-up tight, one of them in a dull red and blue, and looking both disapproving and envious of the activities of the summer). Yet the fury and frenzy are conveyed to us, justifying Henri's complaint of fanaticism, by the speed of cutting and juxtaposition of sounds and images in the scenes of the cell after he has left. Perhaps this is further reinforced by the powerful image of Yvonne selling Humanité Nouvelle. She is in dark glasses, against dark green foliage, speaks and moves mechanically, in a pose of alienation from whoever she is addressing.

The most substantial judgement on the politics and violence of *La Chinoise* is made by Jeanson. We cannot conclude from this that the film is hostile to assassination and terror as such. True, no adequate account is taken by the perpetrators of the human meaning of the deaths in the film. The simplification of strip-cartoon violence, assimilated into the consiousness of the young revolutionaries, preclude that. 'What's the man's name? Shokolov, no Sholokov' and Veronique then shoots the occupant of room 23 instead of room 32, and has to go back and shoot a second man, to kill the Minister. But a point the film implicitly makes here is that the revolutionaries have no more and no less indifference to life than the society they fight. For them, supporters like the West of 'just wars' (but less hypocritical about it), the deaths of Vietnamese peasants are what matter, not the deaths of a Minister of Culture and the unfortunate and unseen occupant of a mistaken hotel room. They invert the attitudes of the bourgeoisie, for whom the assassination would be shocking, an atrocity, whereas the Vietnamese can die in thousands without a qualm. With its strip-cartoons, a feeling for guns as extensions of the self which the revolutionaries have learned from the American cinema (Yvonne, Veronique and Johnson are all shown firing) La Chinoise shows us in visual terms how revolutionary consciousness is formed in the inverse image of its enemy.

What Jeanson does defend is the belief that a death can only be justified by reasons that have been considered and weighed. He defends in the film, as he has in life, the assassinations of the Algerian F.L.N. because they were undertaken, by young girls, as necessary to a revolutionary war. Yet Veronique is accused of contemplating 'a string of murders', of planning to kill people without possible good. The film, in its implicit assault on pacifism as a bourgeois hypocrisy (Mao's 'a revolution is not a dinner party' is quoted, Johnson says he is for peace in Vietnam as he fires in his tiger's head) resists swinging all the way over to a morality of violence as an end in itself.

Jeanson presses the imperatives of rational theory, responsible work, membership in a real community, for any genuine revolutionary action. You cannot create revolutions, only participate in them, he tells Veronique. Only in such a context could deaths be justified. The elements of adolescent acting-out in the cell's projects are 'placed' by contrast with Jeanson, and by Veronique's subsequent admission that it was all a fiction, but nevertheless the beginning of learning, of a Long March. *La Chinoise*, in the person of Jeanson, contains its own negation. Even in formal terms this is so. The whole lengthy dialogue between Veronique and Jeanson is shown in a train, showing only the two faces and the moving landscape through the window. The scene is carried on words, yet has such an important balancing weight in the film. But how appropriate, that Jeanson's rational argument with the young people should be in words, while they seek a total language of image, movement and sound.

But *La Chinoise* cannot simply be resolved into an argument about violence. Rather, Godard explores a quality of violence in the experience of the young comrades. The violence mediated to them by society and especially by its culture. The therapy of violence created in response to this in the theatre. The destructiveness and despair of the adolescents themselves, in the suicide and project of the assassination. The recognition of a necessary violence, in a real as against pretended or wished-for revolution, of which Jeanson alone can recall an authentic experience, but which the Chinese Cultural Revolution forcefully communicates from so far away.

La Chinoise makes real these contradicting facets of violence in our situation, and pretends no final resolution of them. *La Chinoise* is a film about a didactic process, but we can say that only about art is the film itself unequivocally didactic. The necessity for aesthetic as well as political revolution is the enacted meaning of *La Chinoise*. Just as the problem of revolution, in France in 1967, is complicated and self-contradictory ('you don't think that France in 1967 is like Russia in 1890, do you'? Jeanson asks Veronique) so the art which explores this situation is an art of contradictions and fragments.

North East London Polytechnic.

1. The literary criticism of F. R. Leavis is perhaps the most influential example and defence of this position. Even given Leavis's great interest in social context, and extremely sensitive consideration of social issues, his commitment remains wholly to a problematic of quality and standards, both moral and aesthetic. This concern with judgements of quality was carried into English work on the criticism of popular culture, for example Stuart Hall and Paddy Whannel: *The Popular Arts*, Hutchinson, 1964, and Richard Hoggart's work.

2. See, for example, the overall emphasis of a recent collection of essays on the state of current sociology, J. Rex (Ed.) *Approaches to Sociology* Routledge and Kegan Paul, 1974.

3. There are numerous examples. (Among them, M.F.D Young (Ed.): *Knowledge and Control* Collier-MacMillan, 1971, and Open University Course Team: *Schools and Society* Routledge and O.U. Press, 1971.

4. See the useful account of recent developments by Stanley Cohen in M. McIntosh and P. Rock (Ed.): *Deviance and Social Control*, Tavistock, 1974; and a fuller account in I. Taylor, P. Walton and J. Young. *The New Criminology*, Routledge and Kegan Paul, 1973.

5. For a debate on the implications of this subjectivism for cultural studies see the debate between A. Shuttleworth and Stuart Hall in *Working Papers* in Cultural Studies, No. 1, (1971). Alan Dawe's paper *The Role of Experience in the Construction of Sociological Theory*, in *Sociological Review*, Vol. 21, 1973, raises some related questions.

6. E. P. Thompson: *The Making of the English Working Class*, Penguin, 1968.

7. R. Williams: *The Long Revolution*, Chatto and Windus, 1961. See also his *Base and Superstructure*, in *New Left Review*, 82, Nov-Dec. 1973.

8. L. Althusser: *Lenin and Philosophy and other Essays*, New Left Books, 1971 especially *Ideology and Ideological State Apparatuses* in that volume.

9. Perry Anderson: *Considerations on Western Marxism*, New Left Books, 1976.

10. Peter Wollen: *Signs and Meaning in the Cinema*, Secker and Warburg, 1969.

11. The consideration of works of literature as highly complex ideological forms is a main theme and method of a recent structuralist approach to literature, Terry Eagleton's *Criticism and Ideology*, New Left Books, 1976.

12. See Phil Slater: *The Origins and Significance of the Frankfurt School*, Routledge and Kegan Paul, 1976.

13. On this idea of the inherent uncertainty facing Marxists in practice see M. Merleau-Ponty: *The Adventures of the Dialectic*, Heinemann, 1974.

14. A basic statement is in R. Barthes: *Elements of Semiology*, Cape, 1967. J. Culler's recent *Saussure*, Fontana, 1976 is also useful.

15. P. Wollen: op.cit., and Peter Wollen (Ed.): *Working Papers on the Cinema: Sociology and Semiology*, British Film Institute, undated.

16. The journal *Screen* has since 1973 devoted itself to the task of establishing the 'theoretical object' of the study of film, that is, a properly constituted semiology of film. This work draws heavily on semiology and linguistics, on Althusser, and on Lacan, and has given especial prominence to the work of Christian Metz. It has not been possible to discuss the theoretical issues raised in that discussion in this paper. However one may note that much of the material is extremely difficult, and that it is hard to judge at this point whether the theoretical (theoreticist?) approaches being developed by the *Screen* group will prove fruitful in the understanding of specific films, or genres of films. Screen is published by the Society for the Education in Film and Television.

Art and Reality: Gangsters in Film and Society

Frank Pearce

Introduction[1]

In 1943 Humphrey Bogart was visiting troops in North Africa. German radio publicised his visit by claiming that American morale was so bad that the wicked American gangster Bogart had been sent to Africa to entertain the troops. It was not only the Germans who saw things this way, for one day when he ran out of cigarettes, he walked up to some GIs in a jeep and bummed a cigarette from them. One man recognised him, and, as he lit the cigarette, leaned over to ask quietly, 'How are the boys doing?'

It took Bogart a second to get it, then he said,

'Okay. They're fine.'

'Do you think Bugsy'll take the rap?' The G.I. asked.

'Yeah.'

'I thought so. And Lepke? Will he burn?'

'Sure he'll burn.'

The soldier drove off and, needless to say, he had been in the rackets back home.[2]

Louis 'Lepke' Buchalter did indeed burn; he was electrocuted in March of the following year. His capital offence of murder was only one of a long list of criminal activities ranging from bootlegging through to labour racketeering. Benjamin 'Buggsy' Siegel was a colleague in the latter enterprise and they had rich pickings in Hollywoodland. They collaborated with the studio heads to keep out militant unions though in the end they squeezed too hard, and their men were imprisoned for extortion; they were replaced in the union by honest but oh-so-right wing Roy Brewer following the typical pattern of labour racketeering. But in the meantime Siegal supplied the film colony with women, drugs and gambling and was also a good friend of Longie Zwillman racketeer lover of Jean Harlow herself immortalised in *The Public Enemy* (1931) as the enigmatic blonde in the life of screen gangster James Cagney. Yet another good friend of Siegel was George Raft, Paul Muni's coin flipping sidekick in another of the early cycle of these films, *Scarface*, (1932). Originally when still carrying the extra 'n' as George Ranft he had been third hand in a gambling club and though he became a star he never stopped running errands for the big men of crime. Is it any wonder that the soldier was confused?

And there is more. Joe Schenck a founder of Metro Goldwyn Mayer was a good friend of Arnold Rothstein and helped him acquire a "piece' of Lowe's giant theatre chain. Buggsy Siegel's dream was of an oasis: he built it in the Nevada desert – Las Vegas the city of suckers. Money was also provided by Frank Costello, Joe Adonis and Meyer Lansky. Soon after in the home of star(let) Virginia 'Sugar' Hill, Siegel was shot dead; the killing has been immortalised in a gory photograph showing blood pouring from his right eye. In the sixties Howard Hughes, ex-studio head of RKO, moved into Las Vegas, a significant investment since he was always on the far right in American politics and had been a major supporter of the House Un-American Activites Committee during the purge. The chairman during the first post war hearing of the H.U.A.C., those in 1947, was J. Parnell Thomas who joined the Hollywood Ten in jail the following year; his crime – fraud. Another guardian of Hollywood morals, Will H. Hays. author of the Hays Code which insisted that all those 'crime does not pay' endings should be stitched on to occasionally fine movies had in fact accepted bribes when Paymaster General in Harding's administration. His organisation employed mafiosi Johnny Rosselli as a 'labor conciliator'. Many years later Rosselli served time for his part in the labor union shakedown racket that Willie Bioff and George E. Browne organised and fronted for Buchalter; later still Rosselli was used by the CIA in the Bay of Pigs fiasco, and was part of the penumbra of racketeers around Nixon. Gangsters were sometimes informal consultants on movies, Rosselli was even a producer, and they undoubtedly brought influence to bear many years later on the scripting of the *Godfather*, (1972). A more insidious influence however is possible. The major rackets after the twenties were undoubtedly gambling, prostitution, drug peddling and milking corrupt unions, yet relatively few gangster films have dealt with these activities. Was this perhaps because they were all too close to home?[3]

Most of the remarks so far relate the activities of real life gangsters to the actual activity of film making and to the lives of the film makers. The question of the relationship between the reality of syndicate activities and their portrayal by Hollywood is more germane to this piece and will be dealt with later.

First I would like to address a few remarks to the issue of the relationship between art and society. The framework used in this piece starts from the position that art is not so much a *reflection of reality*, but a *reflection upon reality* this has been well argued by Suvin and Mirowski and clearly informs the work of Brecht. It is compatible with the appreciation of the achievement of a wide range of artists in different media throughout history.[4] Reality is not self evident – there is no such thing as a naive, pre-conceptual apprehension of the world. We experience and know the world through socially derived categories which are themselves constantly open to revision as our conditions of existence and our knowledge are transformed through history. This applies both to our taken-for-granted knowledge and its counterpart – science upon which intellectual work has been expended.[5] To explore the issues in which they are interested, artists use as raw materials objects, situations and experiences taken from 'reality' and relocate them in a different context, that of the art object.[6] One can see this in painting, theatre and film; for example John Ford in his *She Wore a Yellow Ribbon* (1949) uses the Western myth as a locale to explore the dilemmas posed by a commitment both to public life and to the family. In gangster films, as Robert Warshow has argued in a seminal essay, film makers have been able to confront the urban industrial nature of twentieth century America. The first section of this paper pushes these ideas to their limits and this in turn leads to a consideration of the image of individual and society found in these films.

Here George Lukács's ideas on the relationship between the individual and the typical in art have some utility because, after all, most Hollywood cinema can be accurately described as 'novelistic'.[7] Insofar as art reflects upon reality it helps us to interpret, assess and understand it, particularly when we realise that we are not apart from it and that we ourselves are every bit in need of exploration as are inanimate objects: Great art usually provides us with a new vision, it entails revelation. Sometimes, as in the case of Balzac, a reactionary political stance does not diminish its power to do so: at other times it most certainly does and the racist/cold war thinking that informed many of these films precluded their providing us with a deeper understanding. A long section of this paper is addressed to this problem of ideology, since the images of society, the explanations of criminality and the implicit guides to action found in these works must be assessed adequately if they are to be treated with any seriousness. Ideology as a term has little concrete meaning if the specific ideologies being considered are divorced from a dialectical consideration of the world which they purport to define and explain, so embedded within the latter part of the paper is a theorisation of the 'real' role of organised crime within American society.

The Gangster and the Urban Nightmare[8]

'The gangster is the man of the city, with the city's language and knowledge, with its queer and dishonest skills and its terrible daring, carrying his life in his hands like a placard, like a club. For everyone else, there is at least the theoretical possibility of another world – in

that happier American culture which the gangster denies, the city does
not really exists; it is only a more crowded and more brightly lit
country – but for the gangster there is only the city; he must inhabit it
in order to personify it; not the real city but that dangerous and sad
city of the imagination which is so much more important, which is the
modern world. And the gangster – though there are real gangsters – is
also and primarily, a creature of the imagination. The real city, one
might say, produces only criminals; the imaginary city produces the
gangster: he is what we want to be and what we are afraid we may
become.'
Robert Warshow: *The Immediate Experience*, p. 131.

Warshow's assessment of the gangster film has proved seminal for
most of its students. It is easy to see why. German expressionism created
the world of strange perspectives and long shadows through the use of
specially constructed sets in early films like *The Cabinet of Dr. Caligari*
(1919), *Metropolis* (1926) and *The Testament of Dr. Mabuse* (1923), but
exposure to the American film industry soon showed the limitations of
such theatricality. After reaching America, Fritz Lang, director of the
latter films, soon realised that mood and the strangeness of the modern
world was better conveyed by filming real but anonymous city streets,
by focusing on the flickering lights and often on the driving rain, and
that by doing so with much more poetic efficacy, universal moods of
loneliness and alienation could be conveyed. In films like *You Only Live
Once* (1937) he used these raw materials to create compelling but
mysterious images – in one scene a bank robbery is carried out with
bombs and gas masks but its perpetrators never reveal themselves, they
always remain hidden; another film maker, Max Nosseck, would use an
identical scene eight years later in his film *Dillinger* (1945). Perhaps
nowhere has the fantasy quality of the city been better shown than in
Jules Dassin's *Night and the City* (1950). Here Richard Widmark plays
Harry Fabian, a mean petty crook who involves himself in the
racketeering side of boxing in a London more connected with that
portrayed in *Brighton Rock* (1946), or *The Threepenny Opera* (1933), than
of post World War Two. Widmark's familiar haunted face becomes
almost archetypal as he runs terrified through the streets. He can find
nowhere to hide in the vast geometric mosaic and his agony reminds us
of all of our vulnerability in a world where we cannot escape the all
seeing eye; they can always plot our position and we know that we are
statistics in somebody's file.

In this unnatural man-made world of ruthless competition only those
so tough as to be dehumanised can survive. The iconography in the
films shows clearly the isomorphism between the gangster and his

locale. Cars patrol the streets: their long bonnets passing each other with a terrible inevitability. Suddenly machine guns spit out their straight lines of death. After a few minutes of frantic activity there are corpses scattered around, both friends and enemies are simply left behind and the survivors, their jaws still set firm, still wearing their boxy sharp suits and their wide brimmed hats glide off like tigers into the distance. In their mirrors we see arriving on the scene the same cars but this time with wailing sirens; it is the police. The gangsters' world is divided up and his views are separated one from another; his experiences are framed through apartment windows or through car windscreens. Everything is cut off by these parallel lines found everywhere in the urban industrial world – discovered for art by the camera. Colin McArthur has provided a useful enumeration of the elements that go to make up this iconography.[9] Firstly, there are 'those surrounding the physical presence, attributes and dress of the actors and the characters they play' – the stars and back up men like James Cagney, Edward G. Robinson, Humphrey Bogart, Richard Widmark, Lee J. Cobb, Rod Steiger, Jack Palance and Lee Marvin.

These actors and their typical roles evoke a whole world of relationships through which they realise their ambitions, and we know how they do so from the way that they hold themselves and the ways in which they move against and away from others. The gangster's world is made of crooked politicians, bent cops, elegant but slippery night club owners, beautiful molls who are often untrustworthy and ultimately losers, and this is counterpointed by the good cop, often solitary and grim, but a man whose masculinity lies in his integrity rather than in his violence. The smart aggressive clothes are important for the screen characters but are also an essential element in the appeal of these films. The second element of the iconography, the milieu, is the industrial city. The gangster is a functional type for that environment. But within the American ideology as so well exemplified by film makers like John Ford and John Huston and in a long tradition of social movements from village America – the child savers,[10] prohibition, etc., this is defined as an unnatural world. If the unnatural creature who can survive in the city finds himself confronted by naked natural forces he is powerless. In Huston's *Key Largo* (1948) the gangster's leader Rocco, played by Edward G. Robinson, is extraordinarily tough and ruthless particularly in personal relationships yet he is terrified by a storm on the Miami coast. He is almost reduced to whimpering. Bogart made his name in another somewhat stagey film, *The Petrified Forest* (1936), which explicitly addresses these questions. Actually Bogart, who plays Duke

Mantee, the leader of a gang on the run, provides a nervous performance which is overshadowed by Trevor Howard's assured exploration of the flippant cynicism of the disillusioned intellectual, Adam Squier. He makes Gabrielle Maple/Bette Davis, the waitress in an isolated country cafe, fall in love with him whilst philosophing on the kinship of intellectuals, industrialists and gangsters: he sees their individualism as inseparately linked with an arrogant belief in a superiority of their artificial lives over those more in tune with mankind's place in the world of nature. Nature, Squier asserts, is fighting back by creating massive neuroses in modern man, a clear reference to the irrational forces loosed within fascism. Yet Squier himself is arid, less human than Mantee who risked discovery for a rendezvous with his love, because after winning Gabrielle he helps her to realise the least important part of her dreams – her visit to Paris – providing the money from a life policy which he realises by persuading Duke Mantee to kill him, thus absurdly depriving her of the natural consummation of her love.

Raoul Walsh's *Roaring 20s* (1939) further develops these themes. A group of first world war soldiers returns home to find unemployment their reward. They have an opportunity to enter the rackets and do so. They rise fast, particularly Cagney, the plucky tough dynamo behind them all. He falls in love with a 'good girl' who is obviously fated for the lawyer in their team. Cagney is warned of this by his moll, Gladys. George, Humphrey Bogart, another war time comrade, joins their team when they hi-jack his boat. Cagney may be tough and rather immature and unrealistic – he never stops 'carrying a torch for that broad' – but he is a normal man with guts. Bogart is so cold, vicious yet detached as to be almost psychopathic. When the going gets violent the lawyer opts out taking Priscilla Lane, Cagney's belle, with him – they both owe their start to Cagney but do not recognise their debts or their implication in the violent side of his business. At the Wall Street crash George behaves like a ruthless businessman and, in the manner of the large corporations, buys out the small man, Cagney, getting his taxi business for a song and leaving him just one cab. Thanks to the resources available to members of his class, the lawyer prospers in the District Attorney's office and George because of his own ruthlessness still rides high. Only Cagney, the small man with guts, falls by the wayside. He is defeated by the system to which George and Nick, the lawyer, are so well adapted. It is a doomed system as is made clear in an extraordinary scene with a 'March of Time' overvoice. It is 1929 and a ticker tape machine fills most of the screen, it is truly gigantic for many human beings are seen scurrying around its base. It suddenly changes into a pyramid which a wind reveals to be simply paper. The screen frames two skyscrapers and then the image distorts and they dribble away too. The urban industrial civilisation is as frail as the paper money on which it is built. Cagney gets his revenge on George but thereby guarantees his own death. He died on the steps of a church cradled in the arms of his barfly who tells an inquisitive policeman who wants to know his identity 'This is Eddie Bartlett: he used to be a big shot.' Eddie may have talked tough but ultimately he was flesh and blood and therefore vulnerable.

In many other movies the psychopathic violence of some gangsters is made clear. Few scenes equal in brutality that in *The Big Heat* (1953) when Lee Marvin/Vince Stone disfigured Gloria Grahame's face with scalding coffee; an exception is Altman's reference to this scene in his own film *The Long Goodbye* (1973) when a mobster breaks a coco cola bottle in the face of his mistress. Mickey Rooney's *Baby Face Nelson* (1957) is a portrayal of a man often out of control with violent rages. But there can be few more disturbed characters than Cagney's Cody Jarrett in *White Heat* (1949). The violence is always latent within him, liable to expression at any time and usually in a sly effective way. The film provides a surfeit of explanations of psychopathology – his father and brother were mad, when a child he faked headaches to gain his mother's attention. Later he develops the pain of real ones, and then there is the buried agonies of an unresolved oedipal fixation. He is kind and attentive to his powerful mother but to his wife detached and domineering, treating her as an object – 'she belongs to me'. After his mother's death, following a classical Freudian pattern he seeks out as a love object another man, the detective that has infiltrated his gang. Throughout the film there is a strong stress on the police use of technology – radios, telephones and police cars to track the criminals.[11] The gang plans to enter the chemical plant which they intend to rob by using a petrol tanker-cum-Trojan Horse. When they crawl inside it the difference of scale makes it seem as if they are administering to it rather than using it for their own ends. Inside the plant the robbery goes wrong thanks to the machinations of the spy in their midst. A shoot out takes place but nobody can destroy Cagney. His pathology makes him superhuman and invulnerable – the sharpshooting detective who deceived him earlier – puts two or three bullets into him and asks in exasperation 'What's keeping him up?' The only power that can destroy him is that of technology itself; and when he shoots his submachine gun into the refinery he is killed by the explosion. The police are not identified with this victory but rather are driven back by the flames.

The treatment of these themes is not to be read literally but rather symbolically. They are representations of the essence of the relationships between objects and men in a world where nature has been transformed but not as an aid to man's self-development, the fusion of mankind's telos and materiality has produced an oppressive cage that dwarfs and intimidates him. Marx commented on the relationship between the worker and the productive forces in the following way:—

> 'Every kind of capitalist production, in so far as it is not only a labour process, but also a process of creating surplus value, has this in common, that it is not workmen that employ the instruments of labour but the instruments of labour that employ the workmen.'[12]

Here we have man described as the resident in an alienated world where his products control him. He lives in a re-ified world – he accepts this situation as natural and things have become so autonomous that they move according to the laws of their own motion, and not those of man. And, as Raoul Walsh's films make so clear, this is not simply true of the means of production but of the whole environment that man has created for himself – the whole nightmare of the city. Walsh felt this acutely after witnessing the impersonality and inhuman scale of destruction found in the second world war when the old values of individual heroism, courage and comradeship were marginal to success. To survive, human beings had to be deformed because if they were too human they would be frustrated and crushed by all that surrounds them.[13] In these terms the ultimate gangster film is not the somewhat mediocre fare provided by *The Godfather* (1972) or *The Valachi Papers* (1972) but the T.V. movie *Duel* (1972). For here we have a man in America's commodity of commodities – an automobile – being chased by a monstrous freight truck and ultimately destroyed by it. We never see the other driver and when at the end it catches up with the car it seems not to matter that the driver, Dennis Weaver, escapes because the battle is between two machines not their servants; so, having pushed the car over the cliff, the lorry follows after it.

Explanations of Criminality

While some gangster films glorify violence and others simply adopt a police attitude towards crime as for example, *The F.B.I. Story* (1959), other films try to understand the gangster's motivations and his world. Reference has already been made to those which stress some sort of psychological explanation of his behaviour, and there are of course others who have the view that the criminal is made not born. *You Only Live Once* (1937) and the *Roaring Twenties* (1939) both see gangsters as criminals by default, people who had little opportunity to go straight in a world of high unemployement. Gangsters are above all people the same as you and I, as those who are pushed and pulled by what confronts them; they are seen both as individuals and types, as are the host of minor characters. Perhaps the finest of this genre is *High Sierra* (1941) in which once again Humphrey Bogart plays a gangster, Roy Earle, who is on the run.[14] His toughness is a tool of his trade for there is a certain proportionment about his violence. He meets an old family of Oakies and develops an interest in their grand daughter, Velma, a girl who has a club foot. He provides the money for her to have an operation which rectifies the fault in her foot. But when he declares his romantic interest in her he is rebuffed. Having the use of both feet, the same as anyone else, she indulges her desire to have a good time and turns out to be no angel, just an ordinary and high spirited girl. There is no sentimentality in the portrayal of her or of Bogart/Earle the gangster, they are shown as real people with ordinary passions and ordinary feelings. Similarly, the police in the film are shown in a complex manner; as men doing their job, but also as authority figures – moreover these men enjoy the power they can exercise by animating these cultural artefacts. There is good reason for people to be suspicious of them. In films like this, and in a whole cycle of Bogart films – like *The Big Sleep* (1946), *Dark Passage* (1947), and many others – there is a recognition and celebration of the common man. An American egalitarian ethic is pervasive, the writers and film-makers portray them as members of their community and not as outsiders. One has only to compare the majority of British films right up to the early sixties to see the contrast between the two cinema industries.[15] The Hollywood cinema of the late thirties and forties had a relationship to American people roughly equivalent to that of Dickens to the English common people. Arnold Kettle commented on Dickens's writing in the following way:

'Somehow in a Dickens novel we are all, including the reader, equals. Because there is no exclusion there is no contempt and no superiority. We look degradation in the face and see humanity there. So we can judge and enjoy at the same time. Our partisanship enlarges our comprehension and our inclusive sympathy strengthens our partisanship.'[16]

These films were made at a time when the ideal of democracy was in a critical phase. The failure of capitalism in the thirties and the joint war effort with Russia in the forties meant that democacy was not identified with American capitalism. The celebration of the common man meant that his interests were held to rise above those of any government or any system. The films of Whyler and Huston were much in that vein in the thirties and forties. Yet contrast the presentation of gangsters in William Whyler's film *The Desperate Hours* (1955) with that in *High Sierra*. In *High Sierra* there was no objectification of the gangsters, there was a recognition of their diversity, their frailty but they had their strengths as well as their weaknesses. In *The Desperate Hours* Bogart again played a gangster on the run who with his companions takes over a house and its inhabitants. A personality and power struggle develops between him and the man of the house, who is a banker. All Bogart's resentments are portrayed not as being class consciousness but rather as petty envy. At the end of the film, the banker beats Bogart at his own game and takes the gun off him, demonstrating that not only is he superior in the everyday competitive struggle in the commercial world but also in the struggle on the level of brute force. Thus implicitly the unequal rewards in American society are vindicated as expressing some kind of natural law. Needless to say by this time the democratic ideal was identified with the American political system, and, of necessity with American capitalism.

The McCarthyist witch hunts changed the face of Hollywood so that in the fifties the best that could be expected was irony, as in Robert Aldrich's *Kiss Me Deadly* (1955) where Mickey Spillane's character, Mike Hammer, was filmed so that the audience did not identify with him, they looked at him objectively and shared any reasonable person's horror at his fascistic activities. Indeed it was mainly in examining such subjects as the conflict of the generations, in *Rebel Without a Cause* (1955), or in complex melodramas like Sirk's *Imitation of Life* (1958) that any kind of critical edge was maintained at all. Other seemingly hard hitting films, as I will show below, were nothing of the sort.

Ideological Lacunae in the Populist Tradition

An unusual feature of *The Petrified Forest* was that one of the gangsters *happened to be* black. He was an individual and no more highlighted when on the scene than were the other gangsters. But late in the film the gang captured a rich couple, the Chisholms, and their chauffeur Joseph. True to the times, this chauffeur was black and there is a very telling confrontation between the two black men. The gangster mocks the flunkey for being an Uncle Tom and there is a strong contrast between his easy looseness and the wooden, puppet-like stance of the other. This confrontation underlies the awful choice facing black people at the time

– either to be cast in the white man's image of them as inferior and slightly ridiculous but thereby being able to live within society, or to be themselves at the cost of living outside it. This investigation of black people's dilemna is unique. Much more typical is the instant vaudeville provided by Algernon/Willie Best in *High Sierra*. There is affection in the presentation and an element of self parody in the acting but nevertheless as opposed to the fine observation of the individual/typical (Lukács's sense) this is a stereotypical portrait of black people.[17] The populist ideology had a concept of the people and their needs and a recognition of the separateness from them of the state and the economic institutions, but its concept of 'the people' at its worst degenerated to Ku Klux Klan purism (as in the case of Griffith's) *Birth of a Nation* and at its 'best' simply ignored black people.[18]

> During the period of reconstruction in the South, from 1876 until the late '90s, Southern Populists like Tom Watson adopted in theory and practice a policy of racial equality and intimate co-operation with black radicals. He told the two races, 'You are made to hate each other, because upon that hatred is rested the keystone of the arch of financial despotism which enslaves you both.'[19] But the alliance was fragile, broken with the triumph of the Jim Crow movement. Black people were viewed as a different species, not to be understood empathically as other human beings but rather seen externally, as non-rational and inferior, treated as outside the moral and physical community of American society. Miscegenation was viewed as un-American.

Built into populism was a dangerous anti-human category. In the Cold War of the late '40s and early '50s the populist ideology equated radicalism with Communism, which because of its obvious Russian connection could be seen as un-American and therefore as outside its community of discourse. Populism, like all acceptable political currents, defensively identified with the extant American system; those not making this identification were seen as necessarily defective, their beliefs as not requiring understanding. An indication of this defensive world view can be found in Section 2 of the Internal Security Act, 1950, which included the following two paragraphs:

> '13. There are, under our present immigration laws, numerous aliens who have been found to be deportable, many of whom are in the subversive criminal or immoral classes, who are free to roam the country at will without supervision or control.'
> '14. One device for infiltration by Communists is by procuring naturalisation for disloyal aliens to use their citizenship as a badge for admission into the fabric of our society.'[20]

The Korean war reinvoked the anti-Asian racism, found in World War II films, and this was always on tap as would be seen later in the Vietnam lingo of 'gooks', etc., and its glorification in such films as *The Green Berets* (1968). For America the Second World War was primarily fought in the Pacific against the 'Japs'. Even some leftists like Dalton Trumbo fell into the trap of using racialist language about Asians as for example in *A Guy Named Joe* (1943). (The record in relation to anti-semitic and anti-black prejudice was of course impeccable). There was a certain lack of critical edge in their appreciation of 'the people' that led many populists whether left or liberal into sentimentality.[21] The weakest element in *High Sierra* is the treatment of the relationship between Bogart/Earle and Lupino/Marie. Earle initially softens towards her because they both respond to a dog, Pard, introduced into the film by Algernon. Pard becomes their dog – they possess each other through another animate being – their potential child; he is potential but not real because he also represents a degree of undefensive humaneness that they as outlaws cannot afford to feel. At the end of the film Pard's barking makes Earle come out of hiding to call Marie and thereby fatally exposing himself to a police sharpshooter. Marie asks a policeman 'Mister what does it mean when a man crashes out?' Surprised he says, 'That's a funny question for you to ask now sister. It means he's free.' The film ends with a shot of her looking relieved repeating 'Free, free'. She knows that with his boyhood rural home gone forever, Roy Earle could only be free outside that nightmare society, outside that time. The sentimentality is found in the way the dog's role is stressed.

Women, characteristically, are treated sentimentally by Hollywood; even in Walsh's films they tend to gain *valid* purpose in life only from their relationship with men.[22] This is also true of the strong women played by actresses like Lauren Bacall *To Have and Have Not* (1945), *Big Sleep* (1946), *Dark Passage*, and Joan Crawford *Mildred Pierce* (1944), Barbara Stanwyck *Double Indemnity* (1944). These weaknesses came from the built in limitations of the ideology informing the understanding and practices of the medium. The potential for change was nevertheless there – the finest films like Polonsky's *Force of Evil* (1948) portrayed a complex set of relationships between people and situated day to day activities within a wider socio-structural context. This film tells of the rationalisation of the numbers racket, paralleling the development of monopoly capitalism in legitimate business. The big money boys engineer the winning numbers on the 4th July knowing that there will be heavy betting on those derived from the date and the year. The small operators are cleaned out and can only survive by selling out to the big gamblers. The parallel with the 1929 crash and subsequent clean up are obvious. John Garfield, the architect of all this is the willing servant of his employers, even though this means complex negotiations with his brother (Thomas Gomes) who has a small numbers business, also with his brother's secretary (Beatrice Pearson) whom he skillfully charms. The coercive strategies and scintillating but confusing methods he uses dazzle her into loving him – there are few more poignant explorations of the coercive underpinings in romance except perhaps Douglas Sirk's *Tarnished Angels* (1957) or *The Bitter Tears of Petra Von Kant* (1973). Eventually the brother gets killed, grief stricken by the finality of this act and rehumanised by his contact with the girl, Garfield goes to the police, thereby leaving behind his chance of wealth and thus of necessity accepting the difficult lot of ordinary people. The H.U.A.C. hearings of 1947 and their aftermath put paid to this potential. By 1954 hundreds of people in the film industry had been designated as Communists or fellow travellers, and Hollywood drifted into the sterile '50s. Many of the best talents were black listed and/or émigrés.[23] Many of those who had opposed H.U.A.C., even some who had chartered a plane to Washington in October 1947, stopped protesting. Lauren Bacall and Humphrey Bogart voted for Eisenhower in 1951; William Wyler made *The Desperate Hours* (1955); Gene Kelly cleared himself of the taint of the blacklist by commending 'Irving Brown's program in France in which he is doing an especially fine job of persuading members of French labor trade unions to the anti-Communist position of the American labor movement.'[24] Brown's 'persuasion' included financing Corsican gangsters to intimidate and kill Communist trade Unionists in Marseille.[25] He did this with money provided by the CIA and he was connected with a key figure in the Hollywood trade union movement, Roy Brewer. Brewer had not only undertaken Gene Kelly's political re-education but also that of John Huston which probably helps explain the disappointing quality of much of Huston's work since his early successes. He co-scripted *High Sierra*, and directed *Across the Pacific* (1941), *The Treasure of the Sierra Madre* (1948), *Key Largo* (1949) and *The Asphalt Jungle* (1951), after this he did little that was significant, until *Fat City* (1972). Brewer had helped clean the gangsters out of the International Alliance of Theatrical Stage Employees and Motion Picture Machine Operators of the United States, IATSE, after they had guaranteed that this would be a non-Communist union. He had then gained the support of the producers who had dealt with the gangsters and their struggle to keep out the militant socialist unions from the industry. If they had to have unions, they wanted them tame, because the Wagner Act of 1935 gave the workers the right (a) to decide whether they wanted a union and (b) to choose which union should represent them. The post World War II period saw heroic efforts to organise the film industry by the militant and radical CSU (Conference of Studio Unions). One dispute in 1945 led to the use of hoses, clubs and tear gas bombs as the police cleared a picket line, outside the Warner brothers' studios. This period was one of massive working class uprisings with strong socialist elements throughout the country and a real potential for the spread of socialist ideas.[26] The response was manifold – direct repression, the encouragement of right wing unions and a massive cultural assault, blocking out tendencies running counter to the hegemonic ideologies of capitalism. Hollywood, the dream factory, was a pivotal place and the government, the right wing press (Hearst and Hughes), and right wing elements in Hollywood combined, with the New York financiers controlling Hollywood to censor dreamland.

The '50s: Propaganda and Pseudo-Realism

There was, as a result, a dearth of films dealing with social reality – a massive production of banal sugar plums and some hysterically anti-Communist films. In 1950, a good year for McCarthy, MGM released *Conspirator* where an unwary Elizabeth Taylor unwittingly married a Communist; such 'miscegenation' resulted in dire consequences for all, thus Miss Taylor 'symbolised the very seduction of American innocence which increasingly would become McCarthy's message to the country.'[27]

Not only the innocent were under attack, so were the most worldly wise – the criminals. In *Pickup on South Street* (1953), Samuel Fuller showed a sad mix of good dramatic sense, of general perceptiveness, but with a caricaturing weakness when dealing with Communists. He traced Richard Widmark's inadvertent involvement with Communist spies when he steals a handbag in a New York subway. As the film unfolds a contrast is drawn between the humane personal loyalties felt even by the sneak thief and the cold detachment of the obviously smug and over-intellectual 'commies'. But the latter are only ciphers, they have no real presence and consequently the film is lopsided and ultimately unconvincing. The direct attack on Communism continued all through the '50s and into the '60s, as did movies that drew heavy analogies like *Invasion of the Body Snatchers* (1956). But there are also a few that addressed themselves to the social problems once attended to by radical populists. After his brilliant interpretation of *A Street Car named Desire* (1950), and once again using Brando, Elia Kazan turned to the New York docks and the problem of labour racketeers. He wanted to get back in touch with the everyday world of America and when interviewed he said '*On the Waterfront* is a good example of this contact with reality because it is about living issues. And furthermore, it's about an issue that was being decided as we made the picture.'[28] Kazan agreed that 'it related to the gangster films that summed up real American life on the screen', for, he said, 'The first breakthrough into working class life came through the gangster films. They were the first view from underneath'. To what extent does this film tell us about the conditions of the docks, the state of the unions and the condition of working class life? Seen in purely formal terms, *On the Waterfront* (1954) is a very compelling movie. Kaufman's photography is superb and the performances of Brando, Eva Marie Saint, Rod Steiger, Lee J. Cobb are themselves a vindication of the method school of acting. The film is an account of a young punk, Terry Malloy/Marlon Brando, who gradually realises that the mob who has employed him as an errand boy has not only exploited the people in the community but also him. In a very moving scene with his brother, Charley/Rod Steiger, he keeps referring back to the days when he was an up and coming boxer and when he could have won a fight – and thus retained some sense of self worth – if he hadn't thrown it for the gambling interests; as a result he was left with nowhere else to make a living but on the waterfront where he depended on the largesses of his brother and the mob. In the film Terry meets and falls in love with Edie Doyle/Eva Marie Saint whose brother was killed by the mob. The tensions he feels about this gradually increase during the film and come to a head when his own brother is killed on the instructions of Johnny Friendly/Lee J. Cobb. These incidents plus the promptings of Father Barry/Karl Malden lead Terry to testify before the Waterfront Crime Commission. Later he comments on his action saying – 'I was rattin' on myself all these years, and I didn't know it . . . I'm glad what I done'. His action is shown as one of individual heroism since he knows that he breaks the waterfront code by turning stoolpigeon; many of his former friends literally turn their backs on him and make cutting comments. His testimony calls into question Friendly's power though Terry remains an outsider. But he has found his dignity. He tells Edie 'I aint a bum. I'm going to get my rights' and in the closing section of the film he goes to the waterfront where hiring takes place and is pointedly passed over for some old winos. He confronts Friendly only to be beaten up by his henchmen. But by now

the other stevedores are the audience who name their condition for a
return to work – 'If Terry walks in, we walk in with him'. Father Barry
badgers Terry into staggering towards the loading boss.

> 'With the climax, the social moral seems to become almost overt. In
> the doorway of the shed stands the overseer; Terry lurches to a stop
> before him. Authority, well dressed, paunchy, complacently in control,
> confronts its weary, pain-racked subject. It opens its mouth, to shout
> an order: 'All to work!' In this relationship, we can only suppose, the
> ordinary human impulses of generosity and compassion are irrelevent.
> To pity sheep on their way to the slaughter-house would be the merest
> simple-minded sentimentalism. It is with this charitable thought that
> the film comes to an end. The priest and the girl smile. The last
> image, powerful and grim, is of the iron portcullis, descending to shut
> the workers away in a shadowy and remote world of toil.'
> 'Whether intentional or not, the symbolism is umistakable. There is, it
> is true, a shot of Friendly, vainly trying to assert his authority again,
> jostled aside by the dockers as they move forward to work; but there is
> not much that is positive in the image; it is an almost an aside.
> Nothing expresses a sense of liberation. The impact is made by Terry's
> battered face, the overseer, the priest and the girl, the expressionless
> dockers, the portcullis.'
> ' . . . It is a conclusion that can only be taken in two ways: as
> hopeless, savagely ironic; or as fundamentally contemptuous,
> pretending to idealism, but in reality without either grace, or joy, or
> love.'[29]

These words of Lindsay Anderson may seem unduly harsh,
particularly when at one point in the same article he describes the last
sequence of the film as 'implicitly (if unconsciously) Fascist'. Can such a
view be vindicated? A good starting point is to analyse the film in
relationship to the real history of dockland struggle.

In the film, working class passiveness, their collaboration with the
rackets and their distrust of the authorities are all shown as examples of
irrationality. It is against this backdrop that Terry's exemplary heroism
must be seen. But was this the situation? Is this an accurate
characterisation of what was going on in New York docks? While there
is no doubt that the International Longshoremens Association of the
AFL was a corrupt union tied into the rackets, this was far from
inevitable.[30] On the West Coast, Harry Bridges has successfully
organised a clean but radical waterfront union, and there were many
clean, radical unions in New York City itself, but that of course was the
problem. The American ruling class has ruthlessly opposed the
development of working class political consciousness. When
unionisation has seemed inevitable they have always supported the

most reactionary elements in the movement; they were more willing to negotiate with Samuel Gompers and his followers in the AFL than the rival breakaway CIO. In the New York docks there have been many rank and file movements demanding a real union but they were repressed by the mobsters with the connivance of the municipal and federal authorities, and of course the shipowners and the truckers. In 1939 Albert Anastasia murdered Peter Panto, insurgent leader of the Brooklyn Longshoremen; District Attorney William O'Dwyer admitted his knowledge of this to Marcy Potter, a member of the local radical organisations and the American Labor Party, but Anastasia was never prosecuted for this crime. A few years later, in 1945, Local 791, strongly influenced by the Communist Party led opposition to a sweetheart contract, and won their battle. Their leading militant however was expelled from the union and then, 'fell and hurt himself' at work: not too surprisingly these terrorising tactics forced him to repudiate his Communist associates. When rank and file members successfully challenged the validity of wage agreements in the courts, seven in all including the Supreme Court, no official action was taken so in 1948 they came out on strike.

Truman slapped on a 80 day Taft Hartley injunction and the following year a congressional bill reversed the Supreme Court decision. There is little doubt that the authorities recognised that the gangster-dominated unions would control the threat from socialist trade unionists. In 1953 Thomas Dewey wrote and thanked the leader of the ILA, Joseph Ryan, for what he had done to 'keep the Communists from getting control of the New York waterfront'. Dewey had made his early reputation as a racket buster but after failing in his attempt at the Republican candidacy for the President, made his peace with the big boys of crime – he imprisoned Lucky Luciano in 1936 for compulsive prostitution but paroled him 10 years later for his contribution to America's war effort. Naval intelligence collaborated through him with the rackets to police the docks against sympathisers with the German and Italian war effort. In doing so they strengthened the criminal elements in the docks.

The Catholic Church was not only publicly and virulently anti-Communist and often hysterically right wing as in Father Coughlin's radio broadcast; it also actively opposed socialism in the trade union movement. There is a distateful irony in showing a priest as a saviour of the workers since the historical role of Catholicism has been to weaken the working class's defence against monopoly capitalism. Perhaps it is not surprising that Father Barry is the weakest character in the film and

Karl Malden's sermons and exhortations not only lack plausibility but are on the whole very much out of touch with the situation and sensibilities shown in the film.

This analysis then suggests that the presentation of corruption and the pretence at social conscience was little more than a gloss. In 1952, Kazan and Budd Schulberg, the scriptwriter, had been major stoolpigeons in the H.U.A.C. investigations. There was quite widespread revulsion against the major testifiers in Hollywood itself. One cannot help but think that the scene where Malloy steels himself to face his workmates is a transmutation of Kazan's own difficulties at facing the other actors, directors and producers in Hollywood after he had sung – one can imagine him and his wife dressing for a Hollywood party and steeling themselves for the difficult occasion.

If Arthur Miller's original script had been used one wonders what differences might have resulted. For example Kazan defends the lack of any background to the gangsters' action by saying that, 'Budd and I wished we had been able to go deeper into the social structure which supports the gangsters. On the other hand, if we had gone more into that, we would have lost some of the unity of the film.'[31] As early as 1931 in Wellman's *Public Enemy* much more stress was placed on the corrupt powerful men whose collaborations subtended organised crime – Edward G. Robinson was overwhelmed by the urbane 'Big Boy', the real controller of his world. *Force of Evil* has already been mentioned and there are other films that deal with this issue.

The greatness of novelists, a parallel art form to film, often lies not only in their concrete evocation of life but also in the maturity of their understanding of it, the ways in which individuals relate to their own and other milieux and how these are affected by social structural constraints, for example in George Eliot's *Middlemarch*. It is surely not too much to ask the same of narrative film makers.

At this point let us return to the film itself. Kazan shows a clear sensitivity to working class life and the changes wrought in the inarticulate Terry through the growth of his love, and his self awareness rudely increased by the death of his brother are all authentic, yet there seems a disjuncture between all this and the last sequence. Terry is shunned by his workmates when he returns for the shape-up after testifying. Nobody acknowledges him, not even Pop Doyle/John Hamilton and yet he and others were there in the court encouraging Terry. When Terry 'calls' Johnny Friendly it has just been established that the mobster is on the defensive, his name plastered over all the papers and patently weakened. He is weak and the capitalist introduced in the last scene is shown as strong – he looks like a 'heavy' but with a more intelligent manner; he remains ironically similar – wearing the same kind of clothes as Father Barry has pointed out differentiates the workers from the parasites. Yet no such conclusion is drawn – the only reference to the relationship between business and the rackets are a mention of 'Mr. Upstairs' and a short scene involving three characters and a T.V. screen. In the foreground is a cigar-smoking plutocrat watching the crime commission hearing, in the background a homely old lady, obviously his wife, and a butler who is told – '. . . If Mr. Friendly calls I'm out. . . . If he calls any time I'm out.' The scene is not only brief but rendered marginal by the reverberations from the emotive exchange that has just taken place between Terry and Friendly who has just tried to assault him in court.

These fragments start to build into a pattern if one looks again at the last sequence. Terry and Friendly start brawling and when the fight is obviously not going the mobster's way his 'torpedoes' involve themselves. Some of the stevedores make half hearted attempts to intervene but don't; yet a few minutes later Pop Doyle has the courage (and luck) to knock Johnny Friendly into the water. Father Barry will not allow anybody to help the beaten, bleeding Terry: his resurrection has to come from him alone and only he saves them all. This is the point. Father Barry and Edie Doyle both represent pure spirituality moving from innocence to experience, but they also continuously juxtapose their abstract morality against the pragmatism of the waterfront ethics and the real situation. Their morality and the appeals to the workings of American democracy can only seem plausible by turning the complex social drama into a morality play. By looking away from the real dilemmas and solutions in the situation, by forcing the material so that Terry can become a Christ figure going into his 'father's house', the house of capital – again ironically symbolised at the end of the film by a door closing them in – they do violence to the richness of all that has gone before. Sadly it seems that this Jewish intellectual, Elia Kazan, could only reconcile himself with the bleak America of the '50s with a Waspish sleight of hand.

Conclusion: Gangsters in American Society

There are vey few films which treat the subject of labour racketeering even though in the 1957 Appalachian meeting of racketeers, labour racketeering was second only to gambling as to the most common form of syndicate activity. It is true that in Samuel Fuller's somewhat flat film *Underworld U.S.A.* (1959) labour racketeering was shown as one of the syndicate activities but there was no real investigation of this. If there was only one way however in which knowledge of labour racketeering informed Hollywood movie making, it was much more in terms of an attitude towards gangsters and criminals than as specific treatment of the topic. The fifties saw many public airings of the dangers of organised crime, Kefauver's Crime Commission 1951, the revelations at the Appalachian meeting and above all, the McClellan Commission's investigation of labour racketeering itself. In this spectacle, major drama was to be found in the confrontation between Robert Kennedy, the special prosecutor for the Commission, and Jimmy Hoffa, head of the Teamsters union. The clash is often portrayed as if it was one between good and evil; but this is of course an over-simplification. It was as much one between amoral, aggressive, self-made man and a sincere liberal who had been given everything: Hoffa was from the working class, Robert Kennedy was the son of a millionaire. This was made clear at one point when Kennedy demanded to know why Hoffa paid his officials of the Teamsters union money to stay at hotels. Hoffa angrily pointed out that his men only had the money that they got from their wages, they didn't have any inherited fortune on which to live.[32] But what has this got to do with gangster movies? Phillip French in his book, 'Westerns', conceives of there being four different kinds of westerns, namely, the John F. Kennedy Western, the Goldwater Western, the Johnson Western and the Buckley Western. He argues that in the fifties and sixties one could characterise the different themes and styles of Westerns in terms of the political persona projected by these different individuals. In his view the Kennedy Western would express optimism. This argument can be displaced or moved to the gangster movie, except that what one sees is the Kennedy horror at the gangsters' whole life style. The classic case where this fits is the 1959 Robert Wilson movie *Al Capone* where Rod Steiger plays him as a gauche overweight thug. He plays Capone in the way that Robert Kennedy saw Jimmy Hoffa. Matched against him, in film as in 'reality', is a man of integrity, a man of wry humour and one who would not soil himself by having anything to do at any level at all with Al Capone. In a way what one had in practice in the McClellan Committee hearings and in the movie portrayal of gangsters is the contrast between absolute individualism and the face of corporate capital.

Elsewhere, in *Crimes of the Powerful*, I have analysed in detail the historical background of the growth, sustenance and transformation of organised crime in America. Here I will simply present a brief overview. Although there had long been gangsters in America they did not become a real power in its life until the twenties when Prohibition opened up a massive illicit market for those tough and efficient enough to exploit it. Gambling then and later, provided profitable returns; in the forties narcotics became lucrative. These activities were to a large degree tolerated by the State, whereas robbery and other crimes against the propertied were severely dealt with. At the same time certain capitalists used gangsters to harass and intimidate workers. There is indeed a long history of certain fractions of the ruling class using gangsters like Al Capone, Arnold Rothstein, Little Augie, etc. to prevent unionisation or failing that to infiltrate unions, setting up 'paper locals' to intimidate and exploit the workers.

The passing of the Wagner Act giving workmen the legal right to set up a union of their choice made the latter strategy of more importance. Socialism was a real force particularly amongst the organised working class and there was little doubt of the long-term threat it posed for America's real masters. Nor were these fears and repressive strategies confined to the marginal industries, for one of the most notorious examples was Detroit. At first General Motors, Fords and the other companies opposed unionisation with every weapon they had – using both their own and the state's repressive forces. Eventually after the Great Flint Sit-Down Strike, General Motors capitulated but Ford continued its machinations. It had a 3,000 strong private army including many gangsters but it also worked on a different tack. In a subsidiary firm to the motor industry gangsters had successfully gained control of the union locals violently ousting the previous incumbents, who were socialists. When Fords eventually capitulated to the unions they intended to install these men as heads of their locals, and then expand this strategy to the whole industry. In the even rank-an-file organisation was too strong and they were defeated: moreover Communists were voted in as the Ford's union officials. Whilst the ruling class was willing to use organised crime when it furthered their interests they opposed it when it appeared as a threat. Thus the McClellan investigations into labour racketeering were, at least in part, inspired by the spectre of an 'Alliance of certain racketeers and Communist dominated unions in the field of transportation as a threat to national security', (as one classified Congress report was entitled).

In the international arena too, there has been collaboration between organised crime, certain fractions of capital, right-wing politicians and governmental bureaucracies such as the CIA. This is true in France, Italy, Vietnam and Cuba: Meyer Lansky, alleged head of the National Crime Syndicate was a staunch friend and supporter of Batista. So was

Richard Nixon.[33] Indeed this network of relations is the key to any real understanding of the debacle that was Watergate. In the 1968 and 1972 elections Nixon was supported by all the important fractions of capital including those connected with organised crime.[34] However he began to develop an increasingly autonomous administration based on an extreme right wing bloc. He could rely on the $60 million collected by C.R.E.E.P., his political appointments and his allies in the security bureaucracies, his expansion of directly controlled sections of the Justice Department – the Law Enforcement Assistance Administrations' budget was increased from $63 million in 1969 to $1.75 billion in 1973 – and through his indifference to Senate and Congress shown by waging an unconstitutional war. His administration and he himself were closely associated with leading underworld figures – through business partnerships, friends, investments and political organisations: men like Meyer Lansky, Frank Costello, Micky Cohen, the Cellinis, Moses Annenberg, Al Polizzi, Marco Reginelli and Lewis Rosenstiel. These men were rich from gambling, prostitution, narcotics, labour racketeering, Wall Street finangling and legitimate business like real estate, and construction. True they had a certain power and made strategic alliances but their real economic base was insignificant compared to that of the Rockefellers or the DuPonts. This Nixon discovered to his cost when he favoured organised crime and 'cowboy' capital at their expense. Then he had to go, for like his mobster friends he was, after all, simply a servant.

The films about organised crime have generally looked away from its connection with capitalism. Part of the reason for this is undoubtedly the ideological confusion of many film-makers but there is another reason too. Although Marxism does not argue that all forms of consciousness – including art – are simply determined by the economic base, the evidence seems overwhelming that whatever is incompatible with it has scant chance of survival.[35] Thus we find hints of political conspiracy in *Godfather Part Two* (1974) and inter CIA rivalry in *Days of the Condor* (1975) but the best we can expect on Watergate is the so-partial *All The Presidents Men* (1976). Sadly it seems unlikely that the gangster genre will ever come to maturity as an account of the role of organised crime within American life.

London

1. I am grateful to John Dennington, Jackie Wright, Tony Woodiwiss, Stuart Wooler, Robin Marriner, Mike Brake and Stefan Ronay for their advice, criticism and help in producing this paper.

2. Joe Hyams: *Bogie*, London, Mayflower, 1973, p. 83.

3. Documentation can be found in the following sources: – Hank Messick: *The Beauties and the Beasts: The Mob in Show Business*, New York, McKay, 1973; Kenneth Anger: *Hollywood Babylon*, San Francisco, Straight Arrow, 1975; Malcolm Johnston: *Crime on the Labor Front*, excerpted in Gus Tyler (ed.): *Organised Crime in America*, Michigan, Ann Arbor, 1967, pp. 197-204; Charles Ashman: *The CIA-Mafia Link*, New York, Manor Books, 1975.

4. Darko Suvin: 'The Mirror and the Dynamo' and Stefan Mirowski 'What is a Work of Art' in Lee Baxandall (ed.): *Radical Perspectives in the Arts*, Harmondsworth, Penguin, 1972; Bertholt Brecht: *The Messingkauf Dialogues*, London, Methuen, 1963; – Also see Colin McCabe: 'Realism and the Cinema', *Screen*, Vol. 15 no. 2, 1974.

5. Cf. Stephen Toulmin: *Human Understanding*, Vol, 1. New York, Oxford University Press, 1972, and the sections on the philosophy of science in my M. Phil. thesis *A Marxist Analysis of the concepts of White Collar Crime and Organised Crime*, Department of Sociology, University of Leeds, 1974, pp. 88-106.

6. See Terry Eagleton: *Marxism and Literary Criticism*, London, Methuen, 1976, chs. 3 & 4.

7. G. Lukacs: *Studies in European Realism*, London, Merlin, 1972. On the 'novelistic' in film see Stephen Heath: 'On Screen in Frame, Film and Ideology' in *Quarterly of Film Studies*, Autumn, 1976.

8. Although the comparison is a little far-fetched since few gangster films really achieve greatness I have nevertheless used as my principle of selection one somewhat akin to that of Leavis when examining novelists in *The Great Tradition*, Harmondsworth, Penguin, 1966, p. 10; concentrating on the films that 'not only change the possibilities of the art for practitioners and readers, but that . . . are significant in terms of the human awareness they promote: awareness of the possibilities of life'.

9. Colin McArthur, *Underworld USA*, London, Secker & Warburg, 1972, ch. 2. Although this is probably the best book available on this genre it is quite obvious that my arguments differ markedly from those of McArthur. Other books worth consulting are John Gabree: *Gangsters: From Little Caesar to the Godfather*, New York, Pyramid, 1973; William K. Everson: *The Bad Guys*, New Jersey, Citadel, 1972; John Baxter: *The Gangster Film*, London, Zwemmer, 1970.

10. See particularly Tony Platt's *The Child Savers*, University of Chicago Press, 1969, and his 'The Triumph of Benevolence' cyclostyled.

11. In *The Mob/Remember that Face* (1951) an excellent film about the waterfront racket. Broderick Crawford, posing as a mobster, attaches a tin of fluorescent paint to the back of a gangster's car taking him to a rendez-vous. The drip provides a tell-tale trail easily picked up by the police. However, this perfect plan is thwarted by the chance intervention of another mechanical device, the night-time street cleaning truck which erases all trace of the paint.

12. Karl Marx: Capital, Vol. 1, Moscow, Progress Publishers, p. 433.

13. See the interview with Raoul Walsh by James Childs 'Can you ride a horse' *Sight and Sound*, Winter, 1972-73, Vol. 42, no. 1.'

14. This was scripted by John Huston and W. R. Burnett and was a faithful interpretation of the radical novel by Burnett.

15. See George Perry: *The Great British Picture Show*, London, Paladin, 1975.

16. Arnold Kettle: 'Dickens and the Popular Tradition' in David Craig (ed.): *Marxists on Literature: An Anthology*, Harmondsworth, Penguin, 1975, p. 234.

17. cf. George Lukacs: *op. cit.*

18. See Eisenstein's comments in his essay 'Dickens, Griffith and the film today' in Sergei Eisenstein: *Film Form*, London, Dobson, 1963.

19. C. Vann Woodward: *The Strange Career of Jim Crow*, New York, Oxford University Press, 1957, pp. 44-45.

20. *Internal Security Act of 1950*. 81st. Congress, 2nd. Session., ch. 1024, 23 September 1950.

21. See the essay on Dalton Trumbo by Richard Corliss in the volume he edited on *The Hollywood Screenwriters*, New York, Avon Books, 1970.

22. This is made explicit in *The Strawberry Blonde* 1941, and is expressed complexly in *The Revolt of Mamie Stover*, 1956, see Pam Cook and Claire Johnston: 'The Place of Women in the Cinema of Raoul Walsh' in Phil. Hardy (ed.): *Raoul Walsh*, Edinburgh Film Festival, 1974.

23. These included the Hollywood Ten – Dalton Trumbo, Abraham Polonsky, Ned Young, Lester Cole, Edward Dytrych, Ring Lardner, Jr., John Howard Lawson, Albert Maltz, Samuel Ornitz, Adrian Scott; and Robert Rossen, Jules Dassin, Joseph Losey, Joseph Strick, Carl Foreman, and Larry Adler. See particularly *Film Culture 50-51*, Summer/Fall 1970; Gordon Kahn, *Hollywood on Trial*, New York, Arno Press & The New York Times, 1948 & 1972; Walter Goodman: *The Committee*, New York, Farrar Strauss & Giroux Inc. 1968; Geoffrey Ryan: 'Un-American Activities.' in *Index 1, 2, & 3* 1973: the 1975 film by David Halpern , Jr., *Hollywood on Trial*, 1976 provides documentary material and has a commentary by John Huston which suggests his change of heart.

24. See John Cogley: *Report on Blacklisting: One, The Movies*, New York, Arno Press & The New York Times, 1956 & 1972, p. 159.

25. See W. McCoy: *The Politics of Heroin in South East Asia*, New York, Harper & Row, 1972 pp. 44-46.

25. John Cogley: *op. cit.*

26. Art Preis: *Labor's Giant Step*, New York, Pathfinder Press, 1972.

27. Andrew Dowdy: *The Films of the Fifties: The American State of Mind*, New York, William Morrow, p. 16.

28. Michael Ciment: *Kazan and Kazan*, London, Secker & Warburg, 1973, pp. 104-105.

29. Lindsay Anderson: 'The Last Sequence of On the Waterfront' *Sight & Sound*, Vol. 24, No. 3, Jan-March 1955, p. 128.

30. Documentation for this analysis will be found in Frank Pearce: *Crimes of the Powerful: Marxism, Crime & Deviance*, London, Pluto Press, 1976, pp. 141-146.

31. Michael Ciment *op. cit.* p. 104.

32. United States Senate Select Committee on Improver Activities in the Labor and Management Field, 1957.

33. Hank Messick: *Lansky* London, Hale, 1973.

34. See the analyses in Les Evans & Allen Myers: *Watergate and the Myth of American Democracy*, New York, Pathfinder Press, 1974; Michael Myerson: *Crime in the Suites*, New York, International Publishers, 1973;' 'Nixon and Organised Crime', *North American Congress on Latin America & Empire Report*, Vol. VI, No. 8, October 1972.

35. I have argued this in relationship to nineteenth century literature in Frank Pearce and Andrew Roberts: 'The Social Regulation of Sexual Behaviour and the Development of Industrial Capitalism in Britain' in Roy Bailey & Jock Young: *Contemporary Social Problems in Britain*, Farnborough, D. C. Heath, 1973.

FILMOGRAPHY

Birth of a Nation, 1916, Dir. D. W. Griffith.

The Cabinet of Dr. Cagliari, 1919, Dir. Fritz Lang.

The Testament of Dr. Mabuse, 1923, Dir. Fritz Lang.

The Threepenny Opera, 1931 Dir. G. W. Pabst.

Public Enemy, 1931, Dir. William Wellman.

The Petrified Forest, 1936, Dir. Archie Mayo.

You Only Live Once, 1937, Dir. Fritz Lang.

Roaring Twenties, 1939, Dir. Raoul Walsh.

High Sierra, 1941, Dir. Raoul Walsh.

Strawberry Blonde, 1941, Dir. Raoul Walsh.

Across the Pacific, 1942, Dir. John Huston.

A Guy Named Joe, 1943, Dir. Victor Fleming.

Double Indemnity, 1944, Dir. Billy Wilder.

Mildred Pierce, 1944, Dir. Michael Curtiz.

Dillinger, 1945, Dir. Max Nosseck.

To Have and Have Not, 1945, Dir. Howard Hawks.

Brighton Rock, 1946, Dir. John Boulting.

The Big Sleep, 1946, Dir. Howard Hawks.

Dark Passage, 1947, Dir. Delmer Daves.

Key Largo, 1948, Dir. John Huston.

Force of Evil, 1948, Dir. Abraham Polonsky.

The Treasure of the Sierra Madre, 1948, Dir. John Huston.

She Wore a Yellow Ribbon, 1949, Dir. John Ford.

White Heat, 1949, Dir. Raoul Walsh.

Conspirator, 1950, Dir. Victor Canning.

A Streetcar Named Desire, 1950, Dir. Elia Kazan.

Night and the City, 1950, Dir. Jules Dassin.

The Asphalt Jungle, 1951, Dir. John Huston.

The Mob/Remember That Face, 1951, Dir. Robert Parrish.

Pickup on South Street, 1953, Dir. Samuel Fuller.

On The Waterfront, 1954, Dir. Elia Kazan.

The Desperate Hours, 1955, Dir. William Wyler.

Kiss Me Deadly, 1955, Dir. Robert Aldrich.

Rebel Without A Cause, 1955, Dir. Nicholas Ray.

The Revolt of Mamie Stover, 1956, Dir. Raoul Walsh.

Invasion of the Body Snatchers, 1956, Dir. Don Siegel.

Tarnished Angels, 1957, Dir. Douglas Sirk.

Baby Face Nelson, 1957, Dir. Don Siegel.

Imitation of Life, 1958, Dir. Douglas Sirk.

Al Capone, 1959, Dir. Robert Wilson.

The FBI Story, 1959, Dir. Mervyn Leroy.

Underworld USA, 1959, Dir. Samuel Fuller.

The Green Berets, 1968, Dirs. Ray Kellogg and John Wayne.

The Godfather, 1972, Dir. Francis Ford Coppola.

The Valachi Papers, 1972, Dir. Terence Young.

Duel, 1972, Dir. Stephen Spiegelberg.

Fat City, 1973, Dir. John Huston.

The Long Goodbye, 1973, Dir. Robert Altman.

Godfather Part Two, 1974, Dir. Francis Ford Coppola.

Day of the Condor, 1975, Dir. Sidney Pollack.

All The President's Men, 1976, Dir. Alan J. Pakula.

The Demonic Tendency, Politics and Society in Dostoevsky's The Devils

John Orr

The Devils is the most politically controversial of all Dostoevsky's novels. It contains a vicious caricature of Russian liberalism, and open condemnation of the revolutionary ideas of its epoch. Most Marxist literary critics have preferred to ignore it, rather than face the daunting task of condemning it in terms of their own theory. Georg Lukács, perhaps the most celebrated Marxist aesthetician, has discussed Dostoevsky's early work at great length and ignored the later novels almost completely. The greater the political content of Dostoevsky's work, the less time Lukács finds to discuss it. For a theorist who emphasises the important relation of literature to politics, this might seem remarkable. As we shall see, there are very important reasons for Lukács's sin of omission, one of them being that Dostoevsky's novel fits into his genre of "critical realism" remarkably well, and cannot be dismissed in terms of naturalism or modernism, the two categories which Lukács applies to decadent bourgeois literature.

There is another good reason. *The Devils* is an *Ideenroman* which has absorbed and transformed into creative literature the progressive social and political currents of its epoch. It cannot therefore be dismissed as a purely reactionary polemic against revolution. For the execution of the novel lies in the transformation of those very ideas and tendencies Dostoevsky is criticising into art. Ostensibly the novel attacks the liberal and revolutionary ideologies of the 1860s in Russia. Artistically these ideologies are indispensable to the achievement of the creator. They are instrinsic to the novel, not a hostile external force to which the writer 're-acts'. The insight into the generational conflict between the 'fathers and sons,' the liberals and the revolutionaries of the sixties, possesses a totalising perspective on Russian politics and society denied to the respective protagonists who provide the novel with its thematic content. It is this feature of Dostoevsky's work which is vital but often, conveniently, overlooked.

Because Dostoevsky took a topical terrorist outrage of the time as the main theme of the novel, it has been dismissed as a piece of journalistic sensationalism or at best a patchwork of documentary fact and hysterical fantasy. As is well known, the theme is based on the assassination of a student, Ivanov, by fellow-members of his secret revolutionary circle acting under the orders of their leader, Sergei Nechayev. The murder took place in 1868, towards the end of a turbulent decade in Russian intellectual life. Nechaev justified the creation of the revolutionary group as part of a network of world-wide secret groups pledged to revolution. Although Nechaev was an emissary of Bakunin, the claim was a total fiction. In the novel the villain and the victim, Peter Verkhovensky and Shatov, are based on Nechaev and Ivanov respectively. The actual incident became a scandal in revolutionary circles. Bakunin disowned Nechaev and Marx expressed disgust at the whole affair. Yet Nechaev in a rather barbarous way, had inaugurated the cult of the professional revolutionary, pledged to absolute secrecy and ruthlessness. Dostoevsky himself sensed this very clearly. The virtue of his literary talent was to locate this phenomenon within the changing culture of Russian society. Thus he did not extrapolate it as a sensational issue. He used it as a springboard for a search, part sociological, part metaphysical, into the nature of a new evil bearing an organic relationship to the society which had produced it.

He cannot be accused, as Lukács accuses Zola, of the naturalist fallacy of descriptive journalism which strips literary characters of their authentic subjectivity. The process of characterisation in *The Devils* is a complex one, but one central feature is apparent. Most of the major characters have their model in real life. But this is merely the starting-point of characterisation, not its ultimate purpose. There is no real point in using a criterion of literary realism which consists in comparing Peter Verkhovensky with Nechaev, his father Stepan with the Russian liberal Granovsky, or Karmazinov with Turgenev. For two things concern the author here – the authenticity of character in relation to setting, and the authenticity of the relations between characters in the development of the plot. This is achieved by Dostoevsky not through documentary knowledge, but through experience. Like Koestler and Solzhensitsyn who were to follow him, it is the experience of revolutionary activity which artistically motivates him. The novel has a contemporary setting, but many of the features of the revolutionary conspiracy and its conspirators can be traced to Dostoevsky's membership of the Petrashevsky circle in St. Petersberg twenty years previously. As an outsider to the Nechaev conspiracy, he is confronted nonetheless by a familiar, not an alien world.

This is crucial to the success of the novel, to the interior viewpoint of revolutionary activity which he portrays with such devastating accuracy in the account of the meeting at Virginsky's. Yet he refrains from indulging purely in the politics of disillusionment, the weakness of so many lapsed revolutionaries in their efforts at literature. Instead he conforms, not always intentionally, to the dictates of great literature. In writing he explores the nature of something *which is not yet known to him.* The vast, and necessary disparity, between initial intention and ultimate achievement is clearly demonstrated in the notebooks of *The Devils.* To sense the full force of this disparity we must first look at the polemical context in which the novel was written. It was directed against the two opposing and often conflicting forces we have already mentioned, the Russian liberals and the Russian revolutionaries, both of whom Dostoevsky, the Russian Orthodox slavophile, detested. It was also an attempt to transcend the literary offerings from these two sources. *The Devils* can be seen as an artistic response to two novels in particular – *Fathers and Sons* and *What is to be Done?* Dostoevsky clearly senses two opposing trends in literature – reflecting political trends – which he violently dislikes. Both find expression in the controversies convulsing Russian aesthetics at the time, and are immortalised in the clash between Pavel and Bazarov in *Fathers and Sons.*

Dostoevsky regarded the writings of Turgenev as superficial and sentimental, the product of gentry upbringing which contrasted vividly with his own existence as a "literary proletarian". They were inauthentic for two reasons. They were based on western influences foreign to Russian culture and on a class privilege Dostoevsky resented and despised at the same time. Indeed he saw Turgenev's most positive literary creation as being the nihilist, Bazarov whose utilitarian repudiation of art contained everything that Turgenev hated. Turgenev's opponents, the Russian social critics grouped around the magazine *The Contemporary*, were equally anathema to Dostoevsky. He hated the philosophical materialism which Cherneshevsky and Dubrolyubov had extracted from Feuerbach. Even more he despised the rationalistic psychology of Claude Bernard which had given them a brief for the future goodness of man in a rational society. The idea of literature expressed in Cherneshevsky's *What is to be done*, as a blueprint for future living based on a rational utopia appalled him. He knew, and indeed said, that literature was a form of expression he resorted to because his ideas and emotions could find no other satisfactory outlook. Its quality derived from this unique predicament. Cherneshevsky, who seemed to regard literature as secondary to material life, aiming at a reproduction of it, devalued the unique nature of the creative act by pretending that art could be expressed in a political language.

There was a complex dilemma in Cherneshevsky's position here which is relevant not only to *The Devils* but also to the whole of Soviet socialist realism and much of the politically conscious art of the west. Cherneshevsky divides the artistic endeavour equally between *mimesis* and *Tendenz.* While the artist must endeavour faithfully to reproduce existing reality, he must also portray a rational design for a just future society. *What is to be Done?* resolves the dilemma of expressing both simultaneously by jettisoning *mimesis* in favour of *Tendenz.* It is in no sense a realist novel. The characters of Lopukhov and Kirsanov are practically interchangeable: the decision of Vera Pavlovna to reject one in favour of the other is never convincingly explained. The seamstresses' co-operative is a paternalistic experiment in petit-bourgeois socialism, while Rakhmetov, the one distinctive character in the novel, is a 'new man' who arises in a complete social vacuum. Cherneshevsky was interested less in the credibility of his characters than in the practical example they set for future generations of Russian revolutionaries. He was not to be disappointed. It became a bible for Lenin and Plekhanov, and Lukács found himself in the embarrassing position of having to praise it despite its complete flouting of Hegelian aesthetics. But the problem remains. How does the novelist genuinely express the dialectic tension between actuality and tendency? Dostoevsky to his credit achieves it in the very novel which denigrates the theory's progenitors. He correctly assessed the situation in a letter to Maykov: 'What I am writing now is a tendentious thing. Let the nihilists and Westerners howl that I am a reactionary. To hell with them.' He further explained the literary process of *Tendenz* in sociological terms showing his rejection of naturalistic methods. 'Having taken an event,' he wrote, 'I tried only to classify its possibility in our society and precisely as a social event, not as an anecdote, not as a description of a peculiar occurrence in Moscow.' 'The tendentious thing,' 'the social event', vague though they sound, eventually produce a remarkable work of art.

The demonic *Tendenz* of the novel also explains the inadequacy of two specific criticisms levelled against it. The first, ironically, was from the pen of a critic of the tendentious school, the populist Mikhailovsky. In a phrase now famous, he complained of Dostoevsky's 'cruel talent' for portraying marginal social misfits and psychopaths to the detriment of ordinary people. But the tendentious nature of the novel shows quite convincingly how actions, taken out of social context, can seem exaggerated and abnormal, but in social context 'as a social event' seem distinctly plausible. Dostoevsky was a prophet of revolutionary terror and saw how the isolated events affecting a handful of people in one generation could be transformed into a catastrophe affecting millions in generations to come. His frightening vision of the moral relativity of 'abnormal' behaviour is one which affects us all, and it is ultimately realistic.

A second, more common criticism of radical critics, is the surfeit of polemic in his novels for his reactionary slavophile ideas. Were they not part of a creed doomed to failure with the onset of the Russian revolution? What then is their relevance to the modern socialist world? Scrutiny of the major novels, however, shows a distinct lack of conviction in Dostoevsky's literary expression of his political ideas. Unlike the *Diary of a Writer* where he rants on without restraint, the literary characters expressing slavophile yearnings are flawed, often unconvincing and always overshadowed by their enemies. Aloysha Karamazov is the intellectual inferior of this brother Ivan. The visionary thoughts of Prince Myshkin are accompanied by epilepsy. In *The Devils*, Shatov whose ideas are closest to Dostoevsky's own, remains tormented by disbelief. A devoted follower of Christ, he cannot assert a genuine belief in the existence of God. His ideas are put in the shade by the cruel Darwinism of Shigalyov and the metaphysical reflections of Kirilov, neither of which they ever rival in poetic intensity. The very ideas which Dostoevsky upheld in his later life, are undermined in his major novels, just as later they are undermined by history itself. Only when the demonic *Tendenz* defeats the moral *Tendenz* does his literature spring to life.

A further difficulty in evaluating the demonic *Tendenz* arises from a dilemma which confronted the Russian social critics in their criticism of specific authors. How far should one approve the *Tendenz* as a conscious literary plan and how far could it be ascribed to unconscious creativity? Cherneshevsky in particular often claimed that artists could unconsciously create the right *Tendenz* even though they were not consciously aware of it. But the conscious/unconscious dichotomy presents problems. Are great writers really unaware of the significance of their work in any absolute sense? The process of creation which Dostoevsky's notebooks reveal shows us something of what happens.[2] Growing consciousness is part of the craft of fiction, of the creation of characters and the realisation of plot. But it is a process, not a static attribute. While no writer can ever hope to have thought out in his own mind all the plausible interpretations of his work, he is more conscious of its *Tendenz* at the end than at the beginning. This is demonstrated in Dostoevsky's own method of creation. His characters start off as abstract social stereotypes, often based on real-life models. The notebooks reveal, to start with, a student, and engineer and a prince. The ideas and sentiments they are meant to embody are written out in advance of the narrative. Only later do they turn into flesh and blood, to become the famous characters – Shatov, Kirilov and Stavrogin.

This is the crux of Dostoevsky's method and one which totally eluded Cherneshevsky. Initially the ideas lack context and the characterisation is flat. The characters become *realistic* in the process of being *fictionalised*. It is the creative act of inventing imaginary people, organically related to one another, which is the key to literary realism. Cherneshevsky uses plot and narrative as clumsy contrivances to enable characters to express ideas. In Dostoevsky narrative action *is* the realisation of sentiments and ideas, but not necessarily those which it was his original intention to express. This is precisely because of the dialectic tension between actuality and tendency of which there is no trace in Cherneshevsky. Despite the sluggish opening to the novel with its defective first-person narrative, the tension is generated by the dramatic entry of Stavrogin, and heightened by the appearance of Peter Verkhovensky. From then on it provides the key to the novel.

II

We have already mentioned Shatov's doubt and his failure of nerve, by means of which Dostoevsky's slavophile yearnings become artistically flawed. The flaw however is transformed into a realistic portrayal of Shatov's weakness as a person, his capacity for allowing himself to become a political victim. The disparity between original intention and artistic effect in Nikolai Stavrogin is even greater.[3] Like Myshkin, he was intended as a great Christ-figure of modern times and transformed into something radically different. His potential as an aristocratic saviour-hero of modern Russia is never realised. Indeed he consciously repudiates the role out of scorn for humanity. Moreover Stavrogin is not the embodiment of the Nietzschean aristocratic ideal of the *Uebermensch*. He is a sympton of decay. His attitude towards his fellow-men is dominated by 'rational malice' as reflected in the biting of the governor's ear, and not by Christian compassion. Instead of being a messiah, Stavrogin generates suppressed charisma and a terrible sense of waste. In the end the recognition of his failure leads to a rational and calculated suicide.

The creation of Peter Verkhovensky deviates equally from the author's original intention. The notebooks are dotted with references to him as a blunderer and a political amateur, blind to the consequences of his own action. In truth Verkhovensky's cunning and manipulative powers allow him to orchestrate the whole development of the revolutionary debacle. It is his remarkable political energy which gives the narrative action its increasing momentum as the plot unfolds. Peter as the villain of the novel has that remarkable dominating presence traditionally reserved for the hero, while the hero, Stavrogin never attains heroic stature. The portrait of Peter's father, Stepan, which is closer in realisation to Dostoevsky's original intention than any of the others, also changes dramatically at the end of the book. Whining, conciliatory and afraid, he comes at the end of his life to recognise his own deficiencies. The citing of the biblical parables on his death bed is moving and poignant, and Dostoesvsky rescues Stepan's humanity when it seemed that over the course of the novel it had all been whittled away.

The same tension of actuality and tendency is reflected in the setting of the novel, but in the obverse way. Ivanov's assassination took place in Moscow but *The Devils* is set in a large provincial town. Here Dostoevsky purposely uses a closed setting to demonstrate the organic interdependence of the establishment and the revolutionaries, how their actions mutually reinforce their respective political positions. He also portrays the different social layers of the population hierarchically intertwined all the way from von Lembke, the governor to Fedka, the convict. In the large anonymous setting of the big city, this would have been impossible. While the vigorous assertion of political ideas and metaphysical breast-beating is typically a feature of the intelligentsia of Moscow and St. Petersberg, its expression in a more confined, and more unlikely setting, nonetheless generates an atmosphere of claustrophobia crucial to the *denouement*. Here, ironically, fidelity to the actual history of the outrage would have undermined the quest to portray its social relevance. Dostoevsky manages to convey an atmosphere of provincial chauvinism and cosmopolitan *Weltschmerz* at one and the same time. The fire following the governor's fete engulfs the whole community thus establishing a link between the destructiveness of Verkhovensky's conspiracy, the agitation of the Spigulin workmen and the fate of everyone.

The close interdependence of all sectors of the community is reinforced by the actual blood relation between Stepan and Peter Verkhovensky. Here the archetypal liberal and the archetypal revolutionary of the 1860s are literally father and son. It is a bolder step than either Turgenev or Cherneshevsky were prepared to take. But it is not gratuitous. It remains a concrete symbol of the conflict of generational ideologies while at the same time containing a profound psychological insight into the relation of the weak father to the contemptuous son. Thus the relationship operates on two levels – that of a clash of ideas and that of clash of personalities. But the former does not have the balanced conflict of arguments between Paval and Bazarov. It is a garbled clash of attitudes cast adrift from their intellectual moorings, vulgarised by personal obsessions. Stepan's gibbering weakness, his desire not to give offence, are answered by Peter's amoral contempt. Because his father is so weak, rebellion is no longer necessary, and scornful manipulation takes its place.

The fiasco of the Governor's fete, the worker's strike, the arson of Fedka, and the final assassination of Shatov, comprise a microcosm of social collapse. But such a collapse is not a result of planned revolutionary activity. The revolutionary circle at Virginsky's is amateurish and consumed by internal strife. Were it not for Verkhovensky they would have no importance at all. Their active role commences only when the fire has done its damage. For it is only then that Verkhovensky can persuade them to assassinate Shatov. When everyone has been thrown into a state of bewilderment by the act of arson and the murder of the Lebyatkins, Verkhovensky bullies the revolutionaries into protecting themselves from incrimination by an act of further incrimination – Shatov's assassination. It is the organisational master-stroke of collective self-destruction. The group is arrested for a crime it did not need to commit, but which it had committed to avoid arrest for other outrages of which it was innocent. It thus becomes implicated in a self-fulfilling prophecy by default. It becomes part of a revolutionary conspiracy it was too impractical to undertake until it was actually accused of already having done so. This is Verkhovensky's major achievement.

Another remarkable feature of his intrigue however is the brazen openness of his methods. He conspicuously flatters the governor's wife and through her, forces the governor to the same dependency upon him that Virginsky's circle are trapped into. Lembke relies on Peter to assure him that fears of a revolutionary conspiracy are exaggerated while the revolutionaries rely on him to assure them of their own importance. They are then helpless as he manipulates events to destroy them all. Both are demoralised by the distrust he sows with such malevolent energy. The crucial link between establishment and underground, he sets them both on to their parallel roads of destruction. His effectiveness invalidates both radical and conservative stereotypes of revolution. His famous claim 'I am not a socialist but a rogue' cynically subverts the revolutionary belief in the unity of theory and practice. His puppet-like control of his chaotic fellow-men invalidates the conservative view of collective conspiracy. He brings the town 'to the point of collapse', at the same time as all his own schemes end in disaster.

While Peter is the actual link between underground and establishment, Stavrogin is the potential link. His charisma attracts everyone but he denies them all in turn by his calculated indifference. The role he plays in the novel raises the whole issue of moral responsibility. Just as Ivan's amoral rebelliousness precipitates the confused homicide by Smerdyakov, so in *The Devils*, Stavrogin's indifference to moral standards is the catalyst for the final fiasco. Stavrogin influences the situation largely by virtue of what he does not do. He makes no attempt to stop Peter's intrigues, or halt the assassination of Shatov. He does not honour his duel with Gaganov nor sustain his passion for Lisa. His hypocritical involvement with Mary Lebyatkin is a calculated insult to respectable society. Where Peter resorts to blackmail, Stavrogin has sensuality and power. But he witholds them completely. The sense of loss in his character stamps its final imprint when he refuses to take on the role for which Peter has directed the whole conspiracy. He spurns the offer of becoming a new revolutionary Tsar, and so ruins all of Peter's plans. The reader is startled, if not shocked, by the chilling way in which Verkhovensky worships him:

'Stavrogin, you're beautiful.' Verkhovensky cried almost in ecstasy. 'Do you know that you are beautiful? What is so fine about you is that sometimes you don't know it. Oh, I've made a thorough study of you!' I often watch you without your being aware of it. You're even simple-minded and naive – do you know that? You are, you are.' I suppose you must be suffering, and suffering too because of your simple-mindedness. I love beauty. I am a nihilist but I love beauty. Don't nihilists love beauty? The only thing they do not love is idols, but I love an idol. You are my idol!' You don't insult anyone, and everyone hates you; you look upon everyone as your equal and everyone is afraid of you. That's good. No one will ever come up to you to slap you on the shoulder. You're an awful aristocrat. An aristocrat who goes in for democracy is irresistible. To sacrifice life – yours and another man's – is nothing to you. You're just the sort of man I need. I – I especially need a man like you. I don't know of anyone but you. You're my leader, you're my sun and I am your worm.'[4]

The words echo Shatov's despairing admiration 'Stavrogin, why am I condemned to believe in you forever?' But they are more. They combine the perverse quasi-erotic worship of the admirer with the complex qualities of the man he admires. Verkhovensky's hysterical adulation finds a historical echo in the diaries of Goebbels where he records his meeting with Hitler. The tone, the eroticism, the desire for submission are practically identical. The qualities admired however are different 'You don't insult anyone and everyone hates you; you look upon everyone as your equal and everyone is afraid of you.' They are those of an emergent leader of revolutionary communism, whose leadership is hated by his enemies, revered by his comrades. This is Stavrogin's potential – to emerge as a natural leader of men within the context of an egalitarian ideology. Verkhovensky's adulation is fascist, while Stavrogin's charisma is much closer to communism. The relationship of the two men brings to mind the famous lines of Yeats: 'The best lack all conviction, while the worst are full of passionate intensity'. Peter's malevolent energy heightens as Stavrogin's capacity for action decays.

Yeats's idea of 'the best' however is not quite appropriate, because Stavrogin never attains a true dimension of goodness. He cannot, either under the conditions of terrorist conspiracy, or in Russian society as it actually exists. But by doing nothing he shares complicity in the devaluation of values, to use Nietzsche's phrase, which Peter carries through so ruthlessly. Verkovensky is the prototype of the fascist revolutionary of the twentieth century, not an embryonic Leninist. He is certainly anti-bourgeois, but sees revolution as a conscious means to dishonour and a force for permanent destruction. Among his greatest talents is that of making the revolutionaries compromise their own principles. Thus at the end Kirilov's metaphysical suicide becomes merely a convenient alibi for the assassins through his scheming. Having made the poignant claim that 'All man did was to invent God so as to live without killing himself', Kirilov then signs a false confession to Shatov's murder at Peter's instigation. With Stavrogin the incapacity of goodness is a mirror of the power of evil. With Kirilov the incapacity to act according to one's principles is a further mirror of that power. The historical stage is set not only for terror but for fratricide. The despairing vision of modern slavery set out by the sedentary Shigalyev, is transformed during Stalin's time into horrifying reality. The agents of the transformation are the revolutionary intelligentsia who, to borrow Nadezhda Mandelstam's phrase, 'have burnt everything out of themselves except the cult of power'. *The Devils* then becomes the most prophetic political novel of modern times.

The social underpinnings to Dostoevsky's prophetic vision are never neglected. His sociological insight into Russian society rivals that of Tolstoy's, and is certainly superior to that of Turgenev or Cherneshevsky. Provincial Russian society is pre-bourgeois in *The Devils*. The culture of pecuniary self-confidence, of family